Dismantling the Master's Clock

Dismantling the Master's Clock

On Race, Space, and Time

Rasheedah Phillips

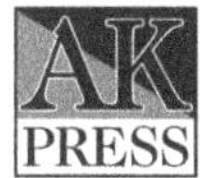

Dismanlting the Master's Clock: On Space, Race, and Time

ISBN: 9781849355612
E-ISBN: 9781849355629
Library of Congress Control Number: 2024939488

AK Press
370 Ryan Ave. #100
Chico, CA 95973
www.akpress.org
akpress@akpress.org

AK Press
33 Tower St.
Edinburgh EH6 7BN
www.akuk.com
akuk@akpress.org

The above addresses would be delighted to provide you with the latest AK Press distribution catalog, which features books, pamphlets, zines, and stylish apparel published and/or distributed by AK Press. Alternatively, visit our websites for the complete catalog, latest news, and secure ordering.

Previous publication credits:
An earlier version of Chapter 4, "Time Zone Protocols," was published as "Counter Clockwise: Unmapping Black Temporalities from Greenwich Mean Timelines" in *The Funambulist*, "They Have Clocks, We Have Time" 36, July/August 2021. A version of this text also appears in the anthology *As for Protocols*, eds. Re'al Christian, Carin Kuoni, and Eriola Pira (Amherst: Vera List Center for Art and Politics at The New School and Amherst College Press, 2025).
An earlier version of Chapter 5, "Race Against Time," was published as "Race Against Time: Afrofuturism and Our Liberated Housing Futures" in *Critical Analysis of Law* vol. 9, no. 1 (2022): Special Issue, Afrofuturism and the Law.
An earlier version of Chapter 6, "Project: Time Capsule," was published as "Project: Time Capsule" in *Survivance*, a collaboration between the Solomon R. Guggenheim Museum and *e-flux* Architecture (June 2021).
Poems by Camae Ayewa featured in Chapter 6, "Project: Time Capsule," were originally published in "Project: Time Capsule" in *Survivance*, a collaboration between the Solomon R. Guggenheim Museum and *e-flux* Architecture (June 2021).

Cover design by Crisis

Printed in the USA on acid-free paper

Dedicated to all who embody the essence of freedom—people, land, time, and space—and to the enduring liberation and unwavering pursuit of justice for oppressed communities around the world.

Contents

Acknowledgments

This book pulses with the rhythm of collective histories, stories untold, and futures yet imagined, a testament to the resistance against the linear progression of time that often fails to acknowledge the fullness of our beings and the myriad of possibilities within our realities.

My deepest gratitude extends to the ancestors whose whispers of wisdom have guided this exploration. Their stories, the ones that navigate the treacherous waters of existence under the watchful gaze of a clock not of their own design, always strengthen and uplift me. It is through their resilience that this book seeks to unravel the tapestry of time itself, questioning its constructs, and reweaving it with threads of our own making.

I am profoundly grateful for the community of thinkers, writers, and activists who have ventured beyond the confines of accepted narratives with me. Your courage to seek answers in the shadows and to challenge the notion that time is a neutral container has been instrumental in shaping this work.

To the readers, who embark on this journey not just through time and space, but into the very essence of our realities and existences, your willingness to challenge the power structures embedded within our understanding of time offers hope for futures reimagined. This book is a product of our collective yearning for space-times that acknowledges the plurality of our yesterdays and tomorrows.

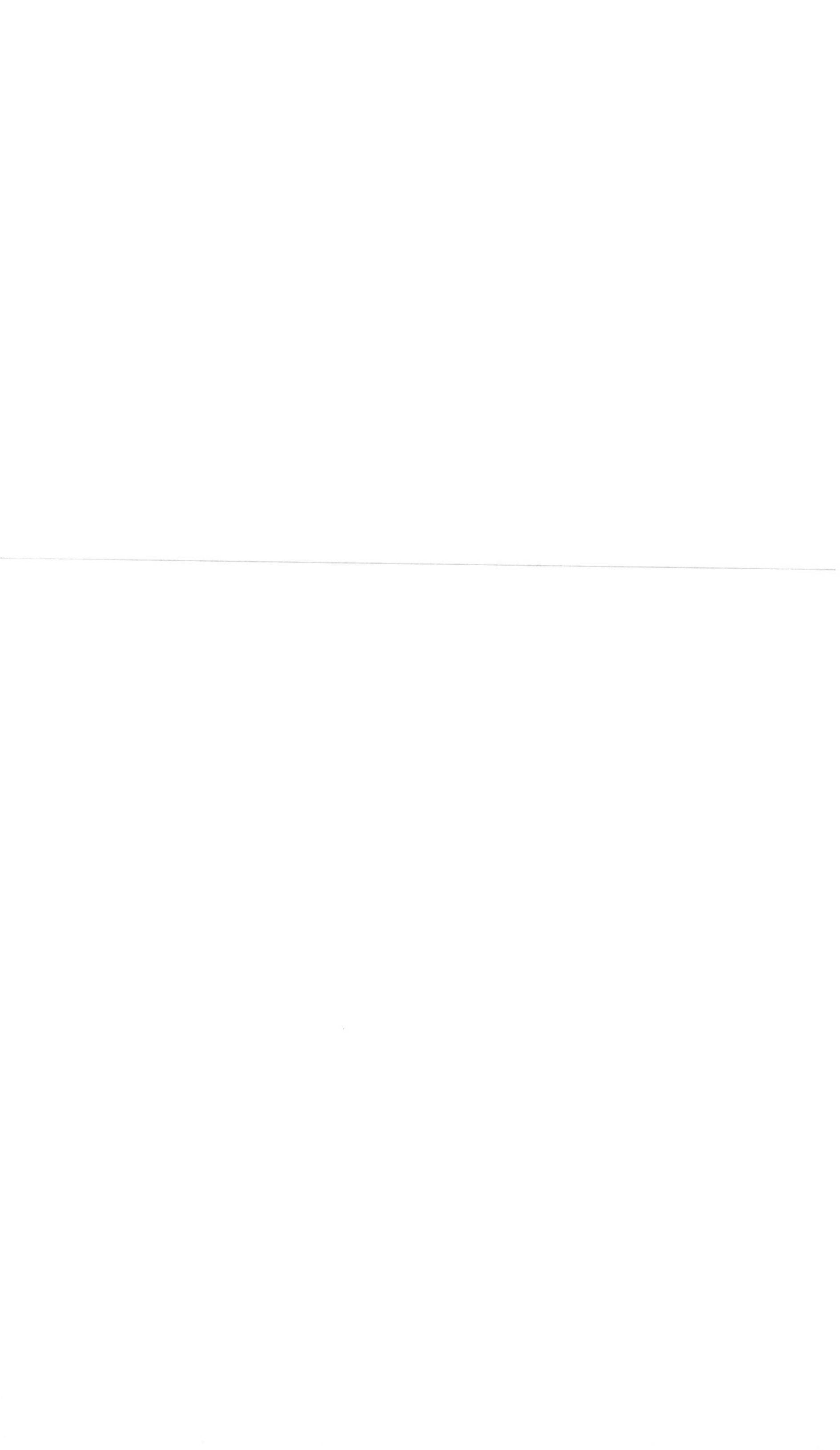

INTRODUCTION

Chapter 0

Echoes of Futures Past

Most people, when asked, might acknowledge that time harbors a subjective dimension. Experiences of temporality can diverge significantly—even in the course of identical events, where one might perceive its passage as either dilated or accelerated in comparison to another person experiencing the same event. This duality highlights a profound dissonance in our conception of time: although we recognize time's subjective nature, we overwhelmingly defer to it as an objective measure, a physical constant within which we orchestrate our lives.

The ubiquitous presence of the clock—on a smartphone or wristwatch—continually asserts itself as the definitive gauge of time. This reliance belies a deeper truth: that time, far from being a mere succession of moments measured by the ticking of a clock, is fundamentally embedded in the fabric of our social, cultural, and political realities. It is shaped by, and shapes in return, the cultural norms, societal dynamics, interwoven global and local politico-economic systems, and other factors that transcend chronological measurements. Yet, this more nuanced understanding remains overshadowed by the dominion of conventional timekeeping, relegating time's vastly multifaceted essence to an afterthought lost to the relentless forward march.

Such reflections on the nature of time became profoundly personal as I entered a new phase of my life, a moment delineated on the Gregorian calendar as the last week of August 2005, when I found myself navigating uncharted temporal and spatial dimensions while seated in a cramped lecture hall during orientation for first year students at Temple University Law School. Even though I was only steps away from the familiar and vibrant world of my undergrad years, and a few blocks away from the North Philadelphia apartment my six-year-old child and I called home, I might as well have been in a parallel time stream. In this cramped and sterile lecture hall, I was markedly different. As one of the few Black students and a young single parent sporting a turquoise-dyed frohawk, several visible tattoos, and face piercings, I was starkly out of sync with the competitive, conservative ethos that permeated this space. Surrounded by rows of solemn peers, some clad in formal business attire, and greeted by the stern expressions of professors and administrators, I experienced a significant metaphysical reorientation in understanding—a shift in space-time that had underscored my entire journey through the landscapes of identity and academia This feeling of misalignment positioned me ahead of, or apart from, the conventional timelines and trajectories that such institutions typically support. My transition into law school was not just a physical relocation but left me with a profound sense of temporal isolation. Unlike the linear progress of career trajectories and life milestones typical of other law students, my own timeline marked by parenthood and my individualized expressions of identity deviated sharply. This highlighted a deeper, underlying disjunction between us that I believe extended to our very perceptions and experiences of time itself. Each moment in this setting reinforced my experience of otherness, challenging the temporal norms and prompting me to reflect on how institutions of this kind recognize and interact with diverse temporalities.

Simultaneously, the unfolding tragedy of Hurricane Katrina added an acute layer of temporal and existential dissonance. The harrowing images and reports of devastation and governmental neglect resonating from the Gulf Coast spoke to a national moment of crisis. This backdrop of mass death, displacement, and trauma magnified my feelings of uncertainty, helplessness, and questioning about the future trajectory of my professional and personal life. This period marked a critical juncture, challenging my temporal perceptions and compelling me to navigate the complex layers of individual identity and collective historical experience.

A few weeks into the semester, my new friend and law school classmate Sakeenah handed me her worn and well-loved copy of *Kindred* by Octavia Butler. I had talked with her about my obsessions with time travel that traced back to the earliest fringes of my memory, stemming from the early days of my childhood where I devoured the science fiction of Bruce Coville, Christopher Pike, and R. L. Stine like they were oxygen. These tales stretched the fabric of possibility, inspiring me to craft my own narratives of little girls transformed into Barbie dolls and aliens hidden in plain sight as authority figures.

But since then, I had purposefully distanced myself from the mainstream, traditional sci-fi culture that captivated me as a youth. As an undergraduate student, courses like Black Psychology and The Black Child, The Black Woman and Black Philosophy catalyzed a seismic shift in my worldview and opened my eyes to Blackness and its many manifestations across racial, cultural, gender, and social spheres. These classes gave me language, theory, and frameworks that allowed me to scrutinize and question the representation of Black people in broader cultural and societal narratives. It was for me a visceral awakening to the exclusion that existed within the speculative realms I once cherished; a stark realization that these stories lacked any semblance of my own culture, history, or identity as a queer Black woman.

And yet, when Sakeenah placed *Kindred* in my hands and I took in the cover and opened the first pages (not really knowing who Octavia Butler was at a time when the internet was not omnipresent and "Googling" wasn't yet really a thing), I immediately had the sense that the book would take me on a journey unlike any other—one that would challenge everything I thought I knew about time travel and how it functioned.

In *Kindred*, Dana, a young Black woman, finds herself unexpectedly hurled back two centuries to a plantation in the antebellum South. Here, she encounters a forebear destined to become a slave owner, whom she must repeatedly save to preserve her own lineage. This narrative diverges sharply from typical time-travel stories that focus on the ramifications of altering the past from a predominantly Eurocentric perspective, emphasizing instead the survival and continuity of family lines through acts of salvation. As the legacy of slavery involved the systematic destruction of Black familial bonds through forced separations and the denial of lineage, Butler's narrative confronts this lost connectivity, illustrating the enduring struggle for identity and heritage in the face of historical obliteration. *Kindred* also reworks the well-known paradox of time travel depicted in many of the stories and movies I enjoyed, commonly known as the grandfather paradox. This paradox poses a theoretical problem for time travelers; if one goes back in time and prevents their grandfather from meeting their grandmother, they themselves would never be born, thus creating a temporal contradiction. This paradox often appears in storylines featuring white protagonists relying on the use of sophisticated time machines, a concept that has fascinated Western audiences since H. G. Wells's *The Time Machine*. These plots are typically designed to illustrate the limitations of our current understanding of time, causality, and the fundamental laws of the universe, reinforcing a deterministic view of time that contrasts with real-world, emerging quantum perspectives that recognize *a reality replete with complexity, nonlinearity, and infinite possibilities*.

However, *Kindred* elegantly circumvents this paradox by not fixating on the technicalities of time travel nor on the causality of Dana's interventions in the past. Instead, the novel focuses on how these temporal incursions affect her life, her relationships with family members, and her sense of self. By deviating from conventional time-travel devices and centering Dana's body as the conduit for temporal displacement, Butler offers a critique of the historical and ongoing exploitation of Black people, their labor, and their time. This revision to the traditional form of the paradox is not merely a narrative choice but a profound commentary on the commodification of Black bodies and on the deep, intrinsic connections that form one's ancestry through genetic memory and cultural heritage. Butler's reorientation of such time-travel narrative frameworks celebrates these connections that were too-often broken and eradicated from the formal historical record yet are vital to understanding the nuanced identities and unique temporal experiences embedded within Black communities.

Encountering Butler's narrative strategy in *Kindred* was a revelation. It showed me that time-travel narratives could escape the confines of linear logic and surface deeper, more meaningful, themes and times concerning identity and legacy. Her work was like holding up a mirror that reflected and amplified the social and cultural complexities of being a queer Black woman.

But beyond that, her work rekindled a sense of wonder and possibility within me that I thought had been long extinguished since childhood—the tantalizing idea that maybe, just maybe, time travel could one day become a reality, and that time itself was much more fluid than we ever imagined. This rejuvenation of hope stemmed not only from the fluidity of time as it was presented in the narrative but also from seeing a reflection of myself within the protagonist and in her experiences. Her struggles and her history resonated deeply with me, making the concept of time travel feel tangible, as if it could be woven into the fabric of my own reality.

This visceral connection I felt to the character of Dana bridged the gap between the fantastical elements of the story and the palpable world around me by anchoring the narrative in a distinctly Black reality, one often marginalized in mainstream depictions of "reality." Through Dana's experiences, the notion of traversing through time forward or backward became conceivable, almost within my reach. The narrative thus masterfully blurred the distinctions between fiction and reality, suggesting that our perceptions of time and possibility are not fixed but are malleable and subject to our imaginations and representations. In this way, Butler's storytelling doesn't just entertain; it radically expands the horizons of what we consider possible, illustrating the transformative power of seeing oneself mirrored in a representation of the world that bends the very concept of time itself. This form of creative surrealism becomes a vehicle for rearticulating the contours of Black existence and resistance against the temporal and spatial constraints imposed by oppressive hegemonic structures. Through her speculative worldbuilding, Butler invites us to redefine our collective understanding of Black possibility and of reality itself.

Butler's storytelling, along with the works of other Black sci-fi and speculative creators such as Tananarive Due and the writers featured in Sheree Renee Thomas's *Dark Matters* anthologies, emboldened me to explore my own ideas on time travel, quantum physics, and societal constructs and to integrate my explorations into stories that were reflective of my own identity and perspectives. Not long after graduating from law school in 2008 and starting as a public interest attorney in legal services, I began taking creative writing courses at the local community college, leading to the stories that would later make up *Recurrence Plot: And Other Time Travel Tales* (2014). This self-published anthology is a fusion of theoretical concepts and fiction, challenging the conventional, linear perceptions of time and engaging readers with alternative (often regarded as esoteric) scientific notions.

The structure of *Recurrence Plot*, which intersperses time-travel experiments within its narrative, aims to fuse the fictional realm with the reader's reality, expanding on the reader's understanding of the fabric of time not just as a literary technique but to see their realities reflected and reshaped within. Each story, while distinct, contributes to an exploration of personal and collective memory and trauma through the lens of time travel and temporal displacement. With its experimental layout—featuring "choose-your-own-adventure" segments and augmented by various media such as a short film, a traveling installation, and a soundtrack—the book extends its potential to transform and influence real-world perceptions and experiences beyond traditional literary confines. *Recurrence Plot* prioritizes characters often overlooked in mainstream speculative fiction, invoking themes rooted in my own experiences as a young parent, advocate, and North Philadelphia resident, and addressing issues such as teen parenting, depression, foster care, the juvenile justice system, and systemic racism. This representation of Black temporalities was intended to validate and elevate the experiences of those frequently marginalized, not only for inclusivity's sake but to foster a sense of possibility, agency, and potential.

At its core, *Recurrence Plot*, disguised as a science-fiction art and literary project, was really a means of demonstrating how real-world experiences can intertwine seamlessly with the realms of science fiction. This project testifies to the blurred lines where fiction intersects with reality, illustrating that the speculative can often mirror, and illuminate, the actual. More critically, the collection was born from my fervent explorations into the quantum mechanics of time and engages dynamically with Black temporalities—the concept at the heart of this present book. Black temporalities refer to the rich, multifaceted, and often contentious modalities through which time is discerned, lived through, utilized, and valued within Black communities. These temporalities do not only encompass chronology but also the cultural, historical, and social dimensions of time in Black life. Ultimately, my book *Recurrence Plot* proposes that the intersection of quantum temporal theories and the lived temporalities of Black people and Black cultures—the transformative potential inherent in the confluence of scientific inquiry and cultural epistemology—might not only illuminate novel *understandings* of time but could lead to a profound *reimagining* of time itself, with significant implications for the future. These same questions and aspirations have also breathed life into this new book, *Dismantling the Master's Clock*, which takes up the speculative research lab of my fiction with essays on what both science and culture teach us about the evolving discourse of time and its transformative possibilities for Black liberation.

Weaving Quantum Threads through Black SpaceTimes

The soundtrack accompanying *Recurrence Plot* was created in collaboration with musician, artist, poet, and activist Camae Ayewa and marked the inception of what would soon blossom into Black Quantum Futurism (BQF). Our shared passions and dialogues on quantum physics, time, astronomy, philosophy, Eastern religions, myth, matrilineal societies, and the pursuit of social justice for Black people catalyzed further creative explorations. Together, we continued experimenting with text, sound, and visual art, spanning across mediums, including zines, collages, soundscapes, and experimental videos. These projects led to the formation of the core principles of BQF, forged from an amalgamation of quantum physics, the temporal consciousness of the Black and African diaspora, and the spatial politics and poetics of Black existence.

Black Quantum Futurism is not just a theoretical framework or a set of practices; it represents both the architects of this concept and those living by its principles, collapsing the boundaries between theory and application. When we embody these theories, we become both the cartographers and the terrain, mapping temporal and spatial features that manifest in personal, communal, and societal realms. BQF challenges and disrupts the normative, hierarchical structures inherent in linear time, particularly as they pertain to the racialized oppression of marginalized Black communities. Our goal is not to simply dichotomize linear time as negative and circular or non-normative temporalities as inherently positive. Instead, BQF critically examines the complex history of how time has been utilized across diverse fields—science, history, politics—to control, define, and advance colonialism and global capitalism. BQF explores the multifaceted forms and dimensions of time, especially as experienced outside the scientific and Western sociocultural frameworks, with a particular emphasis on Black temporalities. Black temporalities present a lush, layered, and multidimensional consciousness of time, distinct from the linear progression typically emphasized in Western thought. This consciousness is vividly portrayed in the works of such visionaries as Octavia Butler, whose narratives bend time and reality, Kodwo Eshun, who explores the futurisms embedded in Black culture, and Zora Neale Hurston, who intertwines folklore with the temporal experiences of the African diaspora.

The works of these thinkers and cultural workers exemplify the complexity of temporalities that embody the experiences, legacies, and perceptions unique to Black and African diasporic cultures. For instance, the Ghanaian concept of *Sankofa* emphasizes the importance of reaching back to historical and ancestral knowledge to construct the future. In Afrofuturism, time is often conceptualized as cyclical or spiral, defying linear constraints and embracing the notion that past, present, and future are not sequential but interconnected and simultaneous. This book will journey through these fertile temporal landscapes, exploring how Black temporalities manifest through storytelling, music, and cultural practices, each contributing to a distinct yet interconnected understanding of time and existence. This approach not only enriches our comprehension of temporal experiences, but also highlights the inherent interconnectedness of time, culture, and identity within the African diaspora.

In adopting "futurism" as a central term for our theory and practice, Black Quantum Futurism intentionally navigates the future in all its multifaceted nature, understanding it as an expansive space that is not only forward-looking but entangled with multiple temporal dimensions. The word *future* designates a time or temporal space that is not now but is situated ahead of us and is distinct from times that precede the one we are currently in. Its etymology, originating from the Latin *futurus*, meaning to grow or to become, suggests that the future is not just a time yet to come but a space of growth and becoming, always inherently intertwined with both the past and the present. This understanding enables us to see time not as a singular, linear path but as a web of interconnected moments, wherein the past, present, and future coexist and mutually influence one another. BQF thus fosters ways to conceptualize time, grounded in a deep exploration of Black temporalities and quantum perspectives, that enables our moving away from the mechanistic tick-tock rhythm of conventional clock time that predominates in Western thought. Time, in quantum physics, emphasizes possibilities and fluidity over strict hours and minutes. Through this lens, we recontextualize history, memory, culture, and potential future possibilities. We can also reclaim the concept of the future, liberating it from the constraints of a Eurocentric and limited imagination, thus re-envisioning it as a vibrant, multidirectional expanse ripe with more possibility than we can ever know. In this reconceptualization, we are not merely passive observers of time; instead, we actively participate in reshaping and redefining our relationship with time and space—both in the world around us and within the broader cosmos—to arrive in a more just reality.

Crafting Temporal Sanctuaries for Black SpaceTimeMatters

From 2011 to 2017, I organized an event called The AfroFuturist Affair in Philadelphia from a deep-seated need for community and representation. This initiative began with a vision, realized on October 28, 2011: The AfroFuturist Costume and Charity Ball. This inaugural event, of what would become an annual ritual, was a dynamic confluence of Black artists, authors, musicians, and performers who all engaged with science-fiction and AfroFuturist themes within their creative, community, and activist endeavors. A sensory explosion of live art, performances, themed food, AfroFuturist visuals and sounds, attendees, adorned in costume, brought to life their futuristic identities and co-created a space-time that was as much an invocation as it was a celebration. The proceeds from this event supported local non-profits that worked in service of women, children, unhoused people, and others. And the themes of these balls, such as Black Holographic Memory, the Museum of Time, and Dark Phase Space, beyond merely artistic prompts, were invitations for participants to engage with these concepts through the vehicle of their performances and costumes.

The AfroFuturist Affair thus transcended its role as an annual celebration, becoming a robust platform for year-round events, artistic, cultural, and educational collaborations, and even a small publishing outlet that produced *Recurrence Plot* and the subsequent volumes of the Black Quantum Futurism series. This platform not only provided an affirming space where people from diverse backgrounds—Black, Brown, Indigenous, Trans, queer, and beyond—could freely play with their identities and artistic visions but also solidified itself as a real-time crucible for communal and cultural transformation. Here, the theoretical was rendered tangible, where we established a practical approach to communal space-time making and the pursuit of spatial agency and temporal autonomy where participants could help craft and celebrate alternative temporal narratives.

For most, temporal autonomy—the ability to perceive and navigate time on our own terms—is curtailed by the institutional constraints of rigid workplace schedules, the chronological cycles of political systems, and the often-linear narratives dominant in the scientific paradigms developed by figures such as Einstein, Newton, and Galileo. This monolithic timeline imposes a uniform Western ontology on our lived experiences and perceptions, negating any of the variant temporal realities of other cultures and communities. The political and existential stakes of this lack of temporal freedom cannot be overstated: For individuals and communities whose experiences and histories diverge from the dominant narrative of progress, and particularly for Black communities, this has led to misrepresentation, existential erasure, and political marginalization. Those of us who would question and reimagine these dominant temporal frameworks seek a shift that is not merely theoretical but one that holds the potential to fundamentally transform how we structure our societies, acknowledge histories, and envision futures. In challenging such temporal constraints, we engage in a radical act of temporal autonomy.

Philosopher and physicist Karen Barad's concept of "spacetimemattering" critically informs our understanding of temporal autonomy.[1] In Barad's framework, space, time, and matter are not separate, distinct entities but exist in perpetual "intra-action," challenging our conventional understanding that entities exist independently before they interact. Uniting space and time and matter into a single term—spacetimematter—emphasizes the ways in which the three are critically entangled and co-constituted by one another. Barad highlights how space, time, and matter interweave to create symbiotic relationships that collaboratively shape reality. "In fact," they argue, "intra-actions not only reconfigure spacetimematter but reconfigure what is possible."[2] In other words, spacetimematter is the recognition that the elements of a complex system are not just interacting components but active participants in creating the system itself. Barad's perspective dismantles the illusion of scientific knowledge as an *objective* construct and compels us to reckon with the irreversibly entangled network of cultural, historical, and power-laden contexts that mediate scientific inquiry. Consider the entrenched Cartesian dualism of mind and body, endemic within Western scientific discourse. Far from being an impartial truth, this dualistic notion reinforces a particular worldview and set of power structures. Embracing Barad's approach encourages a more nuanced view of the universe, one for which interconnectedness is acknowledged as a fundamental aspect of how we comprehend and interact with the world around us.

When we apply these insights on intra-action to the construction of race, it becomes evident that time itself, typically considered an impartial backdrop, is in fact a socially and politically charged construct. Drawing direct parallels to Barad's "spacetimemattering," our concept of "Black SpaceTimeMatters" encapsulates the unique navigations of Western linear time and space by Black communities. Black SpaceTimeMatters is a deliberate departure from linear chronologies, echoing ancestral conceptions of a deep space-time that contrast starkly from our everyday world but are deeply felt within our subjective experiences. These ancestral conceptions saw time as an interconnected web where past, present, and future coexist and influence each other, where history and future possibilities are felt and experienced simultaneously. Black SpaceTimeMatters uplifts Black temporalities as unique relational space-times, in which Black communities and individuals intra-act with time, space, and matter in specific ways that diverge from hegemonic Western scripts. We claim time as a living, dynamic force that can be bent, stretched, and molded according to the needs and experiences of the community, encompassing the rhythms of daily life, cultural practices, and historical narratives. By embracing these alternative conceptions of time, Black SpaceTimeMatters fosters a stronger connection to heritage and identity, empowering Black people and communities to navigate and shape their temporal realities beyond the demands of dominant temporal frameworks.

BQF's exhibition "Community Futurisms 002: Black Space Agency," held in April 2018 at Icebox Project Space in Philadelphia, was a group art show and set of community-based cultural programming exploring the themes of spatial agency and temporal autonomy. This included a community film screening and sci-fi reading called Black Space/Time Matters. The event screened the film *Afronauts* by Nuotama Frances Bodomo and the "Space Traders" episode of *Cosmic Slop*, depicting a story written by Derek Bell where aliens come to Earth requesting that the United States government exchange all of its Black people for advanced technology and gold. Marking the fiftieth anniversary of both the Fair Housing Act and the founding of the North Philadelphia-based Progress Aerospace Enterprises, one of the first Black-owned aerospace companies in the United States, the "Black Space Agency" exhibition interlaced historical events, such as civil rights, the Fair Housing Act, and the space race, with perennial issues including affordable housing and gentrification. Juxtaposing these elements, the show aimed to ignite collective remembrance as well as critical reflection of past, present, and future struggles for spatial agency and temporal autonomy.

It is my contention that Black communities inherently construct and inhabit our own dynamic and textured temporal-spatial realms. Past and future, along with dimensions that defy conventional temporal categorization, are here held seamlessly in a state of superposition. In quantum physics, superposition refers to the concept that a particle exists in multiple states simultaneously, until the particle is measured or observed. In the context of Black temporal-spatial experiences, past, present, and future are overlapping, coexisting dimensions that challenge and resist collapsing into the oppressive, linear timelines of a so-called objective white gaze. This phenomenon is not simply a community response to adversity but should be recognized as a manifestation of African ancestral space-times. The dynamic and layered nature of these space-time realms reflects a cosmology that predates colonial disruption, one that encapsulates an ontological continuity and a way of being that is inherently fluid, resilient, and multifaceted. The communal time experience within Black communities emerges from a mosaic of intersecting timelines, stories, and rhythmic patterns. Such interplay re-engineers our shared temporal infrastructure, making distinctions between past, present, and future irrelevant. In this expanded temporal landscape, Black individuals and communities are ever present, defying normative constraints of time that are often wielded by dominant social and political forces to erase Black history, limit our futures, and confine us to narrow, inadequate instances of the present.

When Black SpaceTimeMatters, it transforms our understanding of time and space from a neutral backdrop into a field actively shaped by and implicated in Black experiences. This shift in understanding has real-world consequences. It demands a reevaluation of urban planning, social policy, and historical narratives, and urges us to recognize and address the specific needs, histories, and aspirations of Black communities. By centering Black experiences in discussions of time and space, we open new avenues for justice, liberation, and belonging, making visible the often-overlooked dimensions of Black existence and resistance.

The lens of Black Quantum Futurism can be crystalized into a robust set of principles for confronting systemic inequalities, historical, present, and future. These guiding principles are Temporal Abundance; Inclusive and Expansive Future Visioning; Past, Present, and Future as Open Possibilities; and Reparative Temporal Justice.

Temporal Abundance challenges the Western notion of time as scarce or finite. It urges a shift to viewing time as a plentiful resource that can be equitably distributed. It advocates for the creation, reclamation, resourcing, and redemption of Black SpaceTimeMatters.

Inclusive and Expansive Future Visioning fosters futures that are inclusive and liberatory, emphasizing the role of marginalized communities in shaping these futures. The future is recognized as fluid, rather than predetermined. We advocate for expansive futures because we have the power to shape them. This principle also highlights the importance of acknowledging and navigating temporal conflicts in our personal, familial, and communal lives.

Past, Present and Future as Open Possibilities posits that history and the future are unfixed and open to reinterpretation and influence. In this way, the past can be revisited and recontextualized. It can impact the present and future. This is a dynamic understanding of time, where the relationship between past, present, and future is open to individual and collective agency.

Reparative Temporal Justice embodies the principle of addressing and rectifying deep-rooted temporal inequities stemming from systemic oppression, particularly those impacting past, present, and future generations of Black communities, as well as other marginalized demographics. Reparative Temporal Justice involves acknowledging the cumulative, long-lasting effects of injustice over time and initiating solutions aimed at correcting both immediate disparities and their enduring historical impacts. Ultimately, Reparative Temporal Justice is a commitment to reshaping a future in which time is a liberatory resource, not a tool of oppression.

This engagement with the temporal dimensions of social construction and oppression actively reconstructs our perspective of time. Through such endeavors, we not only reclaim Black temporal autonomy but also challenge the very architecture of time and space as it is dictated by dominant narratives. Thus, Black SpaceTimeMatters becomes a transformative framework, a means through which Black existence and resistance can be articulated, celebrated, and perpetuated across generations. In embracing this paradigm, we affirm that the full spectrum of Black temporalities is not only valid but vital in the ongoing quest for justice and equity.

Time in Our Own Image: Reframing Black Temporal and Spatial Narratives

In her pivotal essay "The Master's Tools Will Never Dismantle the Master's House," Audre Lorde challenges us to reconsider the methodologies and frameworks we employ in our quest for liberation, arguing that the very tools of oppression cannot be used to achieve our liberation. This finds a resonant echo in the present book, where the conventional, Eurocentric conceptions of time, the master's clock, much like the master's tools, represents a hegemonic structure that imposes its own narratives and systems of organization upon Black life, extending beyond physical or economic domains and penetrating the very fabric of how time is perceived and valued. Western temporal norms privilege progress and futurity, often at the expense of cyclical, relational, and pluralistic understandings of time that are intrinsic to many Black and Indigenous cultures. The insistence on a singular, dominant temporal framework is an element of the master's house, a conceptual edifice that perpetuates inequality and erasure.

The historical embodiment of the master's clock can be traced back to the era of slavery, where the synchronization of time was not just a matter of coordinating actions but a mechanism of subjugation. The master's clock—in the form of a grandfather clock in the plantation house or a large bell on the plantation grounds—regulated the lives and labor of enslaved Africans, dictating their waking hours, work periods, and brief moments of rest. This literal and metaphorical clock set the tempo of daily life, enforcing a power dynamic in which time itself became a calculated tool of oppression.

Today, the legacy of the master's clock is evident in the global supremacy of Western timekeeping practices, which prioritize efficiency and productivity over all else, often disregarding the communal, holistic, and cyclical time concepts that are prevalent in many non-Western cultures. *Dismantling the Master's Clock* seeks not only to expose these colonial underpinnings of the master's clock but also to propose a reclamation and reconstruction of time that aligns with Black liberation. This re-envisioning is essential for true emancipation and the demolishing of the oppressive structures that continue to govern our lives.

In the pages that follow, I tease out the relationship between time and social reality, examining how our understanding of time is both shaped by and shapes cultural, social, and legal frameworks, particularly as regards Black communities. Drawing on personal anecdotes and cultural analysis, I critique the systemic biases and constraints imposed on Black existence by societal constructs of time and space. In doing so, it is crucial to acknowledge that this work is both deeply personal and inherently political. My very existence is inextricably linked to these constructs—my ethnicity, gender, and sexuality are constantly defined with reference to these constructs, and my ability to measure up to the normative standards embedded within them. My experience as a housing advocate also vitally informs my understanding of how systemic structures, especially those related to housing and civil rights, intersect with temporal, spatial, and racial issues. Additionally, through my artistic endeavors as a writer, interdisciplinary artist, and cultural producer, I have blended art, creative research, and advocacy, creating space-times that both challenge dominant temporal norms and foster Black communal ways of being. This fusion of diverse experiences has granted me a uniquely informed perspective on the struggle against the master's clock and toward a temporal framework that truly honors Black temporalities as autonomous and foundational.

The essays in *Dismantling the Master's Clock* amplify overlooked temporal and spatial practices within Black communities, revealing these as sites of resistance, innovation, and transformation. Rather than merely deconstructing flawed paradigms of space and time, I also seek to rebuild. This work is dedicated to reconstructing these concepts and to proposing methodologies, both strategic and artistic, that can build a foundation of more just and holistic access to time. This journey is not an easy one—it requires us to confront uncomfortable truths and unlearn ideologies that permeate to the roots of unquestioned precepts of social and physical reality. The following chapters present new tools for reimagining (and repairing) temporal dimensions across past, present, and future, in the pursuit of rebuilding a more equitable society.

Nonlinear Knowledge Production

The collection of essays in this book are conceptually interconnected yet bound by no linear logic or sequential order, despite the presence of chapter numbers. I invite readers to explore the essays in any sequence that resonates with their personal interests and intellectual journeys.

The first chapter, "CPT Symmetry and Violations," draws from my experiences as an artist in residence at Conseil Européen pour la Recherche Nucléaire, or the European Council for Nuclear Research (CERN)—the world's largest particle physics laboratory. CPT stands for Charge, Parity, and Time reversal symmetry. In simple terms, it is a theory that suggests under certain conditions, the laws of physics remain consistent even when three fundamental properties are reversed: charge (switching from positive to negative), parity (flipping spatial coordinates), and time (reversing the flow of time). This chapter investigates the intriguing phenomena that occur when this symmetry breaks or is violated—these are moments that offer glimpses into the universe's more unusual, yet nevertheless real, behaviors. Drawing from my dialogues with a diverse group of physicists, engineers, and astronomers at CERN, I relate their scientific insights and the seemingly abstract and distant world of quantum physics to the lived experience of Black temporalities. By juxtaposing CPT, as charge-parity-time symmetry, and CPT, as "Colored People's Time"—a tongue-in-cheek reference to the stereotype of Black punctuality—the chapter links the cutting-edge scientific findings with social and cultural perceptions of time.

If traditional notions of time and space lose their meaning in the quantum world, chapter two, "Bending the Arrow of Time," argues that this disjuncture serves as a powerful metaphor for understanding Black temporalities. Studying how African societies and community traditions across history have understood space-time consciousness as rooted in interconnectedness strongly parallels the observation of quantum particles that exist in states of fluidity and intra-action rather than linearity. These various conceptions of time across the African continent prefigure scientific models like CPT symmetry that debunk the notion that time flows only in a forward direction. Challenging the traditional, one-directional "arrow of time" breaks open possibilities in which time is more generative and can flow in multiple directions, even symmetrically and simultaneously. The implications for our perceptions of race, class, and temporality illuminate how disruptions to "normal" patterns in both science and society can be revelatory.

Further, I discuss philosopher John Mbiti's concepts of Zamani and Sasa, describing how time is experienced both personally and across generations, such as is found within the Bambara/Mandinka and Dogon societies of Mali, who view time not as a chronometric measure but as an inherent rhythm integral to life's cycle. I highlight the role of West African griots in time-binding, likening their preservation of collective memory and history through storytelling to energy conservation in physics. Zora Neale Hurston's unique poly-temporal awareness and her understanding of local time practices in her all-Black hometown of Eatonville, demonstrate how personal experiences profoundly shape one's own perception of time, which is visible in everyday phenomena across time and place, such as in Black hair rituals and Black and African traditional divination practices. Finally, I apply the tenets of Black temporalities to cosmic phenomena, particularly black holes and the information paradox that continues to defy scientific understanding, to dispute Western conception of light and darkness and reinterpret black holes as transformative forces. Black and Afrodiasporic epistemologies can offer us new ways of understanding these enigmatic cosmic entities.

Chapter three, "CPT Symmetry and Violations of Black Space-Time," unravels the historical, social, and cultural threads that have woven the concept of "Colored People's Time" (CP Time) into the fabric of Black life through literature, music, material culture, and film. CP Time, often viewed pejoratively, is not just a simple cultural idiosyncrasy but encompasses a vast spectrum of cultural, social, and political dynamics across a maze of historical, present-day, and possible future contexts. This interplay of race, power, and temporal perception is fundamental to the histories of colonialism, white supremacy, and slavery throughout which CP Time has endured as the symbol of a profound struggle for temporal sovereignty for Black people. The chapter highlights the material history of oppression linked to time regimes and timekeeping, while spotlighting the inventive and sustained modes of dissent to these within Black communities. By reframing CP Time as a site of cultural and temporal self-definition, this chapter invites not just a counternarrative but also encourages our continuing vibrant, political re-envisioning of time, wherein Black experiences offer new insights and dimensions to our spatiotemporal realities. In this way, I see CP Time as a pivotal element in the ongoing discourse of Black temporality, spatiality, and significance and enriches the global understanding of time itself.

Chapter four, "Time Zone Protocols," explicates the geopolitical history and implications of global time zones, retracing the colonialist agendas of the International Meridian Conference of 1884 that led to the system of international standard time we use today. I show how such chronometric frameworks have been wielded against non-Western societies, supplanting more culturally resonant traditions of temporal demarcation and forcing them into a global framework that ignores local rhythms and needs in favor of homogenization and managerial expediency. National policies such as Daylight Saving Time (DST) reveal the systemic violence through which time regimes have bolstered colonialist and global-capitalist power structures. The invention of the chronometer, a type of clock that measures longitude on ships, and its role in European imperial expansion and the colonization of continents like Australia and Africa, highlights how timekeeping technologies and clocks, much like maps, embody specific political notions of time and boundaries and inscribed dominant values onto the natural world.

I first began developing the idea of the project called *Time Zone Protocols* in 2020, during an artistic research fellowship at The New School, as an exploration into time standardization protocols, and on the proceedings of the International Meridian Conference (IMC) in particular, to identify their impacts on marginalized Black communities in the United States. A critical examination of these historical political agendas and the tension between global uniformity and local particularities spurs us toward a reassessment of our relationship with time that is able to integrate a diversity of temporal perspectives. The outcomes of the IMC, and its establishment of the Greenwich prime meridian, was fraught with political disagreements and colonial power plays. Similarly, my research also touched on the parallel forces of the Berlin Conference (1884–85), during which imperial European powers negotiated the colonial division of Africa. These events solidified Western dominance by synchronizing disparate cultures under a single temporal matrix, often without their consent. My project *Time Zone Protocols* assessed Daylight Saving Time as another tool of state violence and capitalist labor production linked to the nation-state and global war machine and sought interventions to mitigate its harmful effects on the body and mind.

In 2022, the Vera List Center for Art and Politics presented *Time Zone Protocols* in the form of an exhibition and the three-day hybrid Prime Meridian Unconference. This event became a collective Black SpaceTimeMatters laboratory, where we participants co-created new methodologies to "unmap" Black temporalities from the hegemony of Greenwich Mean Time. This collaborative effort was designed to symbolically invert the objectives of the 1884 International Meridian Conference to produce an archive of alternative guidelines and resolutions, new time zones and tools, each rooted in Black temporal technologies and communal ethos. These were disseminated for communal application and liberation and continue to be available at www.timezoneprotocols.space.

In chapter five, "Race Against Time: Legal Dimensions of Racial Time Unmapped from Our Housing Futures," I probe the intersections between time, race, and housing, foregrounding the insights of housing-insecure and time-poor Black people and communities to expose time's disciplinary role within legal paradigms. Black spatio-temporalities provide the methodological lens for illuminating these complex relationships, enabling us to oppose the punitive, Eurocentric temporal frameworks embedded in legal discourse and foster more equitable housing policies in their place. I have observed firsthand in my career how time is a critical element governing every aspect of legal practice, from mundane tasks like documenting hours to defending tenants in eviction court. This insight lays bare the economic and temporal inequities faced by my clients along lines of gender, race, and class, underscoring the privilege of time in our society and the critical role it plays in gaining access to justice or resources. I have seen how short eviction notice requirements and the time allowed for tenants to vacate a home are severely misaligned with the time actually needed to secure new housing, disproportionately affecting Black women and families. Default judgments, a repercussion of tenants' inability to meet rigid court schedules due to conflicting time demands, highlight the broader societal issue of "time poverty"—the severe constraints on the availability of time experienced by certain communities.

Such constraints and repercussions trace back to time as a measure of the use- and exchange-value of enslaved people. This minute control over time, which continues in various forms into the present, was not just a means of labor regulation but a fundamental aspect of racialized oppression, shaping the daily lives and even the futures of Black individuals. Historic tools of temporal and spatial segregation—exclusionary zoning laws, redlining, and other racially restrictive covenants—have systematically dispossessed Black communities over generations, leading to the contemporary phenomena of gentrification, displacement, and redevelopment. These processes, driven by market forces, ultimately foreclose access to the future for these communities.

In contrast, adopting Black temporal frameworks and integrating the principles of Black Quantum Futurism can inform a shift in housing policy and find new ways to create, resource, share, and redeem time. Throughout my career, I have employed community lawyering principles to support initiatives that have been identified by the community. Key to this has been the development of oral history and oral futures projects like BQF's Community Futures Lab, which brings community members into critical dialogue about housing and gentrification. Through a Black speculative lens, together they can visualize alternative communal futures, prioritize community vision, cultural preservation, and equitable resource allocation.

In chapter six, "Waiting, Wading, Weighting Time," I further explore sociopolitical mechanisms of control through the concept of "waiting time" as a distinct form of temporal oppression leveraged against Black communities as it has been historically and is presently weaponized. "Waiting time" describes the deliberate and strategic use of time as a tool to delay or deny liberation, such as the example of Juneteenth, a pivotal event in the legacy of US slavery. Yet even in circumstances when complete liberation seemed elusive, the rich empirical and metaphysical knowledge of African epistemologies have enabled Black communities to subvert, resist, and reconfigure clock time and achieve varying degrees of temporal autonomy and spatial agency. In this context, I explore how events or information attain their status as facts and explore the biases in conventional understandings of both time and truth. When modes of communication such as reading, writing, drumming, and the use of traditional languages were outlawed, enslaved Black people invented alternative methods to share information via informal networks, ensuring awareness of significant developments and communicating information across multiple scales of time, from the immediate (in the fields) to the future (plans for meeting or escape routes)—reconfigurations of the master's space-time that highlight community resourcefulness. The knowledge conveyed to Harriet Tubman through her visions of the future exemplify a form of what I call "wading time," a term drawn from the spiritual "Wade in the Water." This identifies a dynamic approach to truth embodied in Black narratives and oral traditions, which values collective memory and experience of the community over the individualistic and empirical validations of Western scientism. I extend this analysis to consider "weighting time," identifying temporal-spatial measures such as curfews that regulate the boundaries of time and space for Black people, which are particularly enacted amid societal upheavals such as the COVID-19 pandemic and the uprisings against police brutality that swept across the country in 2020. Through these lenses, I illustrate how temporal oppression continues to shape and constrain Black lives, while also highlighting the enduring resistance and ingenuity of Black communities in reclaiming and redefining time and space.

Chapter seven, "Project: Time Capsule," contends with the cultural and historical significance of time capsules. As the carriers of predominantly mainstream historical narratives, time capsules are often vehicles of exclusion that elide Black voices from the record. I look at a series of time capsules unearthed from affordable housing sites, as well as alternative time capsules in the form of potter's fields, church cornerstones, monument bases, and artifacts found in archaeological studies of slave plantations, and examine the role these play in reversing the exclusion of Black history from the chronicles of Western progress. By broadening our scope to recognize the unique and often-overlooked artifacts particular to Black historical experiences, "Project: Time Capsule" calls for a radical reevaluation of how history is remembered. Each of these offerings holds invaluable insights into the lives of Black people, both intimate and social, and brings to the forefront the need to address temporal and material disparities in historical representation. I view these varied artifacts as sites of memory and resistance, where the act of remembering serves simultaneously as a form of historical rectification and as a foundation for future narratives that are more representative. As a reflection on the nature of history, memory, and the persistent underrepresentation of Black narratives in the historical tapestry, this chapter seeks to make tangible the political potential of reimagining how we engage with the past, which will pave the way for future generations to inherit a more accurate and just historical narratives and offer equity and reconciliation in the present. Here, again, the conventional, linear idea of history gives way to a reality more layered, with the radical potential to work toward justice across all times.

This book ultimately posits that by decolonizing time—by breaking free from the master's clock that has been instrumental in sustaining systems of oppression—we can forge new pathways for liberation that are attuned to the realities, histories, and futures of Black communities. The act of reclaiming both time and *the nature of reality itself* is a profound step toward manifesting temporalities where Black experiences and knowledges are centered. The hegemonic regimentation of time facilitates social control and surveillance, contributing to the disenfranchisement of Black people and communities. Following Lorde's assertion that liberation requires new strategies, new theories, and new tools that are generated from within the communities seeking liberation, *Dismantling the Master's Clock* offers a challenge to envision and enact change that transcends the limitations imposed by the master's constructs. We are called to imagine a future where liberation is not only possible but is crafted with instruments of our own making. This future demands self-definition, creativity, and resistance in the face of systemic injustices. The connection between reclaiming time and Black liberation positions Black temporalities not as alternative possibilities to the present but as essential realities that dismantle oppressive structures and pave the way for truly free futures.

CHAPTER 1

CPT Symmetry and Violations

The Entanglement of an Acronym

Clocks are tools that tell us the time, but that obscure the answer to the question of what time is. —**Kevin Birth, *Objects of Time***

What is time? I think not one single physicist in the world has an answer to this question . . . . Time just flows. —**Michael Dossier, interview with author at CERN, 2020**

The law that entropy always increases holds, I think, the supreme position among the laws of Nature. If someone points out to you that your pet theory of the universe is in disagreement with Maxwell's equations—then so much the worse for Maxwell's equations. If it is found to be contradicted by observation—well, these experimentalists do bungle things sometimes. But if your theory is found to be against the second law of thermodynamics, I can give you no hope; there is nothing for it but to collapse in deepest humiliation. —**Sir Arthur Stanley Eddington, *The Nature of the Physical World***

During the summer of 2013, while researching for my first self-published book of speculative fiction, *Recurrence Plot: And Other Time Travel Tales*, I encountered the acronym CPT, which stands for (C)harge, (P)arity, and (T)ime, and is a cornerstone concept in quantum physics. As I stared at this acronym written in my notebook, my mind immediately flashed to an alternative CPT, one that I was all too familiar with: (C)olored (P)eople's (T)ime. This term, often used derogatorily, implies a perpetual shared lateness among all Black people, a stereotype long wielded against us. This link reinforced my understanding that time is not only a physical dimension but also a fundamentally inequitable social construct.

One of the short stories in *Recurrence Plot* depicts a journey to Geneva, Switzerland to the Large Hadron Collider at CERN, which houses the largest particle physics laboratory in the world and is a pivotal hub for exploring the complicated relationship between physics and time. When I received the news of BQF's selection for the Collide Residency through Arts at CERN in 2020, it felt like a destined convergence of past imaginings and future realities. The Collide Residency meant two months of immersive research alongside physicists at CERN, followed by an additional month in Barcelona to work on an art project of our choosing.

BQF's project, *CPT Symmetry and Violations*, was a multifaceted exploration of the varying scales and dimensions of time and temporality: personal, interpersonal, communal, global, and cosmic. At its scientific core, CPT symmetry in physics represents a foundational symmetry of physical laws under transformations of charge, parity (spatial inversion), and time. The potential violations of CPT symmetry are not just theoretical curiosities; they suggest groundbreaking possibilities about the universe's fundamental nature, especially under extreme conditions where conventional laws might not apply. The residency was an opportunity for us to explore how quantum physics reshapes our conception, experience, and measurement of time, transcending traditional, linear constructs.

Through the project we sought to extend a dialogue between the quantum realm and everyday realities. By intentionally paralleling the scientific concept of CPT with the culturally significant notion of Colored People's Time, the project aimed to confront and deconstruct racialized perceptions of time and punctuality that have historically marginalized, stereotyped, and oppressed Black communities. This approach bridged the often-esoteric world of quantum physics with the palpable realities of race and space-time, implying the potential to break from conventional, linear perceptions of time that have historically marginalized Black communities.

In this light, quantum physics becomes a prismatic lens through which we can reimagine time itself not as a rigid, inexorable flow in a predetermined forward direction, but instead as a malleable dimension, open to reinterpretation and transformation. Such a shift in understanding time has significant corollaries, not just for science but for addressing societal inequities. If time can be perceived differently at a quantum level, this opens discussions about the inequities entrenched in our conventional perceptions of time. It encourages us to question how time, as a social construct, has been used to enforce norms and hierarchies, and how a quantum-informed perspective could inspire more equitable frameworks for organizing our lives, and understanding reality.

Here, the very fabric of reality is woven with threads of quantum potentiality, offering a tableau for revolutionary change and a profound reclamation of agency over the forces that shape our lives and destinies. Embracing a quantum-informed view of time extends to the very ways we perceive and interact with the world around us. By shifting our understanding of time from a deterministic to a participatory framework, we open possibilities for liberation from the conventional constraints imposed by a linear perception of time. This liberatory potential means rethinking not only societal structures but also personal and collective consciousness. It suggests that our engagement with time can be an act of creation and innovation, where temporal boundaries are not barriers but horizons to be explored and expanded.

For two months, I lived on CERN's campus after which my partner, and other half of BQF, Camae Ayewa, joined me for the Barcelona portion of the residency. We collaborated with over thirty theoretical and experimental physicists, engineers, and astronomers to learn about their diverse investigations into the nature of time in physics.

Classical physics, rooted in the works of Newton and others, deals with the macroscopic world—the realm of everyday experiences. It describes a universe where time is constant, flowing uniformly and independent of observers or events. Here, time is akin to a real number line: continuous, linear, and seemingly boundless. Classical mechanics, for example, treats objects and forces in a deterministic way, where the future state of a system can be predicted with certainty given its current state, assuming ideal conditions without external influences. In this view, time is absolute, serving as an unchanging stage against which the drama of physical phenomena unfolds.

The shift from classical to modern physics and the realms of special and general relativity, introduced by Einstein, challenged the classical notion of time. It proposed a universe where time is relative, woven together with the fabric of space into space-time. This integration means that time can dilate or contract depending on the gravitational field or the relative velocity of the observer, departing from the classical idea of time as universal and immutable. Einstein's theories marked a profound shift in understanding not just time but also space itself, fundamentally altering the conception of the universe from a static stage to a dynamic, interwoven continuum of space-time.

The residency research focused on studying CPT symmetry and violations, and CERN scientists' research into quantum theories of gravity and other phenomena. These interactions provided insights into the quantum perspective, where time's nature shifts dramatically. Quantum physics is the science that studies matter and energy at its smallest scales—the level of atoms and subatomic particles. Here, the deterministic nature of classical physics gives way to a world of probabilities and uncertainties, encapsulated by Heisenberg's uncertainty principle, which tells us that nature places a limit on what we can know, contrasting sharply with the predictability implied by classical physics. Quantum theories suggest that fundamental aspects of reality, including time, may operate differently than our macroscopic intuitions imply. This journey through the physics of time, from its classical perception as a one-dimensional continuum, to its interdimensional role in relativity and quantum realms, highlights the ongoing philosophical and scientific evolution of the concept of time.

CERN utilizes particle physics to probe into the fundamental constituents of matter. Here, the Standard Model of physics provides a framework that explains much of what we observe in the universe. Yet it covers only a fraction of the known universe, leaving open questions about the unification of forces, the nature of gravity, and the potential for new physics at higher energies. My time at CERN, including visits to the Antiproton Decelerator offered a unique perspective on these investigations into the mysteries of the cosmos, including why gravity is the weakest force or why matter dominates over antimatter in the universe.

Transitioning from these high-energy experiments to the historical backdrop of Geneva, I was able to further explore the legacy of domains of time, in the bells and clocks deep in the hills of the Jura Mountains. This stark contrast illuminated the multifaceted nature of time itself. In Geneva, the dance of history and mechanics in timekeeping opened a window to a past where time was not just a scientific concept but a symbol of power and control. This exploration continued in Barcelona, where my investigations continued to reveal the role of time measurement as an instrument of social control. The historical context in both cities underscored a critical need: to reimagine time not solely through a scientific lens but also through cultural and social perspectives. The discussions, in-depth research, and interviews I gathered at CERN form the basis of this chapter—an attempt to connect the nonlinear dots between the enigmatic nature of time in physics and its depth of influence on our daily lives and societal structures and systems that we are ensnared within.

Reflecting on time's essence and its seeming "flow," poets, philosophers, scientists, and everyday people—across diverse cultures and epochs have likened it to a river moving at its full power, sweeping us into its relentless current. In Plato's *Cratylus*, Socrates recounts the words of Heraclitus of Ephesus, "that everything gives way and nothing stands fast, and likening the things that are to the flow of a river, . . . you cannot step into the same river twice."[1] Heraclitus's doctrine, as interpreted by some, illustrates how stability and change are concomitant. This idea has evolved an apocryphal interpretation that perpetual change encapsulates the notion of time as a continuous and irreversible flow.

Echoing this sentiment, Marcus Aurelius, the Roman emperor and Stoic philosopher, observed in his *Meditations*: "Time is a sort of river of passing events, and strong is its current; no sooner is a thing brought to sight than it is swept by and another takes its place, and this too will be swept away." This imagery is echoed by Leonardo da Vinci, the Renaissance polymath, who mused in his notebooks: "In rivers, the water that you touch is the last of what has passed and the first of that which comes; so with present time." These reflections highlight the ephemeral nature of the present, underscoring time's relentless passage. In contemporary discourse, the metaphor retains its potency. As noted by Peter Manchester, in modern cinema, "the river has become a cliché for the passage of time, its surface a stock symbolic visualization of time's enigmatic imaging of things timeless and archetypal." This ongoing relevance of the river metaphor underscores its profound impact on our understanding of time's passage."[2]

Modern physics extends the classical metaphor beyond our mere perceptions into a more granular understanding of time's physical nature. The theoretical physicist Michio Kaku points out that in Albert Einstein's theories, time behaves "more like a river, which meandered around stars and galaxies, speeding up and slowing down as it passed around massive bodies." This modern interpretation reveals that the river of time, as it flows through the cosmos, is not uniform but variable, influenced by the gravitational mass of celestial bodies.

In the Western context, this artistic, philosophical, and scientific engagement with time as a river significantly shapes our early cognitive development, seeming an almost instinctive framework for time. From a young age we are taught, and may even seem to experience, time as propelling us forward into the next moment, day, month, or year. Studies in cognitive development reveal that children begin to grasp the concept of time by age three and are often introduced to the rudiments of clock reading by age five. This early education in time perception serves to align young minds with the societal constructs of punctuality and time management. Friedman and Laycock's "Children's Analog and Digital Clock Knowledge" research highlights the developmental stages of learning clock time, indicating how embedded these temporal constructs become in our psyche from a young age.[3]

This ingrained notion of time as a continuous flow is the bedrock of the mechanics of cause and effect, and the bedrock of reality and history. In his book on Isaac Newton, James Gleick writes that, for Newton, "time was a flowing thing," for which he sometimes "made up his own notation . . . calling these functions 'fluents' and fluxions': flowing quantities and rates of change."[4] This harkens back to the thoughts of earlier philosophers like Aristotle, who wrote that "not only do we measure the movement by the time but also the time by the movement because they define each other," and demonstrates the long-standing interdependence in our understanding of motion and time.[5]

In contrast, our everyday time markers (calendar months and clock time) maintain a cyclical rhythm of recurrence; yet events within time rarely themselves repeat in a literal sense, highlighting a disconnect between our perception of cyclical time and the reality of linear progression. Dropping a vase or a glass mug is a classic example. Odds are you are unlikely to witness its shards spontaneously reassembling mid-air and the mug reversing itself back into your hands. Though it is not impossible—given *enough* time, the universe is predicted to reset to its initial conditions—it is statistically improbable, as nature seems to prefer a forward direction. Such a simple, everyday accident succinctly demonstrates the unswerving, unidirectional arrow of time in our physical reality and the irreversible nature of certain phenomena. The arrow of time represents the idea that time flows in one direction only, from past to future, with events following an irreversible chain of cause and effect. Various phenomena (heat flow, the expansion of the universe, the aging of living organisms) manifest to us this arrow of time. Another way to picture the arrow of time is to simply imagine warming up a hot bowl of soup. As the steam rises from the surface and fills the air, the soup gradually cools down. Left untouched, it will reach equilibrium with the surrounding environment, becoming lukewarm. This is the arrow of time in the form of heat flow.

In the case of complex systems, the arrow of time typically kicks in when the system becomes sufficiently large or macroscopic. What is this macroscopic level? It is not seeing the trees for the forest. It is the moment when we shift our gaze from individual particles (grains of sand) to focus on the grand assemblage they form (a sandcastle or a whole beach). Then the physics of the sandcastle would be governed by the arrow of time because the behavior of complex systems is determined by statistical mechanics, a mathematical framework describing the collective behavior of many interacting particles or microscopic components. However, the macroscopic behaviors of systems are emergent properties that do not simply sum up microscopic behaviors but arise from complex interactions at smaller scales. At the macroscopic level, therefore, the behavior of a complex system is determined by the statistical average of the behavior of its individual components rather than the behavior of any individual component. In other words, the strength of the sandcastle isn't determined by how one grain moves but by the combined motion of all those grains coming together in a coordinated dance. Foreclosed from reversing its course, the arrow of time creates the conditions that lock us into the present. Here, the future bears no influence upon our current actions, and our current actions hold no sway over the past. The arrow of time presumes an arrow of progress pointed straight ahead, one that we need always to be on the right side of and move forward in lockstep with—or else be left behind. This tendency is encapsulated in the second law of thermodynamics. Thermodynamics, at its core, is the study of energy, heat, and work, and their interplay in various systems. It explains time through its second law, which states that entropy, or disorder, in an isolated system tends to increase over time. This principle anchors our understanding of time's unidirectional flow, a concept fundamental to scientific thought. The second law of thermodynamics holds that, over time, the total entropy, or disorder, of an isolated system always increases. Imagine you have a kitchen junk drawer full of various electronic cords. When you first organize them, they might be neatly coiled and separated. However, over time and with use, these cords tend to get tangled and disordered. In an isolated system (like the universe, or our kitchen drawer), entropy, or disorder, naturally increases over time. It is far more likely for the cords to become tangled (increase in entropy) than for them to spontaneously untangle and organize themselves. This increase in entropy is what directs the flow of time; it is like an invisible hand that guides the progression from order to disorder, shaping how we perceive the passage of time. In this context, scientific laws bear striking resemblance to traditional legal rules and statutes. Both articulate a series of rules or principles elucidate the operation of specific systems or phenomena. Legal laws created by governing bodies are prescriptive and regulate the behavior of individuals and society. In nature, scientific laws serve as foundational descriptions of natural phenomena, meticulously derived from empirical observations and experiments. These laws do more than just describe; they also provide a framework for understanding how nature behaves under various conditions. As Historian and Philosopher of Science Thomas Kuhn argued, these scientific laws "set puzzles and . . . limit acceptable solutions."[6]

Both types of law, legal and scientific, are designed to be convenient, interpretive, and offer steadfast benchmarks intended to be applied to constantly changing scenarios. However, these laws are not immune to external influences. They are often shaped by political, economic, and societal factors, reflecting the control and perspectives of those in power and the prevailing norms of society's institutions. In essence, both legal and scientific laws distill consistent patterns observed in their respective realms—the natural world for scientific laws, and the social world for legal laws. This distillation aims to predict and explain how elements, within our universe or society, interact and function.

As you prune away at any given scientific law in search of its foundational reasoning, like the laws of thermodynamics, you will ultimately arrive at a set of axioms, principles that were established through rigorous observation and analysis, often by esteemed thinkers and scientists across various disciplines. An axiom stands as a self-evident truth, accepted as valid without requiring proof. An axiom can serve as a cornerstone, or a fundamental belief that exists beyond the realm of doubt, from which other truths are derived. We either accept an axiom as an indisputable fact or undertake the difficult, perhaps impossible, task of substantiating it.

But foundational axioms don't inherently prove their own validity. And it is crucial to remember that the axioms derived from observations of nature aren't nature itself; instead, as theoretical physicist Werner Heisenberg pointed out, they represent "nature as exposed to our method of questioning." This highlights the crucial point that axioms, and our understanding of them, are shaped by our own perspectives and methodologies.

Furthermore, what is deemed self-evident can change over time (and has), evolving with the development of new knowledge and ideas. Perception of an axiom is substantially molded by cultural, historical, and individual contexts in which it is considered. While they form the bedrock of scientific and logical reasoning, axioms are also reflections of our ever-changing understandings of the world around us.

Thermodynamics, for instance, while primarily concerned with energy, heat, and entropy, offers a macroscopic view of the universe that is irreversible. Established as a fundamental scientific law, thermodynamics has significantly molded our modern comprehension of time, ensnaring humanity in a linear progression since its inception. Developed in the nineteenth century during the Industrial Revolution, a period rife with scientific discovery and technological advancement, thermodynamics was largely formulated by scientists like Lord Kelvin and Rudolf Clausius. These scientific pioneers, operating within the sociohistorical context of rapidly advancing industrial society, laid down principles that have since been regarded as unassailable within the scientific community. Their work solidified the concept of entropy and the irreversible arrow of time, principles that have become axiomatic in physics. As unshakable as they may seem, human experiences of time are far more nuanced and subjective than what thermodynamics suggests. They encompass psychological, cultural, and personal dimensions that defy the linear progression of thermodynamic time. Our perception of time can be elastic, influenced by emotions, cultural practices, and individual experiences, which are not accounted for in the thermodynamic framework. This discrepancy highlights the limitations of scientific laws when applied to the human experience. However, the perspectives, principles, and axioms of time ingrained in Eurocentric education as a key pillar of scientific understanding, shapes our conventional worldview.

As a result, while thermodynamics remains a cornerstone within the scientific community, their application to the broad nature of human temporal experience is limited. The axioms are taught as essential doctrines in schools, shaping our basic understanding of the world, and much like laws governing human conduct, they are rarely questioned or scrutinized. As with challenging laws governing human conduct, contravening the laws that govern time is viewed as socially and scientifically unacceptable, and "unlawful" within the scientific realm.

What if the foundational principle of thermodynamics, the second law, which dictates the irreversible increase in entropy, appears to contradict another fundamental principle in physics—the law of time symmetry? How do we reconcile these seemingly opposing aspects of the same universe?

If the foundational law of time in thermodynamics contradicts the principle of time symmetry, it suggests that our understanding and structuring of time, both scientifically and socially, might be based on an incomplete or even flawed interpretation. This realization opens possibilities for alternative temporal frameworks that could have significant societal and political ramifications. It urges us to envision a world where time is not a rigid, linear progression but a dimension with more fluid and equitable possibilities. Such a reimagining of time could lead to more inclusive and flexible societal structures and political systems, challenging the status quo and offering new ways to conceptualize progress, productivity, and community.

The Symmetry in CPT: Why Time May Not Actually Prefer a Direction

> *Linearity or simplicity does not dominate in nature. Complexity is the order of things in the universe.* —**Reginald Crosley, *The Vodou Quantum Leap***

Many of us are first assigned to create timelines in social studies or history class. This provides some of our earliest indoctrination of time as a linear procession, as a sequential understanding of events in world and national history and even our own lives. Typically, a straight, unbroken line stretching from past to present to future, the timeline embodies the familiar narrative of time's unidirectional flow, with major events as points on the line, where time moves forward ahead of us and comes up from behind us. In the realm of contemporary science, a similar concept emerges, referred to as the "world line," which traces a path from past to future, embodying the notion that time surges forward, leaving the past behind as it propels us moment to moment into the future.

Recognizing the potential political consequences of this understanding, we must consider how our culturally ingrained perceptions of time influence our societal structures and worldviews. By taking seriously the notion that time could be nonlinear and multidirectional opens possibilities for alternative frameworks in understanding history, progress, and human interaction.

Reevaluating the concept of time beyond the linear model opens new avenues for understanding social progress and for decolonizing scientific knowledge. This paradigm shift could pave the way for more equitable and inclusive societal structures, breaking free from the constraints of a linear, progress-oriented perspective that has long dominated Western thought. Historian Reinhart Koselleck contends that this perception is a fiction linked to the Enlightenment and the notion of progress.[7]

The linear portrayal reflects not only the dominant chronological framework but also serves as a vivid representation of causal asymmetry, the principle that cause always precedes effect. This dynamic unfolds as a sequence—A, B, C, D, where A triggers B, and D results from C. This linear comprehension of time, stretching inexorably into the future while leaving the past behind, carries with it an inherent imbalance or asymmetry: the notion of later events like D influencing earlier events C, B, or A appears implausible, as time remains steadfastly oriented forward, refusing to cast its glance backward. Such a dominant temporal orientation reveals more about our cultural and social constructs than about the nature of time itself.

Echoing Koselleck's analysis, philosopher of science and historian Thomas Kuhn argues that the structure of scientific revolutions is itself profoundly influenced by scientific narratives that "make the history of science look linear or cumulative."[8] These conceptions of time are entangled with the legacy of colonialism and of the Eurocentric worldview that has been instrumental in shaping the "empirical" science that often bolsters racist and colonialist narratives of progress and development.

At the microscopic level (at the level of particles), this assumption of asymmetry begins to falter, where we find that the concept of causal asymmetry is little more than a projection of our own temporal biases. As we dive deeper into quantum physics' most steadfast rules, concepts, and frameworks, one concept emerges that challenges what we believe we know about time's unidirectional flow: CPT symmetry. It becomes clear that linear causality is a construct that we have ingrained within our language and our methods of recounting events.

CPT symmetry, or charge-parity-time symmetry, is a fundamental principle in physics that highlights the consistent nature of the laws of physics, where the physical description of a system remains unchanged under the transformation of the particles into their antiparticles under the execution of operations charge (conjugation), the reflection of space (parity), and the reversal of time (time reversal) on that system. If you compare the results to the original description of the system, they should be identical.

To understand this, let's first consider what we mean by a "physical description of a system." In basic terms, this can be thought of as a set of equations or rules that describe how particles in that system behave, such as how they move, interact, and change over time. It is like having a recipe or a set of instructions that tell us everything about what's happening inside that system. Now, when we talk about executing the operations of C (charge conjugation), P (parity or spatial inversion), and T (time reversal) on this system, it is akin to altering some key ingredients or steps in our recipe and seeing if the outcome remains the same. For example, imagine if in our system recipe, we replace positively charged particles with their negatively charged counterparts (charge conjugation), flip the spatial layout like looking in a mirror (parity inversion), and then run the entire process backward as if rewinding a video (time reversal). CPT symmetry suggests that after making these transformations, the final state of our system should match the original. It's like saying, no matter if we swap the charges of particles, flip the entire setup in a mirror, or reverse the flow of time, the fundamental rules governing the system's behavior remain unchanged. This concept is not just theoretical; it has been tested in real experiments.

The concept of CPT symmetry, first confirmed through experiments in the late 1940s and early 1950s and solidified through the works of Julian Schwinger, Gerhart Lüders, and Wolfgang Pauli, has become a bedrock principle in modern physics, indicating that the laws of nature are consistent even under fundamental changes. The experiments conducted to confirm CPT symmetry involve observations and measurements of particle interactions and decay processes. Scientists observed how particles behave normally and then compared these observations with situations where the particles have undergone the transformations of charge, parity, and time and found that, in line with the principle of CPT symmetry, the outcomes of these experiments were consistent, supporting the theory that the fundamental laws of physics always remain the same under these transformations.

CPT symmetry is a principle rooted in experimental evidence that has transformed our understanding of the fundamental nature of reality, with far-reaching impacts on various fields, from particle physics to cosmology.

This principle, however, does more than just advance our understanding of physical laws; it challenges the linear and forward-driven conception of time that has been a mainstay in Western scientific thought. By suggesting that the laws of nature do not inherently favor a forward progression of time, CPT symmetry undermines these narratives, challenging the deeply ingrained notion of linear causality in our language and methods of recounting events and offering a more equitable and nonlinear understanding of time and causality.

On a warm September afternoon, I was in conversation with physicist Helga Timko in the courtyard of one of CERN's sprawling campus restaurants. When I asked her about CPT symmetry, Dr. Timko sketched a formula in my notebook, explaining, "Physics is about observing nature in nature. We have energy conservation and momentum conservation, and if you want to write it down mathematically, it turns out that energy conservation is the consequence of the symmetry of time because time is the conjugate variable of energy. Momentum conservation is the consequence of a symmetry in space because space is the conjugate variable of momentum."

Dr. Timko's explanation reveals that energy conservation is a consequence of time symmetry, just as momentum conservation results from spatial symmetry. If, following the first law of thermodynamics, energy cannot be created or destroyed, only transferred or transformed, CPT symmetry indicates that the total energy and momentum in a closed system remains constant across time, whether in its conventional flow or in theoretical reverse.

Put another way, if a particle collides with its antiparticle, they annihilate each other. Despite this, the total energy and momentum of the system in which they collide will remain unchanged. If you skipped a lot of your senior year of physics in high school, where they may have covered this principle, you have still no doubt heard it in countless science-fiction films as the reason why a time traveler from the future cannot come into physical context with their past self. In the 2020 film *Tenet*, for instance, the main character, a spy called the Protagonist, is debriefed by a soldier named Wheeler before he moves (not travels) backward in time via a turnstile that inverts entropy. Wheeler instructs, him, "The number-one rule: don't come into contact with your forwards self." After the Protagonist rejects wearing a protective suit, she warns him that if any of his "particles come into contact" it would mean "annihilation." To which the Protagonist replies, "That's bad, right?"

While touring CERN's experiments, I gained insights into how CPT symmetry sheds light on the imbalance of the existence of matter and antimatter in the universe. It suggests that that despite being created in equal amounts initially, matter and antimatter didn't completely annihilate each other, leaving a surplus of matter. Slight differences in their properties might have led to their unequal annihilation, meaning that when matter and antimatter collided, they didn't completely cancel each other out. Instead, a small surplus of matter remained, which constitutes the observable universe we see today. This subtle disparity, possibly a consequence of CPT symmetry, helps scientists to better understand the universe's composition.

Parity, Power, and Prejudice: Mapping the Herstory of CPT Violations

Time has a history. —**Karen Barad, *Meeting the Universe Halfway***

Shifting our focus, the exploration of violations of CPT symmetry unveils another crucial aspect of the universe's inner workings. Each component of CPT symmetry—charge conjugation (C), parity (P), and time reversal (T)—represents a distinct phenomenon. While no complete violations of CPT symmetry have been found, the discovery of violations in combinations of the individual symmetries is particularly intriguing. Notably, violations of C symmetry, P symmetry, and CP symmetry have been observed in processes like the decay of subatomic particles. Far from being mere anomalies, these violations provide deep insights into the asymmetrical aspects of our universe coexistent with its fundamental symmetry. What might seem like imbalances or contradictions are evidence of a non-traditional model of the universe at play.

This context provides a backdrop for appreciating the groundbreaking work of Chinese American physicist Chien-Shiung Wu. Tucked away in a quiet corner in CERN's vast library, I sifted through historical narratives, learning Wu, a pioneering Chinese American physicist, first confirmed the violation of parity in a 1956 experiment. The "P" in CPT, parity refers to the concept that the laws of physics should remain consistent when observed in a mirror. Imagine a universe as seen in a mirror—if parity is conserved, the behavior of particles in this mirror universe should be identical to our own. This principle of mirror symmetry was long thought to be a fundamental aspect of nature until its violation was discovered. Wu's experiment revealed that certain processes in nature, specifically within the domain of subatomic particles, do not adhere to this mirror symmetry. In other words, the behavior of these particles in a mirrored scenario would differ from their behavior in our universe, contradicting the long-standing assumption of parity conservation in particle interactions.

Wu's groundbreaking work earned her the moniker "the First Lady of Physics." Her name translates to "strong hero," in many ways encapsulating her unyielding drive in a field monopolized by white men. However, despite her monumental contributions to our understanding of CPT theorem and particle physics, Wu was notably passed over for the Nobel Prize multiple times.[9]

Born in Liuhe, China in 1912, Wu relocated to the United States to pursue graduate studies when she was twenty-four years old, ultimately securing a PhD in physics at the University of California, Berkeley, in 1940. The path was not smooth; she encountered and overcame significant challenges, including those she confronted due to her gender and ethnicity. Yet, her talent was too glaring to be suppressed. Following a brief teaching stint at Smith College, Wu transitioned into a research role in the physics department at Princeton University, serving under the guidance of the eminent physicists Eugene Wigner and Edward Teller.

Her particular skill in designing experiments did not go unnoticed during World War II. She was recruited to the Manhattan Project, a top-secret initiative led by the US government aimed at developing the first atomic bomb. Despite more well-known names, such as Robert Oppenheimer, becoming the subject of blockbuster films,

Wu's work was indispensable. Despite being reluctant to discuss her role, Wu made groundbreaking contributions to radiation detection, uranium-enrichment processes, and nuclear fission—elements critical to the creation of the devastating atomic bombs dropped on Hiroshima and Nagasaki in 1945.

Following the war, Wu shifted the focus of her research to beta decay, a subatomic event in which a neutron decays into a proton while emitting an electron and an antineutrino in the process. Her experiments substantiated Enrico Fermi's earlier theories on beta decay and provided the first experimental evidence of photon entanglement in 1949. These successes began to establish Wu's reputation as a go-to for elegant design of experiments.

It was in the watershed year of 1956 when theoretical physicists Tsung-Dao Lee and Chen-Ning Yang approached their colleague Wu at Columbia University with a hypothesis. They speculated that weak interactions—those governing processes like beta decay—might not actually conserve parity. As theorists, Lee and Yang were initially hesitant to fully commit to the idea that parity conservation could be violated by a scientific experiment. Their reticence reflected much of the scientific community's views at that time, which saw the conservation of parity as a fundamental symmetry underlying all of nature. However, Wu's reputation as a successful experimentalist preceded her. She agreed to work with Lee and Yang in 1956, later recounting, "This was a golden opportunity for a beta-decay physicist to perform a crucial test, and how could I let it pass?"[10]

Wu's meticulously designed experiments would provide the empirical evidence that confirmed the theory. In an ironic twist, her male colleagues Lee and Yang won the Nobel Prize in Physics in 1957 for their theoretical work on parity violation, while Wu, whose experimental expertise made the theory a verifiable reality, was left out of the award. Despite her pivotal role in elucidating the key principles of the CPT theorem and providing groundbreaking experimental evidence for its parity violations, Chien-Shiung Wu remained marginalized. This oversight is emblematic of a broader narrative of systemic inequality and reflective of an issue pervasive in the scientific field, where contributions from women and people of color are frequently overlooked or undervalued—a direct legacy of the colonialist and patriarchal biases that are deeply ingrained in the history of "empirical" science. Profoundly cognizant of these biases, Wu emerged as a formidable advocate for women in science, challenging the status quo and advocating for inclusivity and recognition.

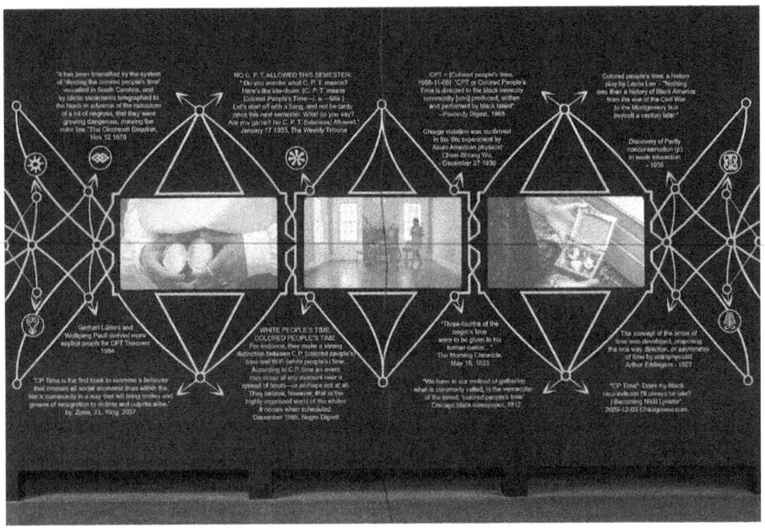

"CPTimeline" installation, with the speculative three-channel film *Write No History* on screens, by Black Quantum Futurism (2021), as part of the solo exhibition *CPT Reversal* at REDCAT (Los Angeles).

Over time, Wu's contributions have thankfully received the celebration and honor they merit, including prestigious awards such as the National Medal of Science and the Wolf Prize in Physics. Additionally, an asteroid was named in her honor in 1990, signifying her stellar contributions to the field. At CERN, a place where streets bear the names of eminent scientists, Route Wu stands as a testament to Chien-Shiung Wu's indelible mark on the world of physics. Her story stuck with me throughout my time there.

Transitioning from the historical to the contemporary, my discussions at CERN with theoretical physicist John Ellis further unveiled the intricacies of CPT symmetry and its potential violations. Over tea he explained his research and recounted how he'd once collaborated with CERN's experimenters to explore the theorem's bedrock. The plan was to investigate prospects of finding experimental evidence for a CPT violation (where change, parity, and time symmetry are all violated simultaneously, instead of a violation in individual or combinations of C, P, and T) which might offer physicists further insights into the foundations of quantum field theory and the symmetries and behaviors governing the universe.

One such area of exploration led them to the rigorous study of kaons, subatomic particles that manifest a unique duality. Dr. Ellis expounded on the kaons' unique composition, made up of strange quarks and antiquarks, allowing them to act as both particles and antiparticles simultaneously. This characteristic makes them an excellent test bed for examining C, P, and T transformations:

> There are two types of kaon that are particularly interesting to me. One is a strange quark [with] a different type of antiquark, and the other one is a strange antiquark with a quark. These are particle and antiparticle, and you get from one to the other by a C transformation. Then you can look at their evolution in time and its force in time, back in time—that's a T transformation. You can also bring the P transformation into the game. So, particle and antiparticle, reverse direction of time, put things in a mirror, and you should get exactly the same thing.[11]

This research, while deeply embedded in theoretical physics, extends beyond the laboratory walls. Walking through the campus back to my room after our talk, I think more on the potential for these theories and experiments to radically alter our grasp of time, causality, and the fabric of reality, moving from theoretical abstraction to tangible, real-world reverberations.

Dissecting the Arrow of Time: Everyday T-Violations in CPT Symmetry

Order is subjective—in the eye of the beholder. Order and confusion are not the sorts of things a mathematician would try to define or measure.

Or are they? If disorder corresponded to entropy, maybe it was ready for scientific treatment after all. —**James Gleick,** ***The Information***

The trajectory of absolute time is a full circle, manifested as forward or backward arrows on local or fractional space-time. —**Reginald Crosley,** ***The Vodou Quantum Leap***

Classical physics, grounded in Newton's laws, usually adhere to time-reversal symmetry, which states that time should be able to flow in either direction without affecting physical laws. This symmetry is codified in the CPT theorem, a concept from particle physics, primarily applicable at the quantum level, which holds that CPT transformations (simultaneous flips in charge, parity, and time) should leave fundamental physical processes invariant (meaning that they do not change). Focusing on time in the CPT acronym, this means that if a physical process occurs in one direction of time, it should also be possible to reverse the process and obtain the same results. Phenomena like a pendulum's swinging motion or the bounce of a ball are theoretically time-symmetric events: if you record either of these and watch them backward, they should appear identical.

However, the arrow of time that we perceive at the macroscopic level throws a wrench in the whole time-symmetric system. Specifically, the arrow of time generates in us the feeling and perception that we as humans "have no way of moving forwards or backwards in time ourselves, and we want to step back from time, but it is not under our control," as CERN physicist Michael Dossier noted in our interview. The asymmetry between the past and the future on the macroscopic level appears to be a violation of time symmetry. There are some processes, like aging, birth, or car crashes, that seem to only occur in one direction of time, breaking time's otherwise normal symmetry in the universe.

To put it another way, the same equations that describe matter and radiation plunging to their deaths into a singularity at the center of a black hole can be flipped around to describe matter and radiation exploding from a singularity, spreading out through space-time to birth a universe. However, once we, from our vantage point, begin to observe what are called large systems, or macrostates—like galaxies, star systems, or even the thermodynamic state of a gas—that pesky arrow of time shows right back up to reassert itself, facilitating our concept of causality. A macrostate can be thought of as the broader, observable state of a system, determined by macroscopic properties such as temperature or volume, rather than the detailed positions and velocities of particles. For instance, consider a balloon filled with gas; the macrostate of the balloon is defined by its overall properties like volume and pressure, irrespective of the countless ways the individual gas molecules can be arranged to achieve these conditions. This asymmetric characteristic of the arrow of time aligns with a T-violation of CPT symmetry, raising fundamental questions about the nature of time and reality itself. For example, the asymmetry suggests that the future is fundamentally different from the past, privileging one over the other, and that the universe is constantly moving toward a state of increasing entropy or chaos. The arrow of time is also important in the context of cosmology and our understanding of the origins of the universe. Some physicists propose that the linear arrow of time may have in fact originated from a fundamental asymmetry in the early universe. I asked Dr. Timko why time flows in only one direction according to thermodynamics.

> Dr. Timko: Yeah, we don't really know why. We just observe that it is like this—we are aging, we cannot get younger. It is just a fundamental thing. Then we build it into the axioms of our theories. So, the way it works in physics is that you have laws, physical laws, and they are really just observations. It is observed that time is one directional. It is observed that energy is conserved, and so on and so forth. And then you just believe, and you don't really . . . Of course, you ask yourself the question, "Why?" but you don't really have an explanation.
>
> Rasheedah: Yeah. I guess "Why?" is the philosophy part of it.
>
> Dr. Timko: I mean, we would like to dig more into it, but I think we don't really have the answer yet. If we had the answer, we could get all young again and so on.

The origins of the laws of thermodynamics trace back to the mid-seventeenth century, though the Industrial Revolution of the nineteenth century marks their most significant evolution. Mechanical engineers, predominantly during the Napoleonic wars of France, sought to enhance steam engine efficiencies, which led to advancements in the understanding of thermodynamics. French mathematician and engineer Nicolas Sadi Carnot developed the concept of thermodynamic irreversibility in a theory published in 1824. Carnot's observations on the efficiency of heat engines led to the understanding that certain thermodynamic processes are irreversible, meaning they cannot occur in the opposite direction without adding energy into the system, laying the groundwork for the second law of thermodynamics. Later, Lord Kelvin and Rudolf Clausius built on Carnot's theories. Kelvin introduced absolute zero and the Kelvin temperature scale. By 1850, Clausius had introduced theories on mechanical heat and, by 1865, had coined and defined the concept of entropy, noting that it could "never decrease in a physical process and can only remain constant in a reversible process."[12] He also began developing the foundations for the first and second law of thermodynamics, stating that "the energy of the universe is constant; the entropy of the universe tends to a maximum."[13]

James Clerk Maxwell further developed the concept of entropy, culminating in his "Maxwell's Demon" thought experiment in 1867. He proposed a hypothetical creature capable of detecting and controlling individual molecules in a gas or liquid. The creature would be able to reverse a normally irreversible process by separating hot molecules from cold ones without expending energy, which would violate the second law of thermodynamics. This thought experiment continues to cause much debate and influence real-life experiments and theories on the fundamental characteristics of thermodynamics and whether its laws can be broken.

Arthur Eddington, a British physicist and astronomer, would continue this work in the next century and is credited with coining the term "the arrow of time" in his 1928 book *The Nature of the Physical World.* Eddington uses the term to describe the one-way flow of time, characterized by an increase in entropy. He theorized that the arrow of time is a fundamental part of our experience of the world and is intimately connected to the second law of thermodynamics, suggesting that entropy in a closed system can only increase over time.[14]

With a few notable exceptions, the pioneers of thermodynamics typically distanced themselves from the broader existential and societal ramifications of their theories. Clausius, for instance, purposely kept ontological beliefs about the motion of heat particles separate from his theories on thermodynamics because. According to Craig Callendar, Clausius did not want to "(in his own word) 'taint' the latter with the speculative character of the former."[15] An ontological perspective might have bridged the gap between the abstract, statistical nature of thermodynamics and the tangible, observable phenomena of heat and energy transfer, thus providing a fuller awareness and understanding of nature and the physical world. Nor did Lord Kelvin have the philosophical or societal consequences of the theory in mind when he wrote on the second law of thermodynamics in 1862, reflecting that the impact of the universal tendency toward dissipation would result in "a state of universal rest and death."[16] Yet, these theories inadvertently influenced popular culture and psychology. Writer and journalist James Gleick observes that Lord Kelvin's bleak outlook "imprinted the second law on the popular imagination."[17] The consequences of universal heat death and entropy showing up in stories like H. G. Wells's *The Time Machine* and in the theories of Sigmund Freud, reflect a growing public fascination with the concept of time and its irreversible flow.

Conversely, theorists like Luigi Fantappiè, who challenged scientific norms, often faced significant pushback, illustrating the risk involved in proposing unconventional ideas. Born in Viterbo, Italy, in 1901, Fantappiè made significant strides in mathematics, especially in topological algebra and theories of complex variables. His introduction of "analytic functionals" extended function theory to new domains, laying foundations for later advances in distribution theory and quantum field theory. Fantappiè's foray into theoretical physics, particularly his unified theory combining elements of relativity and quantum mechanics, though speculative, didn't gain as much traction as his mathematical contributions. His concept of syntropy, proposed as the opposite of entropy, suggests a universe characterized by increasing order and complexity. This idea, while remaining at the fringes of mainstream acceptance, continues to spark discussions in fields exploring system complexity and evolution.

To many non-physicists, the nature and direction of time seem definitive. But, as my talks with CERN scientists around time's nature revealed, the reality is neither straightforward nor settled among physicists and philosophers. In conversation with me, scientist Michael Dosser acknowledged that scientific questions of time and in what direction it moves, or even what time is, are not so easily answered in the work and life of a physicist: "I have no idea what time is; I know how to control the sequence of things that occur in tiny slices of time and to study the phenomena that happen within, but I can't change the ordering, I can't go backwards, and I can't change my subjective perception of time." I asked theoretical physicist Dorota Grabowska whether and how her work influences her thoughts and experiences about time as a human, to which she responded: "Thinking of time as a physicist is very different to how I think about time as a human. As a quantum field theorist, time goes forwards and backwards. It is reversible; there's no arrow of time. Obviously, as a human, there is. How you go from having no arrow of time in fundamental physics to having an arrow of time in our human scale is a massive question, and we don't know the answer." As Dr. Grabowska alludes, there is an ongoing, perhaps eternal debate among physicists and philosophers concerning the intrinsic nature of the arrow of time and the extent of its degrees of freedom. This term, "degrees of freedom," essentially refers to the number of independent variables or parameters that define the state of a system. In the context of the arrow of time, it pertains to how many independent ways time's progression can influence or be influenced by the physical state of the universe. While some experts contend that the arrow of time is an essential component of the universe, defying quantification into a specific number of degrees of freedom, others propose that it has a connection to the universe's initial conditions, suggesting that the arrow of time can be linked to a finite number of degrees of freedom.

One theory is that the arrow of time is connected to the number of possible starting conditions or scenarios that can lead to a particular outcome. For example, imagine a cup of hot coffee left in a cold room, or return to that bowl of hot soup you made at the beginning of this chapter. Over time, both substances naturally cool down, but they won't spontaneously become hot again. This common observation reveals more when we think about time and its direction. The cooling down of the coffee or soup happens in many ways at a microscopic level—the tiny particles in the coffee or soup move around in countless configurations, all of which result in the coffee or soup losing heat. On the other hand, these particles don't spontaneously arrange themselves in a way that would make the coffee or soup hot again. There are far fewer ways, at this tiny particle level, for this spontaneous heating to occur.

In scientific terms, we're talking about "microstates" and "macroscopic" states. A "microstate" is all about the specific, tiny details of the particles' arrangements and movements. The "macroscopic" state is the overall situation we can observe, like the coffee being hot or cold. The arrow of time concept suggests that the direction of time—why we see the coffee cool down but not heat up on its own—is connected to the number of these microstates that match up with the observable situation. In simpler terms, there are many more ways (microstates) for things to cool down than to heat up spontaneously, which is why we seem to observe time moving in the direction of cooling down rather than heating up.

In the quantum world, time's subtleties become increasingly nuanced the further you go into the microscopic level, even to the possibility of reversing quantum changes using special protocols. Experimental physicists at the University of Vienna and the Institute for Quantum Optics and Quantum Information (IQOQI) Vienna have implemented a universal rewinding protocol designed by theoretical physicists that demonstrates the ability to achieve, or revert, changes in a quantum system without working from prior knowledge of their evolution.

Time-reversal techniques in fields like acoustics and signal processing further illustrate the malleable nature of time. If a wave travels from point A to point B, its time-reversed counterpart could travel back from point B to point A while obeying the same physical laws. This principle has found applications across multiple scientific domains, including medical imaging, telecommunications, and seismology, further challenging the singular, universal conception of time and underscoring its context-dependent nature.

Other experiments have shown that quantum particles display a feature called retrocausality. The concept of retrocausality in quantum mechanics, which suggests that present actions can influence past events, challenges traditional notions of time and causality. This concept has been explored in various experiments, demonstrating that quantum particles seem to exhibit behaviors that imply a form of retrocausal influence. For instance, in experiments based on John Bell's work in the 1960s, correlations observed between particles suggest that the choice of measurement setting by experimenters can affect the properties of particles back at the source, prior to the experimenter's decision being made. This phenomenon suggests that the particles "know" about future measurements, thereby exhibiting retrocausal behavior. Theoretical work by physicists such as Matthew S. Leifer and Matthew F. Pusey further deepens the discussion by challenging the compatibility of time symmetry (the idea that physical processes can run the same forward and backward in time) with the principle of no-retrocausality (the assumption that future events cannot influence past events). Their work suggests that holding onto the principle of time symmetry might necessitate accepting retrocausality, as attempting to maintain both time symmetry and non-retrocausality leads to contradictions. This work underscores the potential necessity of retrocausality to preserve the fundamental symmetry of time in quantum theory, while also aiming to maintain consistency with Einstein's theory of relativity.

The exploration of retrocausality hints at profound implications for our understanding of the universe. If retrocausality is a feature of the quantum world, it could indicate that the current framework of quantum mechanics is incomplete and that retrocausality might be a missing piece that could help make the theory more complete. Speculatively, the presence of retrocausality, potentially leaving signatures in cosmological data, could even suggest that during certain eras, such as near the Big Bang, there might not have been a definite arrow of causality.

Such theories and experiments fundamentally challenge the supposed "uniformity" and "objectivity" of scientific concepts, particularly time, and highlight the limitations of the standardized, hegemonic narratives of time that we in the West are conventionally taught. The disconnect between the scientific understanding of time and our lived experiences reflects a broader tension between empirical science and human reality. This tension is rooted in historical scientific practices that often ignored or dismissed non-Western, non-male perspectives, reflecting colonialist and patriarchal biases. Ongoing debate about the nature of time challenges these traditional scientific narratives and opens possibilities for alternative understandings that are more inclusive and representative of diverse human experiences. This reevaluation of time and reality in scientific discourse is a crucial step toward dismantling the long-standing biases embedded in the field and embracing a more holistic and equitable approach to understanding our universe.

More specifically, the traditional portrayal of time in science as a rigid, unidirectional force has been used as a regulatory tool, shaping societal norms and expectations. This has particularly affected marginalized Black communities, who have historically been denied the agency to define their own temporal experiences and realities. The potential of quantum physics to redesign time offers a pathway to rectify these historical injustices, allowing for a reimagining of time that acknowledges and incorporates the diverse experiences and needs of these communities. It is not just about providing creative control over temporal modes in the present but also addressing historical "debts" related to time and freedom.

CERN serves as a hub for the collaborations of hundreds of scientists from institutions worldwide, with many that investigate scales of time of all kinds, from wormholes and black holes to quarks and particles. Visiting the groundbreaking experiments, including ALICE, CMS, and the Large Hadron Collider, for which CERN is known, underscored to me the contextual and experiment-dependent nature of time. Time within the scientific community does not adhere to a singular, objective, and universally accepted definition. Instead, its interpretation is fluid, varying significantly across different experiments and areas of physics. In reality, and as my conversations reinforced, the application of concepts like time in science is heavily influenced by specific contexts and the nature of the specific investigation.

Recognizing the diversity and subjectivity in scientific concepts like time is crucial in dismantling the hegemonic structures within the field, and in moving toward a more inclusive and representative approach to understanding our universe and our place within it. This resonated deeply with my understanding of Black and Afrodiasporic cultural contexts, where time is experienced and perceived in a similarly diverse and context-dependent manner. These observations at CERN thus reinforced the idea that both in physics and in cultural contexts, time is a fluid and adaptable concept, shaped by the perspectives and purposes of those studying or experiencing it. This is the fundamental idea underlying Black Quantum Futurism and Practice. As will unfold throughout the rest of the book, I propose a practical application of these concepts in the political, metaphysical, and reality-altering conditions that produce an alignment of quantum physics with Black temporalities. Taking lessons from Karen Barad, my approach challenges the traditional use of metaphor in describing the intersection of quantum physics and cultural temporalities. Metaphors, while useful in bridging concepts, often fall short in capturing the transformative potential of praxis, if not obscuring it altogether. This work is about actualizing a new temporal reality, one in which the rigid, linear constructs of time are dismantled in favor of a more equitable, holistic understanding that encompasses the diverse experiences, histories, and future trajectories of Black and Afrodiasporic peoples. Throughout the book I will continue to offer real-world possibilities for reimagining time and reality, while addressing historical debts and the ongoing impact of colonialism and racism on perceptions and experiences of time.

CHAPTER 2

Bending the Arrow of Time

DR. TIMKO: *But if you really want to go into the time frame of the particles traveling at the speed of light, for them there's no "the time doesn't exist" and "the space doesn't exist." They are at any time, at all the places. That's where we get into this quantum world. So, from outside, you see this thing making circles. But if you could hop onto this proton, and just travel with the proton, the meaning of time disappears. You are just everywhere at the same time.*

RASHEEDAH PHILLIPS: *And "at any time" would mean even going back to the Big Bang as the starting point of time?*

DR. TIMKO: *[Time] just disappears. It just doesn't have any meaning anymore. So, present is the future and is the past. It is just anywhere at any time or nowhere at no time or whatever you like to call it. It just is unified, you know?* **—Interview with the author at CERN, 2021**

The bridge would be finished in a few more days—you just weren't bred with the patience found in Willow Springs. Time, for its own sake, was never a factor here. The crops, the weather, the seasons—they all controlled behavior much more than your elaborate digital watch.
—Gloria Naylor, *Mama Day*

In the African American folktale "Br'er Rabbit's Race with Br'er Turtle," Br'er Rabbit, confident in his swiftness, agrees to a race. Yet, in a clever twist, the turtle enlists his kin to aid in an elaborate ruse. By dressing each family member identically and positioning them strategically along a path marked by hills and valleys, the turtles create an illusion of continuous progress. Each time Br'er Rabbit encounters a turtle ahead of him on the path, it seems as though Br'er Turtle is perpetually in the lead. This culminates at the finish line, where the real Br'er Turtle waits, appearing to have far outpaced the rabbit. This loop of misdirection contrasts starkly with its Classical counterpart in Aesop's fable of "The Tortoise and the Hare," where the hare's laziness leads to his downfall, imparting a moral of steady diligence over swift complacency. Instead of valorizing individual speed and linear progression—hallmarks of the Western "arrow of time"—in the African American folktale, the turtle employs a strategy of collective effort that disrupts the linear narrative. That multiple temporal events can coexist and influence each other exemplifies the cyclical and relational conceptions of time and of success as the product of collective support and shared wisdom.

This folktale reflects Black and Afrodiasporic temporal forms of consciousness that are deeply ingrained in processes of community, nature, and the cosmos—a resonance that aligns with the enigmatic principles of quantum physics. From ancient African traditions steeped in cosmology and spirituality to contemporary understandings of quantum physics, there has always been a deep understanding of time within these cultures. Philosophers, historians, and scholars such as John Mbiti, Molefi K. Asante, Ama Mazama, and John Henrik Clarke have shed light on this holistic worldview, where people within that society are tightly intertwined with their cosmic position. This echoes the fundamental interconnectedness found in the quantum world, where every particle exists in relation to each other. This concept of space-time consciousness is woven into the very fabric of Black and Afrodiasporic cultures.

Karen Barad's theory of "agential realism" offers a compelling framework that aligns with this embodied sense of unity.[1] Barad suggests that entities, including humans, do not pre-exist their interactions. Instead, they emerge through specific "intra-actions," a term they introduce to signify the mutual constitution of entangled agencies. This notion challenges the classical view of independent, pre-existing entities that interact in a linear, cause-and-effect fashion, proposing instead that phenomena (including the entities and their properties) emerge from their intra-actions. Drawing from Niels Bohr's quantum mechanics interpretation, agential realism proposes an ontological perspective where the universe is comprised of phenomena that are indissolubly the product of intra-acting agencies. The paradigm shift from interaction to intra-action emphasizes a reality where boundaries and identities are dynamically co-created within an ongoing network of relationships.

The synergy between agential realism and African temporal consciousness is striking. Both perspectives advocate for a reality where the nature of entities, their characteristics, and even time itself unfold through relational processes. This shared emphasis on emergence and relationality highlights a cosmos where all elements, from the smallest particles to vast celestial bodies, are part of a continuous exchange, echoing the African understanding of a cosmos where every part is in constant dialogue with every other and the very fabric of reality are co-constitutive, co-emerging from their mutual entanglements and interactions. This perspective not only reinforces but also deepens the enmeshment at the heart of Black and Afrodiasporic temporal consciousness, offering a quantum-inspired lens to view the rich tapestry of time and existence within these communities.

This chapter elevates Black temporalities as distinct and profound ways of engaging with time, space, and matter. These modalities are not just alternative temporal frameworks but are rich, relational space-times where Black people engage with the universe in ways that diverge markedly from dominant Western narratives. In numerous African, Black, and Afrodiasporic cultures, time is not simply a linear sequence of events but a rhythmic series of recurring cycles, reminiscent of the ever-cycling seasons and the lunar phases. Within these paradigms, the universe and natural world's rhythms—from the grand celestial dances of planets and stars to the intimate cadences of human heartbeats, breaths, and blood circulation—are a manifestation of the harmonious nature of time. Ancient African civilizations, attuned to these rhythms, were not mere observers but active participants, developing sophisticated systems of calendars, zodiacs, and mathematical frameworks. Their perception of time, as fluid and cyclical, mirrors the universe's dynamic and recurrent patterns, suggesting a time fabric far more flexible and interconnected than previously acknowledged.

The exploration of this perspective yields insights with far-reaching and transformative consequences, especially concerning the traditional concept of the arrow of time. A comparison of Western and African temporal concepts reveals a stark dichotomy between the static, linear timeline of the West versus the dynamic, living temporality of African cultures.[2] This dichotomy mirrors some of the fundamental differences between classical physics and quantum physics. In classical physics, characterized by its deterministic framework, events unfold in a predictable, sequential manner. This perception is akin to the Western view of time as a straight, unchanging line moving from past to future. In contrast, in the quantum realm, the outcomes of events are not strictly determined by their antecedents but are instead shaped by a spectrum of possibilities and uncertainties. Rather than following a predetermined trajectory, quantum phenomena exist in a state of potentiality, where multiple futures are possible.

In this chapter's exploration of Black SpaceTimeMatters, we will see how African, Black, and Afrodiasporic temporalities present a profound integration of aspects that mirror characteristics of quantum phenomena, with an emphasis on the qualities of uncertainty, potentiality, and the nonlinear flow of time. I draw parallels to the everyday realities of African practices, rituals, and traditions. Exploring phenomena within Black SpaceTimeMatters, such as the symbolic status of Zora Neale Hurston, the cultural significance of Black hair in relation to time, and the innovative conceptualization of Black holes through an Afrodiasporic lens, further illustrates the depth and breadth of Black temporalities. These examples underscore the critical role of African-derived temporal frameworks in showing us what is possible in the world and reality when we depart from Western-centric, linear notions of time and embrace local, communal, and cultural frames of time.

In discussing these concepts here and throughout the book, it is essential to clarify the overlaps and distinctions between the terms "African," "Black," and "Afrodiasporic." As I will use them, "African" refers specifically to the diverse traditions and philosophies originating from the African continent, spotlighting specific countries and societies. "Black" encompasses the global community of African descendants, acknowledging their shared heritage and the diverse cultures arising in different contexts. This text often uses "Black" to particularly refer to the traditions, practices, and concepts that have evolved within Black American communities. "Afrodiasporic" highlights the cultures and temporal perspectives of African descendants living outside Africa, underscoring the global dissemination and adaptation of African traditions. While these terms are sometimes used interchangeably to underscore their shared roots in African consciousness, precision in their application is sought to elucidate the nuances among these traditions.

Crossing Temporal Boundaries: African Perspectives and Quantum Insights

> *If we knew how a tree contracted into a seed, then we could predict the future. This is like saying that if we can understand the retrograde process of development then we can predict the future . . . . The future is always present as a seed, so if I know how a tree contracts to a seed than I can also predict how the tree will develop from the seed. If we know the kernel point of a situation we can predict its consequences.* —**Marie-Luis von Franz,**
> ***On Divination and Synchronicity***

While late philosopher John Mbiti's description of African conceptions of time in his 1969 book *African Religions and Philosophy* drew criticism for its seemingly reductive Eurocentric misconceptions of African temporalities, his clarification in the 1990 edition counters these misinterpretations. Mbiti's delineation of the Swahili concepts of Zamani and Sasa, as two significant ontological dimensions of time, is particularly enlightening. In these contexts, time is experienced both personally and through the societal lineage and collective social memory that stretches back generations before their births and extends beyond their own lifetimes.[3]

Within Zamani, a macrotime realm, events unfold with a unique kind of reverse causation that defies traditional linearity. As events occur, they don't simply progress forward, but instead retreat into the Zamani realm where they are recontextualized, becoming part of a broader, interconnected historical tapestry. It is essential to recognize that this form of backward causation does not equate to reverse linearity or the reversal of forward causation, they are instead reinterpreted, gaining new meanings and significance within the broader continuum of past, present, and future.

Consider a community ritual celebrating a child's birth. This event is not just recognized as a new beginning but also as an extension of an ancestral lineage, interweaving the child's life with the threads of generations past. This is retrocausality at work: an event reshaping the fabric of time by integrating into and altering the context of past events, rather than merely following them.

Retrocausality is a fascinating phenomenon that challenges our conventional understanding of time and causation. It suggests that the present can be influenced by the future, just as it is by the past. A compelling example from the realm of quantum physics is the behavior of entangled particles. When particles become entangled, a change in the state of one particle instantaneously affects the state of the other, irrespective of the distance between them. In retrocausality, an entangled particle can seemingly send a signal backward in time to the moment of its entanglement. This retroactive influence does not break the speed of light barrier; rather, it traverses the shared path of the entangled particles in space-time. This implies that the present state of the particle is not only the result of past actions but is also tied to future interactions.

Sasa time more closely mirrors the Western concept of the present, but is, according to Dr. Nikitah Okembe-RA Imani, "much more nuanced including the immediate past and the immediately impinging future (just around the corner reality)."[4] It is a temporality where the present is a confluence of moments, a nexus where what has just happened and what is about to occur coalesce. In Sasa, a falling leaf is observed not as a discrete moment but as part of an ongoing process: the leaf's fall signifies the imminent arrival of autumn, hinting at the future's turn while still resonating with the rustle of other leaves that have just fallen. It is a tangible, palpable present, where the leaf's descent is both a current happening and a bridge to the imminently approaching season, as well as a reflection of the just-concluded summer. In quantum terms, the leaf's journey is akin to a particle's wave function, which doesn't just describe a single state but encompasses a range of potential states. As the leaf descends, it is not merely a consequence of gravity acting at that moment; it is a culmination of past factors (such as the tree's growth cycle) and a predictor of future events (the onset of autumn). This is similar to how a particle's present state reflects its past interactions and hints at future probabilities.

While Zamani time overlaps Sasa time, Zamani time extends into the eternal past and Sasa extends into the immediate past, with both recognizing that the past is not a discrete entity. In both Zamani and Sasa, the future as a dimension is conceptualized as "potential time," actualizing or coming into existence only when conditions and experiences align. This parallels the quantum concept of superposition, where particles exist in all possible states simultaneously until observed. In quantum mechanics, the outcome of any event isn't predetermined but is modified by the act of observation and measurement. Those events are not tethered to any specific chronometric reference, in other words, they do not depend on some specific clock time or calendar date for their manifestation. Instead, time—as in, the "right" time for an event to occur—depends on the quality of the event and the person experiencing it, manifesting when conditions and experiences align.

Dr. Imani's perspective underscores this, writing that potential time "is speculative and its character and existence is prefigured and determined by the actions that individuals and collectives take within the working realms of Zamani and Sasa."[5] This echoes the quantum principle of entanglement, where entangled particles remain connected so that the state of one instantaneously affects the state of another, no matter the distance of the two particles. This concept suggests that events are interconnected in a nonlinear, nonlocal manner, much like how the African conception of time views the past, present, and future as interconnected realms rather than distinct, sequential phases. Events, though seemingly separate, are intrinsically connected across time. Again, to take the example of the falling leaf is entangled with the past (its origin and growth) and the future (its impact on the ecosystem), just as entangled particles share a connection that transcends spatial and temporal boundaries.

Once the future event transpires, it intertwines with Zamani and Sasa time. And in this, "there is no need for a 'feedback' loop since there is no 'back' there to feed to. Even the eternal past is understood as immediately and presently accessible."[6] Moreover, the absence of a "feedback" loop in this concept, where the past is immediately and presently accessible, again recalls the quantum physics notion of retrocausality. In the context of Zamani and Sasa, this means that future events could inform or reshape the past, a notion that aligns with the quantum theory where past, present, and future are not strictly linear but are interdependent dimensions of time. Reginald Crosley, in his 2000 *Vodou Quantum Leap*, highlights that the classical rules of physics appear to dominate the day-to-day interactions of humans. Classical physics, rooted in Western paradigms of time and space, operates under principles such as Newton's laws of motion, which describe a predictable, deterministic universe where cause precedes effect in a linear, straightforward manner. This framework tends to dominate our day-to-day understanding of physical interactions.

Crosley argues, however, that quantum-like causality violations are regularly recognized in other worldviews and ontologies, such as the notion of the "premonitory kick" in the Haitian mental construct which "reverse[s] the space-time arrow . . . by letting the future coincide with the present."[7] The premonitory kick acts as an advanced warning system. It may take the form of accidentally hitting your left foot against a door, a bad omen, as opposed to your right foot, a good omen. These events live in the realm of the indeterminate and so are capricious, with many possible interpretations, emphasizing the pivotal role of the observer's beliefs in shaping their reality, aligning with the quantum physics principle that "the observer changes everything."

The observer effect in quantum physics is the changes that the act of measurement or observation will have on a phenomenon being observed. This concept is dramatically illustrated in the famous thought experiment known as Schrödinger's Cat. In the Schrödinger's Cat hypothetical, a cat is put inside of a sealed box with a vial of poison, a radioactive atom, and a Geiger counter. If the atom decays, a random event, the Geiger counter triggers, releasing the poison and killing the cat. Quantum mechanics suggests that until the box is opened, and the cat observed, it exists in a state of superposition, or in this case, a state of being both alive and dead. This paradox highlights the counter-intuitive nature of quantum mechanics, where the act of observation determines the state of a system.[8] Introduced in 1935, this experiment was a reaction to the concept of superposition. In somewhat simpler terms, a particle—say, a photon—initially in a superposition of all its theoretically possible states before being measured, appears to reduce to a single state once measured, giving a result corresponding to only one of its possible configurations. This change of a quantum system from a superposition of states to a single, definite state is called a "wave-function collapse."

Crosley suggests a similar paradigm in everyday life: the interpretation of an event like the premonitory kick can change the reality of that event for the observer, underscoring the profound influence of personal and collective belief systems. Specifically, Crosley describes superstition as "a belief that modulates the reality around the believer," giving the superstition its own role as a fact.[9] He compares this to Carl Jung's notion of coincidence and synchronicity. Jung proposed that synchronicity is the occurrence of two or more events related meaningfully but without a causal connection, suggesting a deeper order to the universe beyond apparent randomness, where coincidences carry significant meaning and are not just events that occurred by chance.[10]

Just as Schrödinger's Cat's fate is indeterminate until observed, in African temporalities, events and moments are not fixed in a linear sequence but exist in a state of potentiality, shaped and defined by the act of remembrance, interpretation, and communal significance. Originating from the Yoruba people in West Africa, the spiritual concept of Ifa is not just a spiritual and divination system; it is a multidisciplinary framework that incorporates aspects of science, epistemology, cosmology, ontology, and even physics and mathematics.[11]

In the Ifa cosmology, the universe is an interconnected network, with each element of the cosmos carrying dynamic information essential for maintaining the system's overall harmony. Here, "information" refers to the essential qualities, functions, and interrelations of each element within the cosmic network which dictates how they interact and contribute to the universe's balance. This concept of dynamic information mirrors the principles of quantum physics, where particles exist in states of probabilities rather than in fixed locations.

Rather than having a definite position, particles are described by a range of possible locations, each with a certain likelihood of being accurate. These probabilities are influenced by numerous factors including observation and interaction, leading to a universe that is not predetermined and fixed but is constantly evolving and interconnected, with each part influencing the whole. The Odu Ifa, the system's sacred texts, are comprehensive guides to moral, spiritual, and philosophical questions, offering a rich reservoir of collective wisdom. These texts, preserved through both oral and written traditions, provide invaluable guidance not only for individual lives but also for the broader community.

The Ifa divination system, particularly through the use of the Opele chain, offers a striking parallel to quantum concepts like superposition and entanglement. The Opele chain, used in divination rituals, consists of a rope or chain strung with half-seed shells, cowrie shells, or similar objects that have two distinct sides, arranged in a pattern along both sides of the chain. When the chain is cast, the specific pattern in which the shells or coins fall represents different messages or answers from the spiritual realm.

In *The Mechanics of Ifa Divination System*, author Ojo Oyebisi draws a comparison between the Opele chain and quantum computing systems. Essentially, Oyebisi points out that classical computers function by storing and encoding data in binary form (0s and 1s), while quantum computing utilizes qubits that can be in a state of 0, 1, or any superimposed combination of these states. This allows quantum computers to hold and process a much larger amount of information than classical computers, and to perform certain computations much more efficiently.

In a similar manner, the Opele chain provides a richer source of possibilities for data than a simple binary system. Oyebsi describes the Opele as a tool designed to reflect the human mind's computational dynamics during decision-making, encompassing a "range of possibilities" and a vast "nonlinear spectrum of potentialities." Each casting of the Opele chain can result in a variety of configurations, or a superposition of possible outcomes, each with its own meaning and interpretation.[12] This is akin to the superposition of states in a qubit, where multiple possibilities coexist until the act of measurement (or, in the context of Ifa, interpretation) crystallizes a specific outcome or result.

Karen Barad's unique perspective on the wave-function collapse in quantum mechanics, offers another view of what may be happening with superposition and the act of measurement that produces a wave-function collapse (transition of a system from a superposition of states to a single state upon measurement).[13] Traditionally, this collapse is seen as a definitive transformation from potentiality to actuality. Barad denies the occurrence of such a collapse and suggests instead that the "reality" of particles in specific states emerges only in the context of their interaction and measurement.

This perspective resonates with the way time is conceptualized in many African and Afrodiasporic temporalities, where time, in this sense, does not collapse into a single, predetermined moment but is continuously created and redefined through communal interactions, rituals, and traditions. Just as Barad views particles in a state of potentiality until they are measured, Black and African temporalities consider time as a dynamic process, shaped by the collective experiences and actions of the community. Black and Afrodiasporic traditions, rituals and ceremonies are not mere commemorations of specific historical events; they are reenactments that bring the past into the present, creating a temporal bridge that defies the apparent unidirectional flow of time.

English literature scholar Geneva Smitherman's observation about the use of "be" in African American Language (AAL) also highlights these distinctive aspects of Black temporal expression. In standard English, the verb "be" is typically bound to a specific tense—present, past, or future. However, in AAL, "be" transcends these conventional time boundaries, indicating a recurring or habitual action without a fixed temporal anchor.[14] When someone says, for example, "She be singing in the choir," the verb "be" isn't referring to a specific instance of singing. Instead, it indicates a recurring, habitual action that happens over time. This use of "be" suggests that the action of singing in the choir is a regular part of her life, not confined to a singular event or limited timeframe.

This linguistic feature mirrors the quantum idea that realities are not fixed but are potentialities that exist simultaneously across different states. By enabling speakers to express continuity and regularity, emphasizing an action that is characteristic or ongoing rather than momentary, this transcendent "be" offers a window into a worldview where events and behaviors are seen as part of a larger, ongoing cycle and a broader cultural understanding of time as something fluid and expansive rather than sequential.

Time and the Community

In many African cultures and societies, the notion of time is often intimately connected to genealogical, astrological, and ecological cycles. For instance, Kassim Koné's examination of the Bamana, primarily based in Mali, reveals that their temporal understanding centers around natural occurrences, such as rainfall or the sun's movements.[15] These societies view time as an inherent rhythm or pacing, often tied to the duration required for journeys between places. The *Encyclopedia of African Religions* provides a comprehensive view of the Bamana people's spiritual practices, highlighting a deep temporal connection in their rituals and beliefs, particularly in their reverence for ancestors. For the Bamana, ancestors serve as vital intermediaries between the living and the divine. The practice of burying ancestors within the family compound is a physical manifestation of their belief in the continuous involvement of ancestors in the lives of the living. This spatial closeness is paralleled by a temporal closeness, as the Bamana maintain an ongoing dialogue with their ancestors through regular libations and consultations.[16] The process of becoming an ancestor is intricate tied to the passage of time, marked by specific temporal milestones. The performance of funerary rites at critical intervals—the first, third, seventh, and fortieth days following death—is not merely a matter of ritual observance but a reflection of the Bamana's understanding of time as a transformative force. Each of these days holds significant symbolic meaning, representing different stages in the transition from the physical world to the ancestral realm. Here it might be said that the pace of time is dictated by one's actions and engagements, rather than by a predetermined clock pace that can lead to either the excess or scarcity of time. In these paradigms, time isn't an independent entity;

instead, time is characterized by relationships, patterns, and rhythms and so becomes an experience that can be created, produced, saved, or retrieved, particularly through ritual and communal practices.

Within these traditions and practices, the historical past and genealogies are conceptualized within contexts of space, place, totemic affiliation, and family names," as opposed to Western notions of "exact chronology, recorded history, dominant figures, royal succession, centralized states, and international relations."[17] From the Akan perspective, a person is not merely an individual entity but a composite of several elements: *kra* (the soul), *mogya* (blood), and *sunsum* (spirit). Additionally, an individual's identity is intrinsically linked to their *abusua* (family from the matrilineal clan) and extends to the broader community, which encompasses the living and the dead. This interconnectedness forms the basis for the concept of *nkrabea*, which is deeply rooted in the family and community context.[18] *Nkrabea* is not just about individual destiny; it's about how an individual's path is interwoven with the destinies of others within their community, or "that each human is unique and has value apart from others, although this value is meaningless without community."[19] This Akan philosophy underscores a temporal continuum where past, present, and future are inextricably linked through familial and communal ties. The idea that one's existence and fulfillment of destiny are contingent on assisting others in realizing their destinies speaks to a belief that individual actions and destinies are not isolated but are part of a larger, communal thread evolving through space-time.

In Malagasy culture, destiny, or *vintana*, is woven to the time of a person's or object's origin. This belief holds that the destinies of beings and things are governed by ancestors, intertwining past, present, and future. For instance, the time of birth of a newborn or the construction of a house determines its *vintana*, or destiny, which then influences future events, rather than disconnected from ancestral or cosmic influences.[20] Similarly, in Sierra Leone the Temne people practice a form of ethnoastronomy, where time is not just a chronological measure but an embodiment of metaphysical concepts. The human body is seen as a microcosm of the universe, representing balance, self-possession, and the interplay between physical and spiritual realms.[21] Communal events, such as the birth of a child, are not just social gatherings but ritually significant moments that intertwine the community's temporal experience with their spiritual and social life. The act of women gathering and clapping hands at the mother's house is a ritualistic marking of time, initiating a series of community and family rituals. This holistic approach to time connects communal, spiritual, and cosmic elements, in stark contrast to the compartmentalized, secular view of time prevalent in Eurocentric cultures.[22]

Africana and Political Science scholar Omari H. Kokole described the fluidity of indigenous African time perspectives and their ability to blur conventional temporal boundaries between past, present and future. This conceptual elasticity resonates with the quantum idea of superposition, where, as explained earlier, particles exist in multiple states simultaneously until measured. The indigenous heritage of time, Kokole explains, "often made no sharp distinction between the past, present, and the future (yesterday, today, and tomorrow)," and was generally "uninterested in the minutia of time."[23] This is a temporality where events and experiences, rather than minutes and hours, compose the contours of time, and where memory is not tethered to a specific calendar date or clock time. Instead, time and date are integrated into the memory itself, becoming part of the fabric of the experience and subject to reinterpretation in future recollections. This approach allows for a more fluid and dynamic interaction with time, where human activity and experiences dictate the perception of time's passage, rather than a strictly linear or mathematically predetermined rate.

The way of life of the Dinka people of South Sudan exemplifies a profound connection to both temporality and spatiality that transcends the conventional chronometric time scale. The Dinka operate with a socialized time, as "compared to a Western regimentation of time which favors the alienation of other people's space, place, and time by private individuals."[24] Their year is divided not by the conventional twelve months but by the rhythm of two pivotal seasons: the dry and the wet. This division of time is fundamentally interwoven with their spatial movements and their sense of home. During the wet season, the Dinka reside in their traditional dwellings, "often scattered among palm trees and fruit trees."[25] This setting is not just a physical space but a temporal haven, where the pace of life is synchronized with the rhythm of nature. Here, time is not measured by the ticking of a clock but by the growth of the trees and the patterns of rainfall. Their homes, amid this lush environment, become spaces of preparation, as they anticipate the arrival of the dry season.

With the onset of the dry season, the Dinka's sense of space and home undergoes a transformation. This change is not just a physical relocation but a temporal shift. Moving to new areas with their herds, they embrace the grasslands, adapting to a different rhythm of life. This transition from wet to dry season locations illustrates a unique understanding of temporality and spatiality. Time for the Dinka is a cycle of seasons, each with its own set of activities, rituals, and meanings. Their movements across landscapes are not merely geographic but are rooted in a temporal narrative that guides their lives. The Dinka's sense of home, therefore, is vibrant and intimately tied to these seasonal cycles. Home is not a fixed location but a series of spaces that they inhabit in accordance with the temporal dictates of nature. This relationship reveals a deep harmony with the natural world, where time is a living, breathing entity that shapes their movements, activities, and the very concept of home itself.

In many African communities, momentous events such as harvests, rites of passage, and communal gatherings are not marked by their occurrence on a specific date. Instead, these events are remembered and anticipated through their significance and impact on the community. This approach to time acknowledges the interconnectedness of events, where each moment is part of a larger continuum of experiences, relationships, and memories. The Adae festival, central to the Akan culture of West Africa, is a profound observance intertwining ancestral reverence with the temporal rhythms of their calendar. It is a period where the *ahene*, or traditional rulers, engage intimately with the spiritual realm, honoring ancestors within the *nkonuafieso*—a sacred space symbolizing rest and ancestral presence.[26] This festival, inherently linked to the concept of rest, mandates a pause from daily work, allowing for spiritual and communal reflection.[27] Adae festivals are intrinsically linked to the concept of time and cyclical nature within the Akan community. The Akan year is divided into nine cycles, each spanning approximately forty-two days, within which the Adae is celebrated twice—Akwasidae on a Sunday and Awukudae on a Wednesday.[28] These festivals are not fixed calendar events that fall on a specific numbered date of observance, but are instead dynamic periods of deep spiritual significance, marking a time when the living connect with the ancestral realm, and encapsulating a cyclical sense of time that reflects the enduring rhythms of culture, kingship, and community. During the festival, time takes on a layered quality as historical events are reenacted and ancestral spirits are venerated, connecting the present Ashanti community with their past and projecting their cultural identity into the future. This temporal blending, where past, present, and future coalesce, underpins the profound spiritual and cultural significance of the Adae Kese Festival, making it a living embodiment of the Ashanti people's understanding and experience of time, and where events are "situated in time as well as in context."[29]

Time-Binding and the Griot

> *No people will prosper without a knowledge of their history that they can respect. This is where you start to use history to tell your time of day, wherever you are.* —**John Henrik Clarke, "The Elder Radical—John Henrik Clarke—Bad Boy of Academe"**

African cultures and societies overwhelmingly operate within the African oral tradition, which the *Encyclopedia of African Religion* defines as a "complex corpus of verbal or spoken art created for the purpose of remembering the past based on the people's ideas, beliefs, symbols, assumptions, attitudes, and sentiments."[30] The griot, as a vital figure in these traditions, appears in various forms across West African societies, including the Mandé, Fula, Hausa, Songhai, Tukulóor, Wolof, Serer, Mossi, and Dagomba. Traditionally part of a social caste, the art of storytelling in griot families is passed down through generations. They are responsible for keeping records of all births, deaths, and marriages in the family or village.[31] Griots in the West African Mandé empire of Mali, dating back to the thirteenth century, are "storytellers, musicians, praise singers, and oral historians," preserving genealogies, historical narratives, and oral traditions, keeping the history and traditions of the empire alive.[32] In the Mandinka culture, the griot serves as a "court poet," documenting historical events of the ruling family through song and acting as the king's spokesperson.[33]

In their role as custodians of cultural heritage, griots act as temporal bridges across generations. Their storytelling transcends narration, functioning much as entangled particles do by remaining inextricably connected despite any distance. This profound analogy is further explored in David A. Grandy's *Everyday Quantum Reality*. Grandy proposes that the principles of quantum entanglement are not confined to the microscopic world of atoms and subatomic particles. He illuminates how these quantum properties manifest in everyday phenomena, such as music and magnetism. In music, individual notes interweave to form a cohesive melody, mirroring the quantum principle where separate elements coalesce into a unified whole. Similarly, a magnet embodies both electricity and magnetism entangled in one object.[34]

According to composer and researcher Daniel Santos Diébaté, griots have a distinct approach to history as compared to Western academics. While academics seek proven facts in archives and books, griots have an active role as transmitters of the past, witnesses of the present, and transformers of both. Values, relationships, and genealogy are their sources of credibility rather than specific dates. Griots, Diébaté reports, perceive time through the "hourglass effect," emphasizing the beginning and end rather than the middle of the happenings they relay. Through their stories, they create a contemporary interpretation of the past, blending old and new values.[35] The stories of griots undergo metamorphoses, adapting to the changing eras while preserving their essence. This process reflects a nonlinear approach to time, akin to the interconnectedness and multidimensional nature observed in quantum physics and traditional African divination practices. As the narratives evolve, they incorporate new interpretations, possibly influenced by events and insights that have arisen since the story was last told, thus forming a layered succession of interpretations. An example of this evolving storytelling tradition is evident in the way that the epics told by griots continue to adapt and evolve, unlike the static epics of other cultures, such as those of the Ancient Greeks. This ongoing evolution allows their stories to remain relevant and engaging for contemporary audiences.

Alfred Korzybski, in his book *Science and Sanity: An Introduction to Non-Aristotelian Systems and General Semantics*, postulates that humans possess an unparalleled ability to "time-bind," that is, to capture, conserve, and transfer knowledge from one generation to the next.[36] This exceptional capability ensures the continuous progression of civilization and culture. At the heart of this process are symbols, especially language, that crystallize our reflections on past events and empower us with foresight into future possibilities.

The griot's process mirrors the principle of energy conservation in physics: just as energy remains constant—neither created nor destroyed, only transformed—the stories and wisdom passed down by griots aren't lost in the sands of time. Instead, the griots' stories, retrieved from the enfolded moments of the communal timescape, undergo metamorphoses, adapting to the tones and tunes of changing eras. The curated ancestral narratives remain ever present, like the conservation of energy in a closed system, a testament to the enduring power of collective memory and the indelible impact of the past on shaping the future.

Zora Neale Hurston's journey as a time binder with involuntary divinatory powers began at an early age. In her autobiography, *Dust Tracks on a Road,* she vividly maps out an experience she had with "the clutching hand of time" at a young age: she was given "knowledge before its time" that left her with a known sense of fate and, like a thief, robbed her of childhood innocence.[37] Hurston describes an abrupt and unwished-for vision that unfolded in her mind's eye of a series of events that would come to pass, including the death of her mother, and indeed, they did so with a grim linearity. It did, however, seed the conditions by which Hurston transformed into a time binder upon the hour of her mother's death, she pinpointed where her wanderings "not so much in geography, but in time" began, and "then, not so much in time as in spirit."[38]

Hurston's temporal rupture, I believe, disrupted the prison of the here and now and allowed her access to both the pasts and futures with the same privileges as she accessed the present. Even her documented number of years on this earth was elusive and subject to her own manipulation—she was, in some accounts, born ten years before the date commonly referenced for her.

Time reckoning, like weather and politics, is always local. Zora Neale Hurston's life in the all-Black town of Eatonville, rooted in her family and communal relationships, also strongly informed her understanding of Black communities' particular relations to time. In the opening lines of her autobiography, she writes that, because "time and place have had their say" in the making of her, "you will have to know something about the time and place where I came from, in order that you may interpret the incidents and directions of my life."[39] Even how Eatonville's settlers described their migration to town "just before, or just after the stars fell" sidestep the conventional marking of time. Other examples of Eatonville's temporality follow. Hurston tells the story of how, on the day she "got born," there were no adults close by to tend to her mother as she was going into labor, as it was the time of year when people were "digging for sweet potatoes, and then it was hog-killing time," which was a "gay time" for the community to gather, provide mutual aid, share food and drinks.[40] Her autobiography travels the routes of her family's temporality through her early years and then the nonlinear journey of her one life, with the autobiography jumping around in time, space, and memory, revisiting past experiences from different stages of her life, and intertwining them with her current reflections, bringing us into a realm where time is fluid, and memories are not constrained by the rigid sequence of events. This approach allows Hurston to explore the depths of her family's experiences in a way that traditional timelines cannot capture, bringing a richly layered understanding of her life but also challenging the reader's perception of time and memory. Hurston's text celebrates that mechanical time and historical progress are not the only ways to measure and understand temporality.

Applying Black Temporalities to Everyday Phenomenon: Unraveling Black Hairstories

She pulled in her horizon like a great fish-net. Pulled it from around the waist of the world and draped it over her shoulder. So much of life in its meshes! —**Zora Neale Hurston, *Their Eyes Were Watching God***

From my earliest memories, I found temporal dislocation—being lifted out of the linearity of the present—in the very Black temporal ritual of getting my hair done. Whether it was the tactile sensation of a comb carving patterns across my scalp to create braids, or my mother winding ballies around my hair, each act of sitting down to be styled was disorienting. I was, and still am, what we call tender-headed in the Black community, and so, growing up with a head of thick hair required me to dissociate often as I sat on a pillow with my head between my mother knees, for what felt like hours, attempting to turn long stretches of detangling pain into microseconds while trying to extend the gentle moments, like getting my scalp greased.

It was in the later years, under the sustained heat of a hair dryer or in the duration of an eight-to-ten-hour commitment to an African hair braider's chair for microbraids, that my oscillations between temporal dimensions became most pronounced. I would enter a liminal space between waking and dreaming, into what felt like a lucid dream, floating in a different dimension of the salon I was in. This profound time distortion was, in part, a survival mechanism and a neurological strategy employed by my brain to cope with the long hours of stillness or of waiting to be cycled in and out of the salon stations and into the stylist chair for the final round.

These experiences inspired the time machine as a hood hair dryer, called the Psychotemporal Transcranial Stimulation Device, or PTSD for short, in my book of time- travel stories, *Recurrence Plot*. The PTSD allows the user to 'functionally' relive not only their own memories with perfect clarity and consciousness, but also the memories of others. Combining two brain stimulation techniques of transcranial direct current stimulation and transcranial magnetic stimulation, the fictional PTSD uses a noninvasive method to stimulate several targeted brain regions responsible for memory and time perception. For a 2016 group exhibition called *Octavia's Attic*, at Live Worms Gallery in San Francisco, I made a replica out of a hood hair dryer that I'd found at an old thrift store, representing time travel in mundane and ritualistic acts, and emphasizing the ways that technologies and everyday objects can serve as mediums for experiencing different modes of time.

The texture and versatility of Black hair is another emblem of Black temporality, subverting linear categorization. In much the same way that Black and African conceptualizations of time—like Zamani and Sasa—simultaneously encapsulate individual and collective experiences, Black hair functions as a canvas for personal articulation and ancestral homage. As Black hair can be twisted, braided, or left free, so too can Black temporalities weave in various notions of past, present, and future. Just as a single strand of hair is part of a larger pattern, discrete events in African temporal constructs form part of expansive cosmological designs.

As a Black attorney with natural hair, I have had to navigate a labyrinthine temporal terrain in professional spaces. Despite appearing in court in professional attire day after day, my Blackness, signaled in part by my hair, has led to recurrent misidentification by clerical staff. Being repeatedly asked if I was a tenant while attempting to sign into the lawyers' list, is not just a slight but a theft, and an indicator of how my Blackness costs me time and necessitates additional emotional labor. Altering my appearance to what is considered more "appropriate" by non-Black people—often judges, opposing counsel, court clerks—has led to a notable shift in these dynamics, revealing the temporal politics of Black hair and its misalignment with social acceptability.

This struggle is not just personal; it reflects a broader societal trend. The 2017 "'Good Hair' Study" by the Perception Institute revealed that Black women with natural hairstyles, such as afros, braids, and twists, were often perceived as less professional and competent than Black women with straightened hair or non-Black women with various hairstyles.[41] This prejudice impacts not only professional opportunities but also imposes a heavy psychological burden and perpetuates the notion that natural Black hair is somehow inappropriate or unacceptable in formal settings.[42] As such, Black people are frequently compelled to engage in the practice of code-switching, altering our behavior, appearance, and the ways we communicate to navigate predominantly non-Black spaces. These occurrences are not isolated incidents but are indicative of systemic biases that permeate various facets of society, resulting in widespread and profound consequences. There are numerous documented instances of Black students facing suspension from school due to their natural hairstyles, athletes experiencing the forcible cutting of their hair by coaches, and individuals being denied employment opportunities, or facing disciplinary actions in the workplace, all due to their natural hair.[43] Temporality, Black hair, and cultural significance was explored in a workshop called "Malleable Futures" presented at "Prime Meridian Unconference." As part of my exhibition *Time Zone Protocols*, artist Ingrid Raphaël highlighted the concept of "Black Hair Time" with participants, observing that "Time slows, shifts." Another participant raised the fact that "It's difficult to braid your own hair," and so this activity becomes a communal sense of time. In contradistinction to Western paradigms where hair is often trivialized as fashion, in Black life, it performs a wealth of temporal functions. It serves as a generational chronicle, registering stages of life and even one's transitions into different forms of consciousness. Just as griots and other keepers of communal memory narrate the histories and genealogies of their people, Black hair carries its own continuum of narratives—of hairstories. It relays legacies of migration, of the juxtaposition of freedom and bondage, and of aesthetic and political choices that shift in response to changing historical, political, and cultural contexts.

Black hair is a symbol-laden language. Following Alfred Korzybski's time-binding theory, each braid, each lock, each adornment serves as a symbol, transmitting a variety of expressions and historical narratives, capturing, conserving, and transferring knowledge. It binds time by preserving traditions, methods, and stories passed down through generations. The rituals involved in hair care, from washing to braiding, echo the cyclical and rhythmic nature of African time, deeply embedded in cultural rituals and traditions. Just as time in these conceptions can be created, produced, saved, or retrieved through ritual, so too can the act of tending to Black hair be a form of "time creation," a rhythmic act that ties one back to their roots, literally and figuratively. The rhythmic nature of African time is echoed in the repetitive, almost meditative actions involved in hair care. The act of braiding, for instance, involves a consistent, rhythmic motion that can be soothing and contemplative. This rhythm creates a sense of continuity and connection, not just across time but also within the community. It is a ritual that often involves multiple generations, with knowledge and techniques passed down from elders to the young, reinforcing communal bonds and shared cultural identity.

As Wayne Chandler writes in his seminal book on African philosophy, history, and spirituality, *Ancient Future: The Teachings and Prophetic Wisdom of the Seven Hermetic Laws of Ancient Egypt*, the cyclical and spherical nature of time is represented "even in the follicles of the human hair," especially of Black people's hair, as it "spiral[s] up and out of the head, creating the individual spiral strands of helical, spring-like shafts."[44] Black hair transcends its aesthetic boundaries into the metaphysical, as a mirror reflecting Black temporal experiences. It showcases the intrinsic qualities of Black time—cyclical yet linear, patterned but unshackled, imbued with spirituality, and rooted in community. In its ever-changing forms, Black hair embodies potential time, manifesting when conditions and experiences align. This makes it a site of resistance, a locus of aesthetic freedom, and a sanctum of spiritual nourishment.

Applying Black Temporalities to Cosmic Phenomenon: Peeking Through Black Holes with Afrodiasporic Temporal Frameworks

> *Shadows (like other holes) can survive the destruction of their originators. Consider a tree that is constantly illuminated as it petrifies into stone. The stone continues the shadow begun by the tree.* —**Roy Sorensen, *Seeing Dark Things***

> *There is the same difference between a hole and a void as there is between deprivation and annihilation. This distinction is so true that holes may be seen as a symbol of all potentialities.* —**J. E. Cirlot, *Dictionary of Symbols***

Shortly after leaving Geneva, Black Quantum Futurism held a solo exhibition at REDCAT in Los Angeles called *CPT Reversal*, drawing directly on my research at the CERN laboratory as well as BQF's long-standing exploration of Colored People's Time. Like the residency, this series of works echoed the themes of time and temporality at various scales and dimensions. *CPT Reversal* underscored the importance of understanding the cultural, social, and historical contexts in which concepts like CPT develop and evolve. By highlighting the interplay between these various dimensions, BQF emphasized the idea that our understanding of time is profoundly rooted in our cultural narratives, scientific theories, and firsthand experiences.

One of the central pieces in the exhibition was the *CP Timeline*, a nonlinear timeline tracing the usage and history of "Colored People's Time" and "CPT" Theorem in books, magazines, and other media. This timeline, displayed alongside the archive of media in which the term is referenced, is more than just a chronological sequence of events. It is a visual and conceptual representation of how these moments in time are not isolated or incidental but are part of a larger, interconnected narrative. This narrative spans personal, interpersonal, communal, global, and cosmic scales, highlighting how time and temporality effect, and are affected by, a multitude of factors. This perspective aligns with the notion that events, cultural shifts, and scientific discoveries are not just happenstance but are part of a broader, interconnected system where each element determines and is determined by others. In the middle of the timeline, we screened a three-channel film, *Write No History* (2021), which centers around the speculative narrative of the Temporal Disruptors, members of an ancient secret society of Black scientists, healers, and writers transporting a quantum time capsule between the future, past, and present. Their pathways diverge and come back together along the timeline, this in contrast to the seemingly singular direction of the flowing water in *River of Time* (2021), a kinetic sculpture made of wood and water that stood in front of it. Even within that sculpture, the water cyclically returns to its own source to keep feeding the river at its undifferentiated beginning and end.

Another central work in *CPT Reversal* was the *Black Hole Viewfinder* (2021), designed to provide a glimpse into the mysterious depths of a black hole. Utilizing an array of lenses, the viewfinder aimed to mimic the distorted visual experience of observing objects through a field altered by gravitational forces. This design premise underscores a critical argument: our current scientific grasp of black holes is significantly hampered by the paradigms we employ to interpret their phenomena.

I contend that these limitations are not merely scientific or observational but are entwined with the broader cultural and philosophical frameworks that shape our understanding of Blackness. By synthesizing Black traditions and Afrodiasporic perspectives, our project calls for a reexamination of the concept, urging us to move beyond conventional associations with physical traits and color and by extension, racial categorizations. In this reimagined context, Blackness is not confined to terrestrial or corporeal boundaries but extends into cosmic and metaphysical dimensions. Western scientific paradigms, characterized by a reliance on the conventional properties of light and a purportedly objective lens, tend to constrict our understanding. In contrast, Black ontologies free us to explore the myriad possibilities of the multidimensional concept of Blackness, which permeates deep space, mental space, and inner space, bringing spacetimematter into deep entanglement.

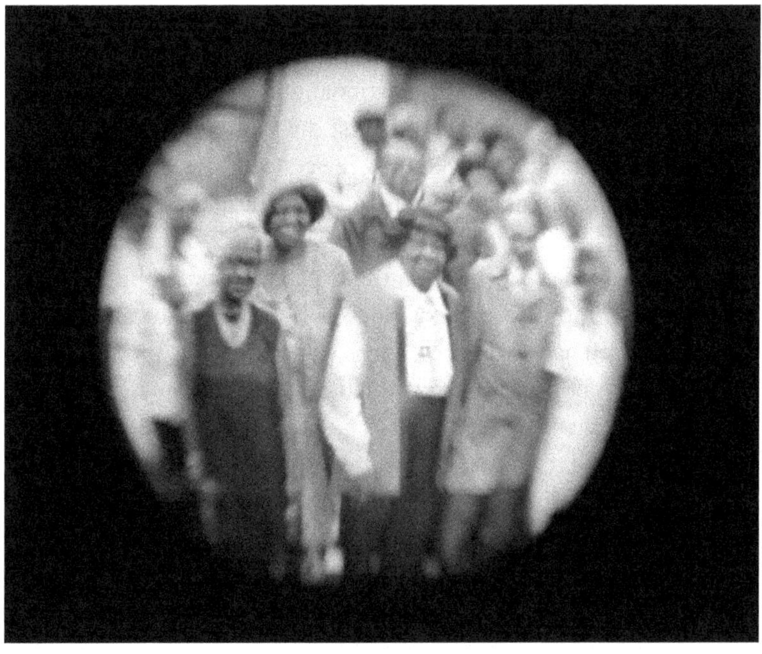

The artwork "Black Hole ViewFinder," through which can be seen a still from the *Mmere Dane Black Time Belt* short film on historic all-Black towns and Freedom Colonies across the United States, by Black Quantum Futurism (2023), as part of the group exhibition *Into the Black Hole* at Het Valkhof Museum (Nijmegen, the Netherlands).

This expansive approach does not simply reconfigure our understanding of Blackness within the cosmos; its uniquely AfroFuturist lens fosters a holistic embrace of the universe and all it holds. This ontological shift enables us to perceive and engage with the cosmos in ways that challenge the very foundations of traditional scientific inquiry and open avenues for a more inclusive and exploratory cosmic narrative. In this view, black holes symbolize not only points of no return but also sites of infinite potentiality.

Chronological Collapse: Black Hole Histories and Potential Futures

I'm playing dark history. It's beyond black. I'm dealing with the dark things of the cosmos. —**Sun Ra, *Space Is the Place***

Black holes are both mystifying and formidable. These regions in space have such an intense gravitational pull that nothing can elude their heavy grasp, including light.[45] First theorized by Albert Einstein's General Theory of Relativity in 1915, the concept of black holes introduced the idea that massive objects can warp the fabric of space-time.[46] Einstein described the relationship between space, time, gravity, and matter, and opened the door to the theoretical possibility of black holes. However, the concept of black holes was so radical that even Einstein himself had strong misgivings, concluding in a 1939 paper that the idea was "not convincing" and did not exist "in the real world."[47] The development of the idea of black holes from Einstein's general relativity is credited to German theoretical physicist Karl Schwarzschild. Schwarzschild found that a hypothetical singularity could literally punch through space-time. This point of no escape, known as the event horizon, marked the boundary beyond which nothing could return.

Initially known as "frozen stars," the term "black hole" was first printed in a January 18, 1964, issue of *Science News-Letter* in an article written Ann Ewing recapping a symposium from the previous year. While it remains uncertain who exactly coined the term, it is widely attributed to American physicist John A. Wheeler, who used it in 1967 to describe end of a massive star once it has exhausted its nuclear fuel and collapsed in on itself.[48] This gravitational collapse is the natural end of the star's life cycle when it can no longer support its own weight through nuclear fusion reactions. The star compresses its mass into an extremely small and dense point known as a singularity, which is surrounded by the event horizon.

Black holes are characterized by their strong gravitational fields, which can affect nearby matter and energy. For instance, a star passing too close to a black hole risks being ripped apart by its gravitational forces in a process known as tidal disruption. Additionally, black holes can bend light around them, a phenomenon predicted by Einstein's theory and confirmed through observations. This bending of light, or gravitational lensing, can make black holes observable indirectly by distorting the light from objects behind them. Another remarkable effect of black holes is time dilation, a consequence of their intense gravity. According to general relativity, time passes slower near a strong gravitational field. Therefore, time near a black hole would appear to pass more slowly compared to an observer at a safe distance. Black holes can also significantly influence cosmic events, having a major role in the evolution and formation of galaxies.[49] Black holes harbor a deep-seated paradox at the intersection of quantum mechanics and general relativity, challenging our foundational understanding of physics. Quantum mechanics posits that information can never be destroyed and must be conserved; it maintains that all physical data about a system, such as the position, speed, and spin of particles, can theoretically be traced through time. On the other hand, general relativity argues that anything entering a black hole is lost forever. According to this theory, anything that crosses the event horizon of a black hole, including light and information, cannot escape, thus effectively removing the information from our observable universe. The fate of this information according to general relativity appears to be destruction, which directly conflicts with the conservation principle of quantum mechanics. Under these circumstances, information is defined as all the data or knowledge contained within an object or system. This includes all the characteristics that make something unique and distinguish it from other things.

Despite various proposed theories and models, the fate of information swallowed by black holes, remains an unresolved conflict between quantum mechanics and general relativity, highlighting a key area where our current understanding of physics is still indeterminate. As such, this paradox shakes the foundations of our understanding of reality and brings CPT symmetry once more to the forefront.

I explained earlier that CPT symmetry—charge, parity, and time-reversal symmetry—forms a cornerstone of our understanding of physical laws, suggesting that the laws of physics should hold constant even when these three variables are inverted. Black holes, while seemingly classical in nature, are not exempt from these quantum principles, though their exact compliance with or deviation from these principles remains a topic of ongoing investigation and debate. At CERN I asked John Ellis about the potential for black holes to disrupt CPT symmetry:

> CPT theorem is a consequence of quantum field theory. If you find a violation of CPT, then you're saying quantum field theory is going wrong in some way. So, then the question arises: How could it possibly go wrong? We had some ideas that in string theory maybe there would be a way of modifying the rules of quantum field theory and, in particular, that maybe you could violate CPT. This is also connected with the speculations of Stephen Hawking and others about black holes where a priori it looks like you could have a violation of CPT. Hawking in later life kind of walked back on that, but I still think it's a possibility that one should consider. So, for me, CPT is still a fair game, and I think it's something that we should continue to probe experimentally.

This ongoing dialogue underscores the necessity of testing these theoretical boundaries, as any potential violations could necessitate a fundamental reevaluation of our understanding and perception of the cosmos.

Celestial Silhouettes: The Interplay of Light and Dark in the Blackness of Black Holes

> *Black is admired, in a negative way, as the colour associated with warfare, ancestral ghosts and above all the untrammeled freedom of the*

forest, away from society and man. —**Alfred Gell, *The Anthropology of Time***

Invisibility, let me explain, gives one a slightly different sense of time, you're never quite on the beat. Sometimes you're ahead and sometimes behind. Instead of the swift and imperceptible flowing of time, you are aware of its nodes, those points where time stands still or from which it leaps ahead. And you slip into the breaks and look around. —**Ralph Ellison, *The Invisible Man***

The discourse surrounding black holes and their implications extends into broader cultural and ontological contexts, particularly in the way we conceptualize light and darkness. Western scientific tradition often frames these as binary opposites, a dichotomy rooted in theological and philosophical narratives where light is invariably aligned with order, clarity, and divinity while darkness is associated with chaos, obscurity, and the unknown. In the Christian Biblical narrative, for example, black is "the darkness before time began," and that without light, "the Earth was without form, and void."[50] The first few lines of the Bible has God creating light by divine decree, and upon seeing "the light was good," God deliberately "separated the light from the darkness."[51] Philosopher Hans Blumenberg interprets this dichotomy that privileges light over darkness as not a primordial state of the universe but rather as a division instantiated by divine command, suggesting that the divine transcends and manipulates this binary. Blumenberg argues that this reading is in fact a "reversal of the initial, dualistic cast that late antiquity gave to metaphors of light."[52]

This view is further complicated by discussions in color theory and philosophy, where black is often dismissed as a non-color, a symbol of negation and absence rather than a substantive entity. In the *Dictionary of Symbols*, "Black sucks in colour and does not return it. Above all, it suggests chaos, nothingness, night sky, night shadows on the ground, evil, anguish, sorrow, the unconscious, and death."[53] Philosopher Roy Sorensen attributes the friction surrounding the status of blackness to an "aversion to negative things," whereas "other colors are seen by virtue of light simulation. The light itself can be colored but cannot be black."[54] These prevailing notions underscore a broader, often unchallenged belief that that darkness lacks the capacity to convey, carry, or retain information in stark contrast to light, which enables us to observe or perceive information. This dichotomy parallels theoretical debates in physics, such as those concerning black holes and information theory. We must consider how such cultural beliefs inform empirical claims in which darkness is seen as less substantive or informative than light.

Building on this, the causal theory of perception posits that our ability to see and perceive objects occurs when a causal chain involving light is triggered—that is, a sequence of events or processes that ultimately lead to the sensation of sight in an observer. For instance, light reflecting off an object and entering the eyes initiates a chain reaction that involves the retina, optic nerves, and brain, results in the perception of that object, of the object becoming visible. This linear causal model in turn introduces the notion of causation through absence. This notion implies that if an object or phenomenon does not initiate this causal chain—for example, if it fails to reflect or emit light that reaches our eyes—it remains invisible to us. . Thus, visibility hinges on the object's interaction with light, implying that our perceptual capabilities are limited to only those entities that actively participate in that cause-and-effect process.[55] This perspective bias underlines the supposed limitations of human perception, as it suggests that any element not engaging in this perceptual causal chain remains outside our visual awareness.

However, the phenomenon of black holes challenges this linear, causal model of perception, suggesting a need to rethink our classical understanding of light and darkness. Black holes, for instance, though invisible in traditional optical terms because they trap all light, reveal their presence through their gravitational effects on nearby objects and the radiation emitted as matter spirals into them. These observations indicate that regions devoid of light—gravitational absences—can still exert significant influence on their surroundings, contesting the long-held view that "absences do not transmit energy or do anything else positive."[56]

Sir Isaac Newton's work positing that darkness is simply the absence of light shaped the classical understanding of light as the primary substance of visual perception, with darkness a mere void where light does not exist. In this framework, then, darkness does not behave dynamically, as light does. Modern quantum theories have since challenged Newton's classical viewpoint through observations of the behavior of light at the quantum scale. Unlike classical particles that travel in fixed, straight-line trajectories, quantum particles of light, called photons, exhibit both wave-like and particle-like properties.

In their work "Diffracting Diffraction," Karen Barad underscores this aspect of quantum light particles to challenge the precept that darkness and light are at odds, arguing that the famous two-slit experiment in quantum physics "queers the binary light/dark story."[57] The experiment illustrates the enigmatic nature of light, which doesn't conform to a simple dichotomy of light versus dark. In the two-slit experiment, a fundamental demonstration in quantum mechanics and optics, particles such as electrons or photons are fired through two adjacent slits onto a detector screen. Rather than form two distinct clusters on the screen corresponding to the two slits, these particles create an interference pattern that manifests as alternating bands of light and dark on the screen.

This interference pattern is essential for unraveling the experiment's impact on our understanding of light and darkness. The pattern consists of alternating bright and dark bands: the bright bands represent points where the waves of particles add constructively (where the peaks and troughs of the waves align), and the dark bands emerge where they cancel each other out destructively (where a peak meets a trough). Remarkably, this interference pattern occurs even when particles are sent through the slits one at a time, suggesting that each particle interferes with itself as if it were a wave, not just a single point-like particle. The concept of wave-particle duality, proposed by Niels Bohr in 1928, arose from trying to explain such phenomena. This concept, the "Complementarity Principle," posits that fundamental particles exhibit both wave and particle characteristics, depending on how they are observed. This duality blurs the lines between the traditionally separate concepts of waves (associated with continuity and spread, akin to light) and particles (discrete and localized, akin to points of darkness), challenging the conventional dichotomy between waves and particles.

Barad's interpretation extends this idea into the realms of cultural and philosophical understandings of light and darkness. By demonstrating that particles and waves are not distinct but intertwined phenomena, the two-slit experiment suggests a more nuanced view where light and darkness are not strictly opposites but part of a continuum. Barad proposes darkness not as "mere absence" or lack but rather as "an abundance."[58] A paradigm centered on Black temporalities and Afrodiasporic epistemologies would also see blackness as abundant. *The Penguin Dictionary of Symbols* states, for example, that "In the West, black is the colour of mourning, yet originally it was the symbol of fertility, in Ancient Egypt, for example, and in North Africa, being the colour of rich earth and of rainclouds. If it is as black as the ocean depths, it is because the Underworld contains the treasury of hidden life and because it is the storehouse of all things."[59]

Reimagining black holes under this new paradigm shifts our understanding of these cosmic entities. They are no longer seen as merely destructive forces that merely negate or annihilate light and information. Instead, black holes emerge as transformative phenomena that actively preserve and metamorphose information This conceptual shift reveals darkness as a potent, active element of the cosmos, one that conserves and reshapes information. In this context, black holes are not just entities that destroy space-time, they also contribute to its creation, evolution, and regeneration.

This understanding of black holes can already be recognized in other everyday phenomena that require cycles of darkness as well as light to grow and change. This appreciation underscores the fundamental balance between these two states, which is crucial across ecological, biological, and even cosmic processes, illustrating that periodicity and contrast is vital, and that growth and transformation often depend on the dynamic interplay between darkness and light. Many plants, for instance, rely on photoperiodism—the response to the length of day and night—to regulate flowering times, seed germination, and other pivotal life cycle events. In this rhythm of life, darkness is not a period of inactivity but a necessary phase that triggers specific biochemical and genetic responses.[60]

Similarly, in animal biology, the circadian rhythms that govern sleep-wake cycles, feeding behaviors, and hormonal changes are also regulated by the cycle of day and night.[61] Several studies have shown that nightshift workers are more likely to encounter health issues that include cardiovascular disease, diabetes, and cancer.[62] This is because darkness triggers necessary physiological processes that cannot occur during light periods, such as the secretion of melatonin which is essential for sleep and immune function. The absence of light doesn't halt activity; instead, it shifts the organism into different modes of operation as crucial as those conducted in daylight.

At a broader cosmological scale, the cycle of light and darkness is foundational to the formation and evolution of celestial bodies. The collapse of dust and gas due to gravity leads to the birth of planets and stars in the cold, dark recesses of space. There, far from the intense radiation of stars, matter aggregates, leading eventually to the ignition of nuclear fusion in stars or the accretion of material into planets. And it is in the darkness of space that the universe's most dramatic transformations occur, such as the death of stars and the birth of black holes, phenomena that reshape the structure of the cosmos itself.

Afrodiasporan discourses do not conceive of space as simply a void, nor of blackness as devoid of information. Instead, both are regarded as sacred, filled with potential and meaning, such as in theorist Christina Sharpe's notion of "blackness anew, blackness as a/temporal, in and out of place and time putting pressure on meaning and that against which meaning is made."[63] The "Space and Time" entry in the *Encyclopedia of African Religions* explains that "Space is . . . a means by which creation and all life forms can exist and interact . . . The Africans have understood that space and time are mutually dependent."[64] Space, in these perspectives, is not a passive backdrop for physical events but an active and integral part of existence, facilitating interaction and ultimately the manifestation of life. Such a holistic view of space, time, and matter resonates with modern physics' exploration of the interconnectedness of these fundamental aspects of reality, as exemplified by the way black holes interact with their surroundings, influencing the fabric of space-time and the flow of information. In both African cosmologies and contemporary physics, the dynamic interplay of elements reveals a more integrated understanding of the universe.

In the context of special relativity and light speed, blackness, interpreted as the absence of light or a non-signal, doesn't violate the principles of special relativity because it doesn't transmit information in the way light does in Western scientific understanding. In philosophical terms, Sorensen's perspective suggests that theoretically darkness, or the absence of light, could move faster than light, since it's not a signal bound by the light-speed limitations that govern physical signals. Darkness, deemed a non-signal that does not travel, analogous to shadow, should, in the Western paradigm of time, theoretically "move" faster than light, since, as a non-signal, "no signal can travel faster than the speed of light."[65] In other words, darkness does not violate light speed, because it is already there before light arrives, not needing to have moved at all. Can something that is always there, waiting for light to arrive and make it not dark anymore, be said to move?

Sorensen answers the question by envisioning darkness as moving at a pace comparable to, if not faster than, light, unburdened by the constraints of physical motion and unaffected by attempts to measure itself or be measured against light. The velocity of darkness isn't predicated on movement; velocity is inherent to its very essence, defying the need for movement at all, a notion which may seem paradoxical or contradictory in Western epistemologies but transcends habituated linear thinking and reliance on causal perception. Therefore, we can understand darkness as enigmatic, challenging conventional logic and scientific principles; emergent, arising from a paradigm that values holistic and non-causal relationships; and deeply interconnected, reflecting a universe where all elements are intrinsically linked, as emphasized in many non-Western—and particularly African—philosophies.

African epistemologies, which place equal value on empirical and metaphysical knowledge, offer a unique lens through which to examine the information paradox. These epistemologies reveal a multifaceted approach to understanding information, especially evident in the temporal dimensions of Black narratives.

English professor Laura C. Jarmon reveals the diverse temporal qualities in Black narratives, especially within oral traditions, highlighting how information is perceived and valued as fact, invention, news, history, myth, narrative, or other classifications based on its temporal context, whether in the remote past, near past, or future.

For example, what is considered contemporary news in one generation might transform into the fabric of oral tradition in the next, highlighting the fluid and revisionist nature of information transmission and its reliance on its local and communal context. This perspective is crucial in societies where myths, for example, are not just stories but hold the status of fact due to their sacred role in defining a community's cosmic place.[66]

The principle of "ubuntu," derived from the Bantu language demonstrates this broad cultural understanding of information. Translated by John Mbiti as "I am because we are, and since we are, therefore I am," this principle introduces a communal dimension to the concept of information.[67] This is in marked contrast to the Cartesian, individualistic axiom of "I think, therefore I am." Accordingly, information is inseparable from the social and cultural context of the community. Here, information is a living, breathing entity, embedded within the intricate social and cultural tapestry of the community.

Echoing Jarmon's insights, the status of any piece of information in Black communal settings is fluid, shaped by the communal process of evaluating and interpreting the narratives and details within their specific local and temporal frameworks.[68] What constitutes contemporary news in one generation may seamlessly transition into oral tradition for the next, underlining the evolving and adaptable nature of information transmission in communal settings. This approach to understanding information reflects a deep interconnectivity and collective consciousness, standing in stark contrast to individual-centric perspectives and enriching our broader understanding of information in diverse cultural contexts.

In the realm of physics, the information paradox grapples with the question of how information is preserved or transformed inside of black holes, which are traditionally thought to absorb and obliterate everything. Both the cosmic scale of black holes and the communal nature of narrative in African epistemologies, deal with how information is conserved, transformed, and contextualized. Black holes, often seen as destructive, can be reinterpreted as transformative entities, mirroring the way African temporalities and understandings of information view the reshaping and recontextualization of information within a community's collective memory and experience.

Eclipsing Hegemony and Harmonizing the Cosmos

The fusion of Black and Afrodiasporic epistemologies with quantum physics represents a pivotal movement toward redefining the constructs of reality, time, space, and matter as understood in the concept of Black SpaceTimeMatters. This amalgamation challenges the hegemonic narratives that have long dominated our perception of the cosmos and societal structures, marking a significant effort in dismantling the Eurocentric biases and entrenched systems of power both ingrained in and upheld by scientific and philosophical discourses.

By interrogating the very notions of time, space, race, and matter, this integration offers a counter-narrative that enriches our cosmic perspective and reveals a fuller and more textured understanding of how time and space are perceived differently across cultures and histories. Incorporating these alternative conceptions expands our scientific and philosophical reckoning of time and space, encouraging a reevaluation of how these dimensions have impacted racial inequality and community development. A more dynamic view of these concepts, informed by Black and Afrodiasporic epistemologies, opens new avenues for reshaping not just our cosmic understanding but the very fabric of our social and political realities through problem-solving, that recognizes the deeper connections between individuals, societies, and the physical world. Failing to take such insight into account risks perpetuating a status quo that limits our scientific and philosophical growth, marginalizing non-Western ways of knowing the world and resulting in the continued loss of valuable perspectives to the detriment of humanity. Thus, the inclusion of Black and Afrodiasporic thought in quantum physics is essential for a truly comprehensive worldview that best captures the multiplicity of human experience and the universe.

CHAPTER 3

CPT Symmetry and Violations of Black SpaceTime

Each society formulates its own understandings of different kinds of temporality, and, in fact, contains varieties of temporal understanding that differ from the dominant interpretations, sometimes consciously articulated as forms of resistance, sometimes subverted and shameful.

—Maureen Perkins, *The Reform of Time Magic and Modernity*

It's terrible to think that a child with five different present tenses comes to school to be faced with those books that are less than his own language.

—Toni Morrison, "The Language Must Not Sweat"

At a 2016 black-tie event for US presidential candidate Hillary Clinton, she stood on the stage between a Black cast member of the hit musical *Hamilton*, Leslie Odom Jr., and then-NYC Mayor Bill de Blasio, when an awkwardly scripted joke began to play out in real time. Hillary Clinton teased de Blasio for taking so long to endorse her, to which he quipped in reply, "Sorry, Hillary, I was running on CP Time."[1] The audience reacted with sparse laughter and palpable discomfort, and Odom, Jr. chimed in to say, "I don't like jokes like that." Clinton jumped in to clarify that de Blasio meant "Cautious Politician Time."[2] Although de Blasio faced some backlash and apologized for the joke, it remains a stark demonstration of how the negative stereotype of "being on CP Time" is still in use.

CP Time, CPT, or "Colored People's Time," is a phrase used to describe Black people as more prone to lateness compared to other racial and ethnic groups. It is a perception that stems from enduring negative stereotypes that portray Black people as being more "laid back," or lazy and unreliable, with a supposed lack of conscientiousness regarding time. Take for example, a long-running "black joke" relayed by American Historian Lawrence W. Levine: "At the time the world was made . . . people were allowed to select their own skin color and hair texture and style. Negro people, arriving late, as usual, had to take what was left."[3] Another joke has a man walking pass a white church and hearing the congregation singing "I'll Be There When You Open Those Gates," only to later walk past a Black church singing "Don't Close Those Gates 'til I Get There."[4]

The concept of CP Time, even when used as an in-group joke among Black people, carries a fraught inheritance. In a 2009 essay titled "CP Time: Does my Black race indicate I'll always be late?" author Nikki Lynette challenges the stereotype that Black people possess a "tardy gene."[5] However, Lynette goes on to share her own experiences where she observes a pattern of business meetings with Black people frequently starting late. Although Lynette concludes that CPT "is not inherently a negative thing," she does lament that the inside joke may have been "taken too far," and that it often turns into an excuse given by some Black people for failing to adhere strictly to clock time.[6]

The stereotype that Lynette challenges, but ultimately affirms, extends beyond mere inaccuracy and humor, serving a more insidious political function. By attributing tardiness to race, the stereotype of CP Time perpetuates a narrative of irresponsibility and unreliability that can have damaging implications. This feeds into broader systemic biases and prejudices, often used to justify discriminatory practices in employment, education, and other societal sectors. When tardiness is racialized, it is not just an individual's punctuality that's called into question, but the professionalism, competence, and worth of an entire racial group. Furthermore, what is typically understood as CP Time—a lack of punctuality as measured by a so-called objective clock—undermines the rich and diverse cultural understandings of time within Black communities, where perceptions of time may differ from Western standards of punctuality. By enforcing a singular, rigid view of timeliness, we risk erasing these valuable cultural perspectives and enforcing a homogenized, Eurocentric, worldview.

The concept of CPT (Charge, Parity, and Time) symmetry in physics can indeed offer a metaphorical parallel to the notion of Colored People's Time (CPT). In physics, CPT symmetry suggests that physical processes remain unchanged when charge, parity, and time are simultaneously reversed. A violation of this symmetry would thus be considered a rare and significant anomaly, pointing toward unresolved aspects of the universe.

Similarly, Colored People's Time is often perceived as a deviation from the normative perceptions of time—effectively, a social violation of "mechanical clock time." In contrast, the findings of quantum physics introduce a realm where time exhibits fluidity and bidirectionality. Our familiar linear experience of time might itself represent a "violation" of a more symmetrical and nonlinear nature of time. This analogy suggests that violations of time may be contextually biased. In the realm of physics, a violation of time's symmetry (like the unidirectional arrow of time) is a subject of fascination and rigorous study, whereas in societal contexts, deviations from linear timekeeping are punished. This contrast highlights a double standard in how we value different expressions of time and timekeeping.

In his book *CP Time: Why Some People Are Always Late* (2007), J. L. King attempts to dissect the origins and implications of CP Time, exploring his own experiences and perspectives on the matter alongside the perspectives of other people he has interviewed. As advertised in the book's description: "Everyone has a story of being the victim of CP time. It's been responsible for the termination of jobs and relationships, and for delaying weddings and even funerals. *CP Time* is the first book to examine a behavior that crosses all social economic lines within the black community in a way that will bring smiles and groans of recognition to victims and culprits alike."[7]Despite its lighthearted approach, King's treatment of CP Time is predominantly critical, framing it as an emblem of disregard for punctuality that he perceives as shameful, trifling, rude, and self-centered behavior. King describes himself as both guilty of and a victim of CP Time, condemning it unequivocally in statements such as, "There is no excuse on why some black people are always late. The fact of the matter is that they have no respect for time." Chapters such as "CP Time at Funerals," "CPT at Weddings," and "CP Time on the Job" reinforce the notion that people who are late are essentially stealing time from others, echoing a view of lateness as a moral failing, a violation of normative time. King's perspective assumes a generalization that lacks nuance and fails to consider underlying reasons for lateness, such as socioeconomic factors, systemic barriers, or personal circumstances, as anything more than excuses.

For instance, consider the impact of economic disparities and systemic barriers on individuals' daily routines. Economic inequalities often force individuals into a state of "time poverty," where managing multiple jobs to make ends meet results in tight schedules and limited rest, making punctuality a challenge rather than a choice.[8] For many in these communities, relying on infrequent or unreliable public transit infrastructure imposes an additional, rigid temporal framework within which they must operate, often at odds with their personal, familial, and professional demands.[9] These situations are not just inconveniences; they are realities shaped by broader socioeconomic, systemic, and structural barriers. As I can attest from my own experiences, for parents balancing childcare, work, and other responsibilities , meeting strict time constraints can often be an overwhelming demand—a challenge magnified by systemic issues such as inadequate childcare, which disproportionately affects low-income families. Healthcare access also presents significant obstacles as chronic health problems and unforeseen emergencies compromise one's ability to be on time. Impacted mental health can significantly affect one's relationship with time in ways that are often invisible to others.[10] These health-related time disruptions are particularly poignant in communities living the effects of a lack of timely and affordable health care.

Simply put, by characterizing lateness as a character flaw or a demonstration of a lack of respect, we fail to acknowledge broader social and historical contexts that may contribute to practices of time, overlooking the role of systemic inequalities, as well as the cultural and subjective nature of time itself.

The disparaging rhetoric of CP Time, with its insensitivity toward non-Western cultural values of time, has deep historical roots and can be traced back to the legacy of colonialism, white supremacy, and slavery in the United States. To comprehend the extent of the stereotype's racist ramifications, we must understand the historical backdrop against which the dominant culture's emphasis on "being on time" was imposed upon marginalized communities. Historically, the concept of time in colonial and slaveholding societies was not just a measure of minutes and hours; it was a tool of control and subjugation. The dominant culture's perception of time, typically linear and strictly regimented, was imposed on enslaved and colonized peoples as a means of exerting control and power. This imposition extended to direct violence and punishment for those who did not adhere to these stringent timekeeping standards. The rigidity of this system often ignored the complexities of individual lives and the nonlinear, more communal approaches to time prevalent in many African and Indigenous cultures.

The oppressive legacy of rigid timekeeping is still evident today. The moral outrage represented in J. L. King's book and often directed at the notion of CP Time and the stereotype of Black tardiness overlooks a critical point: the social, political, and economic systems we live by continue to hinge access to fundamental aspects of human rights, dignity, and security on adherence to bureaucratic timekeeping. This approach fails to recognize the historical and ongoing trauma inflicted by such systems, which have traditionally prioritized efficiency and productivity over human well-being.

In many ways, the emergence of CP Time can be seen as a form of cultural resistance. With CP Time, Black communities reclaim agency and resist the imposition of an external, oppressive temporal framework. This act of reclamation, however, is often misunderstood or misrepresented in mainstream discourse, leading to further stigmatization and misunderstanding. The stereotype of CP Time, therefore, is not just a benign cultural quirk. It reflects a history where non-normative relationships to time were not just dismissed but actively punished. Understanding this context is vital in addressing the systemic inequities that persist today and in challenging the narratives that continue to marginalize and devalue diverse cultural experiences of time.

A Brief History of Time in the Wild, Wild Western Tradition

St. Augustine, the eminent Western religious philosopher, was a pioneering figure espousing a Christian-based concept of time as linear and irreversible. In his magnum opus *Confessions*, composed in Latin circa AD 400, Augustine probes the paradoxes of time, asking, "How can the past and future be, when the past no longer is, and the future is not yet? As for the present, if it were always present and never moved on to become the past, it would not be time, but eternity."[11] This work of the fifth century is often credited with laying the intellectual groundwork for the Western conception of time, a concept itself already embedded within Judeo-Christian religious doctrine.

Building upon this foundation, Western time consciousness stresses fixed events along an irreversible, forward-moving timeline. This linearity is itself embedded within cyclical time—hours, minutes, and seconds, in their abstract numerical form, repeat. Events themselves, however, are unique occurrences that will never be identically replicated in a future moment on this progressive, unidirectional timescale. Though the phrase "history repeats itself" is probably as old as the concept of history itself, it is presumed obvious that what we really mean is that events in history can only ever parallel each other.

In *Time Wars*, Jeremy Rifkin discusses how Western culture encoded its visions of the future within the intertwined realms of religion and politics, seeking to predict and control unfolding events. This pursuit of prediction and control reflects a desire to navigate and shape the future, fundamentally influencing the Western approach to time and historical progression. The Judeo-Christian religious tradition codified a disciplined regimen for work and prayer, governed by doctrine and motivated by a looming sense of eschatological urgency fueled by apocalyptic beliefs. This apprehension of impending doom necessitated tight and efficient management of time to make the most use of it before the future arrived.[12] Ecclesiastes 3:1, for instance, proclaims, "For everything there is a season, and a time for every matter under heaven," while Ephesians 5:16 admonishes believers to "Make the best use of the time, because the days are evil."[13] The effective use of time, in this context, is synonymous with piety and moral righteousness.

These Biblical narratives indelibly shaped Western temporality. For instance, the seven-day creation account in the Book of Genesis not only orders the universe with a linear understanding of time but does so in a step-by-step sequence, establishing a divinely ordained chronology with God as the ultimate clockmaker or architect of time, setting a divine order. In the Old Testament, there are numerous instances where time plays a critical role. The prophetic books, such as Daniel and Isaiah, are replete with visions and prophecies that unfold within a linear timeline, forecasting future events and the fulfillment of divine promises. These prophecies often detail a sequence of events leading up to pivotal moments in religious history, such as the coming of the Messiah or the end of days, reinforcing the concept of a divinely preordained, linear progression of time.

The New Testament continues and expands upon this theme. The Gospels, chronicling the life and teachings of Jesus Christ, are structured around a chronological narrative, tracing his birth, ministry, death, and resurrection. The parables and teachings of Jesus often reference time, using it as a framework to impart spiritual lessons and to emphasize the transitory nature of human life compared to the eternity of the divine.

One of the most striking depictions of linear time in the New Testament is found in the Book of Revelation. This apocalyptic text describes a series of future events, including the final judgment and the establishment of a new heaven and earth, unfolding in a sequential manner. Revelation's vivid imagery and detailed account of the end times underscores a linear, teleological view of history, where all events are moving toward a predetermined culmination. This theological perspective influenced scientific views of the universe during the medieval and Renaissance periods, when the boundaries between science and religion were more openly porous and interrelated.[14]

Early scientists like Isaac Newton, whose works were as grounded in theism as they were on empirical observations and mathematical formulations, adopted a mechanistic view of the cosmos that mirrored the Biblical framework. Newton's laws of motion and universal gravitation can be seen as extensions of this "clockwork universe," governed by immutable laws set in motion by a divine creator. During the early development of the clock itself in Western Europe of the seventeenth century, science historian Jimena Canales writes, "Clocks were symbols of a universal order maintained and set in motion by God himself."[15]

This theistic and mechanistic analysis was soon applied to broader social contexts, particularly during the Age of Exploration and colonization, which spanned from the late fifteenth century through the nineteenth century. Researcher Maureen Perkins highlights how temporal conceptualization was crucial in defining "otherness," which played a significant role in crafting European identities. In *The Colonisation of Time*, Giordano Nanni details how European missionaries and colonizers viewed African time as primitive, and what they perceived as "timelessness" presented a challenge to their authority and control as it was not conducive to the strict schedules and deadlines of industrial capitalism. Nanni describes how missionaries and other European travelers experienced the sense of "leaving time and civilisation behind them altogether" when they arrived upon the African continent.[16] From the "painfully slow" speed that a wagon traveled ("3 miles per hour") to the variable rate that a letter would be delivered ("3 days to 3 weeks"), Indigenous Africans in West African nations had their humanity and intellect clocked, appraised, graded, and grouped in accordance to how strictly they appeared to adhere mechanical clock time, and how civilized they were.[17]

Europeans, missionaries, military officials, and others who considered themselves a part of the educated classes viewed temporal responsibility as a crucial aspect of maturity, dismissing any variance in relationships to time as a sign of immaturity or childishness. Even leisure time, rest time, and playtime expressed to the colonizers "a lack of awareness of temporal regularity and was policed and seen as a waste of work and planning time."[18] In *The Global Transformation of Time: 1870–1950*, historian Vanessa Ogle recounts conflicts between indigenous laborers and those who profited from their labor arising from divergent timekeeping methods:

> The Zulus in the British Naval Colony followed the moon and the stars in calculating the month and divided the year into thirteen moons. One circuit lasted for about twenty-eight days after which an interlunary period followed, a moonless period during

> which people paid respect to the darkness and abstained from work. Colonial officials, employers, and native workers clashed frequently over when a worker was due his pay, as European months followed different calculations.[19]

Christian missionaries enforced clock time particularly when it threatened the coordination of religious meetings and activities, under the dictum that "timeliness is next to Godliness." African societies were coerced through force or education into becoming true Christians and adopting new systems of timekeeping, such as the Gregorian calendar and the twenty-four-hour clock, often at the cost of violently demonizing and erasing indigenous religious practices deemed "backward" and "primitive." The Western timeline and mechanical clock time as its representative were enforced as the standard of civilization, which perpetuated a hierarchy of human worth that placed Indigenous Africans at the bottom of or off the timeline all together, as people operating with metaphorically damaged clocks or no clocks at all.[20]

Constructing the Master's Clockwork Universe

> *The hands are required to work in the cotton fields as soon as it is light in the morning and with the exception of ten or fifteen minutes, which is given them at noon to swallow their allowance of cold bacon, they are not permitted to be a moment idle until it is too dark to see, and when the moon is full, they often times labor till the middle of the night. They do not dare to stop at dinner time, nor return to the quarters, however late it be, until the order to halt is given by the driver.* —**Solomon Northrup, *Twelve Years a Slave***

Advances in science and technology during the scientific revolution, provided detailed precision to a framework that viewed time as a quantifiable and measurable entity. As noted by German historian Gerard Dohrn-van Rossum, "Only since the scientific revolution in the middle of the seventeenth century can one speak of experimentally qualifying scientific procedures and conceptions of time as a scaled continuum of discrete moments."[21] This transition to a view of time as a series of distinct, measurable units, is a shift that has fundamentally altered both the perception and the societal role of time.

One example of this increased granularity in time measurement is the development of more accurate clocks, including the pendulum clock by Christiaan Huygens in 1656. This invention allowed for the division of time into increasingly smaller units. As a result, time began to be perceived not as a continuous flow but as a series of quantifiable moments, laying the groundwork for further scientific explorations. This influenced subsequent scientific paradigms and theories. The concept of entropy in the second law of thermodynamics, for instance, relies on a granular understanding of time to describe the irreversible nature of physical processes. Similarly, Einstein's theory of general relativity, which revolutionized our understanding of space-time, depends on the concept of time as a measurable continuum.

As clocks became ubiquitous fixtures in public spaces around the late thirteenth century, Western society moved toward an even more rigidly structured understanding of time, cementing a mechanical temporality that permeated all facets of Western life. The earliest public timekeeping devices, which were large, mechanical clocks, first appeared in the clock towers of Western European cities. These early public clocks did not have faces but struck bells to signal the hour, serving both practical purposes and demonstrating the wealth and technological advancement of the city that housed them. By the fourteenth century, clock technology had advanced significantly, and clocks began to feature dials and hands, making the measurement of time more precise and visually accessible to the public. This period marked a significant shift in societal attitudes toward time, moving away from "event time" (where activities are done according to natural cues or the completion of tasks) toward "clock time" (where time is divided into equal, measurable units). This mechanical temporality infiltrated every aspect of life, from the organization of work and social activities to the broader economic and industrial systems underpinning the development of capitalism, industrialization, and the bureaucratic state, and reinforcing the importance of punctuality, efficiency, and the regimentation of daily life. The segmentation of time facilitated the rise of regimented work schedules, and the emphasis on punctuality and efficiency that characterize modern Western society.

By the sixteenth and seventeenth centuries, with the advent of domestic clocks and pocket watches, this rigid structuring of time permeated more fully into individual lives, cementing mechanical temporality. This evolution laid the groundwork for the modern, industrialized conception of time as a linear, divisible commodity, incorporated in dominant economic, social, and cultural norms.

In a striking metaphor, Dr. Nikitah Okembe-RA Imani likens the Eurocentric perception of space and time to airport "people movers"—conveyor belts designed to facilitate human transit throughout airports. One boards the people mover at a discrete point, moving inexorably along its finite track toward a predetermined end. Human agency exists only in accelerating one's progress toward this inevitable conclusion; attempting to reverse direction on the people mover is unlikely to yield physical progress against the overwhelming forces pushing toward the future. Although theoretically possible, attempting a reverse course on the people mover is not only socially frowned upon but thwarted by momentum.[22] It is this kind of thought that is at the heart of the second law of thermodynamics, which asserts that entropy, or disorder, in a closed system invariably increases. As noted by sociologist Barbara Adam, "energy is conserved but cannot be reversed."[23] Her remark emphasizes the perceived irreversible nature of time in the physical world and aligns with the principle that while energy in a system remains constant, its ability to perform work diminishes over time.

This law provides a scientific imprimatur to the idea that time has a definite direction, hurtling toward a state of maximum entropy known as the "heat death" of the universe. In this state, energy becomes uniformly distributed, and no more work can occur, leading to a kind of ultimate stagnation. This linear trajectory ultimately culminates in a telos, a climactic and perhaps chaotic endpoint, echoing the apocalyptic prophecies of the religious texts.

Other technological innovations like the first long-distance railroads and the invention of the telegram fundamentally altered human conceptions of time and space. These advances facilitated a shift in Eurocentric perceptions of the future from a concept largely out of humanity's control and within God's near-exclusive domain, to becoming a tangible frontier open to human conquest." In her seminal work *Time and Social Theory*, Barbara Adam shows how the late eighteenth and nineteenth centuries marked a transition from an interest in "quantity and timeless laws" to a new cultural fervor for "change, growth, and evolution," a transformation that occurred almost synchronously across physics, biology, astronomy, philosophy, and the arts.[24]

This reimagined outlook on time and space was not only theoretical but had profound practical implications, particularly evident in the imperialist, settler-colonial projects of the era. These projects are often described in terms of colonization of space and land but also entailed a significant temporal component: conquering the domain of the future. Embodied within the time, day, and month was a white supremacist political, spatial, and temporal imaginary. Historian Stephen Kern, argues that the "annexation of the space of others" and the "outward movement of people and goods" through colonial expansion were essentially "spatial expressions of the active appropriation of the future."[25] Kern cites a telling example from 1839, when British Foreign Minister Lord Roseberry stated that the motivations for colonizing Africa were not about the present, "not what we want now, but what we shall want in the future."[26] Roseberry viewed the future as s resource to be mined; he and his fellow imperialists—positioned themselves as stewards, in the business of "pegging out claims for the future" as trustees "to the future of the race."[27] These same ideas intertwining the spatial and the temporal were mirrored in the growing rhetoric and propaganda of American expansionism, where political leaders and so-called thinkers carved out their visions for the future in time as much as space. A few years before popularizing the term "manifest destiny" in 1845, political writer John O'Sullivan penned an essay called "The Great Nation of Futurity." English professor Thomas M. Allen writes of the essay that "rather than focusing exclusively on the spatial dimension of the Jeffersonian vision," O'Sullivan instead "emphasizes the temporal dimension of national expansion . . . Jefferson's confederation becomes a 'congregation' that stretches into the future as much as it does into the West."[28] This framing emphasized not just the physical conquest of land but also the projection of American ideals and influence into the future. This perspective represented a significant shift in the rhetoric of expansionism. It was no longer just about acquiring territory; it was about shaping the future. O'Sullivan's emphasis on the temporal dimension underscored a belief in the inevitability and righteousness of American expansion, not just across the continent but through time. This blend of spatial conquest with temporal destiny encapsulated a broader narrative in American politics and ideology. It was a narrative that saw the nation's growth and its principles as inexorably linked to the passage of time, suggesting a preordained trajectory that would define the future.

The melding of time and space in the national consciousness served to justify not only the physical expansion of the United States but also the propagation of its values and institutions into the future, reinforcing the ideology of manifest destiny as both a spatial and temporal inevitability.[29] Barbara Adam also highlights this interplay of time and expansionism, noting, "Colonization with time has been achieved with the aid of standard time, time zones and world time, on the one hand, and with the globalization of industrial time and its associated economic values as common-sense norm, on the other."[30] To be more specific, the centuries-long campaign to command the future (in both its temporal and spatial manifestations) could only be accomplished by simultaneously and systematically locking Black people out of civilization and effectively out of time in order to exploit labor and resources.

In his 1785 book *Notes on the State of Virginia*, Thomas Jefferson spends a few pages detailing his observations on the inferiority of Black people to white people, both mentally and physically. He claimed as an immutable truth that Black people were less intelligent, less capable of reason, and more prone to violence than white people. He believed that the differences between the races were insurmountable, unable to be overcome through education or socialization. Jefferson then spends a considerable number of words analyzing what he perceived as the Black sense of time, rhythm, and memory:

> They seem to require less sleep. A black, after hard labor through the day, will be induced by the slightest amusements to sit up till midnight, or later, though knowing he must be out with the first dawn of the morning. They are at least as brave, and more adventuresome. But this may perhaps proceed from a want of

> forethought, which prevents their seeing a danger till it be present. When present, they do not go through it with more coolness or steadiness than the whites.[31]

Amid his racist diatribe, Jefferson momentarily acknowledges a paradoxical symbol of humanity, a glimmer of possibility yet to be proven. He remarks, "In music they are more generally gifted than the whites with accurate ears for tune and time, and they have been found capable of imagining a small catch. Whether they will be equal to the composition of a more extensive run of melody, or of complicated harmony, is yet to be proved."[32] Here, Jefferson subtly highlights a relationship between racial perceptions and the understanding of time. He ultimately advances his conclusion "that the blacks, whether originally a distinct race, or made distinct by time and circumstances, are inferior to the whites in the endowments both of body and mind."[33] These comments are damning proof of the foundational narrative entanglement of race, space, and time that demarcates Black people as a distinct race. Our modern conceptions of race have been long shaped by temporal and spatial factors, particularly if we consider "the collective trauma of slavery as the founding moment of modernity," as writer and filmmaker Kodwo Eshun invites us to do, in echo of Toni Morrison's provocative contention that enslaved Africans, enduring that foundational trauma, should be viewed as the first moderns.[34] The exploitation and regulation of Black bodies has been inextricable in constructing the conceptual framework of the modern world.

Jefferson's ruminations on Black people reflects an observational methodology, a mechanism of "clocking." The term "clocking" primarily refers to the act of recording or measuring time, such as an employee clocking in for work or a scientist logging changes in an experiment. Colloquially, "clocking" also denotes the act of noticing something or someone, or realizing something, often retrospectively. In some contexts, "clocking" can carry a physical connotation, describing the act of hitting someone, in which its metaphorical usage expresses the impact of a physical or emotional blow.[35]

For Black people, however, "clocking" retains a pernicious dimension across its various interpretations. In this context, clocking suggests the measurement of time as a means to assess the movements of Black laborers and ensure that they are conforming to the master's clock. The white gaze, when surveilling Black people, compresses space and time, anchoring Black existence firmly within the reductive confines of a white supremacist chronology. This act of observation serves as a mechanism of disenfranchisement, embedding Black people within a narrative that frequently overlooks our diverse historical and cultural narratives. Simultaneously, this methodology dogmatically enforces a Western, linear, and progress-driven temporal framework as the universal standard and shared governing rubric, dismissing the plurality of time perceptions beyond the Eurocentric view. Such enforcement perpetuates a singular, restrictive narrative on the ways time and progress are valued.

The Quantum Zeno Effect, akin to this process of "clocking," illustrates how continuous observation can inhibit the evolution of a quantum system, effectively freezing its state. Named after Greek philosopher Zeno of Elea's famous paradox involving an arrow that, when observed, never seems to reach its final destination, this phenomenon in quantum physics posits that a system cannot change its state while being watched. By continuous measurement, the state of a particle remains the same as the potential for change is interrupted by the act of observation itself, as in the old adage "a watched pot never boils." Often attributed to Benjamin Franklin's *Poor Richard's Almanack*, this saying captures the experience of time dragging on when one is waiting for something to happen, a perception of time influenced by the frustration of inactivity or impatience. It suggests that obsessive attention might slow the passage of events, highlighting a goal-oriented outlook on time that becomes burdensome when progress is halted.

By analogy, the relentless scrutiny and regulation of Black temporalities under the white gaze "freezes" or severely constrains the dynamism and fluidity of Black temporal experiences. Just as the Quantum Zeno Effect reveals the dramatic influence of observation on the behavior of quantum systems, pervasive surveillance impedes the free evolution of identity and experience. In marked contrast to the watched pot of American proverb is the Sierra Leonean Crio saying, "If you watch your pot, your food will not burn" ("W yu wach yu pɔt, yu fud nɔ go bɔn").[36] In this more generative stance toward the relationship between attention and time, vigilance is seen as beneficial, a nurturing action that ensures desirable outcomes. Rather than emphasize the frustration of waiting, it endorses the rewards of mindful engagement. In this process-oriented view of time, sustained attention is intrinsic to fostering the cycles of life and time a canvas for action and care, rather than merely a countdown to a particular outcome. The diverse ways cultures understand and interact with the phenomenon of time shapes both daily practices and philosophical outlooks on life and its rhythms.

When Black people live beyond the scrutiny of the white gaze, a multiplicity of spatial and temporal states becomes possible. Black existence then extends across various dimensions of space and time, free from the constraints of an imposed timeline. This freedom allows for the exploration and embodiment of a multiplicity of temporal states, reflecting a rich diversity of experiences and perceptions.

Jefferson's sensibilities about time, laziness, and labor align well with another aphorism often attributed to Benjamin Franklin, "Time is money." In his 1748 essay "Advice to a Young Tradesman," Franklin counseled, "Remember that time is money. He that can earn ten shillings a day by his labor, and goes abroad, or sits idle one half of that day, though he spends but sixpence during his diversion or idleness, ought not to reckon that the only expense; he has really spent or rather thrown away five shillings besides."[37] Three hundred years later, the faces of Jefferson and Franklin are stamped onto our nation's currency, and the phrase continues to tie efficiency and productivity to clock time, with implications that extend to the socioeconomic stratification of society.

The mathematics of capital and time acquire additional dimensions given the context of chattel slavery and its enduring socioeconomic legacy. Victims and survivors of this dehumanizing institution were not merely subjected to economic exploitation; their very bodies and the temporal aspects of their labor were commodified, turning every aspect of their existence, from the rhythms of work and rest to the velocity and productivity of their labor, into metrics for maximizing profits.

For the enslaved Black people of 1748, the "time equals money" manifested as a cruel paradox; the privilege of owning time, a fundamental aspect of freedom, was often an unattainable luxury. They could never possess the resource or currency of time; rather, they were themselves transformed into currency, they functioned as the very instruments that produced time and resources for their white enslavers, then, and white society systemically, into the present. It was their labor time, taken by force and in often physically excruciating and violent conditions, that generated leisure time and the privilege to exercise autonomy over their schedules for their white masters.

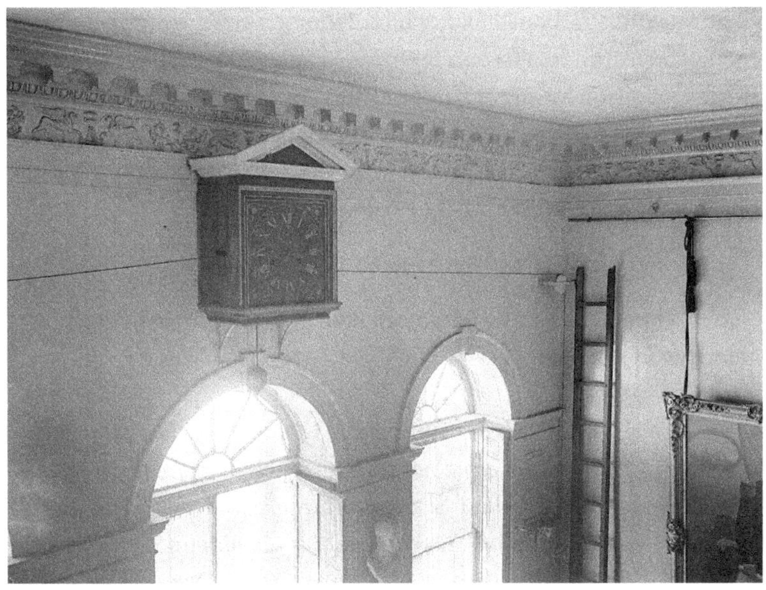

The Great Clock in Thomas Jefferson's Monticello Plantation house, in a photograph taken circa 1914–1918.

In the 1847 memoir of Isaac Granger Jefferson, Thomas Jefferson's formerly enslaved blacksmith recounts that at the Monticello Plantation, "For amusement, he [Jefferson] would work sometimes in the garden for half an hour at a time . . . in the cool of the evening," underscoring the incongruity that enslaved laborers had to work in whatever conditions and at whatever times their masters dictated.[38] Another observation from Thomas Jefferson himself in 1811 poignantly encapsulates the privileged hours of the white slave-owning class: "From breakfast, or even at the latest, to dinner, I am mostly on horseback, attending to my farm or other concerns, which I find healthful to my body, mind, and affairs."[39] His daily supervision of the plantation he experienced as leisurely and rejuvenating, a sentiment predicated upon the backbreaking labor of those he enslaved, labor performed under conditions of inherent violence and exploitation. Consider, too, that when Jefferson designed a Great Clock to be built by Peter Spruck of Philadelphia in 1792 and installed in the entryway to his Monticello house, it was constructed with both an exterior face on the outside of the building and an interior face inside: "On the outside wall, the clock has only an hour hand, which Jefferson believed was accurate enough for outdoor laborers. The inside face of the clock reveals much greater precision by offering not only hour and minute hands, but also a smaller dial for a second hand."[40] In its design, the master's clock made the distinction clear that plantation time was one thing for the slaveowner and another for the enslaved.

Clocks Without Faces: The Forgotten Role of Black People in Crafting American Clock Time

> *About 3 o'clock, A.M. I heard the sound and felt the shock like unto heavy thunder. I went out but could not observe any cloud above the horizon. I therefore conclude it must be a great earthquake in some part of the globe.* —**Benjamin Banneker, *Memoir of Benjamin Banneker***

Despite persistent doubts from white society about Black people's capacity to comprehend or even experience "civilized" time, evidence suggests that Black clockmakers contributed significantly to the development of the clockmaking craft during the antebellum period. Yet the documentation—or rather, lack thereof—of Black clockmakers in the annals of American history is glaring. The figures that emerge in the history books are few, and when they do, their stories are often riddled with gaps. One exception is Benjamin Banneker (1731–1806), a self-taught astronomer, mathematician, and clockmaker born in Maryland. Benjamin Banneker constructed his first, and supposedly only, clock in 1762, without, he claimed, having ever seen a clock before, and using only a pocket watch as his model. Although history reports that he never made another clock after that, this first wooden version, operated for over twenty years until it was destroyed in the mysterious fire that destroyed his home and all his belongings shortly after his death. The almanacs he meticulously compiled were more than just timekeeping tools; they were compendiums of knowledge that included medical advice, tidal schedules, and social commentary.

The other thing Banneker is best known for is his correspondence with Thomas Jefferson. In 1791, Banneker sent Jefferson a copy of his almanac along with a letter challenging the slave-owning Secretary of State to reconcile the ideals of liberty and equality with the reality of slavery. Jefferson's response was short and non-committal, writing in part that "nobody wishes more than I do to see such proofs as you exhibit, that nature has given to our black brethren, talents equal to those of the other colours of men, and that the appearance of a want of them is owing merely to the degraded condition of their existence both In Africa and America. I can add with truth that no body wishes more ardently to see a good system commenced for raising the condition both of their body and mind to what it ought to be, as fast as the imbecility of their present existence, and other circumstance which cannot be neglected, will admit."[41]

In the colonial and early national American landscape, craftsmen such as clockmakers often commanded a respected position in society. Their prestige, was, in some cases, propped up on the foundation of enslaved labor. William Faris, an artisan in early Annapolis, Maryland, for instance, was not only a renowned clockmaker but also an enslaver.[42] Faris's workshop was a composite of diverse talents, including those of an enslaved silversmith and jeweler who likely participated in the crafting of several objects, such as the face of a tall case clock built between 1772 and 1776.[43] On November 9, 1778, Faris advertised the enslaved silversmith as being for sale in the *Maryland Journal and Baltimore Daily Advertiser*, including that "there is very few, if any better workmen in America."[44] A biographical profile of Faris written by the editors of his diary reveals that Faris often acted as a receiver of captured runaway slaves. Advertisements seeking the return of runaway slaves, placed by his brother-in-law and by an unrelated Philadelphia slaveowner, both named Faris as an agent who could have the enslaved person delivered to him if found.[45]

The profile repeats a dangerous myth that is echoed by Florida politicians like Ron DeSantis in the present day, that enslaved Black people benefited from slavery by gaining skills like blacksmithing.[46] The book reinforces the narrative that Faris "made the investment of training a slave in such highly-skilled crafts," and that "slaves who practiced any of the crafts Faris mentioned were rarely found," given that skilled slaves were more likely to do "more utilitarian trades, such as blacksmithing, carpentry, cooperage, ship building, and shoemaking."[47] Contrary to this myth, many enslaved Africans kidnapped from Africa brought such skills with them.

In an article about the life of the enslaved artisan Pompe Stevens, research fellow Caitlin Galante-DeAngelis Hopkins counters these accounts as inaccurate and ahistorical, noting that major museum collections, like the Philadelphia Museum of Art and the Museum of Fine Arts, contain pieces attributed to "master craftsmen" who used enslaved labor.[48] After recounting numerous ads of sale or capture posted by noted silversmiths, Hopkins writes, "None of these slaves' names appear in any museum catalog, but all of their masters' do."[49] Enslaved craftsmen were likely involved in various stages of production, from the initial design to the final assembly and finishing of clocks and other fine objects. Yet, their contributions were rendered invisible, subsumed under the reputation and economic benefit accrued by their owners.

One such craftsman was Peter Hill (1767–1820), a clockmaker and accomplished craftsman formerly enslaved by Joseph Hollingshead, Jr. Like Faris, Hollingshead is credited as having trained Hill, teaching him the skills that would later enable him to become the owner of a clock business of his own.[50] While the National Museum of American History suggests that Quaker advocacy for education and emancipation benefited Hill, his relative invisibility compared to his white contemporaries exemplifies a larger issue: the systemic erasure of Black artisans from the historical record, a form of historical and ongoing violence in itself.[51]

The popular narrative that slave owners imparted vocational skills to their enslaved individuals out of benevolence rather than economic pragmatism distorts the contributions of Black artisans and craftsmen. It conveniently obscures the reality that for slave-owning craftsmen, skilled enslaved labor was a calculated asset that increased production rates, reduced operational costs, and enhanced their social standing. Meanwhile, enslaved artisans, those known and still unknown, had little to no control over the products of their labor, making their economic and social mobility virtually impossible.

Critical to this history of clockmaking is the recognition that timepieces served as symbols of status and wealth, as well as of the conquering of time and space, contributing to the prestige of the profession of watch and clockmaking. Personal timekeeping devices like those made by Virginian clockmaker Joshua Lockwood were unaffordable for the emerging middle class, costing anywhere from four months to three years of the average salary—for instance, in 1759 in Virginia, a teacher' s annual salary was £60. These were luxury items targeted at the wealthy merchants and plantation owners in the Charleston area. Advertisements for Lockwood's watches and clocks featured motifs such as "a slave planting in the arch, the motto 'Success to the Planters;'" themes that "would appeal to plantation owners 250 years ago in colonial America."[52]

Enslaved Black people were forbidden access to their own indigenous timescapes, as well as the temporal domain of the Western progressive future represented by such timepieces. They were generally forbidden ownership of watches and clocks and often had an imposed illiteracy of clock time so that it could not be used as a tool for gaining freedom. In his essay "Time and Revolution in African America," historian Walter Johnson observed that "one of the many things slaveholders thought they owned was their slaves' time; indeed, to outline the temporal claims that slaveholders made upon their slaves is to draw a multidimensional portrait of slavery itself. Slaveholders . . . defined the shape of the day."[53] Indeed, in 1838 *The Essex County Standard* reported that masters had "complete control over the distribution of the negro's time."[54]

Johnson recounts how slave masters controlled even the biographical time of enslaved Africans, as they "recorded their slaves' birthdays in accounts books that only they could see; they determined at what age their slaves would be started into the fields or set to a trade, when their slaves would be cajoled into reproduction," and otherwise "infused their slaves' lives with their own time . . . through the daily process of slave discipline."[55] The temporal domination was so pervasive that even proposals for emancipation, emerging in various forms throughout the early nineteenth century from abolitionists, politicians, and reformists alike, were framed in a way that continued to bind freed individuals to their former masters through the allocation of their time, suggesting, for instance, that "three-fourths of the negro's time were to be given to the former owner" upon emancipation.[56]

This extension of the master-slave dynamic into the realm of timekeeping technology, with the invention of synchronization mechanisms that linked "slave clocks" to a "master clock," in which a master clock relied on slave clocks to keep time, symbolizes the literal and metaphorical ways in which the concept of ownership permeated aspects of daily life and technological innovation in the nineteenth century. Clockmakers of this era, unwittingly contributed to the metaphorical representation of the master-slave relationship, embedding the hierarchies of slavery into the very fabric of timekeeping.[57] Slaveowners further enforced a temporal order by use of sound; bells, horns, public clocks, chants, songs, speech patterns, and the like were used to regulate slave labor on the plantation. Reading through "Slave Narratives" project, held in the US Library of Congress, yields hundreds of references by formerly enslaved Black people to the attempts by slave masters to regulate every waking moment of their lives including when they were allowed to sleep and rest. Interviewees recounted being made to wake up between 3 or 4 a.m., usually by the master blowing a horn or ringing a bell. They were then and made to work until sundown, or past dark. Some recall regularly working until 10 p.m. This control extended into the times of birth, times of death, and even the "time" of emancipation and liberation. As Thomas Ash shared:

> I have no way of knowing exactly how old I am, as the old Bible containing a record of my birth was destroyed by fire, many years ago, but I believe I am about eighty-one years old. If so, I must have been born sometime during the year 1856, four years before the outbreak of the War Between the States. My mother was a slave on the plantation, or farm, of Charles Ash, in Anderson County, Kentucky, and it was there that I grew up.[58]

It is no surprise, then, that as modern-day mechanical clock time and its attendant linear rhythms were forcibly encoded onto enslaved Black people by means of the whip and other physical violence or that some enslaved Africans came to internalize a linear time construct. Abolitionists in 1838 condemned the "arbitrary appropriation of the negro's time" as a fundamental injustice of slavery.[59]

Enslaved peoples both obeyed and resisted clock time as if it were an extension of the slave master himself. Both Mark M. Smith and Walter Johnson detail techniques with which "time could be turned back upon its master," by utilizing such passive strategies as "working slowly, delaying conception, shamming sickness, or slipping off," as well as explicit acts in the form of mutinies, revolts, escapes, poisonings, magic practices, and other spiritual and religious traditions.[60] These practices were not merely acts of physical resistance but also temporal subversion. Smith identifies Colored Peopl"s Time (CPT) as a specific form of temporal resistance among African Americans. He notes,""African Americans can adjust to white time sensibilities, which stress punctuality and are future-oriented, but they can also reject these same sensibilities as a form of protest against democratic capitalism generally, white bourgeois sensibilities specifically, by eschewing the authority of the clock and adopting presentist and naturally defined notions of time." CPT thus encapsulates the rejection of planter-defined time and its enduring legacy, symbolizing a collective resistance.[61]

One potent example of the retention of indigenous African spatiotemporal orientations was the reliance on the North Star that guided many a sojourner through the night toward destinations of freedom. Babies were given names that carried the legacy of venerated ancestors or were named for their day of birth in their indigenous languages.[62] Such practices reflect the resilience of African temporal traditions, persisting despite the systematic efforts of enslavers to impose linear clock time upon them.

Ultimately, the role of Black bodies in a broader system of time regulation was foundational to the rapid industrial and agricultural development of the United States. The strict regimentation of time in the management of slave labor—enforced by overseers, with plantation bells to mark the shifts—mirrored the synchronization required by mechanical clocks. This organization of enslaved people's labor schedules to maximize working hours was not solely about maximizing productivity; it also served to instill a temporal discipline that synchronized human bodies with emerging capitalist technologies, in which time itself became a commodified resource. Moreover, the external, economically driven time structure eroded personal temporalities such that enslaved people had minimal control over their time for rest, family, or community. This system subordinated the natural rhythms of human existence to an artificially constructed economic time, replacing the cyclical, seasonal time commonly observed by agricultural societies with a linear progression of hours, minutes, and seconds, valued solely in terms of labor output.

Chains to Clocks: Temporal Constructs, Race, and the Myth of CP Time

I am that timeless nigga that swings on pendulums like vines
Through mines of boobytrapped minds that are enslaved by time
—Saul Williams, "Sha Clack Clack"

As formerly enslaved Black people transitioned to post-Emancipation life, they found themselves still barred from existential dimensions of the future and much of their real-world manifestation. The Western, linear paradigm of time was embedded in every facet of American life, including the social hierarchy, the burgeoning industrial economy, transportation, and communication. Time did not tick on indifferently; it was weaponized as a form of social and psychological control. The previous conditions of servitude were supplanted by the unyielding, ever-watchful master's clock and, eventually, the regimentation of the industrial punch clock of labor time.

As Black people sought more control over their own labor during the lead-up to and following the end of the Civil War, expressions like "negro time," "negro clocks," and permutations of the phrase "colored people's time" first began to circulate widely, linking Blackness with lateness and lack of productivity. These cultural myths were reinforced through the creation and distribution of racist Americana memorabilia from the late nineteenth century.

Early print references to Colored People's Time include the remark in an anonymous 1867 op-ed that, "The colored people lose time, it is said, attending public meetings. Well, what if they do?—it is their own time."[63] Another op-ed, from 1878, on political divisions between the North and South in the *Cincinnati Enquirer* observes that tensions were "intensified by the system of 'dividing the colored people's time' so-called in South Carolina, and by idiotic statements telegraphed to the North in advance of the massacre of a lot of negroes, that they were growing dangerous, drawing the color line."[64] Soon after Emancipation, the associations grew increasingly pejorative, as references to the "old-time nigger," the "nigger's clock," and the "old-time darkey" surfaced in literature and newspaper articles. White writers lamented the loss of the mythological joyful, docile, Black slave who is "the happiest of all living creatures" and "comes nearer being a joy forever than anything earthly."[65]

The associations between clocks and the enslaved and formerly enslaved continued. Newspaper advertisements listed Black people alongside clocks and other inanimate objects, as possessions. Among taxable property, an 1840 newspaper ad in the *Asheville Messenger* lists "carriages, slaves, clocks, watches, jewelry."[66] Racist caricatures of Black people as clocks were prevalent in American memorabilia from before the Civil War, through the Reconstruction era, Jim Crow, and even into the civil rights movement.

To further institutionalize these tropes of white-proscribed "Black time" and maintain stereotypes that would reinscribe Blackness as inherently inferior, Black people were not only metaphorically but also literally objectified within the racist material cultures emblematic of Americana memorabilia. Postcards, toys, clocks, and other trinkets, conjured a romanticized view of American history, depicting an idealized past when the country was more unified and innocent. This coincided with timekeeping devices like clocks and pocket watches gaining more popularity in the late nineteenth and early twentieth centuries. Industrialization spurred the mass production and consumption of these timepieces, leading to a heightened societal preoccupation with punctuality and time management. Clocks and watches became widely coveted items, appreciated for both their functional utility and aesthetic appeal. "Souvenir Spoons" and other items featuring engraved images of American landmarks, American flags, historical figures, and emblems commonly incorporated small watch faces in their designs. This integration subtly reinforced the commodification of time.

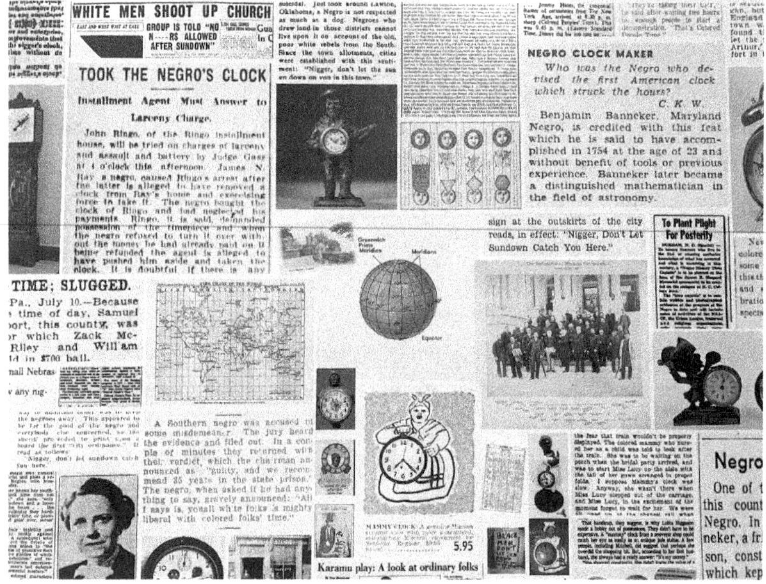

"The Clock, the Bell, the Church," a collage of historical clippings and images, by Rasheedah Phillips (2022), as part of the solo exhibition *Time Zone Protocols* at the Anna-Maria and Stephen Kellen Gallery and presented by the Vera List Center for Art and Politics (NYC).

Images of American nostalgia, including racist Black caricatures, were used to sell products, such as food and household goods, but also appeared in movies, cartoons, and other popular entertainment. Such items often featured a Black figure with exaggerated features, such as oversized lips and bulging eyes. The "Sambo" figure, a recurring trope of a Black man as lazy, ignorant, and happy-go-lucky, emerged in literature around the late 1840s and was commonly used in advertising and other forms of popular culture, including on clocks and watches. "Mammy" imagery, portraying Black women as overweight and contented in their existence serving white families as caretakers, was another gendered racial stereotype prevalent on clocks and watches. That patents for such clocks existed demonstrates the deliberate and profitable mass manufacturing and market for racist Americana.

Antique collector P. J. Gibbs's *Black Collectibles Sold in America* catalogs a 16-inch cast-iron Sambo "winker" figure with a Waterbury clock shaped as a banjo, noting that its eyes move up and down. Manufactured by a company called Bradley/Hubbard circa 1890, the clock is marked as a "scarce" item that ranges in price from $3,300–4,000. Gibbs documents several other clockwork tin toys: "Black figure with cigar in mouth, carrying a cane"; "Black boy being bitten in seat of his pants by dog"; and "Black organ grinder with moving arms." There is a "Dixie Boy Blinking Eye" wall clock, which is "in the shape of a man's head with green hat" and a red necktie that swings as a pendulum, worth $250. The most expensive of these clockwork toys, at $4,500–4,800, is Brower's Automatic Dancer Clockwork Toy, patented in 1873, carved out of wood with a lithograph of a Black man dancing in front of a cabin, with a winding clockwork mechanism set in the back of the clock.[67]

While a nostalgic America continued to yearn for a bygone era where the enslavement of Black people could continue unchallenged, simultaneously refining new ways to continue to oppress, segregate, and marginalize them, a starkly contrasting vision emerged across the Atlantic. Early twentieth-century Italy was the birthplace of Futurism, a movement succinctly summarized by Filippo Tommaso Marinetti's proclamation that, "Time and Space died yesterday," in his 1909 *Manifesto of Futurism*.[68] Anchored in a philosophy that disavowed convention and envisioned an ever-evolving future, Futurism engaged the intellectual currents of the time, notably applying Einstein's theory of relativity to argue that time and space were fluid constructs. This was a profound divergence from the classical Newtonian understanding of absolute time and space. In this progressive vision of temporality, there was no more room for static empires, permanent monuments, or enduring traditions.

This forward-looking philosophy reflected concurrent shifts in industrial capitalism, especially considering the transition from reliance on slave labor to wage labor . Drawing parallels to the laws of thermodynamics, the Futurists found in industrial capitalism a fertile ground for their ideas. As factories adopted advanced mechanization and automation, replacing slave labor with wage labor, an obsession with efficiency became more pronounced. This period saw innovations such as Henry Ford's assembly line and Frederick Taylor's principles of scientific management, both aiming to maximize worker productivity. Marinetti, among other Futurists, expressed a dual sentiment of fascination with the dynamic energy of machinery and caution against the dehumanizing conditions under which laborers worked.

Futurism's ideals were not immune to ideological perversion. While initially politically ambiguous, Futurism's ideals became entwined with Mussolini's fascist regime. This alignment marked a dark chapter in the movement's history, marrying radical visions for societal change with oppressive authoritarianism. The Futurists' admiration of power, speed, and technological progress found a dangerous corollary in fascism's exaltation of war, violence, and dictatorial authority. Prominent Futurists like Marinetti actively engaged in fascist activities and the movement's manifestos and publications became intertwined with fascist propaganda authoritarian ideals, tarnishing the movement's legacy.

The American context began to see "Colored People's Time" evolve into a phrase imbued with both cultural significance and subversive potential. A Black Chicago newspaper in 1912 reclaimed the term, framing it as a form of communal solidarity: "We have in our method of gathering what is commonly called, in the vernacular of the street, 'colored people's time.'"[69] Quickly CPT underwent a semantic inversion within Black vernacular, moving from a stigmatized concept to one that fostered collective identity. However, this reclamation was not without its complications, as evidenced by the swift appropriation of the term by white individuals as an indication of being down or hip, a cookout invitee.

Carl Van Vechten, for instance, a white American writer, photographer, and patron of the arts is perhaps best known for his role in helping promote the Harlem Renaissance movement in the 1920s and 30s and for rubbing elbows with the likes of Langston Hughes, Zora Neale Hurston, and James Weldon Johnson. Though mostly regarded as a friend to the culture and later a staunch supporter of the civil rights movement, one of Van Vechten's works, the 1926 novel *Nigger Heaven*, was widely condemned at the time for its title, its appropriation of

Black vernacular language, and its stereotypical portrayals of Black people as exotic and primitive. In one scene in the book, one character remarks to another that "Perhaps he's keeping C. P. T."[70] At the end of the book is a glossary with the definition "C.P.T.: coloured people's time, i.e., late."[71] Other definitions include "charcoal: negro" and "bull-diker: lesbian."[72]

Mary White Ovington (1865–1951), the daughter of wealthy white abolitionists and women's rights advocates, a suffragist, civil rights activist, and one of the co-founders of the National Association for the Advancement of Colored People (NAACP), also felt entitled to use the term. In 1932, she attended a meeting at a Black Methodist Church and, reflecting on the visit in an essay, recounts:

> One night, the Methodist minister has supper with us, and as I was to speak on settlement work at his church at seven, I watched the clock. But he ignored it, and we did not get to the church until half-past-seven. Colored People's Time is evidently derived from Southern People's Times.[73]

Two years later, in her 1934 essay "Characteristics of Negro Expression," Zora Neale Hurston makes legible how Black communities experienced time in a way that was radically different from the conventions of dominant culture, though never explicitly call it Colored People's Time. For instance:

> It is the lack of symmetry which makes Negro dancing so difficult for white dancers to learn. The abrupt and unexpected changes. The frequent change of key and time are evidences of this quality in music. (Note the "St. Louis Blues.") The dancing of the justly famous Bo-Jangles and Snake Hips are excellent examples. The presence of rhythm and lack of symmetry are paradoxical, but there they are. Both are present to a marked degree. There is always rhythm, but it is the rhythm of segments. Each unit has a rhythm of its own, but when the whole is assembled it is lacking in symmetry. But easily workable to a Negro who is accustomed to the break in going from one part to another, so that he adjusts himself to the new tempo.[74]

Here Hurston regards the lack of symmetry found in Black time and rhythm as a feature, not a bug or a violation. If it is to be regarded as a violation of symmetry, however, a unidirectional arrow of time descending into chaos does not follow, but in fact something else altogether, new and creative, emerges in the paradox created by this entanglement of rhythm and asymmetry. Compare, on the other hand, Hurston's observations to Jefferson's, where he insists that Black people do "keep time" and rhythm well, better than whites.

Such code-switching was recognized but unwelcomed in an ad called "NO C. P. T. ALLOWED THIS SEMESTER" placed in the 1935 *Weekly Tribune*:

> Why wouldn't that be a good moto for us to follow this semester? Do you wonder what C. P. T. means? Here's the low-down. (It isn't original with me) C. P. T. means Colored People's Time—i.e.—late. Let's start off with a bang, and not be tardy once this next semester. What do you say? Are you game? No C. P. T. (lateness) Allowed.[75]

The media continued to propagate negative stereotypes about Black time through the '50s and 60s, particularly in reference to Black people participating in the civil rights and Black liberation movements. As these movements gathered strength and demanded full control of their time, space, and freedom in direct ways, the temporalities of Black people were again more visibly disparaged—just as these references to Black and CP Time cropped up right before, and increasingly after, the end of slavery and during nineteenth- and twentieth-century colonization of Africa.

Jet Magazine in 1958 and reprinted in *Negro Digest* and *Trans-action* in 1965, the article "White People's Time, Colored People's Time" legitimized this false dichotomy.[76] In it, Dr. Jules Henry studied tenants at the Pruitt-Igoe public housing and concluded that the poor were incapable of planning ahead; they lived a "flight from death," their temporalities focused on the moment rather than a future they had no hope of achieving. The article described CPT as disorganized, unreliable—a farce of white organization and precision. What the article didn't show was that many of the predominantly Black residents of Pruitt-Igoe were trapped in a cycle of "time poverty"—a condition where the demands of daily life consume so much time and energy that individuals are left with insufficient opportunities for leisure, self-care, or skill acquisition. This temporal oppression, manifested through long distances between their workplaces and Pruitt-Igoe, inadequate access to public transportation options and other public services, and the fact that residents had to invest time fetching water and dealing with frequent breakdowns of elevators as the housing was maintained with such indifference.

Significantly, the complex was originally designed as segregated housing. Despite legal desegregation, Pruitt-Igoe remained overwhelmingly occupied by Black families as a function of broader patterns of racial segregation in housing markets and urban spaces. Black residents were confined to spaces that were, both metaphorically and literally, decaying. All buildings age but they age faster when they are poorly maintained and when their residents lack the time and resources to fill the gaps left by an absent or negligent state.[77]

Another 1963 article from Journalist Laurie Van Dyke offers a disparaging review of a meeting of Black civil rights leaders, undermining the time-based slogan of the movement:

> "The time is now"—the theme of the current civil rights struggle—does not seem to apply to meetings conducted by Milwaukee Negroes. Some Negroes joke about "CPT" (Colored People's Time). Seldom does a meeting conducted by local Negro organizations start on time—and there often is little concern about how long it lasts.[78]

These movements very pointedly employed references to Black temporalities and time-based slogans in their work. "Now is the time," Dr. Martin Luther King Jr. repeats in his most famous speech.[79] This theme recurs in his speech at Oberlin College in 1965, in which he proclaimed, "The time is always right to do what is right."[80] The Black Panthers created buttons demanding "Free Huey—Seize the Time," and "It's Time to Intensify the Struggle." "The Time is Now" possesses a multilayered resonance as a call to collective action eliciting both urgency and imminence. Rooted in the present, it exhorts us to move beyond procrastination, hesitance, and the inertia of the status quo, demanding immediate and meaningful action. In temporal terms, it invokes a sense of "nowness" that transcends mere chronology, asking us to perceive time not as a distant continuum but as an emergent reality, making palpable the risk that delay could mean forfeiture.

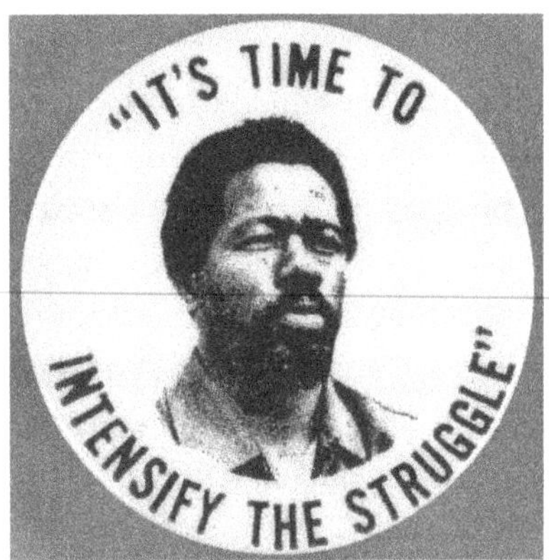

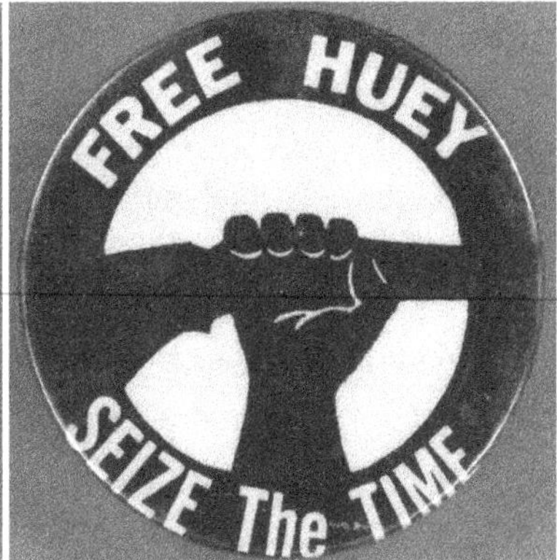

On the left, a protest button depicting Black Panther Party–member Eldridge Cleaver with the inscription "It's Time to Intensify the Struggle." On the right, a button featuring a clenched fist holding a shotgun with the slogan "Free Huey" and "Seize the Time," supporting the campaign to free Huey P. Newton, co-founder of the Black Panther Party, from prison.

As a rhetorical device, "The time is now" succeeds in collapsing future aspirations into the present, rendering abstract goals immediate and tangible. By doing so, it contributes to the construction of what in terms of African temporalities might be understood as a blend of Sasa and Zamani—the immediate present and the vast, indefinite past and future—into a compelling call for action at once urgent and timeless. The phrase serves not merely as a slogan but as a temporal concept, a distillation of collective aspirations into a single moment deemed pivotal for change—*now*. It reconfigures our understanding of time, inciting us to act not out of convenience but out of necessity, thereby altering not just the timeline but the very topology of social evolution. The urgency of *now* is a unique confluence of past struggles and future aspirations, where this moment holds the potential for radical change in the next. This layered understanding of time serves as a critical tool for social movements, framing the present as a pivotal stage from which the long arc of history bends toward justice. This concept of "nowness," or the criticality of the present moment, is further enriched by Geneva Smitherman's reading of the phrase "What time it is." Smitherman explains this Black colloquialism as not just an inquiry into the hour of the day but as a deeper, culturally coded recognition of "the real deal, the truth, what's actually occurring at the moment."[81] Time is entwined with the political and psychological currents of the moment and we must recognize the specific temporal dynamics at play and act with the awareness that the present is indeed the critical juncture for meaningful change.

In the 1960s, the crusade for space exploration occurred in stark contrast to the realities on the ground, where urban renewal and neocolonial practices led to the systemic displacement of Black communities. These policies, often dubbed "Negro removal" by critics, facilitated the razing of Black neighborhoods in the name of progress, resulting in widespread dislocation and the disruption of established social networks.[82] Activists and Black leaders pointedly critiqued the federal priorities and expenditures, contrasting the astronomical investments in space with the insufficient funding for addressing poverty and degradation in Black urban centers. In 1967 at the Southern Christian Leadership Conference, Dr. Martin Luther King Jr. notably highlighted the irony of funding space exploration while neglecting the urgent needs of densely populated slums, questioning the moral and social implications of a society willing to invest more in extraterrestrial endeavors than in the welfare of its own marginalized communities.[83] On July 15, 1969, a day before the Apollo 11 launch, Dr. Abernathy, the vice president of the conference, led a protest at the Kennedy Space Center to highlight the misplaced priorities of spending on the space race over addressing poverty and inequality in the United States. Abernathy's action was not to protest the Apollo launch per se but to draw attention to the country's distorted sense of national priorities, urging NASA scientists to tackle societal problem. An image from the protest printed in the 31 July 1969 edition of *Jet Magazine* shows a Black woman named Mrs. Mattie Gray and her daughter Jackie, who is eight years old and seated in a wheelchair foregrounded against a rocket and holding a homemade sign, that reads prominently "BILLION$ FOR SPACE PENNIES FOR THE HUNGRY."[84]

The discourse in the community continued even after the moon landing. In 1970, Bernice Jones of The Black Panther Party wrote that "America spends over 300 million dollars a year in a race for outer space but cannot afford 300 dollars a month to insure a decent living space for her Black communities."[85] Gil Scott Heron's famous song "Whitey on the Moon" (1970) was also inspired by a speech Eldridge Cleaver gave at a news conference while self-exiled in Algeria, calling the Apollo 11 moon landing a "circus to distract people's minds" from the problems on Earth.[86] This resistance narrative, however, finds scant mention in the popular recounting of the space race, despite the critiques of NASA's diversity or the displacement caused by its expansion, critiqued in both Black and national publications.

The archives of Black newspapers and magazines like *Jet* and *Ebony*, and even national news publications, also reveal widespread critiques of the lack of diversity in NASA employees and of the destruction and displacement of Black communities to build subsidized housing for NASA employees. NASA facilities were spread across the country, with some of the most prominent ones located in areas like the San Gabriel Valley area of Los Angeles County, CA; near Huntsville, Alabama; Greenbelt, Maryland; Hancock County, Mississippi; Houston, Texas, and the well-known Kennedy Space Center in Florida.

The concerns about the displacement of Black communities for NASA's expansion and employee housing were particularly acute in areas like Clear Lake, Texas, adjacent to the Lyndon B. Johnson Space Center. When NASA chose Houston for the space center, it triggered a significant transformation of the city. The arrival of NASA employees catalyzed the growth of new subdivisions to accommodate the influx. By 1965, the population of the area exploded from 6,500 to over 30,000, with subdivisions named "Timber Cove" and "El Lago" cropping up, which would later be known for their notable residents such as astronauts John Glenn and Gus Grissom. Similarly, the Michoud Assembly Facility (MAF) in New Orleans, Louisiana, managed by the George C. Marshall Space Flight Center (MSFC) located near

Huntsville, Alabama, played a role in building and assembling hardware components for space systems. Both these centers, MSFC and MAF, along with other facilities such as the Jet Propulsion Laboratory in California, were focal points of NASA's growth and subsequent need for employee housing.[87]

These expansions inevitably impacted the local communities. While the focus was often on the economic boom brought by NASA, less attention was paid to the displacement of existing residents, especially those from marginalized communities. Partly in response to such criticism, NASA created programs that repurposed spaceship materials for use in "urban" housing and instated campaigns to increase diversity in hiring. Much of this resistance to the space race by the Black community has been largely erased in popular memory.

Reverend Leon H. Sullivan, a civil rights leader and pastor at Philadelphia's Zion Baptist Church at the time, recognized that the Moon landing was one of the ultimate milestones of progress of Western society and a quintessential symbol of humankind's arrival into "the future." In April 1968, just a few days after the death of Dr. Martin Luther King, Reverend Sullivan sat down with one of the white executives at General Electric to discuss how his community could benefit from the space race, telling the executive that "when the first landing on the moon came, I wanted something there that a black man had made."[88] Later that month, Rev. Sullivan and the Zion Baptist Church established Progress Aerospace Enterprises (PAE), one of the first Black-owned aerospace companies in the world. Linking the space race up above to the space race below, just a few years earlier, Reverend Sullivan had co-founded the Zion Gardens Apartments affordable housing project with members of his church, purchasing the building from the owner after learning that Black applicants had been denied housing there based on race.

With members of his church, Sullivan also founded Progress Plaza (the first Black-owned supermarket plaza, which still exists today), Progress Garment Factory, Opportunities Industrialization Center, Inc., Zion Investment Association, and other innovative programs around the country. These initiatives collectively formed what is referred to as Sullivan's Progress Movement, which emphasized the hiring of women and young, unskilled laborers, providing them with training opportunities and jobs in engineering and building parts for NASA and, more controversially, weapons for war.

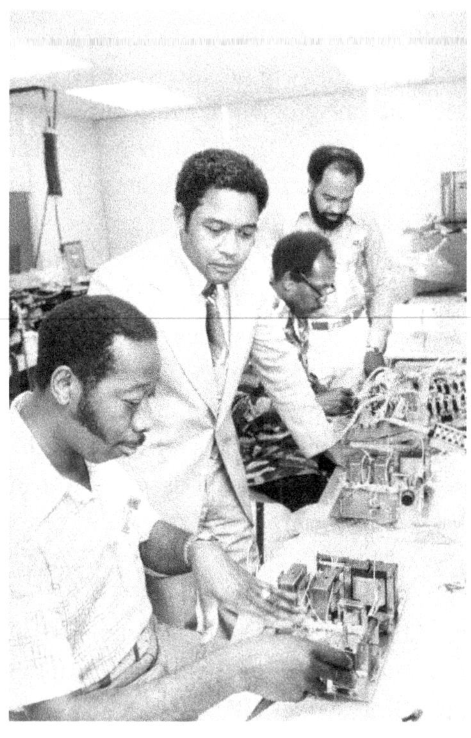

Workers wiring products at the Black-owned Progress Aerospace Enterprises, founded as part of Reverend Sullivan's Progress Movement, from a June 27, 1976, *Philadelphia Evening Bulletin* article.

Some of Sullivan's approaches sparked further controversy, particularly his responses to the Columbia Avenue riots in 1964. These riots, part of a broader wave of civil unrest that swept across American cities in the 1960s, erupted from deep-seated racial tensions and inequalities in Philadelphia. Like the Watts riots in Los Angeles and later upheavals in Detroit and Newark, the Columbia Avenue riots were a palpable manifestation of African American communities' frustration with systemic discrimination, police brutality, and economic disenfranchisement. Sullivan's call for "law and order" in the aftermath of these riots, positioning the riots "as civil destruction rather than civil rights" and at odds with more radical elements of the Black liberation movement and those critical of capitalist frameworks.[89] Sullivan's futurist vision in the Progress Movement should be nonetheless recognized as innovative and sustainable. In the crucible of the space race, within a fervent era of social and cultural upheaval, the zeitgeist was permeated with a narrative of progress and futuristic aspirations. This period was marked not only by the quest to conquer outer space but also by profound social movements seeking to redefine and claim space within the societal fabric for marginalized communities. Sullivan's strategic co-opting of the "progress" narrative and the utilization of "future" in his slogans were acts of temporal reclamation, aimed at intervening in and reshaping the dominant discourse that often marginalized Black contributions and futures. By aligning his initiatives with the broader societal emphasis on advancement and development, Sullivan not only challenged the existing temporal regimes but also crafted a space for sustainable Black communities within the framework of American imperialism and its narrative of linear progression.

Helga Nowotny's observation that on the part of bureaucracies, "temporal control is symbolized by the idea of progress, of economic boom" highlights the strategic importance of Sullivan's approach.[90] Sullivan seemed to grasp the close associations between oppressive temporal regimes, the monopolization of narratives of progress by bureaucracies, and the critical need for sustainable development within Black communities. The technology built at PAE and through other Sullivan projects allowed for hacking into future histories where Black people had already been largely erased—such as in the space race—and helped to ensure our appearances in those histories as they play out on the linear, progressive timeline. Or, to quote Kodwo Eshun, "chronopolitically speaking, these revisionist historicities may be understood as a series of powerful competing futures that infiltrate the present at different rates."[91] By creating revisionist historicities, Sullivan's projects can be seen as cultivating a series of powerful competing futures that permeate the present at varying rates. This approach not only contested the linear, exclusionary narrative of progress but also enacted a form of temporal justice—asserting the presence and significance of Black contributions and futures within the broader historical and societal narrative.

Near the innovative ventures of Reverend Sullivan's Progress Aerospace Enterprises, a rich yet obscured narrative intertwines with the legacy of *Dig This Now* (subtitled "Philadelphia's Only Youth Newspaper"), a weekly newspaper with a circulation of 35,000 birthed from the collaborative spirit of youth gangs in North Philadelphia in 1968, with the guidance of a Temple University student. Nested within the Sharswood Towers—echoing the neglect and systemic racism that plagued Pruitt-Igoe—these youths, emerging from a turbulent period of violence and the aftermath of the Columbia Ave riots, forged a ceasefire. After a particularly bad wave of violence between rival youth gangs in 1967 and '68, and just a few years after North Philadelphia's Columbia Ave riots, the gangs called a truce. Together, the gang members produced and wrote articles for *Dig This Now*, documenting life in their community, exploring issues of local culture, education, and even gentrification years before the word entered popular parlance. Stories included "a mother's view on motorcycle gangs, a column on black history, and descriptions of a neighborhood carnival."[92] One of the gangs would later start an offshoot of *Dig This Now* called *Hip City*, that included articles on ways to reduce violence in the North Philly neighborhood.

The titles of these publications themselves, *Dig This Now* and *Hip City*, are bold temporal and spatial statements, rife with urgency, potential, and inclusion. The term "Hip," as utilized within this context transcends mere stylistic flair to embody a profound temporal resonance. To be deemed "Hip" was to encapsulate being "in the now," fully immersed in the present moment's vibrancy, challenges, and opportunities. This designation signified more than just a superficial coolness or trendiness; it was a marker of acute awareness, a deep connection to the zeitgeist, and an active engagement with the social, cultural, and political currents of the time. In deploying "Hip" as a temporal marker, the young architects of *Dig This Now* and *Hip City* were asserting a deliberate stance of relevance and immediacy. Their engagement with the then-emerging platforms of technology and social media was not merely for amplification, but served as a critical tool for highlighting the intricate web of socioeconomic injustices that plagued their communities. These titles, therefore, were not just names but declarations of intent: to inhabit the present fully, to confront and address its challenges head-on, and to forge a path toward a future where the specters of violence, poverty, and systemic exclusion no longer hold sway. Through this lens, "Hip" becomes a temporal expression of resilience, innovation, and the unyielding pursuit of justice and inclusion, encapsulating the essence of being profoundly connected to the moment, with an eye firmly on the horizon of possibility.

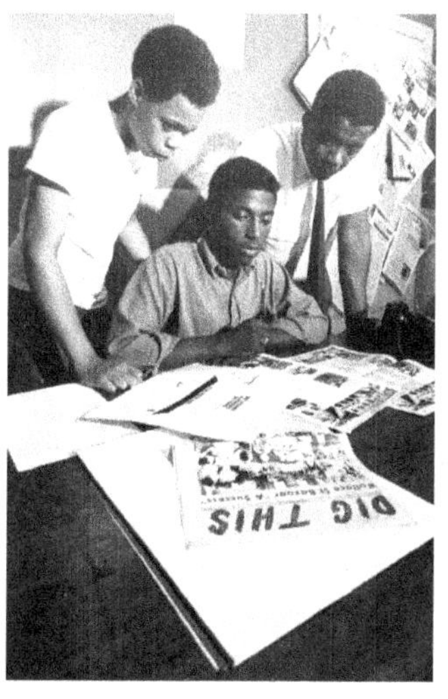

Photograph from an August 16, 1968, *Philadelphia Evening Bulletin* article captioned: "Steven Mixon, 17, Assistant Managing Editor; Nat Goodwin, 19, Advertising Manager, and an unidentified older male pore over an issue of *Dig This*, the newspaper published by the Moroccos Gang."

As Eshun wrote in *Further Considerations on Afrofuturism*, Black futurist imaginaries disrupt the assumed linear progress of time by creating temporal divergences and anachronistic episodes, upending the temporal logics that relegate Black subjects to a prehistoric realm, an archetype steeped in notions of the primitive and the undeveloped, often symbolically linked to an "out-of-time" Africa. This ahistorical narrative frames Africa and its diaspora as permanently lagging behind. To alter the fatalistic rhetoric of a future from which Black people are excluded, we've had to vie for our rightful place within the collective human timescape, underscoring the indissoluble bond between our temporal, spatial, and liberatory pursuits. *Dig This Now* and *Hip City* also embody a long-standing tradition of Black communities seizing print media as a vehicle for our own news and real-time stories, combating the distortions and misrepresentations perpetuated by mainstream media and hacking the trajectory of the future. The existence of separate press and print media outlets has been instrumental in countering negative portrayals and preserving counter-memories and counter-histories of remarkable events. From the pioneering *Freedom's Journal*, established by a group of free Black men in 1827, to the African American literary magazine *Fire!* of the Harlem Renaissance, to the twenty issues of *The Black Panther* published from 1968 to 1973, Black print media stands as one of the most effective technologies for transmitting culture, art, and news. These publications fostered connectivity and engaged in a form of "time-binding"—a process of transcending generational divides through the power of symbols allowing us to channel future insights into our present, enhancing the communal fabric of Black temporalities.

As in Philadelphia, racial tensions in the United States surged to an unprecedented zenith, as cities across the nation were engulfed in riots of escalating magnitude during the 1960s. Civil unrest was further exacerbated by the tragic assassination of Martin Luther King Jr., merely six months after the cataclysmic riots that had ravaged Detroit and Newark. In the aftermath, the National Advisory Commission on Civil Disorders, ubiquitously known as the Kerner Commission, embarked on a mission to dissect the underpinnings of this turmoil, advocating for innovative policies and measures to mollify the burgeoning discord. Part of their analysis highlighted the egregious failure of broadcast television to adequately convey the complexities of racial strife, inadvertently fueling the flames of unrest, particularly within predominantly Black cities like Detroit. The commission criticized the media's portrayal of the riots, denouncing the pervasive bias within white-owned broadcast stations that not only perpetuated a racial schism but also vilified African Americans, thereby exacerbating the societal divide.

In a bold reclamation of Black temporal and spatial sovereignty, on November 6, 1968, a groundbreaking initiative emerged on Detroit's local network, *WTVS*, in the form of a television program titled "Colored People's Time." Tailored expressly for the Black inner-city populace and helmed by African American creatives, this program constituted a deliberate effort to carve out a space within the media landscape that resonated with the lived experiences and aspirations of the Black community. The irregularly scheduled news and social issues was a reclamation of a dedicated Black space-time. It included segments such as "The Poor Do Pay More," an interview with Father William Cunningham, the sponsor of a survey on inner-city grocery prices, and Mrs. Alfreda Rowley, a survey participant; "Git White Overnight," a public service announcement about how skin-lightening creams don't work ("black don't wear off"); and "The Making of a Rioter," a feature that locates the roots of the 1967 Detroit riots in the poor condition of the city's public schools.[93] Yet, less than a year later, a September 1969 edition of *Ebony Magazine* reported, "In Detroit, CPT (Colored People's Time), a black-produced variety and panel discussion show, is going off the air for lack of money."[94] Nevertheless, the program's enduring legacy and its significance within the cultural and media landscape have ensured its survival and evolution. Renamed as "Detroit Black Journal" and later as "American Black Journal," the show has continuously adapted its format and content to reflect the evolving dynamics of the African American community it serves.

The dialogue surrounding CPT intersects intriguingly with futurist Alvin Toffler's seminal 1970s work *Future Shock*, a theory positing that the rapid pace of societal change induces profound disorientation and stress. Toffler's narrative, emphasizing the dissonance wrought by the abrupt collision of new and old cultural paradigms, provides a lens through which to examine the evolution of CPT. According to Toffler, the greatly accelerated rate of social and technological change in our society has produced mostly negative personal and psychological consequences, which arise from "the superimposition of a new culture on an old one" and produce a form of culture shock from which the victim cannot recover.[95] Toffler's diagnosis of future shock as a symptom of modernity's relentless march captures the existential predicament faced by societies in thrall to the notion of perpetual progress—a notion that the Futurists of the early twentieth century, with their exaltation of speed and mechanization, had once heralded as the dawn of a new epoch. This concept of future shock offers a prism through which to view the phenomenon of CPT, as analyzed by Ronald Walcott. Walcott's interpretation of CPT as a deliberate, if subversive, repudiation of "the value-reinforcing strictures of punctuality that so well serve this *coldly impersonal technological society.*"[96] CPT emerges as a nuanced critique of, and resistance to, the linear, homogeneous time of industrial capitalism, which privileges efficiency and productivity over human rhythms and relationality.

The resonance of *Future Shock* extended beyond academic discourse, permeating popular culture through music, literature, and media. These artistic expressions, echoing Toffler's thesis, articulate a profound skepticism toward a unidirectional, progress-oriented view of history, highlighting the disjunctures and disparities engendered by a blind faith in technological salvation. In 1973, Curtis Mayfield released the song "Future Shock," which Herbie Hancock covered as a title track in 1983 as a space-age jazz-funk-electronic fusion. The song envisions a dystopian vision of society ravaged by the very forces of change that were once hailed as harbingers of progress:

> When won't we understand
> This is our last and only chance
> Everybody, it's a future shock

The temporal orientation described in Mayfield's "Future Shock" emerges as a nuanced adaptive strategy, a countermeasure to the relentless forward march of a society that often marginalizes and overlooks the historical and ongoing struggles of Black communities. This orientation of speeding toward the future can be seen as both a reaction to and a coping mechanism for navigating a world where the future seems perpetually out of reach, distorted by the legacies of enslavement and systemic racism. It represents a temporal stance that prioritizes immediate survival and resilience over the uncertain promises of a future that remains heavily influenced by past and present inequalities.

Reflecting similar themes, ten years later, playwright Leslie Lee would write and produce *Colored People's Time: A History Play*, billed as, "Nothing less than a history of Black America from the eve of the Civil War to the Montgomery bus boycott a century later."[97] First presented at New York City's Cherry Lane Theater in 1982, Lee's play counters the dominant narrative of history, revealing layers of Black creativity, resistance, and communal solidarity and contributing to a rich tapestry that challenges the monolithic portrayal of Black life. Composed of thirteen historical vignettes featuring fictional Black characters, the work underscores the nonlinear, cyclical, and sometimes ruptured temporal perspectives that are more responsive to Black historical and cultural realities. Lee invites the audience to perceive time not just as chronological but as emotional, cultural, and deeply intertwined with the social and political movements of Black Americans.

CPT in the Present-ism

The term CPT continued to evolve, and by 2006, received one of its first critical definitions in Geneva Smitherman's *Word from the Mother* as a "reference to the African American concept of time." According to Smitherman, CP Time is "being in tune with human events, nature, seasons, natural rhythms, not a slave to the artificial time of the man-made clock. Being 'in time,' in tune with emotions, feelings, the general flow of things, is more critical than being 'on time.'"[98] The challenge, as Smitherman articulates it, lies in reconciling this culturally ingrained "in time" philosophy with the "on time" demands of mainstream society, which often prioritizes punctuality over the nuances of interpersonal and emotional synchronicity.

However, the interpretation of time and Blackness within dominant cultural, sociological, and medical narratives continue to bear negative connotations, framing Black communities through a lens of deficiency and deviation. The concept of "presentism time orientation" is a recurrent theme in studies exploring temporal perceptions among Black populations, a theory identifying a pronounced emphasis on the immediacy of the present over the significance of the past or future. This orientation, often pejoratively associated with a lack of future planning and tendencies toward immediate gratification, has been misused to pathologize Black individuals as inherently lazy or irresponsible, especially within healthcare contexts.

This problematic framing ignores the broader, systemic injustices that shape these temporal orientations, including environmental racism, disenfranchised infrastructure, and the enduring legacy of segregated neighborhoods. Environmental racism, for instance, exposes Black communities to higher levels of pollution and denies them the benefits of clean air, water, and access to green spaces, significantly impacting their health and well-being. Disenfranchised infrastructure in predominantly Black neighborhoods, marked by inadequate public transportation, substandard housing, and limited access to essential services, further entrenches economic and social disparities. These conditions are not merely coincidental but are the direct result of historical policies such as redlining and ongoing segregation practices that spatially and economically isolate Black communities. Attributing a presentism time orientation to Black individuals, without acknowledging the historical and ongoing context of environmental racism, segregation, and systemic disenfranchisement, oversimplifies complex socioeconomic issues and perpetuates harmful stereotypes and reinforces a narrative that blames individuals for their circumstances while ignoring the systemic roots of those conditions.

Studies highlighting the heightened incidence of heart disease among African Americans often attribute a presentism time orientation as a contributing factor. This perspective suggests that individuals with a present-focused view "may not see the need to take preventative medication or to finish antibiotics when symptoms disappear," or "may delay seeing a physician until symptoms are severe and begin interfering with their work or life."[99] This analysis overlooks deep-seated cultural fears and distrust toward hospitals and medical institutions among Black communities, fears that are rooted in a history of illegal medical experimentation, such as the infamous "Tuskegee Syphilis Study." In this study, Black men were deceitfully denied treatment for syphilis to allow researchers to observe the natural progression of the disease, exemplifying the extreme breaches of ethical medical conduct and contributing to a long-standing wariness of medical systems.

The framing of presentism fails to account for the myriad socioeconomic factors that exacerbate health disparities, including inability to afford continuous medical care, limited access to reliable transportation, poverty, and a history of discrimination within medical settings. These elements not only influence healthcare access and quality but also reinforce a cultural apprehension toward medical institutions, perpetuating a cycle of delayed medical consultation and treatment adherence.[100] Recent advancements in research, policy, and practice are beginning to acknowledge the profound impact of systemic racism and historical trauma on health disparities, recognizing these issues at the individual level of physical, mental, and emotional well-being.

This notion of presentism, within the medical-industrial complex and how it is applied to Black people, can serve to obscure the fact that the concept of presentism, when viewed through a temporal lens, offers a rich tapestry of cultural and spiritual significance. This notion, rooted in Indigenous and African diasporic traditions, emphasizes living in and valuing the present moment. It is a perspective that inherently understands the cyclical and fluid nature of time, contrary to the linear and future-focused orientation predominant in Western societies. Presentism, in its authentic form, is not merely about disregarding the future or neglecting the past but rather is an embodiment of a profound engagement with the present moment as a site of power, healing, and connection. It is a practice that recognizes the present as a space where the past and future converge, where ancestors are honored, and future generations are nurtured. This orientation toward time is echoed in spiritual practices that focus on mindfulness, meditation, and communal gatherings designed to cultivate a deep sense of presence and interconnectedness.

The modern wellness industry, with its capitalist motivations, has often co-opted these spiritual practices without respect for their origins and meanings. For instance, the popularization of yoga in the West often strips away its spiritual roots, focusing instead on its physical benefits, for profit. Similarly, mindfulness and meditation apps commodify practices that have been part of Indigenous and Eastern spiritual traditions for centuries, repackaging them as tools for individual stress relief disconnected from their communal and ethical contexts. This co-optation not only dilutes the depth and richness of these practices but also perpetuates a form of cultural appropriation that fails to acknowledge or compensate the communities from which these practices originate. The wellness industry's emphasis on individualism also overlooks the collective and communal aspects of presentism inherent in Black and Indigenous spiritual traditions.

"Time colonialism" refers to the imposition of a dominant culture's temporal standards upon marginalized communities, for example compelling Black people to align with punctuality norms dictated by corporate America and the global economy, which operates on Greenwich Mean Time. This expectation disregards the disparate access to resources that would enable adherence to such standards. Historic colonizers not only claimed lands and resources but also enforced their timekeeping systems upon Indigenous and colonized peoples, creating a global temporal order that prioritized European economic and social structures. This practice of enforcing time rules can be seen as an extension of colonial control, shaping the rhythm of daily life and work according to the colonizer's homeland, often to the detriment of local customs and needs. In the context of gentrification, time colonialism manifests through the reorganization of urban landscapes to suit the lifestyles and time schedules of more affluent, often white, newcomers at the expense of existing, often predominantly Black communities. These communities are displaced not only spatially but temporally, as their historical rhythms, routines, and connections to the neighborhood are disrupted. Gentrification, in this sense, is an extractivist phenomenon, extracting not only physical space but also temporal autonomy from communities, enforcing a new time order that prioritizes the economic activities and lifestyles of the gentrifiers while displacing the existing social fabric and time customs of the community. Jeremy Rifkin's analysis highlights the restrictive nature of this linear progress narrative on oppressed peoples, confining them within a "narrow temporal band" that renders them unable to plan for their future or influence their political destiny.[101] The future, from this marginalized position, appears "untrustworthy and unpredictable," reinforcing a cycle of disempowerment and exclusion from the broader societal progress.[102]

Cultural and organizing institutions, including corporate entities, educational systems, and certain societal norms, actively enforce the requirement to adhere to punctuality, punishing those who do not conform. This punishment for not being "on time"—where ten minutes late to an appointment might cost individuals their livelihood, children, home, or freedom—illustrates how time is weaponized within a racial and class hierarchy. This form of temporal discipline is markedly different from the enlightenment offered by new age techniques that romanticize "living in the moment," borrowed from ancient spiritual practices and spatiotemporal orientations.

The materialization of CP Time, driven by legal and institutional mechanisms of racist oppression and exploitation, underscores a deliberate and systematic effort to deny Black communities agency over their own temporal domains. The racial segregation of public spaces and discriminatory access to housing and land have evolved alongside and in response to struggles for emancipation, serving to maintain control over Black temporalities. Time, weaponized in service of racial hierarchy, first catalyzed and then sustained the systemic oppression that denied Black communities access to and agency over the temporal domains of the past, present, and the future. This white-proscribed Black time manifested itself in mammies with clock faces built into their cast-iron abdomens and in "Topsy" Blinking Eye clocks.

In *Physics of Blackness*, Michelle M. Wright cautions that "if we use the linear progress narrative to connect the African continent to Middle Passage Blacks today, we run into a logical problem, because our timeline moves through geography chronologically, with enslavement taking place at the beginning, or the past, and the march toward freedom moving through the ages toward the far right end of the line or arrow, which also represents the present."[103] Black Americans today, bound to and by the linear progress narrative, starkly embody these logical fallacies, temporal tensions, and chronological disunities between cultural notions of time, many of us occupying what Rifkin calls "temporal ghettos" as well as physical ones.[104] How we negotiate time and space in relation to the event(s) that forced us upon these shores—the transatlantic slave trade—provides context for the struggles that we continue to endure in the present. We are told that slavery ended, but if so, when? This remains the crucial question particularly with the linear temporal-spatial history of the world still largely intact.

Bending the Arrow into a Circle: Reclamation of CPT into Black Temporalities

BQF's research initiatives at CERN serve as a crucible for interrogating the very essence of time—from a scientific standpoint but also from within the matrix of the sociocultural time of the Black experience. By unraveling what the term "violation of time" implies in the context of both physics and social justice, we enter a multidisciplinary discourse that echoes W. E. B. Du Bois's concept of "double consciousness" to describe the "two-ness" Black people experience in reconciling their identity as both American and Black.[105] This duality can overlay the dynamic between the often-marginalized nonlinear temporalities inherent to Black American cultures and the linear, monochromatic view of time endorsed by dominant Eurocentric frameworks.

In his work "Closure and 'Colored People's Time,'" John Streamas analyzes this dual consciousness as more than just a mechanism for survival but as "also a site in which to imagine and even work toward liberation from racism."[106] Streamas observes how, particularly in literary works by people of color, CPT operates as a narrative tool to encapsulate visions of justice through a "sideshadowing" that allows for the exploration of alternative historical outcomes. Unlike linear, apocalyptic narratives that culminate in a final judgment, narratives informed by CPT often depict a cyclical or alternative sense of time that resists closure, emphasizing ongoing struggle and the possibility of different futures.

Drawing a parallel between the metaphor of double consciousness and quantum physics, Du Bois's "two-ness" can be likened to the quantum conundrum known as wave-particle duality, in which light is coerced into identifying as either a wave or a particle upon measurement. This duality is a fundamental concept in quantum mechanics, illustrating how physical objects can display characteristics of both waves and particles depending on how one observes them. This reductionist act of observation truncates light's intrinsic multiplicity and its ability to exist in a fuller state when not pressed into a categorical choice.

In the classical view, light was debated to be either a wave, demonstrated by phenomena such as diffraction and interference, or a particle, evidenced by the photoelectric effect where light knocks electrons off a material. Albert Einstein's explanation of the photoelectric effect in 1905 proposed that light consists of discrete packets of energy called photons, suggesting a particle nature. Meanwhile, Thomas Young's double-slit experiment in the early nineteenth century highlighted light's wave-like behavior. The quantum theory reconciles these two findings by proposing that light (and, indeed, any quantum particle) doesn't strictly exist as *either* a particle *or* a wave until it is measured. Before measurement, its state is a superposition of possibilities. Scientifically, this means that the very act of observing or measuring a quantum system affects its state. Before observation, quantum entities like photons exist in a state of potential, embodying multiple possibilities simultaneously. This idea challenges classical physics, which assumes that objects have definite properties at all times, such as their position and momentum.

The reduction of all possible Black temporalities, culturally and spiritually derived, to conform to a linear, Eurocentric narrative diminishes their otherwise. By reconciling this "two-ness"—the lived reality within a racialized society and the intrinsic cultural identity that resists such confinement—a powerful call emerges to reimagine our collective temporal constructs. Digging into the quarks and quirks of time, we unearth understandings about both the mechanics of the universe and of our cultural biases within the dominant paradigm.

It is important to recognize that time operates as a multidimensional construct, functioning simultaneously as a device to organize, mediate, and define human interaction and experience. European temporal hegemony works by overwriting African, Black, and Afrodiasporic temporal-spatial experience and identity. This imposition of a unilateral narrative delegitimizes nonlinear and communal modes of timekeeping and reinforces the subjugation of Black communities, establishing a racialized construct of time. CP Time as it has been imposed on us is Black time, temporalities read wrong on the master's clock because they are essentially illegible to the white temporal imagination, within the metric of being "on time."

The notion of Colored People's Time, mirroring the symmetry of the charge-parity-time theorem, can be understood as a metaphorical undoing of the unidirectional arrow of time, bending it back on itself and into a circle. This reconceptualization facilitates a multidimensional temporal landscape that defies traditional linear constraints, and its implications are not merely theoretical but offer a blueprint for emancipation from the very temporal systems that perpetuate the marginalization of Black communities. In a society that continues to marginalize Black people—as "timeless," "uncivilized," "outside of time," or "historically inconsequential"—the dismantling of such temporal constructs is indispensable. This emancipation is more than adjusting histories that have long excluded or misrepresented Black existence but about fundamentally rewriting the temporal rules themselves. Such a liberation would allow Black individuals and communities not only to reclaim their time but to *redefine it*, creating spaces where time bends to cultural rhythms, historical reckonings, and futuristic aspirations uniquely our own. In this reimagined temporal landscape, Black communities would possess the agency to construct worlds that honor their past, cherish their present, and innovate for their future. This holds the potential to not just reshape societal structures but to launch new paradigms of thought, interaction, and existence where Black SpaceTimeMatters and Black experiences are recognized as foundational to the human story.

CHAPTER 4

Time Zone Protocols

I really just can't get down with this whole concept of a "New Year." What does that really mean? Perhaps I am jaded by my skepticism about the concept of time, but to me it is simply a cycle of numbers that shift with the cycle of the sun, an arbitrary date that some Roman in power picked out hundreds or thousands of years ago to be the beginning of a year, a way to demarcate and standardize time for those who abide by our version of it. It's not the beginning of a season. It doesn't reset anything. There is no natural growth nor change. It's just another day, another date, another first of the month. —**Rasheedah Phillips, AstroMythoLosophy blog, January 1, 2008**

History, I have often said, is a clock that people use to tell their political time of day. It is also a compass that people use to find themselves on the map of human geography. —**John Henrik Clarke, "Why Africana History?"**

A global system of twenty-four time zones is used to synchronize activities across and between continents, serving to control the activities of billions of people and billions of dollars across the globe. These invisible borders typically go unnoticed on days not spent traveling at high speeds across them or communicating with colleagues or family members in different time zones. Under scrutiny, time zones reveal more varied and nuanced temporal terrains beneath their homogenizing logic. The international time zone standard ensnares and unravels local temporal fabrics, then divides and orders them to fit a larger global framework. Local time, originally based on the sun's position in a particular location, gives way to the more rigid structure of international time zones. These zones, spanning the globe, are slices of time, each typically an hour apart from its neighbors, designed to standardize time across vast geographical areas. The concept of meridians, imaginary lines running from pole to pole, plays a crucial role here. The prime meridian, set at Greenwich, London, and marked as zero-degrees longitude, serves as the central axis from which all other global longitudes and time zones are calculated.

The Greenwich meridian redefined the global landscape of timekeeping, aligning local temporal practices across distinct cultures and regions within a universal time structure. This global division of time is not an ancient practice etched in the annals of history. Rather, it is a relatively recent construct: Greenwich, in southeast London, was only established as the world's prime meridian after delegates from twenty-five countries gathered in Washington, DC for the International Meridian Conference (IMC) 1884.[1] Prior to this, various prime meridians were used by different countries, each using their own reference lines for navigation and timekeeping, with over two dozen such meridians in use globally. The conceptual, and later material shift, to a singular, standardized meridian was a significant decision that reflected that the "interplay of national and global time was a matter of legislative and bureaucratic time."[2] The IMC represents a pivotal event on the Western timeline for helping to understand the backward- and forward-reaching implications of time standardization and the oppressive global time hegemony that was its founding charter. Prioritizing "commercial and scientific" intercourse between nations, by collapsing capitalist time into natural time through an assimilation standard, the decisions enshrined at the IMC toward the eventually successful project of time globalization has fundamentally altered human relationships to time itself, with immense political, legal, and social consequences.[3] The choice of Greenwich as the world's prime meridian was influenced by several factors. During this period, the British Empire was at its peak, often described as "the empire on which the sun never sets" due to its vast global presence. This extensive influence gave Britain significant leverage at the IMC. The selection of the Greenwich meridian strategically established Britain as the temporal center of the world, reinforcing and legitimizing Western-centric power dynamics and global dominance.

The lens of Black temporalities makes apparent how a global time system disproportionately impacts different communities, disrupts indigenous and localized understandings of time and threatens to erase non-Western temporalities that are deeply intertwined with the cultural, spiritual, and practical life aspects of their people. Through this analysis we uncover not only the hegemonic practices embedded in timekeeping but also the potential for resistance and the reclamation of temporal autonomy by marginalized communities. The quest for temporal sovereignty is a radical act of decolonizing time itself, challenging the uniformity imposed by global time standards and advocating for a pluralistic, inclusive understanding of time that respects and revives diverse temporal narratives.

In 2020, I was drawn to an artistic research fellowship at the Vera List Center for Art and Social Politics at The New School (VLC) with the theme "As for Protocols," and in particular intrigued by their descriptive detail that since "a protocol may also refer to documentation and minutes, the term signals a hybrid time frame of both the past and projection into the future."[4] The theme resonated with my research around time zones and Daylight Saving Time (DST). In reviewing documents from the IMC, I realized that the official 1884 minutes from the conference were subtitled "PROTOCOLS OF THE PROCEEDINGS," with each chapter a distinct protocol.

Over the next two years, as a VLC fellow, I researched and developed *Time Zone Protocols* (*TZP*) as an expansive artistic and creative research project, encompassing an interactive digital archive, an exhibition, and the Prime Meridian Unconference (PMU). Specifically, my work centered on journeying into the labyrinths of political agendas, social contracts, covert rules, and norms—both written and unwritten—that scaffold our contemporary Western-centric time construct.

My research, inherently organic in its approach, sought to comprehend how oppressive time protocols and policies perpetuate structural barriers which tangibly affect marginalized Black communities in the

United States. These protocols are not neutral; they are active agents of historical erasure, contemporary disenfranchisement, which limit the futures of these communities. By dissecting these time constructs, my research aimed to reveal and challenge the structural barriers that deny Black people sovereignty over their temporal experiences—a denial that spans the past, present, and future. My artistic research for this project functioned on multiple registers: as a historical inquiry, as a social critique, and as a visionary exploration. It served not just to uncover and analyze but to subvert and reimagine. By positioning these protocols as forms of research, the project underscored their generative power—the power to create new understandings and to challenge the status quo. In doing so, it opened up possibilities for a more equitable and inclusive temporal landscape, where time is not a tool of oppression but a space of liberation.

The PMU, held April 15 to 17, 2022, convened a multidisciplinary assembly of Black artists, architects, musicians, and scholars specializing in fields ranging from physics and geography to technology and African American studies. Through both virtual and in-person workshops, panels, interactive talks, performances, and plenary sessions, *Time Zone Protocols* and the PMU engaged with specifically Black and Afrodiasporic cultural and communal survival mechanisms. Key to these were the temporal technologies developed, discovered, and reconfigured by Black people and their communities to combat temporal oppression and reclaim agency over time.

These projects quickly deciphered the entrenched power dynamics and vested interests that have circumscribed Black agency vis-à-vis historical legacies, current realities, and aspirational futures. This work upends the reductive view that time is merely an unbiased scientific construct reflective of natural phenomena. Rather than perceiving time as a restrictive force, Unconference participants embraced temporal abundance, empowering a departure from traditional systems of time management.

This chapter elaborates on the research I conducted as part of *Time Zone Protocols* and introduces some of the alternative protocols identified at the Prime Meridian Unconference—protocols that can serve as new scaffolds for realities beyond the constrictions of conventional temporal mechanisms.

Time Zone Protocols

The Land Before Time Standardization: Sea Clocks and Temporal Imperialism

> *The conquest of space and time are intimately connected. European territorial expansion has always been closely linked to, and frequently propelled by, the geographic extension of its clocks and calendars.* —
> **Giordanno Nanni, *The Colonisation of Time***

> *The image—or desideratum or perhaps simulacrum—of cartography is the product of a complex belief system that permeates modern culture: the 'ideal of cartography.' The ideal normalizes "the map," requiring that it be construed only in certain confined and quite unrealistic ways; in particular, the map is understood to be the product of a restricted set of specific practices.* —**Matthew H. Edney, *Cartography***

Clocks are not just devices telling the time but can be viewed as another type of map, one delineating standardized spatial-temporal relationships, effectively creating a uniform framework for understanding time across different geographies and for mapping out a synchronized, shared temporal landscape. As maps structure our perception, clocks structure our perception of time, aligning daily rhythms and activities across the world. There are ramifications, not just in coordinating global activities like trade and travel, but also in shaping the very way we perceive the passage of time.

Like geographic maps, clocks embody, mark, and make visible specific ideas, politics, and boundaries.[5] Technologies and ideas—clocks, maps, time, and global imperialism—are intimately bound. Historian Giordano Nanni emphasizes the pivotal role of horology, the science of timekeeping, in maritime navigation, which contributed significantly to the "discovery" of new worlds. The colonization of the Australian and African continents, for instance, were propelled by the quest for a device capable of accurately measuring longitude. The clock was as essential to imperial expansion and colonization as the ships themselves.[6]

In the context of European colonization and exploration, both Africa and Australia presented unique challenges and opportunities. Africa's vast resources, diverse cultures, and strategic location made it a target for European powers seeking to expand their influence and wealth, while the Australian continent, which remained mysterious and relatively unexplored by Europeans, offered new territories for expansion and exploitation. Before a single prime meridian to rule the globe was forged, cracking the mystery of accurate longitudinal measurement was a critical precursor to the European conquest of space-time. The expansion of European empires to regions like the African and Australian continents, the Indian subcontinent, and the islands of the Caribbean and Pacific over the nineteenth century depended critically on the advancements of timekeeping technologies, including the chronometer. A chronometer is a specialized timekeeping device, distinct from ordinary clocks in its precision and reliability, especially in varying environmental conditions. Originally developed for maritime navigation, chronometers provided an accurate and consistent measure of time at sea, unaffected by the motion of the ship or changes in temperature and humidity. The advent of the chronometer marked a turning point in navigation, transforming sea travel from a perilous undertaking into a precise science, thereby playing a pivotal role in the era of global exploration and colonization. The robust accuracy and reliability of the chronometer made it an indispensable tool for European powers, enabling them to reach and dominate remote regions like Africa and Australia more effectively.

Prior to the seventeenth century, clocks were large and expensive and typically owned and operated only by wealthy individuals or institutions such as governments or religious organizations. It was not until after Dutch scientist Christiaan Huygens invented the pendulum clock in 1656 that clocks became more affordable, more accurate, and consequently more widely available to the public. These early devices, however, were still not fit for sea travel or rough ocean waves.

Over the course of nearly two centuries, rivaling imperial nations with significant navies offered large financial rewards to whomever could develop a reliable method for measuring longitude. Spain did so in 1567 and 1598 and the Dutch Republic did in 1600. Galileo Galilei worked on the problem without much success and Isaac Newton concluded that no clockwork technology could succeed in finding longitude. The longitude problem became a popular obsession captivating people across nations, from renowned scientists to inventors to those thought to be scammers or madmen. The craze bred its own slang: the "longitude lunatics."[7]

In the late 1600s, France and Britain tried another solution to the longitude problem, building observatories from which more accurate astronomical maps and charts might be made. France was first, with the establishment of the Paris Observatory in 1667, and a few years later, in 1676, came Britain built the Greenwich Observatory in Greenwich, London—both institutions would come to play important roles in the Age of Exploration that would unleash conquest and colonization across the world.[8] Historian David Rooney underscores the imperialist motivations behind the establishment of the Greenwich Observatory, pointing out that it was founded during the reign of a king actively involved in the African slave trade. The tools and calculations provided by the observatory facilitated European maritime voyages, playing a pivotal role in the project of colonial extraction and expansion.[9]

The Greenwich Observatory's main instrument was the quadrant. Developed by notable astronomers such as John Bird, the quadrant was a large, angular measuring device designed to ascertain the positions of celestial objects and to enable astronomers and navigators to chart the skies more accurately. Its measurements provided the essential data needed to create more detailed and reliable navigational charts. These charts significantly enhanced the safety and efficiency of long-distance sea voyages. By enabling mariners to determine their geographical position with greater accuracy, the risks associated with oceanic exploration were reduced. However, the problem had still not been fully solved. In 1707, for instance, four warships in an English fleet were wrecked due to severe weather and miscalculations of the fleet's longitude, with an estimated loss of 1,400 to 2,000 sailors.

In 1714, the British Parliament established the Longitude Prize, which offered a sum of 20,000 pounds (about $5 million USD today) to anyone who could determine longitude to within one-half of a degree of accuracy or a margin of error of no more than three seconds every twenty-four hours.[10] British clockmaker and carpenter John Harrison threw his hat into the ring. Harrison had spent many years studying the problem of longitude and concluded that an accurate timepiece was the key to solving it. Between 1730 and 1735, he built his first "sea clock"—a marine chronometer which he called H-1, short for Harrison's No. 1. H-1 was large, occupying a 4' x 4' x 4' cabinet, and heavy, weighing seventy-five pounds. It used a balance wheel and spring to regulate its timekeeping.[11] Although it was accurate, it was too bulky and impractical for use on ships.

Over the next few decades, Harrison continued refining his design, building smaller and more accurate sea clocks, watches, marine timekeepers, and chronometers. His H-4 marine chronometer, which he completed in 1759, was a breakthrough. At five inches in diameter, it weighed three pounds. The H-4 was small enough to be carried on a ship, was less subject to rust on long voyages, and was highly accurate, matching land-based clocks within a few seconds. It operated based on a variety of innovative design features, including the use of a high-quality balance wheel and spring, a temperature-compensated balance, and a jeweled pivot.

One of the key innovations that Harrison pioneered, so to speak, was the construction of the escapement, the mechanism that regulates the movement of the chronometer, out of lignum vitae wood, which contains a unique resin that helps reduce friction. The escapement includes a pallet, a small lever that moves back and forth and allows the clock to tick at regular intervals and needs to be both strong and smooth to function properly. Lignum vitae was judged ideal material for this purpose and this secret ingredient allowed the chronometer to function accurately and reliably in the harsh marine environment, where the motion of the ship could cause damage to the clock's delicate mechanisms.

Lignum vitae (Guaiacum sanctum), Latin for "wood of life," is a dense and durable tropical hardwood tree native to the West Indies, parts of South and Central America, Florida, and Mexico.[12] The tree is sacred to the people of the Caribbean and highly valued for its strength, resilience, and resistance to wear. For centuries it has been a vital material in those regions, used in furniture-making, shipbuilding, the making of games and toys, and machinery. The bark, leaves, and seeds of the tree are also used medicinally, brewed to treat fever, headache, stomachache, and respiratory issues.

The H-4 timekeeper was tested on several voyages, including to Jamaica and the West Indies—where they likely also harvested more lignum vitae—and back, on which it proved to be remarkably accurate. However, in 1764, Harrison encountered several obstacles with the Board of Longitude, the committee charged with determining the winner of the Longitude Prize, made up of mathematicians, astronomers, and naval officers. The board was skeptical of Harrison's work and refused to award him the prize money, citing technical flaws with the timekeeper. Several months later, in October 1765, Harrison was rewarded with a certificate from the board but only part of the prize money.[13] Undeterred, Harrison continued to make improvements and eventually constructed a more accurate timekeeper, the H-5, at age seventy-seven. His accomplishment was undeniable, forcing the board to acknowledge Harrison's success and finally award him the rest of the money on April 8, 1773. Harrison died three years later.

The chronometer revolutionized navigation at sea. With an accurate chronometer, sailors could now plot longer, more extensive voyages. By knowing the exact time at a reference point (such as the Royal Observatory in Greenwich, which later became the basis for Greenwich Mean Time) and comparing it with the local shipboard time determined through celestial observations.[14] Moreover, the chronometer's role in maritime history underscores its significance in the broader narrative of global trade and imperialism. It was not just a tool for navigation but also a linchpin in the mechanisms of empire-building, as it enabled the control of sea routes critical for the economic exploitation of colonies. A replica of Harrison's H-4 chronometer, the K-1, would later aid Captain James Cook's second and third voyages to what is now known as Sydney Cove, Australia. In 1788, six years after Cook's second voyage, the first fleet arrived in what Cook had renamed New South Wales to establish the first British colony on Australian soil. This beginning of European colonization of Oceania led to the systematic displacement and dispossession of Aboriginal people. The resources extracted from Britain's new territory helped to cement its position as a major global power.

Chronometers played a similar role in the exploration, exploitation, and mapping of the African continent. In the mid-nineteenth century, David Livingstone, a Scottish explorer considered to be one of the first medical missionaries to travel extensively throughout the continent, used a chronometer to accurately determine longitude. This device enhanced the precision of his surveys and maps and helped fill gaps in the existing European knowledge of the African continent at that time. Livingstone's expeditions, spanning three decades, focused on gaining a better understanding of the continent's hydrology, as he traveled aboard a small steamship and mapped the nuanced patterns of rivers such as the Zambezi, Congo, and the Nile, and lakes such as Nyasa and Bangweulu.

These chronometers, glorified time measurers built from extracted and stolen sacred wood and with the aura of modern progress about them, along with the establishment of a vast navigational empire via the Greenwich Observatory, enabled European powers to conquer the globe with unprecedented accuracy and to develop more precise maps which paved the way for the increased exploitation of natural resources. Both the chronometer and the observatory were also key technologies in the later establishment of time zones and the destruction of unique local time(s).

From Greenwich to Everywhere: Time Zones as Geopolitical Tools

> *In itself, the adoption of the Greenwich meridian was a marker of British political hegemony in the late nineteenth century: global time zone construction was politically charged from the very start. Thus, the world time zone map became a "world" map because of the European way of looking at global control and for ensuring its impress would be imprinted, permanent and non-negotiable. World maps with a Eurocentric perspective further solidified the Europeans' definition of international time and space.* —**Karl Benediktsson and Stanley Brunn, "Time Zone Politics and Challenges of Globalisation"**

In a Newtonian world, often described as a "clockwork universe," the idea of codifying a global time standard can be seen as the function of an earthly mirror reflecting divine order and control over the cosmos. The historical record of the IMC notes that "the preference for the Greenwich meridian is explained by the reputation and reliability for correctness developed by Greenwich time."[15] But anthropologist Kevin Birth and other scholars refute this claim. Birth argues "Greenwich is the prime meridian because of English imperial and economic power, not because that suburb of London is a good place for astronomical observations."[16] This assertion highlights the underlying power dynamics in the establishment of global time standards, where international time zones emerged as more than just practical innovations. They were instruments in the larger landscape of imperial projects that would serve both rising global capitalism in the nineteenth century and the considerable colonial management that buttressed it. These time zones served as a material expression of Western hegemony, imbued with the values and standards of the dominant culture inscribed upon the so-called natural world.

The global imposition of time zones was fundamentally intertwined with the ideology of the "White Man's Burden." Under this guise, the enforcement of Western time standards was perceived as an advancement or maturation of societies under colonial rule. The adoption of these time zones wasn't just about synchronizing clocks, it was about imposing a specific worldview, one that aligned with the interests and perspectives of colonial powers—a "civilizing mission." International time zones, therefore, would become a form of cultural and political enforcement, a tangible manifestation of the colonial agenda to reshape societies according to Western norms and standards. The implementation and acceptance of these time zones required various forms of enforcement, ranging from administrative decrees to integration into the infrastructure of trade and governance, thereby consolidating the hegemonic influence of the colonizers.

It was within this context of evolving global imperialism that Sir Sandford Fleming, a Scottish-Canadian engineer pivotal in the construction of the Canadian Pacific Railway, became one of the first to propose a worldwide system for standardizing time. Fleming had seen firsthand the challenges of coordinating schedules and timetables across great distances. This experience prompted him to propose a single twenty-four-hour clock for the entire world, referred to as "Cosmopolitan Time" and later "Cosmic Time." In his 1876 memoir, *Terrestrial Time*, Fleming laments humanity clinging to a "system of Chronometry inherited from a remote antiquity," and recounts a story of traveling in Ireland and being delayed by an entire day due to a typographical error in a train's timetable that indicated p.m. instead of a.m.[17] This episode underscored for him the need for a time system that could transcend local idiosyncrasies, resulting in his proposal of a universal twenty-four-hour clock and the division of the world into twenty-four time zones.[18] Fleming crystallized his ideas further in academic papers such as "Time Reckoning" and "Longitude and Time Reckoning," which he presented at a meeting of the Canadian Institute in Toronto on February 8, 1879. Grounded in empirical analysis of shipping data where he observed significant inefficiencies and dangers stemming from the lack of a standardized global time system, he advocated for a prime meridian at Greenwich. These papers received widespread attention, with the British Government disseminating them to eighteen foreign countries and numerous British scientific societies in June 1879. Fleming's influence led to the convening of the IMC in Washington, DC, in 1884.

In November 1883, a year before the IMC, the United States independently initiated its system of time zones. Railroad companies, much like seafaring vessels averting disaster, also face the challenge of managing time to prevent train collisions. amid various local times. Before the standardization of time zones, local time was determined by the position of the sun in the sky at each specific location. This method, based on "high noon" or the time when the sun was at its highest point in the sky, meant that clocks in neighboring towns could differ by several minutes or even hours. Prior the 1800s, when clocks and watches were still too expensive to be household items for the average person, the primary sources for determining the time were the town clock and the sun, with each often indicating a different time.[19] This practice led to the existence of hundreds of local times, with distinct variations such as Philadelphia Standard Time or Charleston Standard Time, instead of a uniform Eastern Standard Time. This meant that communities typically maintained a sense of autonomy and connection to the natural rhythm of their environment, where activities and schedules were aligned more closely with the natural cycles of daylight and darkness.[20]With the development of the railroad in the 1800s, the primary source of time reckoning began to shift to prominently include train schedules.[21] Given that every city or town set its own time, this led to discrepancies even in nearby locations. For instance, 1:05 p.m. in one town could be 1:15 in the next. Railroads operated on their own timetables, not always in sync with local times, leading to unsafe traveling conditions and collisions. One significant accident took place on August 12, 1853, when two trains running on the same line collided head-on. The northbound-train conductor, newly appointed, was using a borrowed watch from a milkman to time his train's schedule. This inaccuracy in timekeeping led to the collision, resulting in the deaths of over twenty people.

Initially a system of regional time zones improved the situation. In the 1850s, as railroads began to expand and play a crucial role in transportation, they started operating under about fifty regional times. Each of these times was set to an arbitrary standard agreed upon by the rail companies. These companies often persuaded regions to abandon their local time in favor of the railroad's operating time, which was more convenient for managing train schedules.[22] But local times still challenged operations like national news, regional event reporting, and other moments when national synchronicity would be useful. A further dramatic shift in timekeeping was necessary, and national committees were formed to grapple with logistical problems, including reconciling "the time difference between local time and railway zone time for over 8,000 stations."[23] This issue gained importance following the completion of the US Transcontinental Railroad in 1869. As rail and telecommunication networks expanded, calls by for a more synchronized and efficient system of timekeeping increased.

By 1881, the confusion caused by coordinating between multiple regional times led to concerns about potential government intervention. Railroad managers, seeking a more efficient and less daunting system, commissioned William Frederick Allen, a transportation publisher, to devise a simpler plan, similar to the one Great Britain had devised in the 1840s. Allen proposed a system of five time zones, with each zone's time determined by the central meridian within that zone. Each central meridian was set at fifteen degrees longitude, or one hour, apart. Allen then launched a successful campaign to persuade railroads, businesses, journalists, politicians, and average citizens to support his time zone plan.

This culminated in what became known as "The Day of Two Noons." On November 18, 1883, major US railroads convened in Chicago to usher in a new era of timekeeping based on a nationwide standard synchronized with the Naval Observatory in Washington, DC. Four standard US time zones were introduced, each separated by fifteen degrees of longitude and offset by one-hour increments, beginning and aligned with Greenwich Mean Time, which was already in use globally but not yet established as the prime meridian. When the clock struck noon on November 18, 1883, the country was officially divided into these four zones, and a revolutionary framework for managing time emerged. Through various means, including widespread media coverage, people across the nation were instructed to stop what they were doing and reset their clocks at noon to the new standard time. As a result, in some places, noon occurred twice: once when the sun reached its highest point in the sky, as per the local time, and again when the clock was reset to the new standard time.

In New York City, the change was initiated by stopping the pendulum of a standard clock for about four minutes. This adjustment was replicated in jewelry stores and watch repair shops, surprising many onlookers who had expected a more dramatic process. In Philadelphia, there was considerable interest in the change, with crowds gathering to witness the clock adjustments at Independence Hall and at railroad stations. The event was marked by a mixture of confusion, curiosity, and some humor, as people grappled with the idea of time being altered so simply at the Pennsylvania railroad station in Jersey City, the transition from local (Philadelphia) time to standard time was made by stopping the clock for one minute and then resuming its operation. New signs indicating "Standard Time" replaced the old ones. Railroads across the city adjusted to standard time, and new timetables based on this standard were issued. Beneath the ostensibly practical aim of standardizing time across the United States lay a matrix of power relations with deep social and racial impacts.

The new time regime didn't just streamline operational efficiency; it further codified the temporal parameters that dictated labor conditions. For Black people only a few decades after Emancipation, as well as for those still ensnared by wrongful imprisonment on minor or exaggerated charges and exploitative labor practices, this shift amplified the abstraction of their labor into units that could be more efficiently quantified, optimized, and controlled, in service of burgeoning industrial age. In the railroad industry, where standardized time was first rigorously applied, the work schedules of Black laborers were strictly regimented. Train schedules, maintenance work, and loading and unloading of cargo were all synchronized to the new standard time, leaving little room for deviation.

This new time regime led to a more rigid and quantifiable system, directly linked to increased efficiency in transportation and commerce. For those in agricultural settings, such as sharecroppers, the impact of standardized time was subtler but no less significant. The rhythms of agricultural work, traditionally aligned with seasonal and daylight patterns, now had to accommodate market demands and transportation schedules dictated by the new time regime. This shift further entrenched the economic disparities and exploitative conditions faced by Black workers in these sectors. The application of standardized time during the post-Emancipation era can be recognized as a manifestation of the "temporal oppression" that English historian E. P. Thompson explored in his analysis of time and labor. The imposition of mechanical clocks, Thompson argued, introduced a new discipline in the workplace that transformed "task-oriented" time into "time-oriented" tasks such that labor became measured and managed in units of time. This managerial shift displaced traditional labor structures and fundamentally altered the worker's experience of autonomy, reshaping the labor landscape.[24] Just as they had during the era of enslavement, Black people found themselves bound to the inexorable ticking of a clock, a symbol of an industrial system managed by entities far removed from their lived realities. The micromanagement of labor, exemplified by the adoption of punch clocks in factories, further institutionalized a regime post-Emancipation where time, and consequently labor, could continue to be rigidly controlled and monitored.

The institutionalization of standardized time in the United States intersected with a pivotal moment in the nation's history, particularly in the context of civil rights and freedoms. This period was marked by the Supreme Court's decision on October 15, 1883, which struck down the Civil Rights Act of 1875. This act was a foundational piece of legislation designed to combat racial discrimination in public accommodations, a beacon of hope during the Reconstruction era for establishing racial equality. However, the court's decision, by an overwhelming majority of eight to one, significantly undermined this effort. It conveyed a stark message: despite the nominal abolition of slavery, Black people would remain subject to systemic discrimination and restrictions, deprived of the autonomy to shape the conditions of their existence in both time and space.

The Supreme Court's decision to uphold racial segregation in public spaces, coupled with the imposition of a standardized time system, crafted a comprehensive framework of control. This framework curtailed the liberties of African Americans in both overt and subtle ways. For instance, the decision in the Civil Rights Cases of 1883 effectively legitimized the segregationist practices that would later be cemented by *Plessy v. Ferguson* (1896), endorsing the doctrine of "separate but equal" and further entrenching racial divisions. The standardization of time, ostensibly a measure for efficiency and unity, also played a role in reinforcing societal norms and schedules that were indifferent, if not hostile, to the unique challenges and needs of African American communities.

These co-occurring events—national time standardization and the legal rollback of civil rights—mutually reinforced structures of systemic ani-Black oppression in post-Emancipation US. Economically, Black people were often relegated to the lowest-paying jobs, which were rigidly structured around the new standardized time, limiting their opportunities for advancement, and further embedding racial inequities. Socially, the segregation of public spaces meant that Black people were excluded from participating fully in public life, a condition exacerbated by the synchronization of public services and spaces to a standard time that did not accommodate their realities. Black SpaceTimeMatters underscores the interconnectedness of temporal and spatial dimensions in the lived experiences of African Americans. The Supreme Court decision, by upholding racial segregation in public spaces, and the standardization of time, by regulating the daily rhythms of life, together reinforced a matrix of control that limited the freedoms of African Americans in both tangible and intangible ways.

Author Jo Ellen Barnett, in *Time's Pendulum*, chronicles how the railroad-initiated standardization of time gradually gained acceptance across the country. Through a concerted effort involving a powerful lobbying and propaganda campaign coordinated among local governments, many cities and towns were persuaded to adapt US Standard

Time within a year. Initially, this adoption did not stem from a legal requirement but rather from a practical and collective acknowledgment of the benefits of a unified timekeeping system. However, the widespread acceptance of railroad time laid the groundwork for legal codification, and "all the states soon [separately] passed legislation adopting the railroad time as the time to be used for all legally defined time."[25] Legally defined time refers to time standards set by law or legislation, such as for commercial and legal activities, or the setting of business hours and government office hours. Eighty-five percent of all towns with a population greater than 10,000 had synchronized their clocks to US Standard Time by October 1, 1884, when forty-one all-male delegates from twenty-five countries in diplomatic relationship with the United States convened in Washington, DC for the IMC.

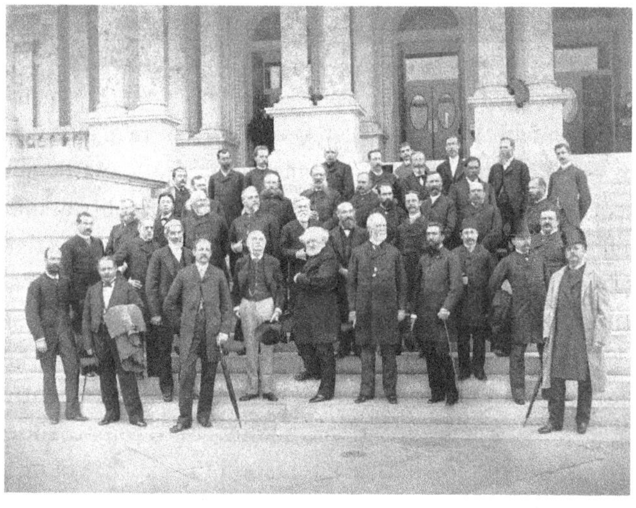

The international delegates to the Prime Meridian Conference, on the steps of the State, War, and Navy Building in Washington, DC, October 1884.

Organized by an act of US Congress "to fix on and recommend for universal adoption a common prime meridian, to be used in the reckoning of longitude and in the regulation of time throughout the world," the IMC followed on preliminary discussions that had been held at earlier conferences in Venice in September 1881 and Rome in October 1883, where at each Fleming had played a crucial role.[26] An international timekeeping system was not just of interest to railroads and ship navigators; it was also critical for astronomers for whom differing time standards and measurements were an obstacle in their work. The IMC set itself an ambitious agenda: the unification of global timekeeping as the linchpin for synchronizing international commerce, communication, and navigation—a monumental task.[27] Prior to this, the United States had been operating with the use two meridians: one in Washington, DC, for astronomical calculations, and the other following the Royal Observatory in Greenwich, for geographic and navigational purposes.

The rest of the world had likewise relied on multiple prime meridians, each nation determining its own landmarks for calibrating time. The IMC, therefore, was not just a scientific endeavor; it was a geopolitical crucible. The conference solidified Greenwich's status, with Fleming's voice a dominant one. Despite varying arguments about the significance of the IMC in the history of global time reform, the conference undeniably played a role in heralding the era of global modern time. It was a product of a dialectic between the scientific quest for universal standardization and the exertions of geopolitical influence, not unlike the predictable movements of a Newtonian celestial clock. The imposition of Greenwich Mean Time (GMT) as the global standard can be seen as a form of temporal imperialism, where time itself was colonized and regulated according to Western industrial priorities. This standardization of time served as a mechanism of control that facilitated global synchronization, aligning global temporalities with Western economic and political interests at the expense of local temporal practices. Such international agreements as those developed at the IMC imposed a linear, progress-oriented view of time that often conflicted with the cyclical, relational, and event-based conceptions of time prevalent in many African and diasporic communities. We continue to uncover the ways such homogenizing temporal structures have contributed to ongoing forms of oppression and marginalization, providing critical perspective on the global narratives of time that dominate our understanding of history.

Liberia and the Temporal Chains of Diplomacy

Despite the US Secretary of State's opening proclamation that the meeting represented "most of the nations of the Earth," the delegate list at the IMC was heavily skewed toward European and South American sovereign nations.[28] Asia had sparse representation, with Japan as its solitary emissary. Liberia was the lone African nation at the table—a country with knotted historical and political ties with the United States.

Liberia's establishment in 1822, by the American Colonization Society (ACS), a white abolitionist group founded in 1816, is pivotal in understanding these ties. The ACS, sought to address the increasing number of free Black people in the US by resettling them in Africa.[29] The organization attracted a diverse membership, including both abolitionists and slaveholders. Liberia was marketed as a relocation hub for free Black people in the US who were willing to move to West Africa. Political figures, including Henry Clay, Daniel Webster, James Madison, supported the mission of the ACS, but they initially struggled to establish the colony. In 1818, their representatives failed to persuade local tribal leaders in West Africa to sell any territory. However, in 1821, a US Navy vessel, led by Lieutenant Robert Stockton, coerced a local ruler to sell a strip of land for the colony. Monrovia, Liberia's largest settlement and eventual capital, was initially named Christopolis. In 1824, it was renamed Monrovia in honor of James Monroe, US president at the time and a supporter of the ACS, reinforcing Liberia's ties to American ideologies and policies.[30] Washington, DC and Monrovia are the only two national capitals in the world that are named for US Presidents.[31] In addition to the settlers from the United States, Africans liberated from slave ships by the US Navy after the abolition of the transatlantic slave trade were also left ashore in Liberia.

By the time Liberia declared its independence from the ACS on July 26,1847, the ACS had facilitated the voluntary migration of several thousand emancipated and free-born Black people. It was a unique case of a nation established by non-Indigenous people gaining independence without a direct colonial ruler. The declaration was a step toward establishing the nation's sovereignty, allowing it to create its own laws and governance structures, distinct from those of the ACS and the United States. The ACS's role in Liberia post-independence included ongoing financial support and guidance in governance and administration. This sustained involvement meant that, while Liberia was politically independent, it was still economically and administratively linked to the ACS and, by extension, to the US. Abraham Lincoln eyed Liberia as a potential solution to the perceived dilemma of integrating emancipated Black individuals into a post-slavery US society reluctant to cede jobs or resources to them. In an 1854 speech, Lincoln expressed that his "first impulse would be to free all the slaves, and send them to Liberia, to their own native land."[32] Under Lincoln, the United States, officially recognized Liberia as a sovereign state in 1862. This recognition was crucial for Liberia's international standing, but it also meant that Liberia's foreign policy and international relations were heavily influenced by the US.

Liberia attended the IMC in 1884 as a sovereign state. Its delegate was ACS Secretary and Liberia's consul-general, William Coppinger, who in 1881 authored a report called, "The continent of the future: Africa and its wonderful development—exploration, gold mining, trade, missions and elevation."[33] Despite the facade of independence, Liberia's continued reliance on the US and the ACS for diplomatic support and economic aid kept the nation locked into colonial space-time relationships with the US government. This relationship was characterized by a power imbalance where Liberia's decisions and policies were significantly influenced by its historical ties with the US and the expectations of the ACS. This dynamic hindered Liberia's ability to exercise full temporal autonomy and spatial agency, as its national agenda was often aligned with the interests of its former patron rather than its own developmental needs.

However, Liberia notably did not adopt GMT until 1972, despite Coppinger voting favorably for it at the IMC almost a century earlier. After the conference, each country navigated its own set of logistical and administrative challenges in adopting the proposed changes and adjusting long-standing local practices tied to the society and economy. In Liberia, local timekeeping was based on the capital's geographic location. The initial system, called Liberia Mean Time, was adjusted to Monrovia Mean Time in 1882, with a slight redefinition in 1919, and was forty-four minutes and thirty-three seconds behind other countries in the same longitudinal alignment.[34] Although eventually succumbing to GMT to facilitate international relations and economic activities, the fact that for over a century, Liberia operated on its own mean time, even if only by forty-five minutes and thirty-three seconds, connotes a measure of temporal autonomy and reflects the country's ongoing negotiation with its colonial past and the pressures of globalization.

Temporal and Spatial Imperialism: The IMC and the Berlin Conference

When the gavel sounded at the IMC on October 22, 1884, the conference had achieved seven landmark resolutions, enshrined in the Final Act of its Protocol Proceedings. Most notably, it endorsed Greenwich as the prime meridian and established a universal day of twenty-four hours starting at Greenwich midnight. Although the conference conceded that local timekeeping could continue "where desirable," it set a standard that would ultimately govern the reckoning of time across the globe, as it still does 140 years later.

The worldwide system that was established in the years following the International Meridian Conference has proved to be enduring, despite radical changes in the worlds of politics and commerce. However, the conference was far from a harmonious affair, fraught with political disagreements. The resolutions were recommendations and adoption was at each nation's discretion, while some scholars claim that "delegates at the meridian conference had no authority to commit their nations to any resolutions."[35] France and Spain both chose to ignore the conference's declaration, instead choosing to adopt time zones based on their own observatories and the time of their capital cities, referred to as "local mean time" in order to differentiate it from Greenwich Mean Time. France, which had lobbied for a neutral meridian unassociated with any continent, eventually adopted the Greenwich meridian in 1911 following a gradual convergence toward this standard among other nations, and contingent upon Britain's adoption of the metric system.[36]

Due to the lack of binding authority and the difficulties of conforming each individual countries' commerce, transportation, time measurement and other national systems to a new time, the resolutions were not immediately adopted or acted on by the representative countries. Several countries officially set their times in coordination with GMT about a decade after the IMC. However, by 1929, this model of universal standard time had virtually global acceptance, and all other longitudes were measured relative to the Greenwich prime meridian, propagating Britain's sociopolitical ideas globally beyond mere timekeeping. The transition placed the British Empire at the center of a global timekeeping mechanism, implicitly endorsing British customs and political ideologies. With international standard time still in use today, "the worldwide system that was established in the years following the International Meridian Conference has proved to be enduring, despite radical changes in the worlds of politics and commerce."[37]

Fittingly, just weeks after the IMC, European powers convened at the Berlin Conference of 1884 with the aim to settle territorial disputes in Africa, an event which has come to be widely recognized as a pivotal moment in the history of the colonization of Africa. Organized by German Chancellor Otto von Bismarck, this meeting involved thirteen European nations, Belgium, France, Germany, Italy, Portugal, Spain, the United Kingdom, Austria-Hungary, Denmark, the Netherlands, Norway, Russia, and Sweden-Norway, and the United States. Also known as the Congo Conference, the meeting sought to prevent military conflict between European nations over African territory and to establish rules for colonization and trade. This had become a point of increasing tension since the mid-nineteenth century, when the European powers had first begun exploring Africa and claiming slices of the continent.[38]

The Berlin Conference of 1884–85 marked a pivotal moment in the history of Africa, setting the groundwork for a catastrophic reshaping of the continent's sociopolitical landscape. European powers, under the guise of the principle of "effective occupation," carved up Africa into territories without regard for indigenous governance structures or cultural boundaries. This allowed them to claim any African territory where they could establish a presence, effectively granting them ownership over the land and its abundant resources. The conference further enabled the imposition of free trade across these territories, allowing European countries to inundate African markets with their manufactured goods, undermining local industries and economies.

The extraction of African resources by European colonizers, under conditions that heavily favored the colonizers, had profound and lasting impacts on the continent. For instance, the exploitation of gold and diamond mines in South Africa, initiated in the late nineteenth century, and the extraction of ivory and rubber in the Congo Free State, particularly during King Leopold II's reign (1885–1908), are stark examples of how European entities drained African wealth.[39] These activities not only stripped Africa of its physical resources but also imposed severe social and economic hardships on its peoples.

Prior to colonization, Africa was a continent with a rich tapestry of political systems, ranging from centralized kingdoms and empires, such as the Ashanti Empire and the Kingdom of Kôngo, to decentralized societies with complicated and foreign systems of governance. These Indigenous political structures were largely dismantled or undermined by colonial rule and replaced with direct or indirect colonial governance models that prioritized resource extraction and exploitation over the welfare of the African people. The long-term impacts of these actions have been profound. The arbitrary borders drawn by colonizers often forced disparate ethnic groups into single nation-states, sowing the seeds for future ethnic conflicts. Additionally, the colonial emphasis on extractive economies at the expense of diversified development has left many African countries vulnerable to fluctuations in commodity prices and dependent on the export of a narrow range of resources.[40]

Imperial Clocks, Colonial Maps: Time and Territory After 1884

The Berlin Conference and the IMC serve as historical parallels, emblematic of the pervasive spread of a temporal and spatial imperialism that underpins the colonial narrative. This dual imposition, one partitioning land and the other segmenting time, has entrenched Western dominance in a manner transcending mere geography or the mechanics of clock-setting, weaving a narrative of control that resonates with the echoes of contemporary disparities.

The Berlin Conference, the notorious symposium of colonial powers, dissected the African continent with geometric precision, oblivious to the ancient rhythms and bonds that tethered its peoples. This surgical partitioning underpinned by a drive to "civilize" and exploit, was a dramatic spatial assertion of hegemony, mapping the world in lines and borders that resonated with the conquerors' creed but were estranged from the reality of the conquered. In parallel, the IMC sought to tame time's fluidity, anchoring it to the Greenwich meridian. This act of temporal imperialism, though cloaked in the guise of navigational necessity and global synchronization, was no less domineering than its spatial counterpart. By imposing a universal standard of time, it did not merely recommend a method for clock-setting; it insinuated a singular, linear perception of time into cultures where time was traditionally understood to be cyclical, seasonal, communal, and event-based. These twin forces of temporal and spatial imperialism were not merely about controlling land or standardizing time. They embedded a capitalist ethos and Eurocentric supremacy into the very fabric of global existence, sidelining Indigenous participation or consent. As historian Vanessa Ogle asserts, "colonized populations are near absent from the correspondence on time changes gathered together in the archives of former colonial power. Attempts to discipline colonized subjects with the help of elaborate timekeeping and time distribution schemes did not leave traces in the circulars mailed back and forth across the Mediterranean, the Indian Ocean, and the Atlantic..."[41] This erasure highlights the insidious nature of such impositions, where the very narratives of those most affected are often obscured or overlooked.

The ramifications of this temporal imperialism are manifold and profound. Cultures that once celebrated time through cycles of renewal and decay now find themselves adrift in the relentless current of clock time, where every minute is accounted for, and every hour must show productivity. This shift has not only alienated individuals from their cultural heritage but also from the natural world, leading to an existential dissonance, in which time is felt as an adversary rather than an ally.

Daylight Saving Time can be seen as a modern continuation of this temporal imperialism. Initially proposed to conserve energy and maximize daylight hours for productivity, DST disrupts human circadian rhythms and imposes an artificial alteration of time that bears little relation to the natural world's cadence. Like the imposition of GMT, DST exemplifies the prioritization of economic efficiency over biological and cultural harmonies, further entrenching the colonial legacy of time manipulation.

The struggle against temporal and spatial imperialism is far from a historical footnote. It remains a present reality, challenging us to reconsider how we measure, value, and live our time in a world still dictated by a colonial past that sought to homogenize the rich mosaic of human existence into a single, linear narrative. Reclaiming the multiplicity of time, then, is not just an act of cultural restoration but a radical assertion of autonomy against the remnants of imperial control that continue to shape our lives. Through such critical engagement, we confront the enduring legacy of colonialism, striving to liberate our conceptions of time and space from the confines of past empires.

Daylight Saving Time

> *Standard time zone boundaries are invisible in the landscape, yet they abruptly delineate a temporal difference of one hour between two large areas located relative to one another on Earth. In most cases, standard time zone boundaries follow political ones and define areas within which daylight saving time (DST)—the seasonal advancement of standard time by one hour—is observed. Moving time zone boundaries and the decision to observe daylight saving time occurs throughout the world for various reasons that result in the synchronization of socioeconomic and political activities within and between communities and the simultaneous separation from others.* —**Rob Kuper, "Joining the Great Plains in Space, Place, and Time"**

> *Most owners of clocks and watches do not know the longitude to which the time of their time zone is calibrated, or the politics about time zone definitions. Instead, they simply note when they cross time zones, and adjust their clocks and watches accordingly.* —**Kevin Birth, *Objects of Time***

Consider a farmer in a remote village, whose day begins with the rooster's crow and ends with the setting sun, now forced to adjust to a factory whistle that adheres to a time zone reflective of a distant metropolis. Or a family whose communal meals, once the cornerstone of their day, are fragmented by shift work hours that pay no heed to local customs or the body's natural hunger cues. Temporal globalization artificially synchronized all local clocks to those of London, or New York, or Tokyo, sidelining personal, familial, and communal rhythms that have sustained societies for generations and disrupting the natural cycles of individuals' lives.[42] This disregard for local timekeeping traditions erodes the fabric of communities, compelling people to live by an imposed schedule that often clashes with their natural sleep cycles, cultural practices, and social bonds. The result is a world where the innate cycles of human life are increasingly at odds with the relentless tick of the global clock.

Geography Professors Benediktsson and Brunn, invoking Reinhart Koselleck's insights, demonstrate how the concept of time zones alters our natural understanding of time. Instead of following the natural day and night cycle, time zones organize time into a system that doesn't always match up with the sunlight visible to us. These zones are supposed to cover areas of the Earth fifteen degrees apart in longitude, but they often follow political borders instead of strict geographic lines. This means some places use a time zone that doesn't fit their actual location on the globe, creating discrepancies that are more political than practical. For example, before 1949, China's size resulted in five different time zones to span the country, but after the Chinese Revolution, the whole country was set to Beijing time. While this decision made political sense, in some places the official time was vastly out of sync with the solar day. As a result of this time zone consolidation, people in Xinjiang, in the west, would start their workday in the middle of the night. To deal with this, the local government then shifted work hours to start later, creating a kind of local time that is again different from the official Beijing time.[43]

This manipulation of time zones for political reasons, as seen in China and elsewhere, often aims to project a semblance of unity or control. In Europe, for example, many countries set their clocks ahead of the geographically "correct" time zone, effectively placing them "ahead of their time." Similarly, Russia's reduction of its time zones from eleven to nine in 2010 further illustrates how time zones are influenced by political and other social factors, rather than a product of strict geographical reality.[44]

The misalignment of time zones with natural longitudinal positions vividly illustrates the intersection of spatial and temporal oppression. Communities perched on the edge of a time zone boundary experience a daily reality at odds with the natural world, coerced into living by a clock that misaligns with the daylight they observe. For those communities and groups whose timekeeping practices are fundamentally intertwined with the cosmos and seasonal cycles, they—find their temporal realities and, by extension, their spatial existences, disrupted by an imposed system. This forced realignment not only erases Indigenous temporalities but also reconfigures their spatial orientations, highlighting the dual facets of oppression. They are forced to conform to a foreign temporal order and spatial hierarchy that disregards these ancestral markers in favor of politically expedient borders.

This mode of temporal oppression and colonialism is used to maintain and reinforce social hierarchies and inequalities, a tactic that includes the manipulation of historical narratives, the erasure of certain groups from history, and control through a narrative of social progress. The intertwining of temporal and spatial oppression is further exemplified in the lived experiences of marginalized communities within modern urban contexts, and is often linked to other forms of oppression, such as racism, classism, and gender-based oppression, as temporal and spatial oppression can exacerbate and perpetuate existing inequalities. The National Equity Atlas, for instance, shows that Black workers who commute by public transportation have the longest commute time out of all ethnic and racial groups. Long commutes, with long waits at bus stops or train stations, makes it challenging for people to get to work on time or take care of their families, sometimes leading to missed workdays, and in turn to decreased wages and increased financial hardship.[45]

Meanwhile, the National Low Income Housing Coalition shows how, in comparison to white households, on average Black and Latinx households work more hours to be able to afford rent and other household expenses.[46] This disparity in time equity—a reflection of broader systemic inequalities—exemplifies how temporal and spatial oppressions are interwoven, with time acting as a silent yet formidable axis of discrimination.

The Standard Time Act: A Nexus of Time Zones and Daylight Saving Time

> *How are the frameworks we've imposed on the natural world in dialogue with natural timelines and frameworks? Miraculous and Horrific things are happening to us, and we can't explain or make sense of them in a linear timeframe . . . the unknown is also its own character.* —**Camae Ayewa, Prime Meridian Unconference workshop, 2022**

Benjamin Franklin is often cited as inventing DST, but this is not entirely accurate. While he did author an essay in 1784 called "An Economical Project for Diminishing the Cost of Light," in which he proposed adjusting people's schedules to better align with daylight hours and so save money on candles, his idea was not implemented, and did not specifically involve changing the clocks. The modern concept of DST—advancing the clocks in the spring and reversing the change in the fall—was first proposed by New Zealand entomologist George Vernon Hudson in 1895. It was later independently proposed and implemented by British builder William Willett in 1907, who campaigned for the idea until it was adopted in the United Kingdom during World War I to conserve coal.

In the United States, the Interstate Commerce Commission had established a system of standardized time zones for all railroads operating in the United States in 1911. However, it was not until the outbreak of World War I that Congress passed the federal US Standard Time Act in March of 1918. It went into effect on March 19, 1918, standardizing the system of five standard time zones—Eastern, Central, Mountain, Pacific, and Alaska—that had initially been established through the railroads in 1883 and subsequent state legislation. They reasoned that the war effort required coordination across multiple time zones, and the military needed a consistent system of timekeeping to coordinate their operations, transportation and communication. The Standard Time Act also enshrined Greenwich as the prime meridian. The US Standard Time Act also established Daylight Saving Time, which allowed for more daylight during the summer months. As in the United Kingdom, DST was linked to War Time, with the aim of conserving resources and energy to support the war effort by reducing the need for artificial lighting. Propaganda posters encouraged people to "Save Daylight and You Save Coal." The message was clear: by using less energy, individuals could support the troops abroad.

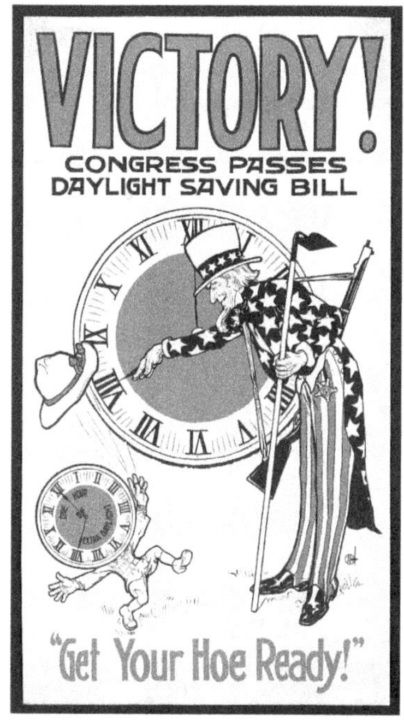

A WWI-era poster sponsored by the United Cigar Stores Company depicts Uncle Sam with a rifle and hoe celebrating the Daylight Saving Bill, 1918.

But in 1919, after the end of World War I, DST was repealed due to public opposition. The act had created time inequities particularly for rural communities: farmers who set their schedule by the sun were forced to adjust to a new sense of time that may not have aligned with the needs of their work or their animals. However, the policy was reinstated during World War II, with new posters declaring, "War Time is Any Time that Saves Time!" An article printed on January 1, 1947, in the *Journal of Geography* called "Slaves of the Time Belts" referred to DST as "War Saving Time"—a time when "to disobey the clock was unthinkable."[47]

Congress passed the Uniform Time Act in 1966, establishing a system of Daylight Saving Time across the country.[48] Today, DST is implemented in the spring or summer months in most parts of the world. In the United States, it typically begins on the last Sunday in March or the first Sunday in April and ends on the last Sunday in October. During DST, the clock time is moved ahead by one hour, so that the sun will set an hour later in the evenings and rise an hour later in the mornings.

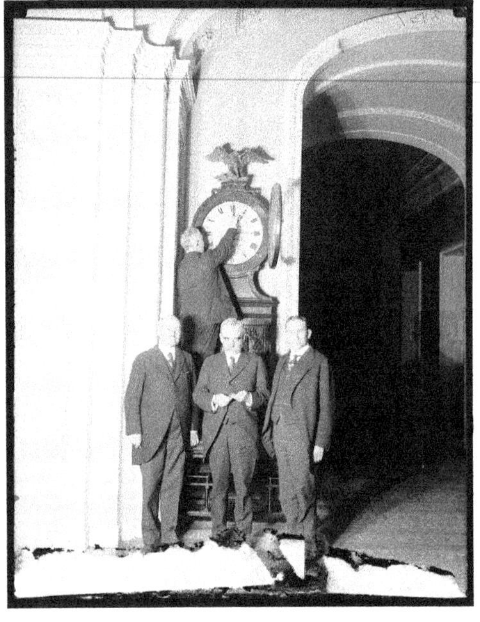

On March 31, 1918, the Senate sergeant at arms turns forward the famous Ohio Clock (also known as the Senate Clock) at the Capitol Building for the first Daylight Saving Time, while three senators look on.

The continuation of DST into the postwar period was influenced by several factors. There was no significant movement immediately post-WWII to get rid of DST, largely because it had become normalized through various societal institutions. The benefits perceived during wartime, such as energy conservation and increased productivity, continued to be touted. Moreover, industries like retail and sports, which benefited from extended daylight hours, also advocated for the maintenance of DST. The later Uniform Time Act of 1966 significantly altered the DST landscape by standardizing the practice across the country, making permanent what had been more of a temporary wartime measure.

Despite these institutional efforts to standardize and normalize DST, the practice has continued to face criticism, particularly concerning its impact on public health and safety. DST is known to affect some people and communities negatively, disrupting the body's circadian rhythms or natural sleep patterns. Difficulty falling asleep, feeling tired during the day, impaired concentration, decreased productivity, and a range of physical and mental health issues, including weight gain, and an increased risk of heart attack and stroke have all been linked to the physical disruption of DST.[49] Some studies have suggested that DST has more significant impacts on public health than previously thought, for example, an increase in car accidents following its implementation. The sudden shift to shorter days and less natural light may lead to an increase in symptoms of depression and the triggers of seasonal affective disorder (SAD). Many of these health problems disproportionately affect Black communities.[50]

Research overwhelmingly shows that Black Americans, on average, get less sleep than whites.[51] According to one study, Black Americans report shorter sleep duration and lower sleep quality than whites—though some studies show Black women as suffering the highest disparities of sleep while others show Black men as the most sleep-deprived.[52] This imbalance in sleep time and quality is due to a variety of factors, including the impacts of discrimination, stress, and socioeconomic status, such as being low-income and having low education.[53] When it comes to DST, there is even evidence that Black Americans may be more adversely affected by it than whites, including evidence that Black Americans experience a greater risk of stroke during the transition to DST in the spring and the several days following, compared to whites.[54]

Furthermore, the negative impacts of DST on sleep can especially affect nightshift and low-income workers, of which both populations are more likely to be Black. Shift workers often have fraught and irregular sleep schedules, and the time change can disrupt their sleep patterns further, or they may be required to work longer hours. In addition, the early morning darkness caused can make it more difficult for people who rely on public transportation to get to work, particularly those who live in areas with fewer transportation options or who have longer commutes. This compounds baseline stress and fatigue levels, further exacerbating the sleep disparities faced by Black Americans.

In "Slaves of the Time Belt," C. G. Stratton questions whether time zones ("time belts") are necessary, speculating that "freed from enslavement to the clock, each community could more effectively utilize the hours of daylight."[55] The Uniform Time Act of 1966 that required states to adopt daylight saving time allows for an "opt-out" process that requires legislation and approval from US Congress. Hawaii is one of the few states that do not observe DST, consistently operating on Hawaii Standard Time (HST) all year round. The decision to opt out of the Uniform Time Act stemmed from Hawaii's equatorial proximity, which results in minor variations in daylight hours across seasons. Consequently, the adoption of DST was seen as superfluous and potentially disruptive for island residents. Hawaii did adopt DST during World War II as a measure to synchronize its timekeeping with mainland United States, enhancing wartime communication and coordination efforts, however, this practice was discontinued after the war, on September 30, 1945, marking the last observance of DST in the state.[56] In addition, Arizona, the eastern portion of Indiana, the US Virgin Islands, Guam, Puerto Rico, and American Samoa have all opted out of DST.[57]

A number of states have considered legislation to either end or make DST permanent, but so far none have been successful. In 2019, the state of Florida passed a law to "lock the clock" and make DST permanent, but the change was not implemented as it did not receive congressional approval. US Senator Marco Rubio introduced the Sunshine Act in 2021, which got voted positively out of the Senate, however, the law never came up for a vote in the House of Representatives. In 2021, the state of California passed a similar law, which still requires approval of Congress.

A study by Pew Research called "Most countries don't observe daylight saving time" notes that only about a third of the world's countries observe some form of DST.[58] Most of the countries that do observe DST are based in Europe, and only a handful of geopolitically European countries (Armenia, Azerbaijan, Belarus, Georgia, Iceland, Russia, and Turkey) do not. With the exception of Egypt, no other African countries observe DST, maintaining instead a consistent official time throughout the year. Efforts to abolish DST have continued to grow worldwide. Clashes of time zones and DST yield geographical and environmental consequences. Currently, the Mountain Standard Time and Central Standard Time zone boundary estrange communities otherwise closely related in terms of climate and land use. Landscape architect and professor Rob Kuper, who has proposed moving the Mountain Standard Time Zone to match the climatic boundary of the Great Plains, highlights two effects of the two different time zones on the people living within them: (1) communities on either side of the time zone boundary may be united by time but disconnected by environmental characteristics, and (2) that the observation or elimination of DST in one state depends on its neighboring states.[59] Kuper suggests that aligning the boundary with isohyets (lines connecting areas with equal rainfall) or the use of aquifers so that the two communities share the same time year round. Reassessing these time zone boundaries, Kuper argues, could lead to better local alignment across numerous factors, such as socioeconomic, ecological, and geological. The main benefits of such a change would allow some states within the geographic boundary, such as Nebraska, to opt out of DST, which residents and politicians of Nebraska have recognized as having detrimental effects (on the other hand, Kuper notes that residents in Kansas appreciate the extra hour of sunlight).

In the modern era, Daylight Saving Time, our biannual state-sanctioned artificial time-manipulation holiday, begins and then later ends again often with little attention, question, or challenge now as our phones and timekeeping devices are programmed to shift automatically. But our bodies keep the time, as the effects of DST exceed the ticking and switching of clocks, impacting our circadian rhythms. These internal timekeepers, synchronized with the natural light-dark cycle, play a crucial role in regulating our sleep, metabolism, hormone release, and even our mood and alertness levels. When DST disrupts these rhythms, it can lead to sleep disturbances, reduced productivity, and an increase in health-related issues. The alteration of time, albeit artificial, underscores the importance of circadian rhythms in maintaining the seamless operation of our internal systems.

Still DST maintains its rule—as a tool of war, of state violence, capitalist labor production, guilt-inducing propaganda, and (white) Western linear time programming. It is essential therefore that we disentangle our temporalities from the nation-state and global war machine's time. In contemporary times, DST's continued enforcement is justified for energy conservation, extended daylight for leisure, and economic benefits. However, these justifications often overlook individual and community well-being, as explained above.[60]

A shift toward local/community timekeeping proposes a reconnection with natural rhythms and a rejection of the one-size-fits-all approach. This enables communities to align their activities with the natural cycle of light and dark, and to foster greater attunement with the environment to potentially mitigate the adverse health effects associated with DST. Embracing local timekeeping allows for the creation of temporal frameworks that respect individual and community health, cultural practices, and ecological awareness. Local timekeeping can also align more closely with cultural practices and community events as communities adjust their schedules to accommodate seasonal festivals, agricultural cycles, or religious observances. As has been highlighted by studies on community-based timekeeping in Indigenous cultures, local timekeeping fosters a greater sense of identity, belonging, and cultural preservation. It offers a way to reclaim autonomy over time and to enable communities to define their rhythms and priorities. This shift can in turn lead to more sustainable lifestyles, improved mental and physical health, and a stronger sense of community cohesion.

From an environmental perspective, tailoring time to natural light patterns can lead to reduced reliance on artificial lighting and potential energy savings. This encourages heightened environmental awareness and sustainable living practices, as suggested by research on the environmental effects of DST.[61] In terms of economic activities, local timekeeping allows for adjustments that can support specific industry needs, such as those in agriculture or fishing, where activities are closely tied to natural cycles. Businesses could also adapt their hours to match peak daylight times, potentially leading to energy savings and a better work-life balance for employees. The economic implications of such adaptations have been discussed in studies examining DST and business operations.[62]

The educational sector could also benefit from this shift. Schools could start later in alignment with students' biological needs, potentially leading to improved academic performance and better mental health, as shown in research on school start times and adolescent health.[63] Local timekeeping also promotes resilience and autonomy, allowing communities to make decisions that best suit their specific needs and circumstances. This self-determination can be particularly beneficial in times of crisis or change, as communities can adapt quickly and effectively, a point emphasized in disaster management studies.[64]

Aligning work hours with natural light and energy levels could lead to a more efficient and productive workforce. Employees working in sync with their biological clocks may experience less fatigue and higher job satisfaction, as indicated by research on workplace productivity and circadian rhythms.[65]

While the transition to local timekeeping presents challenges in ensuring coherence within regional, national, and global frameworks, the potential benefits in health, cultural richness, environmental sustainability, and community empowerment make it an intriguing proposition. The implementation of such a system would require careful planning and coordination, but evidence suggests that the outcomes could be positive for communities and individuals alike.

In 2022, during the *Time Zone Protocols* project, after studying the various propaganda posters used to push DST, I worked with social justice graphic design firm Partner and Partners to create as a form of visual activism and counter-propaganda with a series of posters that included slogans such as “Restore Black Space-Times,” “Restore Black Temporal Realities,” and “We Demand Temporal Reparations Yesterday, Now, and Tomorrow,” based on a set of collages and paintings that BQF had created. I also developed a “DST Tracker and

Chrono-Assessment" tool to assess the impact of DST on the body and mind that includes prompts to foster interventions and intentional practices that can mitigate the harmful effects of DST. The assessment poses critical questions, each crafted to spark deep reflection and proactive responses:

- Investigate the narrative of "saving daylight" inherent in DST. How does this narrative align with or challenge the diverse temporalities, historical narratives, and future visions within Black communities?

- Knowing some of the negative effects associated with DST, what can you do to mitigate the impacts on self, family, or community?

- As DST ends, its temporal adjustment ostensibly aligns with "standard time." How do you interpret the notion of "standard time" and how does this standardization resonate with or disrupt Black temporalities?

- Engage with the notion of "time reclaiming" in the face of DST. What strategies might you or your community employ to reclaim or redefine time as DST ends, especially in a way that resonates with Black temporalities?

Adopting local or community-based timekeeping methods, in contrast to the standardized approach of Daylight Saving Time, offers a range of practical benefits that could significantly reshape daily life. One of the most immediate advantages is the alignment with natural circadian rhythms. Unlike DST, which has been shown to disrupt sleep patterns and lead to various health issues, a localized approach to timekeeping allows communities to sync their activities with the natural light-dark cycle, potentially leading to improved sleep quality, reduced stress levels, and overall better physical and mental health outcomes.[66]

Time Zone Protocols

Disrupting the Prime Meridian's Temporal Order

> *My father and ancestors were agricultural people—had the current almanac in the house. So much of our resources are invested in banks, records, written words and tracking of property that we're divorced from. Would love to see observation of time through the human body- some kind of mapping that honors everybody's time as different. Personal mapping that interacts with other people's maps. Perhaps meditation or song- sensitivities that we haven't ventured into that we can hone and cultivate.* —**Xenobia Bailey, "Protocol 15,"** ***Evolving Time Zone Protocols***

> *Renewed temporalities: We can work with Time and silence to reorganize our worlds in a way oaring renewed temporalities conceptually, materially, metaphorically, spatially to destabilize normative time.* —**The BlkRobot Project, "Protocol 16,"** ***Evolving Time Zone Protocols***

The timeline extending from the so-called end of chattel slavery to the contemporary era serves as a damning indictment of a Western society systematically designed to marginalize Black people's autonomy. This is not a neutral record of events but a weapon wielded against Black lives to curtail our lifespans, exploit our labor, limit our opportunities, and ultimately deny us a future of our own making. Much like a clock meticulously calibrated to run against us, this Western, colonial-capitalist chronology imposes its will with every second, minute, and year that passes, challenging our very right to exist.

Dismantling the monolithic European timeline cannot be accomplished by a single, solitary voice or action, nor even a small group of individuals. This mission to forge vibrant, equitable, and nurturing temporalities, which honor the health, culture, life, and time of both individuals and larger communities, demands the concerted efforts of diverse communities, each contributing their unique temporal and cultural perspectives. It calls for a broad coalition, spanning various times, spaces, and narratives, to set forth new global standards for our temporal experiences. But whereas the prime meridian served to centralize time around a Eurocentric axis, our effort—what I call *Time Zone Protocols*—presents a radical reimagining of time through a Black SpaceTimeMatters framework and using Colored People's Time as an ontological framework. Through this reconceptualization, we engage directly in the re-creation of time, positioning each of us as essential contributors to the universe's expanding narrative.

In 2022, the Vera List Center for Art and Politics presented the *Time Zone Protocols* exhibition and the three-day hybrid Prime Meridian Unconference curated by me as part of my "As for Protocols" Fellowship. This congregation of Black artists, architects, musicians, and scholars across various disciplines—from physics to geography to technology to African American studies—functioned as a Black SpaceTimeMatters laboratory.[67] Black SpaceTimeMatters proposes a vision of time as abundant and equitably accessible, advocating for the creation and nurturing of Black temporal and spatial realms. This paradigm shift not only contests the dominant discourse of limited time but also carves out space for inclusive and expansive visions of the future, grounded in the lived experiences and aspirations of marginalized communities.

TZP is a clarion call for active participation in redefining time itself, inviting us to join in crafting a future where every moment is acknowledged for its unique contribution to the collective human experience. It is a journey toward a future where time is not a uniform, one-dimensional arrow, but a vibrant constellation of moments, each with its own significance. Through this audacious reimagining, we become architects of time, each contributing to the creation of a universe where every second tells a story of diversity, resilience, and unity.

The result of the gathering was an interdisciplinary space-time where participants co-created new methodologies to "unmap" Black temporalities from the hegemonic Greenwich Mean Timeline, an endeavor we saw as symbolically inverting the objectives of the 1884 International Meridian Conference. Unlike the 1884 conference, which sought to impose a monolithic time standard, the Prime Meridian Unconference instead aimed at further pluralizing and dismantling our hegemonic conceptions of time and space. At the PMU, participants didn't just discuss alternate theories; they actively created them, collectively developing protocols, resolutions, alternative time zones, and new markers of time which were then compiled and shared, available for people to put to use in their communities. The PMU suggests that we can effect change now, in our current environment, by rethinking and redefining our relationship with time and space. This approach allowed individuals and groups to experiment with and experience different conceptions of time and space in their daily lives, challenging the normative frameworks that often go unquestioned.

Engaging in such work had immediate and tangible benefits. It trained us to think more critically and creatively, to question the status quo, and to envision alternative realities. This fostered a mind set that open to innovative ideas and different perspectives, essential in a world that is increasingly interconnected and elaborate. It also encouraged a further understanding of how our conceptions of time and space influence our relationships with each other, our environment, and the broader societal structures. This work has the potential to reshape community dynamics. By adopting alternative timekeeping methods or recognizing different temporalities, communities can align more closely with their specific cultural, environmental, and social needs. This can lead to more harmonious and sustainable ways of living, as well as a greater sense of belonging and identity.

Recognizing the PMU's temporal constraints as a three-day gathering, and the desire to extend its impact beyond the typical temporal boundaries of a conference, I explored ways to expand this initiative's reach, both before and after the physical gathering. A few weeks ahead of the Unconference, my partner Camae and I convened the TZP Surveyors discussion group—a gathering of twenty-one people for a series of online meetings that together studied an archive of readings, images, sounds, and videos on various temporal topics.[68] These included time zones, Daylight Saving Time, Colored People's Time, and various social, political, and cultural concepts of time and temporality. Our discussions helped us dismantle colonial and linear notions of time that have habitually rendered Black people "out of time," that is, relegated to a narrow temporal present and denied access to the dimension of the future due to reduced lifespans and reduced possibilities. Agendas, notes, and recordings of these discussions can be found at www.timezoneprotocols.space.

The three days of the PMU itself unfolded as an emancipatory timescape in contrast to the 1884 International Meridian Conference. Organized into two tracks—Photon and Wave—the gathering took place within the large room of the *Time Zone Protocols* exhibition, divided into two rooms only by a set of heavy black curtains. This layout was designed to simulate a live, two-slit quantum experiment on a macroscale. To give a brief reminder of what the two-slit experiment is, it demonstrates the dual nature of light and matter, revealing how particles can display characteristics of both waves and particles. When particles such as photons pass through two slits, they create an interference pattern typically associated with waves, not individual particles. This phenomenon underlines the principle of superposition in quantum mechanics, where particles exist in multiple states simultaneously until observed.

Applying this concept on a macroscale at the PMU created an environment where Black temporalities—seen as living, dynamic, active, and co-created—were central. In this setting, our local space-time became the product of a myriad of intra-acting forces, an active entity shaped and nurtured by all participants. It embodied a field where time and space were fluid and interdependent, influenced by the collective presence and actions of the attendees. The PMU was also not anchored to a specific clock time or calendar date beyond the basic information needed for our meeting in common and sharing the same space-time coordinates. Unlike traditional conferences with their rigid schedules and expectations, this Unconference sought to unravel the time-locked standard of such events. Attendees could freely navigate between the Photon and Wave tracks at will, both online and in the physical space, mirroring the quantum concept of superposition, and to discover novel ways of perceiving time and space within a gathering.

Standing at the center of the room, one could simultaneously experience both tracks, akin to a particle existing in a state of superposition, instead of having to collapse into either Photon or Wave tracks for the duration of the workshop. This allowed for a unique form of interaction and perception, where attendees could resonate with the space in a multifaceted way, experiencing time as a flexible, participatory construct. Standing at the center, I experienced the fusion of ideas and energies, witnessing a living example of how different temporalities and spatialities can coexist, blur, and enrich each other. This experience underscored the Unconference's commitment to challenging the conventional, linear perceptions of time and space, opening up a realm of possibilities for more inclusive and dynamic forms of collective engagement and knowledge creation.

Time Zone Protocols

Our collective foray into nonlinear time produced an anthology of alternative guidelines, resolutions, temporal tools, and new time zones—each rooted in Black SpaceTimeMatters principles, ancestral wisdom, and communal ethos—which were disseminated for communal application. This web of ideas, insights, and counternarratives created before, during, and after the exhibition and PMU shaped the draft Time Zone Protocols.[69] The term *protocols*, as I use it, stands as a non-proscriptive initial blueprint—following its etymological origins from *proto kola*, Greek for "first draft" or "first glue." Our protocols serve as preliminary pathways to be revisited, refined, and recalibrated at future collective junctures, promising a continual evolution toward Black time sovereignty and spatial liberation as it is revisited and reworked by other minds, places, historic moments, and future memories.

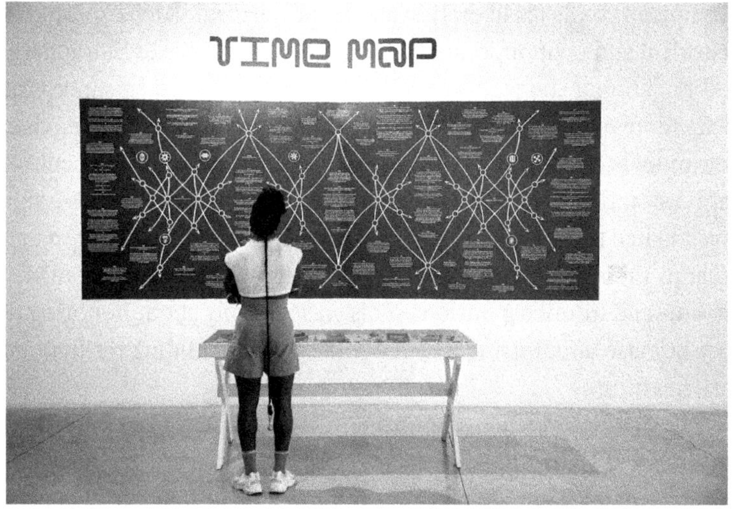

A participant in the Prime Meridian Unconference standing before "TimeMap (Time Has a Complicated History)" by Rasheedah Phillips (2022), part of the solo exhibition *Time Zone Protocols* at the Anna-Maria and Stephen Kellen Gallery, and presented by the Vera List Center for Art and Politics (NYC).

Charting Alternate Temporal Zones for Liberation

The wealth of knowledge and alternative paradigms for time and space that were presented at the Unconference can be likened to a quantum entanglement—each idea, narrative, and counternarrative intertwined and mutually influencing the others. The whole was a collective, subversive reimagining of dominant temporalities, boldly stepping away from the colonial heritage of the Greenwich prime meridian. The gathering promoted Black time sovereignty and spatial liberation These protocols served as blueprints for communities to reclaim and redefine their relationship with time and space, challenging and reshaping the dominant narratives that have historically marginalized Black temporalities and spatialities.

Key workshops at the Unconference were pivotal in this transformative discourse. These sessions provided practical insights into how Black communities can leverage their unique spatial and temporal dynamics as tools for liberation and empowerment. Each explored the historical and contemporary landscapes of Black spaces, illuminating and reclaiming the ways in which these have served as sanctuaries of freedom and resistance. Participants were encouraged to envision new models of community engagement, urban planning, and cultural expression that center Black experiences and perspectives. Sessions investigated the ways in which Black communities can reinterpret and reclaim their past, weaving these narratives into the fabric of their present and future aspirations. This was not only about honoring the past but also about using it as a foundation for building resilient and thriving futures.

The Unconference's commitment to promoting Black time sovereignty and spatial liberation extended beyond academic discourse, inspiring participants to envision and implement tangible changes in their communities. The protocols and ideas generated at the Unconference hold the potential to influence policy, urban development, and community organizing, paving the way for a future where Black time sovereignty and spatial liberation are not just concepts but lived realities. The following is an overview of a few workshops from the Unconference, offering a glimpse into this transformative shared space-time.[70]

Celeste Winston, Assistant Professor of Geography and Urban Studies, presented a workshop called "Black Fugitive Infrastructures and Cross-Time Space Routines." By way of introduction, she thanked people for coming over to her side of the room and explained: "What we're going to be doing today is working through a concept called Fugitive Infrastructure, [and] thinking about the possibilities that it illuminates for shaping black freedom struggles across time. That's where this cross-time space routine term comes in. It's a term that I'm using today to think about how the bodily movements of black people in one particular space happen again and again over time and consolidate into an infrastructure for freedom."[71] Winston's discourse, drawing inspiration from abolitionist geographer Ruth Wilson Gilmore's definition of freedom as a place, pivots around the concept of placemaking as a collective endeavor. Gilmore envisions placemaking as a collaborative process where people unite, bringing together land, resources, and social capacity to manifest freedom. Winston expands on this idea, positing that freedom is not merely an abstract political goal but a tangible reality within our world, observable in both grand and modest spaces where freedom is evident. She asked: "What does it mean to create a space of Black freedom? How can contemporary liberation movements build on the legacy of past, yet incomplete, dreams of freedom?" By examining the geographic practices and knowledge of Black people throughout history, Winston sought to identify and expand those existing places of freedom.

Winston introduced the concept of "fugitive infrastructure," to describe a flexible yet stable architecture that emerges from the necessity to endure hostile environments. She encouraged participants to reflect on current manifestations of anti-Black violence, such as environmental racism, policing, and incarceration. Participants were asked to keep these oppressive structures in mind while envisioning existing places of freedom that demonstrate effective organization of land, people, and resources to counter these oppressive forces. This broke down the concept of "fugitive infrastructure," as an enduring and adaptable system rooted in histories of Black resistance and survival.

Winston connected maroonage, or the act of escaping slavery and creating free communities, with the concept of "Maroon Geography." This extends the timeline of maroonage beyond the end of slavery, seeing it not just as a historical phenomenon but as a continuing practice of Black flight and freedom. She linked historical slave patrols to modern policing practices, exploring how Black communities historically and presently create infrastructures of resistance with examples ranging from escaping police to school truancy. She approaches maroonage as an active stance, not just a response to colonial occupation. Fugitive infrastructures are an antithesis to the rigidity of mainstream temporal and spatial constructs. Winston illuminated how choosing to remain, even temporarily, in spaces abandoned or deemed worthless by dominant white spatial narratives—like marshy, mountainous, or swampy lands—becomes an act of claiming and creating freedom.

Through case studies of resistance movements, Winston presented a protocol that identified the ability of Black flight to establish enduring infrastructures, challenging and altering dominant power dynamics. These examples illustrated how communities can build life sustaining systems amid overwhelming challenges and threats. Participants examined the concept of "holding place," where Black people create geographic refuges and areas of sanctuary. Examples such as block parties and the blasting of go-go music on Georgia Ave in Washington, DC (a site of extreme gentrification and Black displacement since at least 1999) were discussed in the workshop as markers of place and cultural resistance, of maroonage in practice, as were care networks, cooperatives, and other worldbuilding initiatives.[72] The workshop provided a protocol for locating and identifying sites of fugitive infrastructure across time. It encouraged participants to engage with a series of prompts, including identifying present-day anti-Black or violent systems, understanding their historical connections to slavery, colonialism, or imperialism, and critically examining popular calls for reform or abolition and identifying who each originate from.

In exploring similar modes of time related to maroonage, midwife, poet, and mystic Joy Tabernacle-KMT, in a workshop called "Grief Reparations and Temporal Hush Harbors," used the framework of reparations to propose Grief Reparations as an extension of their own praxis of developing "maroon futurisms, liberation, spiritual fugitivity, and very Black space-time."[73] This workshop focused on how dominant white social pathology steals time from and shortens the lifespan of

Black beings and, most blatantly, alienates Black grief time. She defines "Grief Reparations" as giving space, time, resources, and funding for Black people to collectively and somatically process traumatic experiences and death, both natural and unnatural, historical and recent, irrespective of the time elapsed since these events.

During the workshop, Joy Tabernacle-KMT dissected various temporal concepts. "Plantation time" was described as "linear force time" focused on production, characterizing it as inherently antagonistic to Black individuals due to its surveilled and policed nature, and as "a means to a literal end." Common phrases that invoke and reinforce plantation time norms, perpetuate anti-Black sentiments and a distorted historical view include: "Why are you so mad, so upset, so angry?" "That was so long ago." "What do you have to be so upset about?"[74] Another audience member chimed in that it includes "the notion of being on time. As opposed to being in time, being a shaper of time."

In contrast to normative time, "natural time" was defined as being in harmony with oneself, the community, and the natural world, fostering a relationship with the environment and its rhythms. "Ceremonial time," according to Tabernacle-KMT, represents a temporal space that transcends mundane time, linking ancestral, future, and eternal dimensions. Colored People's Time, closely aligned with natural time, is nonetheless constrained, and shaped by plantation time.

Joy Tabernacle-KMT articulated the construction of plantation time as time theft through domestic terrorism, chronic displacement, and pervasive white pathological terrorism, including the undermining of essential cyclical rights such as grieving. This means that "the time that is stolen from black people, from our lifespan actually extends the lifespan of white people because their safety, their comfort, their ability to move unfettered is based upon the policing of blackness."[75] Examples included the disproportionate burden placed on Black children in dealing with life-threatening encounters with police, the reduced life expectancy in Black communities due to medical racism, and heightened stress responses caused by systemic anti-Blackness. Referencing Nicole Van Groningen's article "Racial injustice causes Black Americans to age faster than Whites," Tabernacle-KMT highlighted the weathering hypothesis, which suggests that the persistent stress of racial discrimination prematurely ages Black people.[76] Hailing from Pittsburgh, she highlighted the stark disparities in life expectancy in that city, which studies have shown is notably lower in Black neighborhoods.[77]KMT advocated for Grief Reparations to address these injustices, envisioning a holistic practice whereby Black communities would gain access to critical resources that would allow us to engage in various forms of healing and remembrance practices. This could include ceremonies, rituals, rest, and holistic care, all integral to Black cultural and spiritual practices. Grief Reparations would also entitle Black people to space, time, resources, and funding to enable collective and somatic processing of traumatic experiences and death, offering a means to honor these experiences irrespective of the time elapsed since their occurrence. The reparations, therefore, are not limited to addressing recent traumas, they also recognize the need to heal from historical wounds, acknowledging that the impact of such events can transcend generations.

To actualize Grief Reparations, Joy Tabernacle-KMT emphasized the role of white individuals as accomplices in realizing Grief Reparations by donating wages, labor, or financial resources to Black healing events, funeral funds, and historical preservation efforts. Other specific actions for white allies include contributing wages or retirement savings, donating vacation time or covering shifts for those experiencing Black grief, contributing land and resources for Black ceremonial activities, and supporting Black grief projects without imposing a white gaze. Tabernacle-KMT emphasized the need for white participation in supporting Black funeral funds and historical conservation efforts, including the caretaking of Black cemeteries. She emphasized that white individuals should not be managing plantation grounds and proposed the creation of Black-centered rest spaces in various environments, including nature reserves and urban settings. Holistic, grief, and mental health care were also highlighted as critical areas where support is needed. This could involve funding therapists, counselors, and healers who are culturally competent and sensitive to the needs of Black individuals and communities. Supporting existing Black businesses and staying out of Black neighborhoods unless explicitly invited were also recommended as ways to respect the autonomy and space of Black communities. Moreover, Joy Tabernacle-KMT suggested that white people could donate land and resources to facilitate spaces where Black people can engage in ceremonies, rituals, rest, and healing. This could also include contributing to the establishment and maintenance of spaces like urban sanctuaries, and community centers that are dedicated to Black healing and cultural practices.

The concept of Grief Reparations found a synergistic connection with landscape architect and urban planner Ujijji Davis Williams workshop "Occupying Vacancy: Looking at Detroit's Grassroot Activation of Vacant Land and Structures," which tackled the subject of Detroit's urban landscape, a city often typecast as decayed and abandoned. Williams elegantly contested this stereotype, spotlighting Detroit's renaissance of social and cultural spaces, born from the grassroots initiatives of residents combating years of disinvestment. Detroit residents are reclaiming their neighborhoods, resurrecting vacant land and structures to create green spaces that serve as cultural, historical, and social hubs. Detroit's self-regeneration and the role of "Black spaces" in that resurgence, Williams argues, are physical embodiments of the community's historical lineage, current realities, and future aspirations.

In the context of the PMU's focus on time, Williams shared her unique position at "the precipice of memory and vision, looking back and looking forward at the same time," asking: "How do you do that? You have to look back."[78] Recalling the Ghanaian concept of Sankofa, she emphasized the importance of historical reflection in shaping future aspirations. Williams introduced the concept of eidetic maps, a tool created by landscape architect James Corner, which overlays time-based data on geographical visuals. Williams described how her students applied this method to various sites in Detroit in a class exercise, encouraging them to think about urban landscapes as a confluence of past, present, and future. In the workshop, she showed images from what the students produced in their projects, including one that looked at Lafayette Park, home of Detroit's historic Black Bottom neighborhood, where the image shows there's a big scar that's left both physically and figuratively with the city, as there's this real pull away from the historic fabric to try to fit something that didn't fit there before. The students were looking to the past, looking presently, and then to what's possible. Williams also drew connections to the Black Arts Movement, citing artists Romare Bearden and Faith Ringgold, whose collage mediums uniquely blend historical and contemporary narratives, offering parallels to her approach in landscape architecture. Williams showed images of what it looks like to help communities envision and create Black space, by transforming vacant and abandoned spaces into ones that are active and culturally relevant. "Black spaces" are conceptualized as dynamic environments liberated from racial oppression. These exist on their own temporal and spatial continuum, decoupled from standard metrics of efficiency. This approach to urban planning and community development, inspired by Indigenous and African spatial practices, challenges the grid-like structure of neighborhoods popular in North America. She suggested that the future of Black spaces could offer a departure from the relentless pursuit of efficiency, allowing for a more organic and culturally resonant use of space and time. This rejection of efficiency builds on other aspects of culture, as illustrated by Williams's reference to the slow, deliberate preparation of traditional Jamaican cuisine.

Williams's also touched upon the surveillance and policing of Black bodies in public spaces, where they are critiqued as inefficient or out of place by racialized societal norms. She posited that creating Black spaces is about establishing a relief, a metaphorical exhale from these constraints. This suggests a thematic consistency around liberation and autonomy in spatial use. Williams's reflections on Black space open a realm of possibilities for reimagining urban spaces as sites of cultural affirmation and liberation, unbound by the traditional dictates of efficiency and order. Williams left participants with the profound insight that ultimately, "Black Space is not a definition but a journey and a process. This means a collapsible present-future relationship. Black space happens in its own speed and time and doesn't rely on the normative structure of efficiency."[79]Exploring non-human temporalities, the "Bending SpaceTime with Botanicals" workshop, facilitated by bioregional botanist Asia Dorsey, walked participants through the profound and often misunderstood realm of plant personhood, exploring its transformative effects on human perceptions of relationships, space, and time. At the heart of this exploration was the notion that plants are not merely passive environmental elements but entities with an enigmatic form of personhood, which profoundly influences our own experiences and perceptions. The distinct mobility and temporal influence of plants was explored, via examining their abilities to access and influence multiple timelines based on signals of need.

Looking beyond the physical attributes of plants to probe the intricate synergistic relationships between plants, humans, and our shared environment, the workshop demonstrated that our interactions with the natural world are neither static nor one-dimensional. Lemon balm was highlighted for its ability to soothe anxieties about the future and cultivate a sense of present awareness, emphasizing the profound impact common plants can have on our temporal perception.

Early in the workshop, Dorsey referenced the observer effect in quantum physics, as it relates to plants and humans. She explained that "Time does not and cannot exist without us as observer. It is our physical body that is impacting our perception of time and not only does our physical body impact our perception of time, but our physical body is not alone. Our physical body is in relationship to the physical bodies that are around us, including the physical bodies of plants."[80] This perspective appreciates that our interconnectedness with nature, especially plants, can radically alter our experience of time. As a person with over thirty plants in my home, I can attest to this sense of time alteration by observing a new leaf unfurling from the plant stalk, or in noting the different temporalities related to how often each plant needs to be watered, or by learning how much sun each plant likes.

The workshop integrated social meditative practices with the therapeutic use of plants, particularly highlighting the qualities of lemon balm plant. Dorsey's methodology embraced the deep symbiotic connection between plants and humans, underscoring the idea that this interaction can radically alter our concept of time, shifting it from a linear construct to a relational experience.

Participants in the workshop engaged in social meditation aimed at regulating the autonomic nervous system and the use of an embodiment scale to measure shifts in the perception of reality and the passage of time. A unique aspect of the workshop was the "noticing game," where participants estimated time changes while interacting with each other, without clock-watching. The facilitator captured data while participants focused on their bodily sensations, tensions in the body, and feelings and reactions to their partner in the game, using the prompt, "Being here with you, I notice..."[81] This exercise reinforcing the notion that our understanding of time is inherently linked to our physicality and interconnectedness with nature.

The concept of the "sacred no" was introduced, emphasizing the importance of boundary-setting in enriching both personal and collective experiences. Participants were reminded that choosing not to actively participate doesn't exclude one from the experience; observation itself is a form of engagement. Reflections from the participants also encouraged the obliteration of "colonial time" in shared experiences, highlighting that diverse perceptions of time emerge from relationships. Moreover, the workshop illuminated the idea that increased connection leads to a broader spectrum of temporal experiences, with connection acting as an accelerator of perceived time. The assertion that perceived time equates to actual time, regardless of what the clock reads, fostered a sense of authenticity and presence in relationships.

The "Cloud Time" session, featuring climate scientist Nadir Jeevanjee and architectural designer V. Mitch McEwen, dug into the intriguing concept of experiencing simultaneity through temperature. This discussion explored the idea of "Cloud Time" as an avenue to access a form of planetary temporality. McEwen began the discussion by reminding participants that the planet is mostly water, mostly ocean, and that "when we're talking about climate, we're talking about atmosphere, we're talking about anything planetary, we're really initially talking about water."[82] He situated this in terms of a geography of time, explaining that when you're thinking about the planet in an atmospheric sense, it's tropical ocean space. This is the idea that the temporality of clouds invites us to feel time and to do that in a way that makes temperature and embodiment a part of how time becomes instantaneous and accessible to multiple entities. For me, when we're thinking about instantiating the Black possibility of planetary time—obviously, blackness is already planetary—I think it is important to recognize that the tropical ocean is the space of the planetary, and that temporality through that tropical ocean is always already multiple, in that there is a depth implied in that space.

Central to this concept was the notion that Cloud Time represents a form of multiple temporality that requires active participation and energy engagement and that, unlike mechanical time, is not always accessible. Its dynamic, fluid nature was likened to the flow of water. Understanding and measuring time could be akin to sensing how much has flowed past or through an individual. The discussion raised the idea of "surface time," emphasizing that the surface of the ocean is not merely an access point to deeper layers but rather holds its own distinct, fuzzy state. This suggests that surface time may play a crucial role in reorganizing our perceptions of time. The notion of "instantaneous" events was raised in the context of the deep ocean's delayed response to atmospheric changes. The relativity of what is considered instantaneous was underscored, highlighting the varying time scales on which different environmental elements react and interact.

The session uncovered "fugitive potentials" in our conceptualization of time. This exploration involved reimagining how we measure time, considering unique axes like "temporality of empathy" and collective experiences shaped by weather and temperature. Highlighting these, Mitch presented a two-minute news clip from the initial stages of the Amazon Labor Union's formation. This clip illustrated multiple layers of time:

> AMAZON WORKER: I said, "All right, let's plan the walkout here." Now the media [unintelligible 00:24:55] the car. Telling them "Yes, at noon, March 30th, it's going down." I just kept telling the media that over and over. "Yes, we're playing the walkout." "How many people?" I knew the media wasn't going to come if I would say five people. Of course, I lied.
>
> NEWSCASTER: What did you say?
>
> AMAZON WORKER: 200. I said it's probably 200 people outside. I knew that it wasn't going to be, but I . . . played chess. I checked the weather. I was like, "Oh, it's going to be sixty degrees." I know as an Amazon worker, myself, me, outside eating lunch. I said, "The perception is everything."
>
> NEWSCASTER: What happens on the actual day of the walkout?
>
> WORKER: On the day of the walkout, we got up real early because—I don't even think I slept the night before. I think I

> was like, "Slim Shady, mom's spaghetti," and my stomach was turning. Derek came to get me. It was like we was going across the bridge and in my head I'm like, "Damn we're about to do something. I don't even know what's going to look like. I don't what's going to happen."
>
> All these emotions are going through. We get to the building, and I knew it was real when we saw a helicopter hovering and we saw a row of media vans. I'm like, "Oh, shit. Look what we did?" That's what I said out there like, "Look what we did." That gave me a little bit of confidence. It was funny because when we first started at, it might have been 12:00, 12:30. It takes five minutes to get to the time clock. Media was looking around like nobody's coming out and I had seen it on their faces. I said, "Give me about five minutes."[83]

This clip shifted the discussion of theoretical cloud time to a practical application in a Black context. Mitch led the audience through an analysis of how temporal staging—choosing the right day and time for media impact—is critical. The organizer manipulated both the event's timing and its perceived scale, understanding the media's need for a substantial story. The anticipated warm weather was another strategic element, likely to encourage people outdoors. This sophisticated manipulation of time and perception in organizing the walkout exemplifies the concept of Cloud Time in action, blending linear temporal measurements with a deep understanding of human behavior and media dynamics. It is a vivid example of how time can be stretched, condensed, and manipulated, demonstrating the fluidity and richness of Black SpaceTimeMatters.

Transforming Time Zones into Communal Temporalities

The numerous collaborations across the *Time Zone Protocols* project—including the TZP Surveyors discussion group, the *TZP* exhibition, and the various workshops at the Prime Meridian Unconference all sought to enact a recalibration of our usual understandings of time and space as a critical counter to the enduring colonial and imperial legacies of time hegemony. In ways analogous to quantum entanglement, where entwined particles across vast distances mutually influence one another, TZP championed temporal abundance that recognizes histories, experiences, and temporalities as intra-active and co-constitutive.

The comprehensive digital archive of the project, accessible at www.timezoneprotocols.space, serves as a repository for all TZP materials, including detailed recordings and documents from the PMU and TZP Surveyors discussion group. The site also houses the TZP library, an extensive listing of over 300 books, articles, images, videos, and sounds curated by Black Quantum Futurism over more than a decade. These resources trace the evolution of the political and social agreements, protocols, and rules that have shaped Westernized time constructs, highlighting their oppressive impact on marginalized Black communities in the US. Further, the TZP site hosts interactive experiments such as the Time Zone Generator and the SpaceTime Map. The Time Zone Generator prompts participants for their personal temporal perspectives and memories, inviting them to reimagine the construct of time zones and chip away at the imperialist time colonization project through a richer understanding of time as a diverse and shared experience. The SpaceTime Map provides a nonlinear view of significant temporal sociohistorical events, emphasizing the need to understand the long-standing impacts of time standardization and its role in colonial legacies. The Just in Timekit offers tools, guidelines, and resources for running local discussion groups, drawing from Black Quantum Futurism and adapting frameworks from the Long Time Academy Toolkit, to support participants in restoring or creating new localized space-times and shared temporal principles suited to the unique temporal experiences of Black communities.

Offering alternative methods of being and existing that extend beyond the limitations imposed by mainstream interpretations of time and space, the protocols of time we collectively developed directly undercut the colonial underpinnings of accepted time standards such as those codified by the International Meridian Conference. It opposes not just mandated time, but also the time-centric norms that rule our lives and the political utility of time as a tool of control and punishment, from the ubiquitous 9-to-5 work schedule to Daylight Saving Time.

To witness the application of these principles compels us to acknowledge and celebrate the diversity of temporal experiences, especially those that have been historically overlooked or suppressed. This goes beyond mere opposition to standardized time; it advocates for a profound reconsideration of how time is structured and utilized as a mechanism of governance and discipline. By proposing alternative modes of existence that transcend the constraints of mainstream temporal interpretations, we aim to dismantle the colonial foundations of time measurement. This not only liberates us from the confines of imposed chronologies but also empowers a multitude of temporalities to coexist, honoring the rich tapestry of global cultures and their unique conceptions of time.

CHAPTER 5

Race Against Space-Time

Centering Black Temporalities for Liberated Housing Futures

Time permeates every facet of our lives, subtly shaping interactions within the towering institutions that govern our day-to-day existence. Anthropologist Carol J. Greenhouse describes how "the Western cultural capacity for that belief [in linear time] was established a thousand years ago, or longer, when institutional and social structural changes gave linear time a path from the sacred domain to the domain of the everyday."[1] She argues that this belief becomes "reproduced in the juxtaposition of institutional forms and temporalities which constitute everyday experience in the modern world."[2] The institutionalization of linear time, therefore, is not just a relic of ancient belief systems but guides how we perceive the flow of events and their meaning in our daily lives.

As any lawyer can tell you, this is true of the legal system, where, as law professor Rebecca R. French emphasizes, "time enters every part of how we practice, analyze, project, and balance legal arguments; it is integral to our daily schedule, our client appointments, our classroom teaching time, our court dates, our tickler files, our view of our careers." Despite time's omnipresence in the legal system, "we rarely think about how 'time' actually works, presuming that it is the simple linear measuring device that the clock creates for us."[3] Renisa Mawani adds to this analysis by asserting that "law is fundamentally about time," yet "few have examined how law appeals to particular conceptions of time, whether linear, chronological, circular, or instrumental," while "even fewer have asked how law produces time, how it orders the nomos through its own temporalities, aspiring to assimilate and absorb other temporalities in the process."[4]

Although much has been written about legal constructions of space and race, the function of time and race in this constellation has not been covered with the same breadth, despite playing a profound role in how people—particularly Black, poor, disabled, and other marginalized people—are valued, treated, punished, erased, or underserved within the legal system.[5] Especially underexplored are substantive areas of civil rights, poverty, and public interest law in their temporal contexts, as are the ways in which the nexus of class oppression and institutional racism are reinforced by the union between time and the law. The deeply tangled relationship between race, space, time, systemic devaluation, and the law demands more rigorous scrutiny.

For over a decade I worked as an attorney at Community Legal Services of Philadelphia, where I was a daily witness to the dominance of time within the legal system. In addition to providing legal representation to low-income homeowners and tenants facing eviction and displacement, I led several housing policy advocacy initiatives, working among a team of attorneys, paralegals, and tenant organizers to advance housing rights protections and preserve affordable housing. In this work I often utilized community lawyering practices, a process through which legal advocates lend their expertise to support initiatives identified by the community. The process aims to work directly with impacted communities, developing solutions that resonate with their needs while also helping build community leadership and institutions capable of sustaining power and influence. Incorporating community lawyering into my practice provided a pathway to integrate the Black Quantum Futurism perspective and a critical temporal analysis into the work. This approach combines legal and scientific inquiry with creative research and speculative theory, aiming to challenge and broaden prevailing narratives about time. It serves as an urgent call to reconsider conceptions of time in theory and practice, by amplifying overlooked temporalities and spatial experiences within Black communities, revealing them as sites of resistance, innovation, and transformation.

Merging legal and artistic methodologies, Black Quantum Futurism, with funding for socially engaged artists from A Blade of Grass, created a project called Community Futures Lab (CFL). From March 2016 to April 2017, we operated a community space in a storefront in Sharswood, North Philadelphia, where we developed and practiced a framework called Community Futurisms. This framework aimed to deepen the understanding of the community's dynamics, rhythms, temporalities, memories, histories, and ideas for shared futures. It primarily took shape through creative and informational workshops and "oral futures" interviews, elements of which are included throughout this chapter. CFL was instrumental in connecting with the community on various housing fronts and fights, including campaigns to advance eviction protections and anti-displacement policies in the city, using it as an opportunity to explore the critical nexus of spatial inequity and temporal analysis, and highlighting the imperative to incorporate a nuanced understanding of time and space in housing policy and protections. As a housing attorney, the concept of time was not just a backdrop, but a critical element governing every aspect of my work. This ranged from the mundane task of documenting my hours working on cases, to the immediate necessity of defending tenants in eviction court, to intervening in the trajectory of years and decades involved in preserving fair, safe, and affordable housing. While representing clients who couldn't afford to pay for attorneys, I saw the economic inequities my clients faced presenting themselves temporally as well. Time is, after all, money in this society and is a critical factor in justice and access to resources. Such temporal inequities manifested conspicuously in the eviction process, situated comfortably at the usual intersections of gender, race, and class. This was true in the short (and fully waivable) notice requirements for a landlord terminating a lease agreement under state law and the time allowed for an evicted family to vacate a unit, which often severely misaligned with the time needed to secure new housing. Racial inequities are embedded in the housing system; in Philadelphia, as in many parts of the country, most severely rent-burdened people are single mothers and overwhelmingly are people of color. It is not a coincidence, then, that those who get evicted from rental housing fall along the same racial and gender lines—eviction most frequently impacts Black women and their children, and in Philadelphia impacts Black families disproportionately and regardless of their level of income or education.[6]

Justice on the Clock: Time in Eviction Court

In the heart of Philadelphia, the clock strikes 9:00 a.m. in a bustling eviction court. Outside, Tiffany, a single mother juggling two jobs, races against time, her breath short as she navigates the crowded bus with her toddler. Her struggle is not just against the morning rush but against a system that has already started counting down her days in her home. Meanwhile, inside the court, the wooden gavel falls, marking another default judgment. In that moment, Tiffany becomes one of the countless tenants caught in the unforgiving gears of legal timelines, resulting in impending homelessness. For her, the law's clock ticked in a rhythm unsympathetic to the everyday realities of school runs, job shifts, and life's unpredictability.

Tiffany's story is one of many that demonstrate why there is such a high rate of default judgments in eviction court, where one side automatically loses the case because they were not present in court when the case was called. Reviews of the Philadelphia Landlord-Tenant Court dockets reveal that more than 34 percent of tenants in Philadelphia between 2010 and 2020 had a default judgment entered against them, while over half of all legal evictions are the result of a default judgment entered against a tenant.[7] In eviction court, default judgments are issued swiftly, sometimes only minutes after court proceedings begin and before the judge is even seated. If the tenant is not present in court at 9 a.m. on the dot, they can be evicted in as few as twenty-one days under the strict letter of the law.[8]

It is important here to distinguish between an eviction and an eviction filing. An eviction filing is the initial legal step a landlord takes to begin the process of removing a tenant, often resulting in a court case. An eviction, on the other hand, is the process of legally removing a tenant from a property, which occurs *as a result of* a court ruling, such as a default judgment.[9] This distinction is crucial as not all filings lead to actual evictions, but the threat and stress of the process has significant impacts on tenants' lives, while the court record itself can follow a tenant for life.

Default judgments are often a repercussion of tenants showing up late to or missing court due to conflicting demands on their time, such as getting children to and from school, attending jobs, managing other court dates, navigating disabilities, or dealing with delayed public transportation. These obligations can conflict with the rigid scheduling of court hearings, highlighting a broader societal issue where time is not just a resource but a privilege.

The challenges faced by these tenants underscore the concept of time poverty: the severe constraints on the availability of time experienced by certain communities, characterized by a lack of access to time resources. It also offers a vivid example of how legal frameworks of time, such as those characteristic of the eviction system, can enforce systematic dispossession and insecurity. Through this lens, "time poverty" not only reflects a logistical challenge but a structural inequity that disproportionately affects marginalized populations.

This dialogue on time poverty and eviction intricate ties to the evocative and historical concept of the "deadline," a term analyzed by Danielle Purifoy in her session at the Prime Meridian Unconference called "Dead Line?: On Slowing Down in Black 'Spacetime.'" Purifoy examines the deadline as the latest time by which something should or can be completed while highlighting its connection to the legacy of plantation time. The deadline becomes more than a metaphorical construct but a tangible boundary with severe implications, with its historical usage delineating a perimeter around prisons—beyond which prisoners risked fatal consequences. This chilling origin serves as a stark reminder of the immediate and historical threats imposed on Black lives by such temporal and physical boundaries. In the realm of eviction, the notion of the deadline acquires a heightened significance, representing the severe risks of dispossession that can happen within moments of a judge's ruling, and the disjunction between the eviction process and the pursuit of long-term, secure housing. This interpretation of the deadline magnifies its role as not merely a temporal marker but as a critical determinant of security, stability, and livelihood for those entangled in the eviction process.

In Philadelphia, landlords are allowed to serve court paperwork either in person or by posting it in a visible location, such as on a tenant's door or window. This method, however, is prone to failure for several reasons. Tenants may not receive court notices if they have already left the property, possibly in response to a lease termination notice issued before the eviction paperwork was filed. In some cases, landlords proceed with eviction filings even after tenants have vacated, for reasons such as securing a legal judgment to prevent tenants from returning, punishing the tenant, being unaware of the tenant's departure, or due to simultaneous processes. Additionally, notices posted on doors are susceptible to being removed, soaked through on a rainy day, or blown away by a gust of wind, resulting in tenants being unaware of the pending legal action.[10] The legal system's reliance on such service methods, without adequate safeguards to ensure that tenants are informed, reflects a broader systemic issue where the rights and needs of marginalized groups are overlooked in favor of procedural convenience.

The lease termination notice is also in itself a temporal phenomenon, serving a dual purpose to inform tenants of when they are expected to vacate and to trigger the timeframe for landlords to file a formal eviction complaint. Yet, under the Pennsylvania Landlord-Tenant Act, landlords can include provisions in their lease agreements through which a tenant waives their right to the receipt of a lease termination notice.[11] Waiver of notice to quit deprives tenants of a key safeguard, which is, at its essence, the benefit of time. Many tenants are unaware of this provision in their leases or lack the bargaining power to negotiate its removal before signing. Further, a tenant may have few other options for housing such that they cannot afford to reject a rental offer—despite a lease containing provisions that are unfair, against the tenant's best interests, or even illegal.

The result is a coercive spatial-temporal manipulation that favors landlords' interests and destabilizes tenants' agency, security, and time. Even when tenants are served with a legal complaint for eviction, any waiver-of-notice provisions they may have signed will still often prevent them from raising a timely defense. These legally sanctioned lease provisions to waive notice to quit decrease the little time tenants do have to respond to complaints, secure legal counsel, negotiate with landlords, and prepare their legal defenses. As a result, tenants may present an insufficient defense to eviction or decide not to appear in court at all, leading to a default judgment.

These scenarios reflect a critique of how law asserts its sovereignty and authority by imposing its temporal framework, often erasing or overriding alternative temporalities. The legal system's responsiveness is limited to those temporalities that align with its structure, often ignoring those that do not. In this way, the law's temporal order prioritizes certain interests and narratives, in this case, those of landlords, while marginalizing others, particularly tenants, thereby perpetuating time poverty and its associated injustices.

Colonized Time, Racial Time, and the Time of Progress

In this context of legal and institutional bureaucracy, temporal oppression manifests through the imposition of rigid and standardized time norms and expectations, which may be out of sync with the lived experiences of marginalized Black communities. Strategies of temporal oppression are formidable instruments of control, surveillance, labor regulation, and punishment. These mechanisms, while perfected during enslavement, continue to exert their influence in various manifestations into the present. In political scientist Michael Hanchard's critical examination of "racial time," he articulates a sophisticated understanding of how power dynamics embedded in racial distinctions have historically orchestrated unequal access to institutions, resources, power, knowledge, and opportunities. Hanchard posits that "racial time" emerges from and contributes to the structural inequalities between racially dominant and subordinate groups, effectively using temporality itself as a mechanism of oppression. This manipulation of time—wherein racialized temporal inequalities are established and perpetuated—has profound implications for access to education, economic opportunities, and political power.

Hanchard traces the genesis of racial time to the era of racial slavery, suggesting that the very concept of time was weaponized to sustain a disjunctive temporal reality that favored racially dominant groups while subjugating others. This disjunction is not merely a metaphor but manifests in tangible disparities in the daily lives of individuals within multiracial societies. He illustrates how the unequal temporal access to goods, services, resources, power, and knowledge is recognized and internalized by members of both dominant and subordinate groups, thereby reinforcing racial hierarchies and contributing to a structural effect upon the politics of racial difference. This structural temporal inequality thus becomes a central axis around which racialized experiences of modernity revolve, challenging conventional narratives of progress and equality.[12]

Consider again how racial time's manifestation emerged from the meticulous control exercised by masters over the distribution of time for enslaved people their bodies and their time, through labor, were commodified.[13] Here we see how "the rise of capitalism and the work-clock . . . went hand-in-hand: time became a quantifiable measure of exchange-value in the marketplace for trading in the commodity of human labour, the currency in which the workers' lives—their time, reified—was bought and sold."[14] On most plantations, "the masters ha[d] complete control over the distribution of the negro's time."[15] A staggering average sixteen-hour workday of backbreaking labor continued until 10 or 11 p.m. each evening, and still enslaved individuals remained "on call" twenty-four hours a day with the possibility to be summoned at any moment.

The relationship of Black people and the Western linear time is emblematic of an ongoing conflict, with time hegemony standing as "a reservoir of symbols with which the legitimacy of hierarchies can be defended and reproduced."[16] In this dynamic, "whites are self-positioned as the masters of their own time, as against those mastered by time."[17] It is an enduring dichotomy that illustrates how temporal control has been wielded as a tool of racial dominance, effectively binding Black people's movements in both space and time.

Tools of Temporal and Spatial Segregation

Interwoven with the struggle for emancipation were legacies of discrimination in public spaces, housing, and land in the United States. Known as slave codes, Jim Crow laws, and Black Codes, and showing up in the form of redlining and racially restrictive covenants in the real estate sphere, then through zoning laws, these laws were commonly thought of as spatial segregation that restricted Black people's movements through space. Critical race theorist and law professor Cheryl Harris notes, for instance that "between 1680 and 1682, the first slave codes appeared, codifying the extreme deprivations of liberty already existing in social practice. Many laws parceled out differential treatment based on racial categories: Blacks were not permitted to travel without permits, to own property, to assemble publicly, or to own weapons; nor were they to be educated."[18] Though often framed as spatial segregation mechanisms, these instruments effectively shackled Black people's movements through space *and* time. The laws that were designed to deny Black people the right to vote, restricted where they could live, learn, and work, so attempted to circumscribe the future Black people could manifest as much as access to physical space or rights. Philosopher Charles W. Mills called such laws a "racial regime (racial slavery, colonial forced labor, Jim Crow, or apartheid polities) [that] imposes, inter alia, particular dispositions and allocations of time that are differentiated by race: working times, eating and sleeping times, free times, commuting times, waiting times, and ultimately, of course, living and dying times."[19] To defy or challenge these laws often resulted in arrest or imprisonment, hefty fines, or extreme judicial and extrajudicial of punishments of death and violence against Black people or entire communities. This stark reality represents not just a figurative but a literal deprivation of access to the future for Black people. The potential or actuality of death, as a consequence of resisting these regimes, symbolizes an ultimate severance from the future.

In the early 1900s, towns, cities, and states across the US began enacting zoning laws that regulated land use, building height, and other aspects of growth and development. While these laws appeared neutral on the surface, they were often explicitly designed or used to reinforce segregation and exclusion along racial and ethnic lines. These racist mechanisms of space-time control manifested in several forms, including exclusionary zoning laws, redlining, and racially restrictive covenants, all of which severely limited where Black people could live, work, and own property, effectively segregating them from white communities.[20]

The practice of exclusionary zoning implemented at the local, regional, or state level, was a key tool in this process. Local zoning laws were further reinforced by the federal government's redlining policies of the 1930s. These laws designated certain areas of cities for specific uses, such as residential, commercial, or industrial. Often, the allocation of residential zones was done in a way that segregated Black communities into less desirable areas, away from white neighborhoods. For example, a city might zone a particular area as residential, but with restrictions that only single-family homes could be built there. This type of zoning implicitly favors wealthier, often white residents who could afford such homes, while excluding lower-income residents needing affordable multifamily housing options. With Black families systematically excluded from jobs and other economic opportunities that could support the purchase of single-family residences in neighborhoods with amenities, Black communities were often pushed into areas zoned for multifamily housing or areas closer to industrial zones, which were less desirable due to factors like pollution, noise, and a lack of green spaces.

The impact of such zoning was not only immediate in terms of where people could live but also long-term in its effects on community development and prosperity. Predominantly Black neighborhoods relegated to less desirable zones faced challenges in attracting investment, leading to a cycle of poverty and disinvestment. These areas were often overlooked in terms of infrastructure development, maintenance, and public services. Additionally, property values in these areas were generally lower, which affected the wealth accumulation potential of their residents. Exclusionary zoning thus created a landscape where Black communities were not only spatially segregated but also trapped in a temporal loop of economic stagnation. Their physical location within a city dictated their access to opportunities, resources, and the potential for future growth and prosperity. This systemic segregation through zoning laid the groundwork for enduring racial disparities in housing, wealth, and community development.

Redlining was enforced both implicitly and explicitly, with government agencies, banks, and insurance companies all participating in this discriminatory practice. Exclusionary zoning, coupled with federal redlining policies, significantly contributed to the temporal segregation and oppression of Black communities in the United States. Redlining, initiated in the 1930s by the Home Owners' Loan Corporation and later adopted by banks, involved marking predominantly Black neighborhoods as high-risk for loan defaults, severely limiting residents' access to mortgages and home improvement loans.

Racially restrictive covenants were agreements written into property deeds prohibiting the leasing or selling of property to certain racial or ethnic groups, most commonly Black people. These covenants were explicit tools of segregation, used by white property owners and developers to maintain the racial homogeneity of neighborhoods. The enforcement of these covenants was upheld by real estate boards and neighborhood associations, and even supported by court rulings, until they were declared unenforceable by the Supreme Court in 1948. While the Supreme Court ruled in the landmark case of *Shelley v. Kraemer* in 1948 that such racial covenants were unconstitutional, the practice of exclusionary zoning persists in various forms. These policies and their long-term legacies continue to affect communities of color today, with many neighborhoods still experiencing disinvestment, lack of access to quality education and healthcare, and other barriers to economic and social mobility.

Another particularly pernicious manifestation of racialized temporal oppression coupled with spatial segregation was the existence of "sundown towns." These towns, scattered throughout the United States, were characterized by the deliberate and stringent exclusion of Black people, enforced through a combination of law, custom, and chilling acts of violence.[21] In sundown towns, Black people faced the explicit mandate of leaving the town's limits before dusk and were also prohibited from residing in these areas. Such segregationist practices extended their grip to encompass entire "sundown counties" and "sundown suburbs."

Signs within the city limits openly proclaimed: "Whites only." Local newspapers published warnings stating, "Don't let the sun set on you here, you understand?" These physical markers served as unambiguous reminders of the temporal boundaries imposed upon Black people specifically. The enforcement of these boundaries was brutal and direct, often involving extreme acts of violence. As on the plantations, audible signals like whistles would shrill to signify the time by which Black people needed to leave the area. Failure to comply resulted in severe consequences; shootings, beatings, and lynchings were not uncommon acts of violence inflicted upon those who were perceived to have violated the rules or missed the signs.[22] This was not just a social norm but was enforced through both the actions of residents and, at times, by local authorities. While white citizens assumed the role of enforcers, they faced little to no legal repercussions for their actions, enjoying the privilege of wielding state-sanctioned violence with impunity.

The horror television series *Lovecraft Country* (2020), set in the 1950s, launches with its first episode, titled "Sundown," depicting the harrowing experiences endured by Black people navigating sundown towns. In this episode, the main characters on a road trip pass through a town, ripped right out of the pages of history, that displays a "Whites only" sign. They then find themselves on a treacherous journey through another such town, where the threat of violence tracks their every move. The sheriff pulls them over to inform them that they must cross county lines before sunset at 7:09 p.m. Literally racing against time, while trying to keep under the speed limit to avoid being pulled over again, they exit the county with ten seconds to spare, only to be arrested in the next jurisdiction. This portrayal captures the psychological toll inflicted by temporal oppression and spotlights the pervasive racial time inequities that have sculpted the American landscape.

Together, these mechanisms—exclusionary zoning, redlining, sundown towns, and racially restrictive covenants—formed an interconnected system that sustained and enforced racial segregation in housing. Temporal zoning might then refer to the regulation of time that has been historically used to segregate people of color, particularly Black people, from white communities. Zoning, whether spatial or temporal, or both, creates segregation of space in relationship to time, or of time in relationship to space, with resounding impacts on the social and economic fabric of a community.

These forms of spatial-temporal control and displacement extend far beyond the era in which they were explicitly enforced and into our own. Supported and perpetuated by a range of institutions, including government bodies, financial institutions, real estate companies, and local communities, these historical injustices and forms of trauma continue to cast shadows over Black life. The timeline from the ostensible end of chattel slavery to the present reflects a society minutely designed to systematically disadvantage Black families and marginalized communities.

The impact of these practices results in a contemporary reality of exploitative real estate practices, racial exclusion from housing opportunities, and the resulting housing and land access inequities that are not relics of history but active agents shaping lives today. These modern manifestations appear in the form of realtors and property managers showing Black renters and homebuyers fewer options; in neighborhoods cut off from adequate transportation, grocery stores, or green space, and in the form of policing practices and extralegal violence.[23] They appear as exclusionary zoning and redevelopment practices that displace Black residents from their homes and communities in favor of neighborhoods that become whiter and/or wealthier.[24] This segregation has had lasting effects on the socioeconomic status of Black Americans, contributing to ongoing disparities in wealth, education, health, and quality of life.

Disentanglement and Displacement from Space and Time in Black Communities

> *Obama says he takes the long arc bend toward justice. That's a coping mechanism for leaders at that level. He often says human history is a long novel and we're just trying to get our chapter right, and I resent that. It's true. He's right. But I resent it because for people living in 19121 and other ZIP codes like it, the urgency has never been greater. We don't have the time.* **—Omar Woodard, "There's 'No Time' for the Long Road to Justice"**

> *Gentrification is anti-Black, anti-Indigenous time and space making.* **—Chiekh Athj, Community Futures Lab**

Gathered with about a hundred others amid the early morning chill of North Philadelphia, I watched as a part of the city's history was about to be erased within seconds. Two out of three of the Sharswood-Blumberg towers, which had been part of the Norman Blumberg Apartments, a half-century-old public housing complex, were set for demolition. This event was not just a physical dismantling of buildings; it symbolized the deep-seated issues of race, time, and urban planning converging in a dramatic moment.

As the towers imploded and then crumbled, so did a piece of the Sharswood community's heart. These buildings, though stigmatized as symbols of poverty and crime, were home to generations of families. Their destruction was emblematic of a broader, often-overlooked narrative: how urban renewal initiatives, driven by promises of progress and revitalization, can perpetuate cycles of displacement and racial inequity. Philadelphia Housing Authority (PHA) president Kelvin Jeremiah's spoke these words before the demolition: "Life as we know it is going to change," echoing the sentiments of transformation but at what cost to the community's fabric and history?

As I stood there as witness, I contemplated the broader implications. The plan to replace the towers with new residential and commercial developments, including PHA's new headquarters, was a microcosm of urban redevelopment's impact on communities. It raised critical questions about who benefits from such plans and at whose expense? The acquisition of over 1,300 properties, many through eminent domain, underscored the tension between development and displacement.

Temporalities of gentrification, displacement, and redevelopment in marginalized communities represent a convergence of time, space, and socioeconomic dynamics. These processes often condense time, meaning they accelerate changes in the community fabric at a pace that is disorienting to the established rhythms of life. This rapid transformation can starkly disrupt the shared experiences of time and history within a community. These communal temporalities are rooted in collective memories, traditions, and the lived experiences of residents, forming a vital part of the community's identity. Such urban redevelopment often leads to the erasure of public memory. Historical buildings, local landmarks, or cultural hubs that hold communal significance are demolished or repurposed, effectively erasing physical reminders of the community's past. This loss extends beyond physical structures; it represents a severance of the community's connection to its history and a disruption in the transmission of collective memories and identities.

These redevelopment processes also foreclose access to the temporal domain of the future for current residents. This means that as neighborhoods are gentrified, the original inhabitants often find themselves alienated from the future development of their own community. They may face displacement due to rising living costs or find that the evolving neighborhood no longer reflects their cultural and social needs. The intentions behind redevelopment, whether for affordable housing, market-rate, or luxury developments, do not necessarily mitigate these temporal disruptions. Even well-intentioned efforts can result in adverse effects if they fail to consider and respect the existing temporalities and histories of the communities involved.

Philadelphia, which for many years consistently ranked highest among the top ten most impoverished big cities in America, is a place where gentrification and racialized segregation have manipulated the landscape of Black communities, working to push residents to the edges of the city where they become locked into temporal-spatial ghettos. Housing instability in particular impacts some areas of the city more than others. North Philadelphia—the 19121 ZIP code in particular—is where the highest percentage of the city's poor, Black, and Hispanic residents live in what is called "racially concentrated poverty." It is also where the city's highest levels of evictions and displacement occur.[25] In this area of the city, inequalities related to poverty are magnified. The poverty rate in Philadelphia in 2016, was 26 percent; while in the 19121 ZIP code the poverty rate was at 52.5 percent.[26]

> RASHEEDAH: How would you describe the pace of North Philly?
>
> MR. MCMICHAEL: Well, if you go back ten years, it was questionable. I had hopes in North Philly, but I never realized it was going to move at the pace it moves at now. I think it moves rapidly. With all the development that's going on. I own another property. I get, every week, cards from developers, realtors, wanting to buy my property.[27]

In the 19121 ZIP code, disparities starkly divide the community. As certain neighborhoods within the boundaries 19121 suffer from increased poverty, poor health, and crime, other parts are swiftly transitioning through gentrification. Deteriorating homes, vacant lands, and uninhabitable properties make land deals cheap for out-of-town developers who then demolish the old to erect luxury dwellings and properties priced well above the market average. Within this ZIP code resides Sharswood, a predominantly Black neighborhood, which in 2015 became a focal point for eminent domain and extensive redevelopment initiatives spearheaded by the city and the PHA. Sharswood spans an "arrowhead-shaped" locale bounded by Girard and Cecil B. Moore Avenues, stretching from 19th to 27th Streets. At its heart once stood three towering high-rises and fifteen low-rise, multi-unit dwellings known as the Norman Blumberg Apartments, inaugurated in 1966 under the stewardship of the PHA.[28]

In this compact region, the city's disparities in poverty are accentuated. While Philadelphia's median household income in 2016 stood at $41,449, Sharswood's median income plummeted to $23,790, witnessing a near 28 percent decrease from 1999 to 2013. In 2013 PHA received a grant from the federal Department of Housing and Urban Development (HUD), which they used to develop and implement the Sharswood-Blumberg Neighborhood Transformation Plan (2015), a $500+ million redevelopment project that involved the execution of eminent domain and demolition of 1,300 properties in the neighborhood and the demolition of two high-rises housing nearly 500 families, as well as several dozen low-rise public housing units owned and managed by PHA. Although new affordable housing was desperately needed in the area due to significant neglect and a backlog of repairs of the public housing stock, the plan required homeowners, renters, and businesses to be temporarily and permanently relocated, while historic properties of great cultural significance were demolished, sold, or rendered unusable by neglect.

Sharswood's historical narrative unfurls against a backdrop of transformative epochs, beginning as part of a larger tract of farmland known as the Penn District, with Ridge Avenue, its eastern boundary, serving as a Lenape trail before European settlement. The neighborhood owes its name to George Sharswood, a Justice of the Supreme Court of Pennsylvania who once resided in the area, and a small street in the neighborhood, lined with rowhouses, bears his name as well. By the nineteenth century, Sharswood had evolved into a streetcar suburb offering residence to Irish and German brewery workers (for which the adjacent neighborhood Brewerytown is named).

The early twentieth century marked a significant demographic shift, with Sharswood becoming a hub for African American culture during the Great Migration. Notable residents included James B. Davis of The Dixie Hummingbirds and artist Dox Thrash. The area around Ridge and Columbia Avenue became renowned for its jazz clubs and nightlife, attracting legendary musicians like Charlie Parker, John Coltrane, and Odean Pope. The brief residence of Malcolm X in 1954, during his tenure as a minister for the Nation of Islam, further adds to the neighborhood's historic significance.

Despite its rich cultural legacy, Sharswood was starkly segregated from neighboring white communities, producing substantial risks and inequities for its Black residents. Historical redlining, a discriminatory practice documented in J. M. Brewer's 1934 map and the Home Owners' Loan Corporation's assessments, further entrenched economic and racial segregation in the area. Redlining systematically denied Black people and other people of color access to essential services, including affordable housing, fair mortgage lending, quality education, and healthcare, effectively marginalizing them within their own communities. Describing the history of redlining in the neighborhood, Mr. Warren McMichael, a lifelong resident of the neighborhood who grew up on Sharswood Street and longtime President of the Brewerytown-Sharswood Civic Association before his unfortunate passing in September 2021, shared his insights:

> You couldn't get insurance. The insurance companies stopped running polices. So, you had to go through the state plan to get fire insurance. You couldn't get the regular full policies, homeowner policies. Then also, I think it was difficult getting mortgages at that time. But we always said it was planned obsolescence. Don't know if that's true. As Richard Nixon called it, benign neglect. Because the neighborhood was neglected for a long time. Didn't get services and things.[29]

The Norman Blumberg Apartments, named for a prominent Philadelphia AFL-CIO Council chapter president, were constructed from 1966–67 as a mixture of three high-rise towers and fifteen low-rise apartment buildings totaling 510 units, inside of a neighborhood that just two years before experienced a riot that saw its residents effectively cut off from all resources and their homes stripped of all value.[30] During a period of race riots and Black uprisings across the United States, the 1964 Columbia Avenue Riot lasted two days along a business and residential district that ran through Sharswood. The riot utterly devastated what had been a thriving community of local business owners, artists, and activists of all backgrounds and ethnicities. Most of the district's businesses, such as theaters, grocery stores, restaurants, and furniture stores, could not recover from their losses, and business activity in North Philadelphia declined. The neighborhood continued to experience significant challenges, including a decrease in population, the impacts of deindustrialization, and a reduction in economic investment, contributing to its status as one of Philadelphia's most impoverished areas, characterized by extensive property vacancies and a notably high incidence of violent crime. The turn of the twenty-first century heralded a new era of gentrification, propelled by rising median home prices and property values, alongside Sharswood's desirable location. The neighborhood's adjacency to the already gentrified neighborhood Brewerytown, its proximity to Center City shopping, theaters, restaurants, a major university, high-end supermarkets, and plentiful public transportation made the neighborhood more attractive to speculators and developers, who have launched major urban renewal projects in the area in order to attract higher income, younger, and ostensibly whiter residents to the area. Median home prices in that ZIP code rose by 68 percent from 2010 to 2016, while the property values of homes in Sharswood doubled.[31] The dramatic increase in home prices and property values underscored a shifting urban landscape, where speculative development and urban renewal initiatives sought to redefine the neighborhood's identity and composition.

However, the reasons for targeting the area for the transformation provided by government officials on the public record and in media reports implicitly and explicitly placed significant blame on the marginalized residents of the neighborhood, particularly the ones living in the public housing buildings and the low-income homeowners surrounding those buildings. This narrative of blame became a justification for employing eminent domain, a legal principle allowing government entities to expropriate private property for public use, typically in exchange for what the government deems is fair compensation determined through appraisals and in most cases less than what it would cost to make a person subject to eminent domain whole and therefore able to retain their same quality of life after being displaced. By invoking this principle, authorities posited that the transformation of the area served a greater public interest, albeit at the expense of displacing existing communities. This process, while legally sanctioned, raises ethical and social concerns, especially when it disproportionately affects marginalized populations, reinforcing cycles of displacement and socioeconomic disparity that are being used as the reason for redeveloping the community.

In testimony at public hearings, media interviews, and in op-eds, government officials focused on statistics of the area's poverty, crime, low educational attainment, and high unemployment rates, with the PHA president, Kelvin Jeremiah, dubbing the neighborhood and its residents "by almost any measure . . . a top contender for Philadelphia's worst community," in an op-ed titled "Breathing Life into a Blighted Community."[32] The residents of the area, particularly those living in public housing, were portrayed with all the routine stereotypes of Black people and communities as uneducated, unemployed or implied to be lazy, violent, and as people without a meaningful history, sense of community, and without much that could be hoped for in their future.

In other articles, Jeremiah detailed being held at gunpoint while visiting the Norman Blumberg towers as partly his motivation to embark on the redevelopment project. A *New York Times* piece recounted the alleged incident as, "during an evening trip to the neighborhood in 2013, soon after he became head of the housing agency, [Jeremiah] encountered a man who threatened him with a gun when he refused to buy drugs. After hearing residents' stories of crime in the area, he thought the housing authority ought to focus on the neighborhood." The narrative employs an oft-used pretext for initiating redevelopment efforts in a neighborhood that falls outside the traditional purview of the housing authority's operations. Facilitated by the local government's delegation of its authority, the housing authority, a quasi-federal entity endorsed by the Department of Housing and Urban Development, assumed the role of a developer, thereby instigating displacement.

This narrative, woven into the fabric of the redevelopment discourse, implicitly portrays impoverished Black communities as fundamentally incapable of self-governance, necessitating external governmental intervention. It reflects an entrenched belief in the necessity of a dominant government entity to spearhead the revitalization of areas like Sharswood, as PHA itself has articulated, positing that "the situation in Sharswood is so dire that only a big government player can create conditions for revival on Ridge Avenue." This stance not only questions the community's autonomy but also underscores a contentious approach to urban redevelopment, where the narratives of danger and neglect serve to justify significant transformations that often result in the displacement of existing communities.

The narrative of blight and disinvestment in Philadelphia, particularly in communities like Sharswood, is not just a story of neglect but a result of systemic and structural forces. A report by the Philadelphia Controller's Office in 2020 highlights the historical backdrop of structural racism through redlining and its long-lasting impacts on the community, including poverty, poor health outcomes, and limited educational attainment compared to other neighborhoods in the city. Philadelphia's poverty rate stands at 23.1 percent, significantly above the US average, with median household incomes for Black and Hispanic people falling well below the city's median in 2020.[33]

A study by the National Community Reinvestment Coalition further illustrates the enduring economic struggles of areas historically redlined in the 1930s, with 61 percent still facing economic hardships today. Notably, 94 percent of neighborhoods not redlined remain upper-income, and most redlined neighborhoods are minority-majority today.[34] Between 2012 and 2016, small business lending in Philadelphia reflected these disparities, with redlined neighborhoods receiving 20 percent fewer business loans than non-redlined areas. The loans that were issued in redlined neighborhoods were also significantly smaller, underscoring the ongoing cycle of disinvestment and its throttling effect on business growth and entrepreneurship in these communities.

The mapping of inequality and gentrification in Philadelphia further demonstrates the spatial and economic divides shaped by historical disinvestment and current gentrification trends.[35]

These sources collectively underscore the active process of disinvestment in Philadelphia, rooted in systemic racism and perpetuated by ongoing economic policies and practices. Disregarding this information in policy decisions and redevelopment narratives reinforces a false set of race- and class-based stereotypes that portray the residents of the Sharswood community as uncaring about the neighborhood and indifferent to each other. Stories that run counter to such narratives become largely lost, like this account from a minister at a local church that ran in a city newspaper:

> [The demolition] was quite a sad occasion because some of those people had been there since they were younger. This is something that is affecting them. They've had to leave what they've always known as home . . . Now they're scattered all over the city. A bond that they've had for many years was broken.[36]

The linear progress narrative of redevelopment touted by government entities masks the underlying systems at play and the ways in which the government, developers, and housing providers—either by action or inaction—created or contributed to the present conditions of deterioration. As such, public commentary rarely discusses rising rents and property taxes for their role in gentrification. In a *Newsworks* interview, the President of the PHA placed much of the blame for the community's ills on the Blumberg Towers themselves, promising that "Life as we know it is going to change. It will be forever changed by removing the stigma that was created by this high-rise."[37] This perspective grossly overlooks the broader socioeconomic forces and historical context that have shaped the community's decline. The assertion that the demolition of the towers and the stigma associated with them will fundamentally transform the community underestimates the depth of disinvestment, systemic racism, and economic marginalization that have contributed to the area's struggles.

Further, focusing solely on the physical removal of the towers as a solution disregards the importance of comprehensive community development approaches that address economic, social, and environmental justice. For genuine transformation, initiatives must go beyond physical redevelopment to include access to quality education, healthcare, economic opportunities, and community services that support the well-being and empowerment of residents.

Blaming the towers for the community's ills perpetuates a narrative that externalizes the problems onto physical infrastructure rather than acknowledging the agency's role and responsibility in the disinvestment and neglect of public housing management. It also fails to recognize the resilience and agency of the community members who have lived in and around the towers, often under challenging circumstances. The narrative further ignores the potential negative impacts of gentrification and displacement that can accompany such large-scale redevelopment projects.

The Executive Summary of the Transformation Plan, for its own part, stops short of recognizing PHA and the government's roles in disinvestment in the neighborhood, noting as a point of historical positioning that "as Philadelphia precipitously lost population during the 1980s and 1990s, residents abandoned Sharswood, disinvestment took hold, businesses closed on Ridge Avenue, and Blumberg Apartments became home to a high concentration of the City's poorest families, with hundreds living in high-rise towers that are unsuitable for families with children."[38] Ms. K remembers her displacement from the neighborhood differently, explaining:

> The first time I moved to Sharswood, my mother wanted a bigger house because she had six kids. We were there for twenty-five years, and my mom raised all her kids there. So, when we moved from Sharswood Street, it was because the house was deteriorating, and the back was caving in. So, we had to move to Poplar Street. Then, when I moved to Poplar Street, I stayed there ten years. Things started breaking down, the heater and the stove and stuff like that was going down. Philadelphia Housing Authority did not want to fix it so that was the other reason I moved. Then I moved back to Sharswood, and when I moved back to Sharswood it was just too much for the rent.[39]

Social studies professor Helga Nowotny argues, "Power, exercised by central authorities, establishes itself over space and over time."[40] Inequalities related to displacement are often analyzed in spatial terms, with an emphasis on people displaced from a physical location. However, politicians and government officials strategically employ the language of time and the future to justify their decision-making for redevelopment and urban renewal. In a 2014 commentary in the *Philadelphia Inquirer*, Jeremiah notes that "PHA is making this investment in Blumberg/Sharswood now because, for too long, families in the community were told to wait. The wait is over, and today PHA, with its partners, will build a bridge of opportunity for social and economic prosperity." His words are an apt demonstration of Nowotny's proposition that for bureaucracies, "along with spatial control, the temporal kind is also established, but it still completely follows the imperatives of the organizational needs of the central powers: the temporal control of bureaucracies, which is based on the punctuality that as necessary for maintaining discipline in the army, at school, and later in the factories."

The real impetus for the redevelopment of Blumberg/Sharswood can be traced back to a broader urban renewal strategy that gained momentum in the early 2000s. This period marked a pivotal shift, with the PHA embarking on comprehensive plans to transform the area. By leveraging the narrative of a long-awaited change, officials sought not only to justify the displacement of current residents but also to frame the redevelopment as a long-overdue rectification of past neglect. This strategic positioning is further illuminated by the work of Bahar Sakizlioğlu, who, drawing on Pierre Bourdieu, highlights how "the exercise of power over people's time appears to be a crucial tool for state colonization/appropriation of a space for gentrification."[41] The Blumberg/Sharswood project, therefore, is not merely a spatial reconfiguration but a temporal realignment, wherein the future is colonized to serve the interests of those in power.

Pennsylvania Congressman Chaka Fattah, in the moments leading up to the dramatic implosion of the high-rise buildings in Sharswood, posited their demolition as a transformative act for the physical and societal landscape of the community. "To witness the Blumberg Apartment implosion this weekend is a victory for public housing, for

Philadelphia, and most especially for the residents of the Sharswood neighborhood," he proclaimed. This sentiment was further elaborated in a press release, where he reflected on his long-standing advocacy for the removal of public housing high-rises, envisioning the demolition as a pivotal moment leading to a revitalized Sharswood and a brighter future for its community: "Twenty-five years after I called for the removal of all public housing high-rises in our community, we watch as the demolition of this complex will make way for a revitalized Sharswood, and a brighter future for the entire community."[42]

Fattah's comments underscore the narrative in urban redevelopment, where the physical restructuring of space is seen as inherently linked to positive futures, where power operates not only through the immediate control of space but also through what Kodwo Eshun names as the "envisioning, management, and delivery of reliable futures."[43] However, the critical flaw in Fattah's vision lies in its narrow conception of "community" and who benefits from such revitalization efforts. While the demolition and subsequent redevelopment are portrayed as victories, they often do not account for the dissolution of existing community ties. The experience of the adjacent neighborhood of Brewerytown, which has witnessed significant declines in its Black population amid concentrated private investment, serves as a poignant example. The adjacent neighborhood of Brewerytown has "experienced significant declines in Black population," as one of many "sites of concentrated private investment, while the general area has seen a 65 percent population decline since the 1950s."[44] Targeted investment and gentrification have not benefited the original community members but rather have led to their displacement.

Thus, while Fattah's remarks on the implosion of the Sharswood high-rises highlight a vision of progress and future prosperity, they also inadvertently reveal the complexities and challenges of urban redevelopment. The envisioned future, though bright for some, may not include those who have called these neighborhoods home for generations. This dichotomy brings to light the essential need for inclusive planning and development strategies that truly serve the needs and interests of the entire community, ensuring that revitalization does not come at the expense of its most vulnerable members.

Sakizlioğlu describes the necessity "to bring the crucial element of temporality into the analysis of displacement," allowing a focus on trajectories of neighborhood change that "help us understand not only how residents are affected by displacement even before actual displacement occurs but also appropriation strategies of the state and landlords that put pressures on the residents."[45] This perspective reveals how the deliberate oversight or neglect of neighborhood decline by state entities and property owners contributes to a cycle of deterioration. Examples of such neglect include failing to maintain public infrastructure, overlooking the accumulation of trash and debris, allowing buildings to fall into disrepair, and ignoring rising crime rates. These conditions not only worsen the quality of life for current residents but also serve as a pretext for subsequent interventions like eminent domain and large-scale redevelopment projects. By framing neighborhood decline as a justification for these drastic measures, authorities and landlords effectively manipulate the narrative, positioning redevelopment as a necessary response to self-induced conditions of blight and neglect.

Residents and former residents had an astute sense of the conditions that led to their neighborhood becoming an easy target for projects such as the Transformation Plan. It was part of a pattern of historic disinvestment that has led to the displacement of millions of Black families across the United States in the name of urban renewal. Lawrence T. Brown notes that from the late 1930s to the 1970s alone, "over 1 million households were displaced by federally sponsored actions, affecting at least 2 million Black people and hundreds of Black communities."[46]

In an interview with former Sharswood resident Ms. K, she describes the deterioration of the neighborhood evident not only in the quality of housing but in the quality of relationships and sense of community.

> INTERVIEWER: What were the housing conditions like here when you were growing up?
> MS. K: They were nice, but as we got older, they started deteriorating. That's why we had to move. The block was really deteriorating.

> INTERVIEWER: You feel like the neighborhood as a whole was as well? What do you miss most about the way it used to be?
> MS. K: The people that stuck together and spoke to each other. You know, saying hello, and watching the house if I leave.[47]

Mr. Warren McMichael had a clear sense of when he felt the Sharswood neighborhood began to decline: "After the Columbia Avenue Riot, primarily. That was, what, '64?" He went on to explain, "because you see what Columbia Avenue was, Cecil B. Moore Avenue looks like now. Because when the riot came, they tore up all those stores." In 1987, the city renamed the street to Cecil B. Moore Avenue, after the North Philadelphia-based Black civil rights attorney and activist who represented many of the accused young Black Muslims blamed for inciting the riot, including local activist and educator Shaykh Ali Muhammad Hassan, also known by Absynnia Hayes, who would later go on to open Muhammad's African Asian Cultural Center in the former Sharswood home of pre–civil rights era printmaker and fine artist Dox Thrash (1893–1965) after purchasing it from him in 1959.

Several other residents also highlighted the Columbia Avenue riots as a pivotal moment that forever changed the neighborhood and the communities that called it home. Many had personal connections to the riots, such as family members who had been arrested during or after them, or who had been injured in them. A younger resident of the community, Mr. M., wasn't alive during the time of the riots, but had heard stories from family:

> No. I don't remember it, but I remember my family was just moving up here from the South. They been here for like thirty, let me see. Our brother was two years old.... He would be forty, so my family been up here for thirty-eight years. They told me how Columbia Avenue was. It was a big scene, like a mall. It was like a Broad St. right here in the heart of North Philly. You know how they had the uptown stadium and all that, you know. What I was getting ready to say, how when they started stop and frisk, it started on Columbia Avenue. There was so many people out there, and the drugs, and all the extortion and the crime, to the point, that, I think it was Frank Rizzo that was the mayor at the

> time or the chief of police, started that stop and frisk. And they could pull up on you and make you pull your pants down, and check for your all this, and make you embarrass yourself.[48]

Confirming the communal memory passed down to Mr. M., it has been noted that "the riots also helped to facilitate the political rise to power of Frank Rizzo, who favored more punitive approaches to crime."[49] There was the community as it had existed before the riot and a very different one that existed after.

In *Root Shock*, Mindy Fullilove describes urban renewal projects with redevelopment initiatives "sometimes separated by decades from the demolition phase of a project [that] placed even more unreasonable burdens on the poor and the people of color."[50] The displacement of public housing residents, such as those moved out of the Sharswood neighborhood as part of the Transformation Project, is referred to as "temporary relocation," as is legally required by the Department of Housing and Urban Development.

The great disparity between the intended "temporary" nature of relocation—and the mere months of notice residents typically receive—and the decade-long redevelopment process underestimates the relationship between residents and their living spaces and disregards the essential human need for stability and community. The irony lies in the temporal dissonance between the temporary displacement and the permanent alterations to the neighborhood's social and economic landscape. Under HUD policies, public housing residents technically have a right to return, which means, by the legal definition, they are not *permanently* displaced, while others receive housing choice vouchers.[51] The choice that tenants are forced to make under severe time pressure—whether to relinquish their right to return to the neighborhood in order to receive a voucher or wait for the redevelopment to be completed—often leads to unintended consequences. The extended timeline of the redevelopment renders the return mechanism impractical for many: any number of situations may compromise a particular family's right to return, such as changes in income, health status, family status, or changes to the neighborhood that can no longer accommodate its original residents, such as increased rental rates coupled with the scarcity of affordable housing options. Fullilove writes that "the failure to appreciate the costs that upheaval places on the poor means that grossly inadequate plans are made for resettlement. Issues of community life, transition to new forms of work, emotional pain of separating from a beloved place: all of these considerations are given short shrift."[52] These flaws in the relocation mechanism serve as a stark example of time-related propaganda, where the logistical unfeasibility masks a more fundamental failure to prioritize the rights and dignity of displaced communities.

In public meetings held by PHA on the Transformation Plan, non-PHA residents who owned homes or rented on the private market expressed fears about being unable to return to the neighborhood after it had been redeveloped as mixed-income housing, because there would be a lack of affordable housing opportunities outside of the public housing, which carries a ten-year waitlist and only serves the most severely low-income residents in the city. One resident at a community meeting worried,

> I mean, I'm fifty-nine years old, so homeownership, that's not really in my spectrum. I have a private home, and one day I may want to leave. If I wanted to rent a property but not under the PHA umbrella, will I be able to be eligible, because a lot of times people in moderate middle class, they can't afford it, because the guidelines are so low? That's my concern.[53]

And this fear came true for Sharswood. Since two of the Blumberg high-rise towers and all of the low-rise public housing units were demolished in March 2016 as part of the redevelopment, about half of the 477 households have been able to return to the townhomes meant to replace most of the previous public housing structures.[54] However, changing dynamics of the neighborhood, as described earlier, threaten to keep residents and other low-income people from returning.[55] Fullilove argues that, even if people manage to return, "the elegance of the neighborhood—each person in his social and geographic slot—is destroyed, and even if the neighborhood is rebuilt exactly as it was, it won't work. The restored geography is not enough to repair the many injuries to the mazeway."[56]

The etymology of *nostalgia* derives from the Ancient Greek concept of a pain for home, from the trauma and longing of being removed from your environment (*nostos*, signifying "return home" or "homeward journey," and *algos*, meaning "pain" or "ache"). Coined by Swiss medical student Johannes Hofer in his 1688 dissertation, nostalgia was first used to articulate the intense homesickness felt by Swiss mercenaries stationed far from their homeland and "by 1830s the word was used of any intense homesickness: that of sailors, convicts, African slaves."[57] Its etymology is intimately tied to experiences of displacement, of being pushed out of or torn away from a place where memories and emotions are resonant, rooted in a precise locality and time. Episodic memory is wound up in the places we call home, wrapped around the objects that inhabit them, embedded in the land itself. It is our so-called failure to accelerate quickly enough for the progressive, capitalist timeline and to arrive violently in the futures envisioned by the state that produces our nostalgia. And it is exactly this so-called failure that particularly ensnares marginalized Black people within narrow temporal present(s) under capitalism—bereft of tools, disconnected from resources, with limited and inequitable access to time, memory, and firm roots to place.

The economic and capitalist future constructed by government powers, as Kevin Birth puts it, "limit[s] the imagination and provides an inescapable and non-negotiable structure for the future."[58] Meanwhile, society speeds forward in illusory linear progress into futures that were planned with little to no input of those most impacted by the lack of resources to keep up with this plan. As one former resident shared, the future becomes difficult to see under an imposed temporality of displacement and redevelopment:

> INTERVIEWER: What do you see as the future of Sharswood?
> MS. T: In my future?
> Interviewer: Like the future of Sharswood?
> MS. T: Like I said, I don't know.
> INTERVIEWER: What would you like to see?
> MS. T: That's if I be living. I'm a tell you, let's hope I be out here to see the build. I'm almost fifty years old. I'm hoping to be here to see it.

Creation of Communal Space-Times (in the Face of Hostile Visions of the Future)

> *Regional nostalgia is recalled, utilized and capitalized upon by differently classed subjects in claiming ways in and out of place.* —**Yvette Taylor, *Fitting Into Place?***

> *Well, you know, I live up here in North Philly now. It's a place where you live and love, and it's a lot of memories since this neighborhood has changed. I miss it though. It will never be the same.* —**Ms. E, Community Futures Lab interview, 2016**

Despite being maligned in the media and in public commentary by government officials, current and former residents of Sharswood maintain a keen sense of connection to the neighborhood, one not only tied to their sense of personal identity but to their life stories. As political science researcher Margaret Farrar highlights, place memory is a mode of identity formation that eludes traditional linear time, and instead ties to "a sense of place [that] is inextricably linked to memory formation, which is, of course, crucial to identity formation, both at the individual and collective levels."[59]

INTERVIEWER: What communities would you say you belong to?
MS. K: Sharswood community.
INTERVIEWER: What ways would you say you're connected to it?
MS. K: Born and raised.[60]

What residents considered their community—and more specifically, that of the two demolished high-rises where nearly 500 families were concentrated—is more nuanced than the narrative invoked by government entities. As one local community member, Bryant Jennings, said to the *Philadelphia Inquirer*, residents of the neighborhood had "our own slang, our own language. People who moved away always come back because this is what they knew. And [the demolition] is devastating to a lot of people because what they knew is being torn down."[61] Former residents confirmed this view with us in their interviews at the Community Futures Lab:

MS. T: Yeah, Blumberg was a pretty good place. There's nothing bad you can say about that building. Everybody got along. Like I said, it was one big happy family. Everybody fed everybody's kids in there. Every kid got along in there. It's gone. What else can I say? Well, the hope is now they building up now, it'll be a better place, it'll be a better environment for the kids. Actually, it's going to be a better place.

INTERVIEWER: You'd like to come back to the neighborhood?

MS. T: Well, I'm down here every day, so that's telling me. (laughs)

INTERVIEWER: True! Good point.

MS. T: I'm like, I'm down here three times a week, and like Saturday—well, I come down on Sundays because I go to church down here. And Saturday I might take a breeze through. And then next thing you know I wind up on another Saturday where Blumberg, just watching the buildings, say "oh, what memories in here."[62]

Ms. T's experience of Sharswood accounts for a sense of social time, one that "does not flow at one even rate but goes at a thousand different paces, swift or slow, which bear almost no relation to the day-to-day of a chronicle or of traditional history."[63] She, like other residents and former residents, seems to engage with time in Sharswood in the form of "a local practice rooted in daily rituals and bound up in the particularities of unique physical spaces."[64]

As Carol J. Greenhouse notes, "'community has both spatial and temporal components," where the spatial element defines community as a social field and the temporal element defines community as the historically authentic or original local, regional, or national social form."[65] In coming to understand some of the mechanics of the extremely specific social time and space embodied by Sharswood, one of the prominent phenomena was the decoupling of time from space in the experience of residents, where "social time needs to be understood as multiple and contested, rather than constituting a single dominant order."[66] The quality of time and space are not always traversed evenly and not all communities or people move forward on the arrow of progress at the same rate. Time folds and unfolds into space in infinite configurations.

To an observer from the outside and judging solely by the

socioeconomic conditions of the neighborhood, it may appear as if time stood still within the Sharswood community. The conditions of the neighborhood today are parallel to the socioeconomic stagnation of 1960s North Philadelphia when public housing was first built in the area. The socioeconomic backdrop during the 1964 Columbia Avenue race riots highlights the disparities, the average yearly income then was $3,352, about 30 percent below the city's overall average. Unemployment rates fluctuated between thirteen and 20 percent, particularly affecting youth and laborers at a range of skill levels.[67]

During the 1960s, the housing situation for Black residents in North Philadelphia was critically shaped by the aftermath of suburbanization, white flight, and entrenched discriminatory housing policies. Despite the significant, though not wholly sufficient, strides toward increasing Black homeownership facilitated by antidiscrimination legislation and the decreased home prices resulting from white flight, systemic challenges persisted.[68] Governmental support for white suburban developments, alongside the real estate sector's exploitative tactics in Black urban areas, fueled a cycle of economic disparity and substandard living conditions.[69]

Legislative efforts, including the Fair Housing Act, aimed ambitiously to mitigate these disparities. Yet, the real-world application of these laws often failed to meet their objectives, leaving the promise of enhanced housing access and quality unmet. Initiatives in public housing offered some solace but also perpetuated existing segregation patterns.

Despite the prevailing narratives and conditions, a more nuanced scrutiny of the temporal practices within the neighborhood reveals a deliberate orchestration of intercommunal temporalities—shared communal understandings and negotiations of time that diverge from mainstream linear conceptions. Time has been dynamic in this community—that is, until PHA, HUD, Philadelphia city government and other government agencies began to accelerate time through the Transformation Plan and the swift, external injection of capital over five decades too late for the despairing community. Despite the residents' proactive engagement through civil unrest, the civil rights movement, and local organizations, these efforts were overshadowed by a top-down imposition of time and space that disregarded the neighborhood's layered temporal tapestry. This external imposition operates under the flawed assumption of a unidirectional arrow of time, which presupposes a path of progress as envisioned by dominant forces. As Maureen Perkins observes: "The notion of progress is indeed closely allied to hegemony, since it is defined by those in power. the change they bring is, of course, portrayed as a change for the better."[70]

This perspective fails to acknowledge the rich and nuanced temporal landscape of Sharswood, where progress and time itself are conceived and lived collectively, outside the narrow confines of hegemonic time. Under this scenario, the future, much like space (housing, land, and even outer space), becomes accessible only to those who have the resources to accelerate at the pace determined by the dominant party. In her CFL interview, Ms. E shared the sentiment of not fitting into the projected future:

> They've just been tearing things down. There's a lot of construction here. But hey, I'm here to see everything change so I just deal with it. The old way was fun and exciting, but the new way is not. I feel that I don't belong here. I see a lot of Temple students walk by here. It's not like it used to be. It's more quiet around the neighborhood. I don't hear a lot of noise though. I don't hear no guns shooting. I used to hear the fireworks from the projects, but don't nobody fire them no more.[71]

Incorporating an analysis on temporality, researcher Yvette Taylor's observations in her book *Fitting into Place?: Class and Gender Geographies and Temporalities* highlight how social structures that reproduce class and gender hierarchies create environments where not everyone is able or willing to "fit in" or adapt themselves to "trajectories of future potential" envisioned by urban regeneration and neighborhood rebranding efforts.[72] This critique strongly resonates with the experiences of low-income residents in Sharswood prior to redevelopment, whose societal value, as perceived by governing entities, is contingent upon their capacity to autonomously navigate their futures. They are expected to leverage various networks and forms of capital to envision and actualize a "fulfilling and productive future," essentially to "come forward" and claim their space.[73]

However, this expectation underscores a profound temporality issue, where the ability to project oneself into a future aligned with white supremacist capitalist ideals is not universally accessible or desirable. For those unable to conform to these prescribed trajectories—often due to systemic barriers rather than individual failings—the consequences are dire. Their spaces are appropriated, and their futures are dictated by market and governmental forces, a punitive measure for their failure to ascend within a system that is fundamentally rigged against them.

This analysis suggests that urban redevelopment and gentrification are not merely physical transformations but also temporal interventions. They disrupt established temporalities within communities and impose new temporal orders that prioritize future potentialities aligned with capitalist values. This imposition erases the existing temporal narratives of communities and individuals, especially those rooted in resistance to capitalist exploitation and marginalization. By seizing spaces and predetermining futures, these interventions deny residents the right to define their own temporalities and futures, effectively erasing their histories and potential legacies.

Others, however, have felt a hopeful sense of the future and their place in it despite some of the uncertainties and upheaval.

> INTERVIEWER: How do you feel about the redevelopment in the area?
>
> MS. K: It's nice. It's a big change to the neighborhood, which, change is good. It looks really nice and it's different.
>
> INTERVIEWER: Do you think that it should have been done differently at all?
>
> MS. K: No.
>
> INTERVIEWER: Do you think that things could have been done differently?
>
> MS. K: No, I think it's nice.

Ms. K envisioned a future for the neighborhood that had a layered temporality, inclusive of both the old way and the "new way":

INTERVIEWER: What do you see as the future of Sharswood?
MS. K: It's going to expand. It's going to get bigger. After a while, it's going reach farther down. More houses are going to go down.
INTERVIEWER: What do you think Ridge Avenue will look like in twenty years?
MS. K: Rebuilt with stores. That's what I'm hoping. Busy again, because it used to be so nice coming up here to the fish market, Ridge-o's, Carmens. It was really nice. We used to have a restaurant here called Dirty Mike's and we'd get cheap burgers and roast pork sandwiches.

Youth and younger people from Sharswood—and particularly those who lived in the since-demolished housing towers of the Blumberg Apartments, have other ways of expressing their memories and their sustained temporal connections to the neighborhood. The #ForeverBlumberg hashtag on Instagram will pull up about 1,500 photos and videos of life and times prior to redevelopment. It continues the connections and memorializes the communities of the housing towers thereafter. Dozens of the images are of young people in shirts of varied colors with "Forever Blumberg" in white graffiti lettering, and of a movement coordinated to show up in these shirts to witness the demolition of the towers. The phrase "Forever Blumberg" is itself an obvious expression of temporality—a simple statement that works as a visceral act of resistance against the severance of the social bonds of a shared time and space that the demolition of the towers would enact.

For one former resident, the impact of displacement on youth is particularly pronounced:

Ms. C: And it's really sad that this young beautiful generation of people ain't got nothing to look up to, period. Their homes, and everything they knew. For example, something so wonderful. Projects didn't get torn down in the day. They outlived us. Buildings, buildings didn't do it, so why are you letting somebody tear down? That's all the kids got. That's all they had. And it got torn down. All they knew, basically the one, the ones that was made in that building, all the generations of kids that all they

> knew was these projects got torn down, and they don't know what happened. All they knew is that ever since them buildings came down, they don't know why. But things have been bad since then. They've lost family members. I've lost family members. It's really sad. (Crying) The kids are not happy anymore. And that takes the fun out of things.[74]

Designing Time in Space: Black SpaceTimeMatters in Housing Policy

> *I think that if everyone had safe, secure, and consistent access to housing, people would be able to put down roots and a place. I think it would combat against some of that disinvestment . . . Safe, accessible housing . . . looks like people having more time and energy to put into their community, and to feel some sort of ownership over where they live, to feel some ownership over, . . . what happens in their community.* —**Focus group participant, Philadelphia Renters Report**

As the experiences of the residents and former residents of Sharswood demonstrate, the tricky web of housing, redevelopment, displacement, time, and the temporal domain of the future is impossible to fully untangle. Time, in this context, encompasses the notification period for relocation, decades of investment absence, the rapid pace and length of redevelopment efforts, and the purported temporary nature of relocation. Jeremy Rifkin underscores the disparity in power dynamics, noting that those in control possess the tools and knowledge necessary to forecast and manipulate the temporal dimension of the future, be it through legal or financial means, thus fostering a dependency on state mechanisms. Such tools encompass a range of methodologies and technologies—such as predictive analytics, urban planning tools, financial instruments, and legal frameworks. These tools grant policymakers, developers, and other stakeholders the capability to plan, execute, and control the pace and direction of urban transformation projects, often sidelining the temporalities and aspirations of the affected communities.

Building on this, anthropologist Kevin Birth argues that "the dominant temporality associated with time as linear and consisting of uniform containers is disruptive to alternatives, including temporalities of hope."[75] Instead, the future becomes a monolithic structure, rigid in its form and closed to negotiation or reimagination. This is especially true in the context of housing and community displacement.

The perpetuation of intergenerational poverty within marginalized communities is not solely a result of economic inequality, but also stems from the unequal distribution of temporal resources. This phenomenon manifests profoundly in the context of displacement and gentrification, where the allocation of time resources—or lack thereof—exacerbates socioeconomic challenges across generations. A comprehensive strategy that interweaves spatial and temporal considerations is essential to mitigate these disparities and safeguard affordable housing. Key to this approach is prioritizing time-sensitive strategies that address the often-inadequate notice periods given to tenants at risk of eviction and displacement. Additionally, it entails tackling the protracted timelines that hinder the retention of affordable housing and complicate the preservation process. By adopting alternative temporal frameworks like Black SpaceTimeMatters, housing policy can begin to dismantle the oppressive narratives that have limited and predetermined the futures of Black people and communities. This shift allows for the conceptualization of futures expansive in possibility and powered by hope, resilience, and joy. It illuminates futures previously considered inaccessible, since time itself plays "a role as one of the channels through which defiance towards established order can be manifested."[76] Black SpaceTime tools empower Black communities to strive for futures that they have been systematically discouraged from seeking.

This approach also nurtures housing policies that prioritize community vision, cultural preservation, and the equitable allocation of resources in any neighborhood investment efforts. In this context, housing evolves from mere shelter to a fulcrum for cultural affirmation and community connection.

The lens of Black Quantum Futurism and the incorporation of what I call Black SpaceTimeMatters methodology into my policy work as a housing advocate has been invaluable. I have found ways to operationalize a robust set of principles based on those frameworks for confronting systemic inequalities that span time—historical, present, and future. Among these guiding principles are Temporal Abundance vs. Temporal Scarcity; Inclusive and Expansive Future Visioning; Past, Present, and Futures Are Malleable Constructs; and Reparative Temporal Justice. These guiding principles offer a foundation for confronting and dismantling systemic inequities, providing a pathway toward a more equitable and hopeful future for marginalized communities.

Temporal Abundance in Our Housing Futures

In Western culture, we often say that time is scarce, running low, or running out. When we rely on Black temporal frameworks, time can in fact be created, reclaimed, resourced, and redeemed. To truly embrace this experience of time, we must shift from a mindset of temporal scarcity to one of temporal abundance. This involves challenging the dominant narrative, that resources related to time are limited and finite, and instead insisting on prioritizing equitable and abundant temporal realities for all, and especially those historically marginalized.

In practical terms, embodying temporal abundance includes innovating ways to collaborate with housing-insecure people and historically marginalized communities to prevent displacement and evictions. It necessitates centering their experiences and needs in the process of envisioning and creating more equitable space-times. Including community voices has become increasingly common in housing and community development projects; however, genuine integration of these voices requires providing these communities with ample space and time to strategize creatively and expansively about their futures. This means our strategies for tackling housing insecurity must evolve beyond immediate, crisis-driven responses to embrace long-term, community-focused and community-driven planning that allocates adequate time, space, and resources to plan collectively for their own future space-times.

Key to the Community Futures Lab was our development of oral futures interview questions, some of which are included throughout in excerpted interviews. The oral futures questions were a technique for asking community members to speak futures into existence by envisioning and recalling what was, would, could, or will be., Through these interviews, we projected these collected visions into a tangible reality and preserved them as a permanent record. As displaced Africans in America, our storywave does not carry as far as it did on our ancestral lands. Because of the ways our communities are attacked and eroded, our personal and communal stories typically travel within smaller borders and closed in territories, often tied to the memory of a building or land. If we are pushed off that land, our stories disperse. These oral histories and oral futures are not merely archival efforts but acts of reclaiming Afrodiasporic oral traditions and liberation, restoring the continuity of Afrodiasporic narratives and ensuring they resonate beyond their immediate geographic and temporal confines. By centering these practices, we not only reclaim our time but also reconstruct our stories and, by extension, our futures, in ways that are liberatory, reparative, and abundantly generative.

The oral futurists were self-selected, choosing on their own to walk into Community Futures Lab and be interviewed for the project, after we had done significant outreach and advertisement about the project in the area. We ensured that CFL was always open during the daytime as well as some evening and weekend hours. This approach ensured a diverse range of perspectives were captured to illustrate the richness of temporal experiences within Black communities. We recognized that residents might have little time to spare to contribute to the project given other obligations on their time. One resident explained her desire to participate, regardless:

> Ms. T: I have other things, I have other things on my mind like my doctor's appointment and see they doing a survey on me. And plus, I got a machine at home, so I don't think about that, I be thinking about this machine that I gotta get home to. And these kids. But I like the community, I'd like to come closer to a community.[77]

The oral futures questions were crafted to explore deep themes relating to housing, neighborhood history, future aspirations for the neighborhood and its residents, and broader concepts of time and space. These questions explored the depths of personal and collective meanings of community and the connections to and perceptions of one's neighborhood. Inquiries about the respondent's relationship within Sharswood and more broadly in North Philadelphia sought to uncover historical and cultural shifts, including the impact of significant events such as the Columbia Ave riots and the use of eminent domain. The topic of displacement probed the continuity of community ties amid changes, while questions on housing focused on personal living conditions, comfort, and choices within the housing landscape. Future-oriented questions aimed to gather visions for the neighborhood's trajectory, juxtaposing individual aspirations with communal development. Additionally, the exploration of time, temporality, and space sought to understand the nuanced perspectives on these concepts within the community, highlighting the importance of temporal awareness and its variance across different social contexts. Specifically, the questions include:

What does the word community mean to you?

What does the word home mean to you? What does it look like to you?

How long have you lived/worked in Sharswood?

Was it always called Sharswood?

What was it like when you grew up here/first moved here?

Do you remember the Columbia Ave riots?

How do you feel about the eminent domain and what has happened in the community?

Are you aware of opportunities to be a part of the development of your community?

How has the culture of your neighborhood changed, if at all?

Describe the home you currently live in.

Do you feel comfortable in your home? Why or why not.

Do you think you, or other people in your community, have a choice in where you live? Why or why not?

What are some things currently present in your community that you would hope to continue to see in the future?

Growing up, how did you envision your future self? Is it different from the person you are now?

How do you envision (your respective community) in ten years?

> What do you see as the future of Sharswood?
> How important is time to you? Your family? Your community?
> For you, what does it mean to be "on time"? Is this different from how your family would define it? Your community?
> When you hear the word "past" what comes up for you?

Some interviews happened informally during spontaneous conversations or while at workshops, which encouraged the sharing of experiences and narratives through artmaking to honor the multiple ways that people store and encode memories:

> Ms. T: I write them down. I like to write them down. I like to write. I have a pretty handwriting when I get down to write. Like today, I'm talking to you, I put it in my book what I did today, and you know I got a book about this big. And I write one page at least a day. And I go through the whole book.

Instead of being passive recipients of information, confined by narratives and languages of despair, powerlessness, and crisis, the oral history/oral futures project provided the space-time for community members to participate in critical dialogue about housing, displacement, gentrification, and related issues through a Black speculative lens. In this AfroFuturist container, people who participated in the oral futures interviews could visualize futures of their own making while preserving the historical narratives of the North Philly community.

A diverse array of mapping exercises, such as quantum event maps, housing journey maps, sonic maps, and communal memory maps, serves to untangle the conventional bindings of time and space through art. The choice to employ artmaking in our project was strategic and multifaceted. Artmaking serves as a powerful medium for storing and encoding memory, offering a tangible form for abstract concepts and emotions that are often challenging to articulate through conventional language. By engaging community members in artistic practices, we facilitated a process where individuals could externalize their internal experiences, memories, and hopes for the future. This process not only preserved these narratives but also transformed them into shared artifacts that could inspire collective reflection and dialogue.

Moreover, artmaking in the context of the CFL acted as a catalyst for community engagement. The act of creating art collectively provided a platform for participants to explore and express their individual and shared identities, fostering a sense of agency and belonging. This approach resonated within the community, eliciting enthusiastic participation and feedback. Participants found that artmaking allowed them to visualize and articulate their aspirations for the future in a manner that was both personal and communal, bridging the gap between individual experiences and collective action.

The CFL's integration of art into our framework was also a deliberate effort to challenge and expand the conventional boundaries of legal and policy advocacy. By incorporating artistic expressions into our campaigns for eviction protections and anti-displacement policies, we underscored the importance of narrative, culture, and creativity in shaping public discourse and policy. This innovative blend of art and advocacy highlighted the interconnectedness of legal rights, cultural identity, and community memory, paving the way for more holistic approaches to social justice.

The quantum event map, for example, liberates event memory from the constraints of specific calendar dates or clock times, recasting time into a fluid dimension shaped by remembered experience rather than a linear, unyielding force. In doing so, it invokes quantum theory's notion that the act of observation itself alters the observed reality, influenced by the observer's interaction with their environment. Quantum event maps venture into the construction of communal and personal time around past, present, and future events, acknowledging diverse temporal rhythms and textures.

Drawing upon quantum physics, the map intricate weaves the observer effect into the mapping. Just as the observation of a particle changes its state, the quantum event map posits that the mapmaker, as an active observer of their own memories and experiences, possesses the unique ability to shape their temporal realities. This intertwining of observation and memory creation aligns with the quantum concept of superposition, where events, akin to particles, exist in multiple states or times until observed, thereby collapsing into a single state or temporal moment as remembered by the individual.

The quantum event map also draws inspiration from African and

Asian diasporic cultural traditions of space and time. It focuses on capturing the micro (or quantum) events that tend to occur in temporal unison, or at the same time, allowing mapmakers to sculpt future moments/events or revisit past moments/events through the collective or individual lens. This reflects the quantum entanglement principle, where entities are interconnected regardless of distance, suggesting that events, too, can be entangled in a web of communal and personal narratives that transcend traditional temporal boundaries.

This methodological shift in mapping eschews the traditional anchoring of event memory to fixed points in time, allowing for a dynamic exploration of past, present, and future. It embeds time and date within the fabric of memory itself, allowing for an interweaving where the temporal context becomes an integral, manipulable aspect of future recollections. This enables the mapmaker to "forecast or backcast" events with a degree of autonomy over the temporal context. This reimagining of time underscores the transformative power of observation—time becomes a canvas upon which memories are painted, not a rigid frame or predetermined boundary that constrains them.

By positioning the quantum event mapmaker as the orchestrator of synchronicity rather than a passive observer dictated by chronological constraints, this approach revolutionizes our understanding of temporal interaction. In our workshops, we have groups create communal quantum event maps that allow them to struggle through some of the ways in which a community constructs communal time around a past, future, or present event, composed of diverse and intersecting temporal rhythms (personal and communal) and other event textures and features, such as the moods and emotions present, or the features of the place or location where it is happening. These narratives enable groups to conceptualize events such as remembering a future where housing justice is realized or reflecting on and finding new memories in historical moments like the Columbia Avenue race riots. Such activities have been instrumental in unraveling the phenomenon of space-time compression observed in the redevelopment of the Sharswood neighborhood, shedding light on how communities navigate the intricacies of time and memory.

We also encourage people to make personal quantum event maps, which help mapmakers revisit personal pasts to encounter new features of a past event, to plan and create personal futures, or to explore and recontextualize personal "nows." Participants mapped the "micro" features (such as the sounds they experienced, the colors present, the smells and somatic feelings) of events such as a bike accident they previously had, or their experiences at an Occupy protest. This practice not only facilitates a greater understanding of the multifaceted nature of time and space but also fosters a unique space for individuals and communities to actively shape their temporal narratives. By reimagining their roles from passive participants in time to active creators of their temporal landscapes, mapmakers embark on a journey of self-discovery and communal reflection that challenges conventional notions of memory, history, and future aspirations. Housing journey maps serve as a profound reflection of participants' lived experiences, inviting a deep introspection into how their housing history shapes their identity, conception of home, and connection to community. Drawing from the principles of quantum physics, these maps encourage participants to view their housing journey not as a linear progression but as a complex, intertwined series of quantum states—each residence representing a distinct possibility or reality that has contributed to their sense of self and belonging.

Participants are prompted to chart the quantum superpositions of their past, present, and potential future homes, exploring the multilayered dimensions of their housing experiences. This exercise asks: What narrative does your housing journey weave about you, your identity, your foundational concept of home, and your relationship with the broader community? It challenges participants to consider how their stories resonate with or diverge from those of individuals from marginalized backgrounds, those who have faced displacement, or have been evicted, highlighting the interconnected yet diverse spectrums of housing experiences.

By employing a quantum perspective in our housing journeys, we acknowledge that just as particles exist in multiple states until observed, our housing journeys encompass various potential paths and outcomes influenced by observation and interaction. This approach allows for a richer understanding of how systemic forces, personal choices, and chance encounters converge to shape our housing narratives. It underscores the significance of considering the broader sociopolitical context, recognizing how disparities in power, access, and opportunity can dramatically alter the trajectory of one's housing journey.

Another recurring workshop, "Housing Futures," facilitated visioning sessions with neighborhood residents. These workshops also provided information on housing rights, as well as the opportunity for residents to get directly involved in housing policy campaigns that were currently happening in the city. This included the Assessment of Fair Housing planning process that the city and PHA were undergoing due to a rule promulgated under the authority of the Fair Housing Act. The workshops highlighted initiatives such as the campaign for tenants' right to counsel, aimed at ensuring legal representation in housing matters, and the just-cause eviction protections campaign, designed to shield tenants from unwarranted eviction. Activities like writing, storytelling, and resource-sharing prompted participants to create a collaborative, multi-pronged action plan for shaping the future of housing justice in Philadelphia. This involved solutions for breaking intercommunal cycles of poverty and housing instability using artistic and holistic methods of healing. Through these efforts, the workshops facilitated a direct channel for community involvement in shaping housing policies, thereby fostering a shared endeavor to not only envisage but to actively construct a more equitable future in housing.

The North Philly neighborhood and Philadelphia at large actively co-designed future visions through activities such as creating vision boards, mapping community assets and resources, and asking what kinds of resources they would like to see come into the neighborhood in the future. More than theoretical exercises, these discussions focused on tangible actions that individuals could undertake to drive transformation within their communities. Through discussions after the presentations, workshop presenters collected insights from community members to inform future policy and planning for this and other distressed communities facing redevelopment efforts. This proactive approach challenges the status quo and asserts the essential role of community agency in shaping the future of housing policies and practices.

The stories shared at CFL by the surrounding community paint a vivid picture of the social time within the neighborhood, understood as a local tempo that "does not flow at one even rate, but goes at a thousand different paces, swift or slow, which bear almost no relation to the day-to-day of a chronicle or of traditional history."[78] Residents of Sharswood engage with time in the form of "a local practice rooted in daily rituals and bound up in the particularities of unique physical spaces."[79] It's a reflection of a multifaceted rhythm of life that intertwines with the daily rituals and spatial characteristics of the neighborhood.

In the context of CFL's workshops and interviews, these gatherings have been instrumental in capturing and celebrating this unique temporal experience. For instance, the monthly Brewerytown-Sharswood Civic Association meetings and the annual Unity Day serve not just as calendar events but as communal rituals that embody the neighborhood's distinct pace of life. These are not mere meetings or celebrations but are imbued with a significance that transcends the conventional understanding of time, marking moments of collective identity, memory, and aspiration.

Similarly, the Athletic Recreation Center, a steadfast pillar since 1914, opens its doors daily to over a hundred children for afterschool programs. Housing a father-and-son-run boxing gym, the center underscores the layered, durational aspect of time within the community. It stands as a testament to the enduring legacy and resilience of the neighborhood, offering a space where generational knowledge and skills are passed down and where the community's youth can envision and shape their futures. This center is more than a facility; it is a temporal landmark, encapsulating generations of communal experiences and narratives.

Understanding Sharswood and the surrounding North Philadelphia community, through its affective, layered, durational, and contextual temporalities, challenges the exclusionary, government-sponsored narratives that paint residents as complicit in their own poverty and contests the idea that residents require fast-tracking along a predetermined timeline toward progress. It is within these spaces and through these distinctive practices that the true, dynamic essence of social time in Sharswood is celebrated, fostering a profound reclamation of time that is interwoven with the community's cultural fabric and collective memory. The remembrance of shared histories and the continuity of communal legacies are pivotal, particularly when faced with the widespread phenomena of displacement and disruption. These acts, often disproportionate in their impact on Black individuals and communities, not only sever ties to physical locales but disrupt the temporal continuity that nurtures collective memory and identity.

This nuanced comprehension of temporal dynamics extends into the realm of housing advocacy and preservation, linking closely with earlier discussions on place-based connections and the memory of Black communities. By leveraging legal apparatuses such as ninety-nine-year "ground leases," housing sites may be anchored in affordability across decades. Through this particular legal construct, a temporal continuum is forged, linking the community's rich experiences of time with the vigorous efforts to maintain the neighborhood's cultural and architectural integrity. Such legal frameworks do not merely act as a defense mechanism against the encroachment of market forces but as a proactive measure to embed the community's temporalities into the urban landscape itself. This approach honors and capitalizes on the unique temporal dynamics of the community, employing them as a foundation for robust legal protections and advocacy efforts. It demonstrates a comprehensive approach to urban renewal that acknowledges and respects the intrinsic temporal dimensions of community life, utilizing them as a pivotal axis around which equitable and sustainable urban development can revolve. This methodology serves to both protect the physical space but also preserves the intangible heritage and collective memory of the community, ensuring that the essence of the neighborhood is honored and sustained through successive generations, thus counteracting the disruptive forces of displacement and gentrification. Bridging the gap between the preservation of affordable housing and the broader narrative of community resilience requires a shift in perspective toward embracing non-deterministic futures. Emphasizing non-deterministic futures—visions of tomorrow unshackled from the prevailing narratives of wealth accumulation and instead rooted in the principles of community health, wellness, and sustainability—ushers in a transformative paradigm for low-income and housing-insecure populations.

Non-deterministic futures, a concept that diverges from traditional deterministic outlooks, refer to the idea that the future is not a fixed, inevitable outcome determined by past and present actions. Instead, it is understood as a realm of vast possibility shaped by the choices we make and the actions we undertake in the present.

This approach diverges markedly from traditional models, which typically position housing as a linchpin of financial success based on a wealth-building narrative that often overlooks the essential dimensions of holistic well-being for Black communities. Non-deterministic futures reject the notion that the trajectory of a community must follow a singular preordained path dictated by external economic forces or governmental agendas. They embrace a multiplicity of possible outcomes, each shaped by collective action and grounded in a deep understanding of community needs and desires. This reframing allows us to envision anti-displacement and preservation efforts not just as acts of resistance but as opportunities to actively construct a future in which the cultural, social, and economic fabric of Black communities is not only preserved but thrives. This approach offers a stark contrast to the linear, cause-and-effect model that often dominates policymaking and economic planning.

The CFL storefront, workshops, and interviews fostered a closer understanding of the community of Sharswood and the surrounding North Philadelphia neighborhood. This gave us concrete goals, rooted in our understanding of community needs and desires to use in our housing advocacy roles to dismantle the exclusionary, government-sponsored narratives that seek to paint residents as architects of their own misfortune and complicit in the disinvestment of their own neighborhoods and residential buildings, thus deserving of the gentrification processes that will wipe out the past and move the community into the future that does not include them.

Far from being passive victims of disinvestment or mere bystanders in the face of gentrification, CFL placed community members at the forefront of envisioning futures where they are not only included but central. We invited them to imagine possibilities beyond the constraints of the current system—a system designed to exclude them from the narrative of progress. This shift in perspective is not merely academic; it has profound political and revolutionary implications.

It represents a direct challenge to the forces of gentrification and displacement, asserting the right of Black communities to define their own futures and to claim a stake in the ongoing story of urban development.

The greater aim, then, is nothing short of a reshaping of urban renewal—one that places Black temporalities, histories, and visions at its heart. It is about crafting futures that are not predetermined by the whims of capital or the legacy of systemic racism but are instead co-created by the very communities that have been most impacted by these forces. This is a future where the preservation of affordable housing is seen not just as a policy issue but as a cornerstone of a broader struggle for temporal and spatial justice, cultural preservation, and self-determination. By recognizing and supporting communal temporalities, we open up a space-time for radical hope and transformative action, pointing toward a future where the full humanity and potential of Black communities are recognized, celebrated, and protected.

Revisiting the Past, Reshaping the Future

With Black SpaceTimeMatters in housing policy, the past is recognized as neither dead nor immutable—it is a narrative still being written. Context can be added to the events of the past that can have an impact on the present and future. Decision makers, like landlords and judges, are positioned to determine the relationship of the past to the present and the present to the future for a tenant. Eviction records are snapshots in time that are often manipulated to prevent individuals from accessing housing far into the future. These records remain readily available to the public and to tenant-screening companies for indeterminate lengths of time, even when the eviction filing never led to an eviction or was resolved in a tenant's favor.

Landlords frequently refuse to rent to tenants who have even one eviction filing on their record, regardless of the outcome of the case or extenuating context of a prospective tenant's past rental circumstances, including temporary financial hardships, such as job loss or medical emergencies, which do not predict future rental behavior. A tenant's efforts to rectify past issues, such as repayment of overdue rent or positive rental history prior to or after an eviction filing, can help to demonstrate stable tenancy, offering a more holistic view of a tenant's potential. Tenant-screening companies draw on opaque algorithms that offer renters little opportunity to challenge inaccurate or misleading scores that could be derived from incomplete or out-of-context data. And even if the record is accurate, a payment that is late by a few days becomes a record that lasts years into the future. The reliance on eviction records without context, where past events are seen as deterministic of future outcomes, functions as a time penalty. This penalty not only locks tenants out of stable housing opportunities but reflects and reinforces a system of values that disproportionately penalizes the already marginalized, effectively prioritizing punitive measures over rehabilitation or understanding. It highlights a systemic failure to acknowledge the complexity of tenants' lives and the myriad reasons behind housing instability, instead choosing to perpetuate dangerous time loops of generational instability, exclusion, and inequity that are locked within a linear progress narrative.

Eviction records are rarely a comprehensive reflection of an individual's life. They might reflect temporary hardships—illness, job loss, family crises—now passed. Tenants who exercise their legal right to withhold rent for repairs are also often punished with an eviction filing. This stalemate is ended via a mechanism of power made available to landlords, with the result being a permanent blemish on a tenant's record regardless of the filing's outcome. The long, temporal hold that eviction records carry over individuals more often than not traps these renters in subpar housing and limits their job mobility.

Renters facing eviction records encounter entrenched cycles of poverty, exacerbated by policies from courts and legislative bodies that prioritize transparency. This emphasis makes eviction records not only easy to acquire but also difficult, if not impossible, to get rid of. In Pennsylvania, the legal framework acknowledges multiple legal bases for public access to court proceedings. The US and Pennsylvania constitutions, alongside common law, grant a presumptive right to access judicial records and proceedings.[80] This "principle of openness" underpins the foundational belief in the transparency of both judicial records and court activities.[81] Moreover, common law upholds the public's right to inspect public documents. The intention behind granting access to court records is to enable public scrutiny of judicial operations, ensuring decisions align with legal standards.

This transparency comes at a significant cost to individuals with eviction filings. These records are often utilized punitively, allowing landlords to legally refuse housing based on past filings, irrespective of the eviction's legitimacy or the landlord's previous neglect. This practice serves as a form of extrajudicial punishment, tarnishing reputations and effectively blacklisting individuals based on minimal evidence. The result is a punitive cycle that sidelines fairness, trapping individuals in a state of perpetual vulnerability and hindering their ability to secure stable housing.

In confronting the punitive use of eviction records, my approach as both an advocate and an AfroFuturist artist has been multifaceted, leveraging my dual roles as a housing lawyer at Community Legal Services and as a creator vitally engaged in AfroFuturist expression. This dual capacity enabled me to legally challenge and creatively reimagine the narratives surrounding housing insecurity and eviction's impact on individuals and communities. In October 2020, Philadelphia City Council successfully passed Resolution #200531, introduced by Councilmember Isaiah Thomas, on the matter of eviction-record sealing. The resolution, cowritten by community organizers and housing advocates, primarily from the Philadelphia Rent Control Coalition and Black and Brown Workers Cooperative who had been directly impacted by eviction records from several years before based on an unexpected and illegal mass eviction by a gentrifying developer in 2017, called on the courts and government to create mechanisms for sealing eviction records"[82] Having had an opportunity to represent several of the mass evicted organizers and other tenants in housing discrimination lawsuits, I rejoined their efforts as a legal advocate in support of their fight for eviction-record sealing protections.

One of my first collaborative projects was with Black and Brown Workers Cooperative, coauthoring the policy brief, "Breaking the Record: Dismantling the Barriers Eviction Records Place on Housing Opportunities."[83] This policy brief addresses the significant challenges faced by tenants with eviction records in securing housing, highlighting the disproportionate impact on Black women and their families in

Philadelphia, a reflection of a national issue. It outlines how eviction filings, predominantly in communities of color, exacerbate existing inequalities, further strained by the COVID-19 pandemic's severe effects on these communities, including higher infection and mortality rates, income loss, and housing instability.

The brief advocates for legislative and administrative reforms designed to dismantle systemic obstacles to housing access and alleviate the enduring repercussions of eviction records. Recommendations include sealing eviction records, limiting their consideration in rental decisions, and broadening tenant agreement opportunities, thereby addressing the sustained damage eviction records inflict on a tenant's housing access capabilities—even in instances where the tenant prevails in court or reaches a settlement to remain in their residence. Moreover, it examines the systemic ramifications of eviction records as a matter of racial and gender equity. Authored in partnership with tenant organizers directly affected by eviction records, the report has garnered attention in numerous local and national outlets and spurred the formation of an eviction records sealing coalition that convenes monthly since January 2020.

The Eviction Sealing Coalition harnesses the collective expertise and experiences of over forty-five stakeholders—spanning impacted tenants, organizers, legal and social service providers, social justice advocates, city officials, and landlords—to devise strategies addressing the profound, long-lasting effects of evictions and eviction records on individuals and families. Comprehensive and life-affirming housing policies, including the adoption of eviction sealing and tenant-screening legislation in Philadelphia, aim to balance power dynamics between landlords and tenants.

The coalition places at its core the leadership of individuals directly impacted by eviction histories, with an emphasis on combating racism, gender-based violence, ableism, economic oppression, and on in fostering life-affirming alternatives. Recognizing eviction and its historical impact as one facet of broader housing injustices, the coalition commits to transformative, systemic change through collective action. Key goals include engaging with those who have firsthand experience with eviction, showcasing diverse stories through media and professional storytelling, and advocating for fair, accessible, swift, enforceable, and equitable processes for sealing or expunging eviction records, alongside regulating their usage. During this period, I secured funding as a former fellow of the Atlantic Fellows for Racial Equity to, which supported coalition-building efforts, including funding, story bank training, and providing stipends to for tenant participants in the coalition to enable their participation, attendance at meetings, and engagement despite limited time resources. Our goals also extended to reforming and eventually abolishing the systems responsible for recording and disseminating eviction information, such as court-reporting, tenant-screening, and credit-reporting agencies.

Once the coalition was established and after assessing the political landscape for the most impactful interventions in the shortest time span, we immediately began designing a citywide policy that could work to immediately mitigate the harms of eviction records. Navigating political time within COVID-19 pandemic time, the coalition collaborated with Philadelphia City Councilmember Kendra Brooks to propose legislation called the Renter's Access Act, which she introduced in April 2021. Our efforts to work through political time as a coalition faced challenges, as the customary processes for passing legislation—requiring extensive in-person interactions and hearings—were disrupted due to COVID-19 work-from-home mandates in the city, necessitating the adoption of technologies that altered traditional in-person relationship building critical to a campaign.

However, the campaign also strategically utilized this political time, capitalizing on the emergency tenant protection measures enacted since the pandemic's onset, including state and local eviction moratoriums, emergency rental assistance, and eviction diversion programs. This momentum allowed for the bill to progress through the political process at an accelerated rate, surpassing the typical timeline. Before the pandemic, a rental housing bill in Philadelphia would, based on my decade of experience in housing policy, ordinarily take an average of eighteen months, sometimes longer, to get from inception to implementation.

The Renters Access Act (RAA) was passed by Philadelphia City Council nearly unanimously in June 2021, going into effect ninety days later on October 13, 2021, a little under nine months after our first coalition meeting, after significant public education, political education, and advocacy with city councilmembers by coalition members and others in our collective networks. Tenant testimony was uplifted at the two city council hearings between February 2021 and June 2021.

Designed to break the long temporal chain of eviction records, the RAA mandates increase transparency of the criteria used in tenant evaluations and require the assessment of each tenant's circumstances individually (instead of a blanket ban on any tenant not meeting certain criteria). The mandates provide tenants with options for disputing inaccuracies and prohibit rental policies that reject applicants solely based on their credit score or eviction record.[84] The RAA gives applicants the right to dispute inaccurate information or to seek reconsideration in the case of mitigating circumstances, while requiring landlords to give time for consideration of new information.

By addressing time concerns in the design framework of the Renters Access Act, we deliberately approached the dimensions of past, present, and future as open-ended variables rather than as fixed entities. This demanded a deep reckoning with how historical injustices have actively constructed the current temporal context. It required us to be visionary in our policymaking, setting the stage for future states of being that manifest greater equity in the housing system. Borrowing the insight of physicist and philosopher Karen Barad, we understood that "it's not that the experimenter changes a past that had already been present. Rather, the point is that the past was never simply there to begin with, and the future is not simply what will unfold; the 'past' and the 'future' are iteratively reworked and enfolded through the iterative practices of spacetimemattering."[85]

In practical terms, this meant a mandate that landlords engage in a holistic review of a rental application. It is a philosophical shift that alters our collective understanding of temporality, and that establishes a better collective approach to housing, as well as a collective sense of the unjust barriers to that right. It challenges the unreasonable standard that an eviction record restricts one's housing options indefinitely. Adding nuance to an individual's rental history as only a partial window on the fuller context of their lives, the new mandate destabilizes that history's function as a locked temporal point, a monolithic entity dictating the present.

Applying the rubric of Black SpaceTimeMatters to liberatory

housing futures renders the concept of a deterministic past as antithetical to the human need for housing. In this vision of the future, housing stability is guaranteed for everyone, encompassing access to housing that is safe and healthy, connected to social, familial, and cultural networks, and close to food, green areas, and transportation. To actualize this future, it is paramount to build frameworks that are rooted in the conviction that housing equity is not a distant dream but an immediate reality. The politics of immanence, emphasizing the presence and agency in the here and now, dovetails with this vision, compelling us to acknowledge that equitable housing is not an aspirational goal but a present necessity.

If we treat the future as if it has come to be, activists and policymakers can adopt a mindset in which housing equity is the default, enabling them to reflect on the features of the completed event of universal housing access. Unlike linear deterministic thinking, which limits the openness of future possibilities, this "future perfect thinking," as coined by researchers Lars Fuglsang and Jan Mattsson, imbues the future with a sense of substance and stability.[86] Our collective vision is no longer a future controlled by a select elite but one where stable and equitable housing is a common and universally available good.

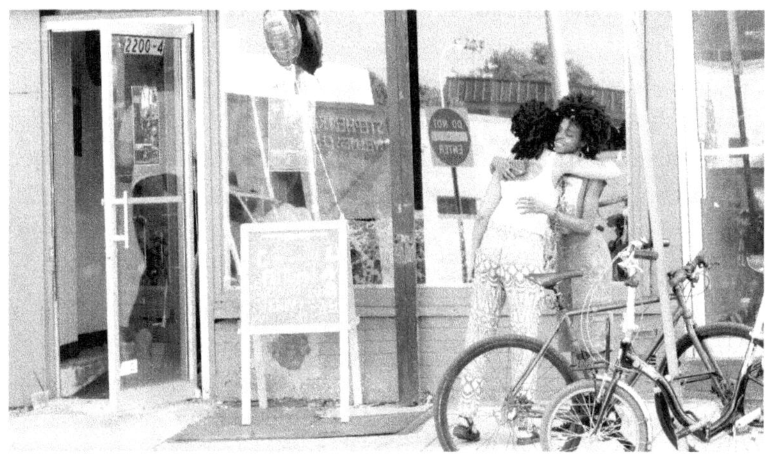

The opening of the Community Futures Lab in North Philadelphia, 2016.

However, realizing this vision necessitates a harmonious blend of imaginative foresight with pragmatic, immediate actions aimed at dismantling the entrenched systemic barriers that perpetuate housing inequities. By synchronizing visions with concrete actions, we can forge a housing landscape that truly reflects the fluid and dynamic essence of time itself, where the narratives of both past and future are actively shaped and reshaped. This iterative process of envisioning and action ensures that the pursuit of equitable housing transcends mere theoretical speculation, grounding it firmly in the realm of tangible and immediate outcomes. Through such a holistic approach, we acknowledge the interlinking of temporal resources and spatial justice, emphasizing that the challenges of displacement and gentrification transcend the present moment. They are inheritances with echoes that ripple through generations, impacting successive epochs and communities.

Repairing Black SpaceTime Injustices in Systemic Time: Directions for the Futures

Time and space are not neutral entities; they are entangled with power dynamics and vehicles through which social inequalities can either be perpetuated or dismantled. Addressing spatialized racism necessitates a commitment to reparative frameworks that integrate reparative temporal justice with spatial justice.

Reparative spatial justice, building upon Edward Soja's work, incorporates a race-class analysis and AfroFuturist visioning. This approach extends beyond equitable spatial distribution to tackle foundational issues of land dispossession and environmental degradation under racial capitalism, imagining spaces and times that fortify communities and foster reparative economies. This holistic doctrine intertwines the spatial with the temporal, probing the "why" behind historical injustices and envisioning the "when" and "how" of just futures. It seeks not only to redistribute tangible assets but also to promote healing, growth, and well-being. Afrofuturism here plays a crucial role, offering speculative tools to envision spaces that are sustainable and free from racial and class oppressions, past and present.

Today, the legacies of segregation, redlining, racially restrictive covenants, and exclusionary zoning persist across the American landscape, while more recent government-sanctioned urban renewal and displacement practices further compounded these racial, spatial, and temporal inequalities. The repercussions of more 150 years of racist policies mean that Black people are often trapped in neighborhoods scarred by poverty, limited access to education and healthy food options, and unemployment to this day. This pattern extends beyond housing alone, as discriminatory zoning, environmental racism, and historic disinvestment have led to a glaring disparity in neighborhood exposure to environmental hazards. Black communities are disproportionately situated near polluting industries and toxic waste sites, exposing residents to hazardous pollutants that have severe health implications, especially for children.

The task at hand is to repair injuries of both space and time for Black communities that have been systematically denied land, housing, and the autonomy to shape their own futures. Doing so requires a multifaceted policy approach aimed at dismantling discriminatory systems, rectifying historical injustices, and fostering equitable access to housing, land, and healthy environments. These approaches recognize the interconnectedness and intra-activity of time and space, necessitating specific yet interwoven strategies, given that spatial considerations are inextricably linked with temporal dynamics. This integrated approach advocates for a reimagining of not only the physical but also the temporal aspects of our socio-spatial fabric, aiming for holistic healing, growth, and well-being.

This perspective provides a conceptual scaffold for a radical rethinking of housing law and land justice, one that is attuned not just to the dimensions of race, class, and gender, but also to the interplays of space and time among them. Freed from the constraints of linear temporality, housing rights and reparative justice can initiate perpetual claims to land sovereignty and housing justice among marginalized communities, offering a blueprint for reimagining both past and future realities.

Charles W. Mills highlighted the importance of "chronopolitical contestation" to acknowledge the enduring impact of past injustices on present realities.[87] This notion refers to the critical engagement with and contestation of dominant temporal narratives and structures that have historically marginalized certain groups, particularly Black communities. This concept underscores the significance of time, history, and memory in the sociopolitical landscape, recognizing that the legacies of past injustices persistently influence present conditions and future possibilities.

The temporal narratives of Black communities emphasize the importance of community, intergenerational connections, and collective memory in shaping not only the present but also the possibilities for the future. Ultimately, by centering Black temporalities, it becomes possible to envision a future where marginalized communities can reclaim their temporal sovereignty, experience temporal abundance, and actively shape the trajectory of their lives in a manner that honors their histories, cultures, and aspirations. We can create futures where Black people are housed, healthy, joyful, and thriving:

> INTERVIEWER: What do you see for the future, for this community, or for North Philly, or for the world?
> MS. C: I see whatever we work hard to do. Speak what we doing into existence. Do what we know that we worked hard at. And do what we were taught. Be mothers. And don't give up on your dreams, and what you set out on. Me, you. Don't give up on that. We going to add new walls to this jawn.[88]

CHAPTER 6

Waiting, Wading, Weighting Time

Waiting Time: Watching the Master Clock for Liberation

wait (n.): early 13c., "a watcher, onlooker," from Old North French wait (Old French gait, "look-out, watch, sentry"), from Old North French waitier (Old French gaitier; see wait (v.)). Compare Old High German wahta, German Wacht "a watchman." From late 14c., as "an ambush, a trap" (as in lie in wait). From 1855, as "time occupied in waiting;" 1873, as "an act of waiting." From the sense, "civic employee responsible for signaling the hour or an alarm by sounding on a trumpet, etc." —**Online Etymology Dictionary**

Nobody didn't tell 'em, but they heard. —**Zora Neale Hurston, *Dust Tracks on a Road***

For still the vision awaits its appointed time;
it hastens to the end—it will not lie.
If it seems slow, wait for it;
it will surely come; it will not delay.
—**Habakkuk 2:3, *The Holy Bible***

But de good Lawd gibs us eyes t' see t'ings dey doan see, an' he comes t' me, a poor brack slave woman, an' tells me be patient, 'cause dar's no wite nor brack in hebben. An' de time's comin' when he'll make his brack chilluns free in dis yere worl', an gib 'em larnin', an' good homes, an' good times. Ah! honey, Iknows, I knows!" **—Aunt Aggy, an enslaved African woman, quoted in Mary Livermore, *The Story of My Life or, The Sunshine and Shadow of Seventy Years***

The stereotype of "Colored People's Time" makes waiting on Black people to arrive the butt of the joke. However, recorded history reveals that the experience of waiting, often involuntarily imposed, is a significant form of temporal oppression, as much sewn into the Black experience in America as time is long in doctor's waiting rooms. This enforced "waiting time" in the Black experience is more than just delayed arrivals or slow service; it represents a psychological and emotional battleground where hope, anticipation, and despair intermingle. It underscores how control over time has been, and continues to be, a powerful tool of subjugation and resistance. "Waiting time" is not just a matter of minutes or hours but spans years, generations, and centuries. Scholar Saidiya Hartman, in her seminal work *Scenes of Subjection*, examines the ongoing afterlives of slavery and the "incompleteness of freedom," articulating how the specters of past injustices continue to haunt the present. How past suffering bleeds into contemporary Black life can be recognized as a form of enforced waiting, where the future is perpetually delayed as a result of the unresolved legacies of the past. This perspective can help us understanding "waiting time" not just as physical delays but as an enduring wait for justice and liberation, where time itself becomes a landscape of struggle.

Take Juneteenth, widely celebrated as Freedom Day. The day commemorates June 19, 1865, when thousands of enslaved Africans held captive on plantations, farms, and other (stolen) land in Galveston, Texas, were finally emancipated—two and a half years after the January 1, 1863, the effective date of the Emancipation Proclamation and several months after the passing of the Thirteenth Amendment, intended to abolish slavery. This delay in emancipating enslaved workers, despite the much-lauded legal proclamation, epitomizes the use of forced waiting as a means of temporal oppression on Black lives.

The Civil War, which began in 1861, was primarily sparked by the secession of several Southern states from the Union, driven by the threat to the institution of slavery posed by the election of President Abraham Lincoln, a Republican known for his anti-slavery views. By 1862, the war was intensifying with exceptionally bloody battles, yet inconclusive in yielding a decisive victory for either side. The Union needed a strategic advantage and a moral impetus to galvanize its cause and demoralize the Confederacy.

Lincoln preliminarily issued the Emancipation Proclamation on September 22, 1862, and signed it formally on December 18 of that same year. It declared that three-quarters of enslaved Africans in the Confederate states were "forever free" as of January 1, 1863, except for some 800,000 slaves across four slaveholding states (Delaware, Kentucky, Maryland, and Missouri) who could opt-in, should they declare loyalty to the Union.[1] In this context, Lincoln's Emancipation Proclamation was a calculated political and military strategy. Despite Lincoln's own personal belief that slavery was morally reprehensible, freeing most but not all of the enslaved Black population was essentially a bargaining chip, a move to preserve the Union and destabilize the economies of rebellious states in the South, which relied heavily on enslaved labor for their agricultural economy, rather than for the stated purpose of securing the freedom of the over 4 million people then in bondage across the country.[2] The demands of the Emancipation Proclamation applied to Confederate states, border states that were in rebellion, and slaveholding territory that had already been seized by the North.[3] By declaring the freedom of enslaved people in the states in rebellion, but not in the border states loyal to the Union or areas under Union control, Lincoln sought to weaken the Confederate war effort while maintaining the fragile loyalty of the border states. As a wartime measure, it was a declaration that could only be enforced through the Union's military conquest of contested terrain.

The January 1 effective date of the Emancipation Proclamation therefore did not in fact mean immediate freedom. It was rather the thirteenth constitutional amendment, passed by Congress on January 31, 1865, that legally abolished slavery and ultimately secured emancipation for all. Even then, Black people still didn't have access to full citizenship rights.[4] In the years following the Civil War, the Reconstruction era sought to rebuild the South and integrate freed slaves into American society. This period was marred by significant resistance from former Confederates, leading to the implementation of Black Codes, laws designed to restrict the freedoms of Black people and ensure their availability as a cheap labor force.

While these circumstances gave the 1862 Emancipation Proclamation "a much greater symbolic than practical effect," enslaved Black people and abolitionists still expected Lincoln to make good on his word and cautiously waited, as "the mere promise of freedom was so tantalizing that it was cause for celebration."[5] On December 31, 1862, enslaved and freed Black people and white abolitionists held Watch Night Services, in which they gathered to pray, sing and wait for the "dawning of freedom."[6] In the North, free African Americans and abolitionists gathered in churches and public halls, where such meetings were less likely to be disrupted by authorities or those opposed to their cause. These spaces were often centers of abolitionist activity, providing a relatively safe environment for the congregants. In the South, the situation was markedly different and more perilous. Enslaved Africans would secretly gather in secluded spots—fields, forests, and plantations—far from the watchful eyes of slaveholders, "while others gathered in churches and private homes for protections from their owners."[7] These meetings had to be conducted with utmost secrecy as any gathering of enslaved people was forbidden and could lead to severe punishment. Despite the danger, enslaved African Americans demonstrated resilience and hope, participating in these services to pray for their imminent liberation.[8]

All night, they watched the master('s) clock at watch meetings and watch parties waiting for the new year to arrive and with it, confirmation by newspaper, telegraph, and word of mouth that Lincoln's Proclamation had in fact been implemented.[9] One "Letter from a Democrat" in the *Chicago Tribune* on December 20, 1862 shows that the public was fully cognizant of this bureaucratic relationship of time to freedom, remarking that "the negroes are counting the days and hours when the 1st of January shall come."[10] The Emancipation Proclamation did indeed go into effect, and January 1, 1863 became the first documented public celebration of an "Emancipation Day, "Liberation Day," or "Freedom Day" in the United States. But, of course, only for some, given that freedom was not evenly distributed.

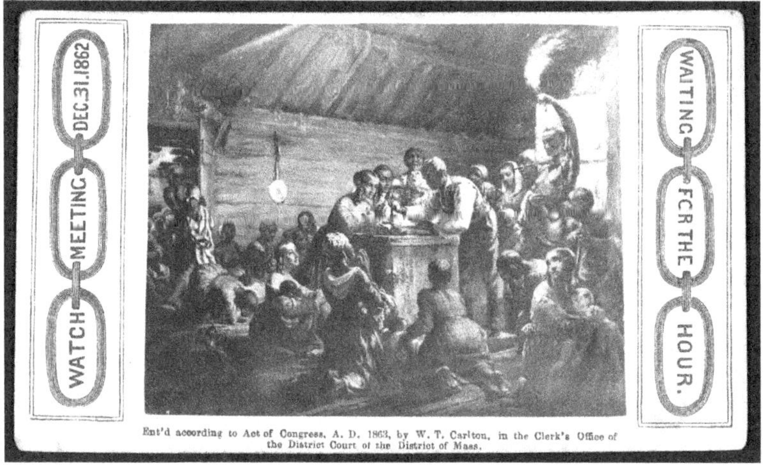

A depiction of a Watch Night celebration on December 31, 1862, awaiting the "effective date" of the Emancipation Proclamation the next morning. It takes the form of a collectible *carte de visite,* which became popular during this era and were meant to be displayed.

January 1 had long held various, often painful connotations for enslaved Black Americans. January 1, 1808 was the date the federal ban on the transatlantic slave trade became effective, and as historian Alexis Mcrossen notes, though "different slave-trade abolition commemorations took place between 1808 and 1831" anniversary commemorations waned as the domestic slave trade flourished unabated.[11] This cruel incongruity, given the systemic enforcement of Black oppression domestically, brought a heightened risk to these celebrations, as evidenced by as a vicious attack on a Black church congregation by a white mob on December 31, 1827.[12]

January 1 was also the date of the violent pre-Emancipation ritual known as Hiring Day or Heartbreak Day, when enslaved people would be torn away from family members and sold, to balance the owners' books if the season hadn't been as profitable as expected. This cruel practice starkly transformed human lives into mere entries in an accounting book, a dehumanizing commodification that tethered the very existence of enslaved people to the cold calculus of business expenses mediated by accounting calendars and fiscal years. This meant that "enslaved people spent New Year's Eve waiting, wondering if their owners were going to rent them out [or sell them off] to someone else, thus potentially splitting up their families."[13] In 1842, an enslaved man named Lewis Clarke reflected that "of all days in the year, the slaves dread New Year's Day the worst of any."[14] January 1, etched in history as both a day of liberation and sorrow, serves as a deeply ambivalent temporal marker, encapsulating the anguish of waiting for freedom to come and the enduring scars of centuries of systemic temporal oppression.

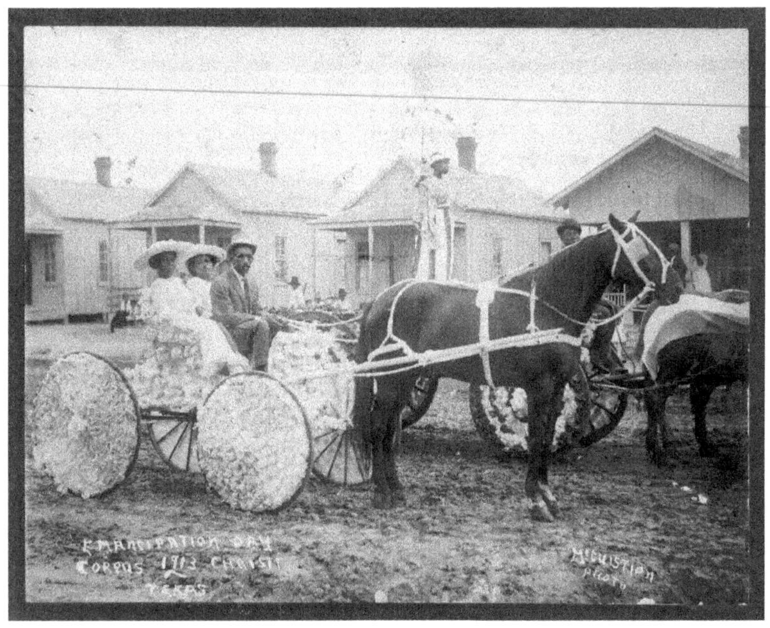

A group of revelers at an Emancipation Day commemoration on June 19, 1913, in Corpus Christi, Texas. In the early 1900s, the anniversary was marked with buggies, carts, and wagons bedecked with flowers and driven along in community celebrations.

Heartbreak Day, Watch Night, Juneteenth, and Freedom Day all mark the many ways that time has been weaponized against Black people. While the Proclamation symbolized a potent ideological shift, its immediate impact on the day-to-day lives of Black people was varied and, in many places, minimal.[15] In regions under Confederate control, enforcement was virtually non-existent, leaving the freedom status of some enslaved people ambiguous until the Union's victory in the Civil War. In some areas, particularly those already under Union control, the Proclamation did lead to immediate emancipation for many enslaved people.[16] However, even then, Masters held on to control until the very last minute. At the Whitney Plantation, there are large marble plaques with quotes by people who were enslaved there. I photographed one by Henriette Butler from the 1940s, in which she recalls the brutal way she was treated: My damn old missis was mean as hell. You see dis finger here? Dere is where she bit de day us was set free. Never will forget how she said, 'Come here, you little black bitch, you!' And grabbed my finger and almost bit it off."

This discrepancy in experiences highlights a significant aspect of temporalities; in some places, "immediate" meant instantaneous freedom, while in others, it translated into an extended period of waiting, often mired in uncertainty and hope. The divergent responses to the Emancipation Proclamation across different regions exemplified the layered and often contradictory relationship between law, time, and social change within the context of Black history, underscoring how temporal dynamics can vary significantly based on geographical, social, and individual factors.

Let us return to June 19, 1865, in Galveston, Texas, when the arrival of Union General Granger and his troops brought the overdue news that the Civil War was over and that enslaved people were *in fact* free, had been legally free for nearly three years.[17] The 1863 Emancipation Proclamation had declared all slaves in Confederate-held territory to be free, including Texas. However, enslavers had increasingly expanded their operations, beginning with the prohibition of the international slave trade in 1808. The domestic trade within the United States began to grow at that time, and Texas became a key destination in this internal market, due largely to its agricultural potential. Texas offered vast tracts of fertile land suitable for cotton, which was the most profitable cash crop of the time and heavily dependent on slave labor. The promise of high cotton profits incentivized the relocation of slaveholders to Texas, where they could acquire land and expand their operations. This agricultural expansion directly contributed to the increase in the enslaved population as slaveholders brought enslaved people with them or purchased more upon arrival to work the land. For instance, one document reveals that Wharton County, Texas, had a population that included 2,798 enslaved individuals by a certain period, illustrating the significant presence and reliance on enslaved labor in the state.[18]

Texas was admitted to the Union as a slave state in 1845. This legal status, combined with its large size and agricultural potential, made it an even more attractive destination for slaveholders from the older slave states. Later, Texas's 1861 Confederate constitution prohibiting manumission would further contribute to the expansion of slavery operations, with enforcement nearly non-existent in the state due to the low Union army presence, in part because it had been the most remote state in the Confederacy.[19] As the Civil War progressed, many slaveholders from states more directly impacted by the conflict sought to move their slaves and operations to Texas to avoid Union raids and the increasing likelihood of emancipation. This migration was a way for slaveholders to preserve their way of life and their economic investments in slavery.

For those enslaved in Texas, this period of waiting for freedom well beyond the policy date of January 1, 1863, created an information paradox where, though they were technically emancipated by the Proclamation, enslaved people were technically "un-informed" of that emancipation by the Western understanding of the term (*informed*: 1540s, "current in information"), amplifying the power dynamics of their captivity. But information still flowed, even under the crushing gravity of slavery. There were many other means by which enslaved people collected and disseminated information among themselves and with distant communities that evaded the enslavers' awareness. An excerpt from Elizabeth Ross Hite's recollections of enslavement affirmed the existence of a clandestine information network: "News? We carried news by stealin' off. Shucks, we knew ev'rything de master talked er bout. De house girl would tell us and would pass it er round."[20] Another account by a woman known as Aunt Aggy alluded to kinds of knowledge that evaded conventional knowledge. "You t'inks I'm mistaken, honey! But I knows t'ings dat de wite folks wid all dar larnin' nebber fin's out, an' nebber sarches fo' nudder."[21] These accounts reveal that being "informed" was a fraught status for enslaved people, laden with the psychological and emotional burdens of knowing freedom was possible yet out of reach and in knowing what is necessary to know to minimize harm, even before escape. Under slavery, being informed was not solely knowing facts but about using this knowledge toward gaining agency and the capacity to act.

Even with other modes of communications outlawed, such as writing, drumming, and their own languages, enslaved Black people invented other methods to share information via informal networks. Work songs and field songs on plantations frequently encoded spatial and temporal markers in their lyrics. In addition to serving as technologies to address physical isolation from each other, across different areas of large plantations or with nearby plantations, to synchronize communal work, and make time pass, these songs, cries, calls, and hollers ultimately communicate layered temporal information across multiple scales of time, in the immediate (there, in the fields) and into the future (plans for meeting or routes of escape).

Historian Lawrence W. Levine describes the "'quitting time hollers' of enslaved Black plantation workers near Edwards, Mississippi," who "sing it late in the evening. About the time they quit, they generally feel good, and they like to sing this kind of thing . . . . If one man starts, well, across maybe another field close by, why they sing that same tune back to him ...Then maybe another man may answer him another tune."[22] One such holler from the Library of Congress was recorded as

Ooooh, the sun going down,
And I won't be here long,
Oooh, the sun going down,
And I won't be here long.
Ooooh, then I be going home.
Ooooh, I can't let this dark cloud catch me here.
Ooooooh, I can't stay here long,
Oooooooooh, I be at home.[23]

Philosopher Casey O'Callaghan's presents a compelling theory that sounds are their own events, characterized by their temporal extension, duration, and localization within specific points in space-time. He suggests that sounds are fundamentally temporal phenomena, undergoing distinct patterns of change in their audible attributes over time. This perspective invites us to understand that when we engage with sounds, be it through music or speech, we are interacting with entities whose identities are shaped by their dynamic evolution through time. O'Callaghan further elucidates those environmental sounds, such as the calls of birds or the crash of falling trees, are identifiable due to their temporal behavior—each sound event begins, evolves, and concludes, embodying change as an intrinsic property.[24]Often, we interpret sounds by attributing qualitative characteristics—such as volume, distance, tone, and pitch—to the phenomena producing them. We can discern the proximity or remoteness of a sound source, gauge its loudness, and identify its pitch. Yet, we synthesize these diverse qualities into a cohesive auditory whole. This synthesis extends to our capacity to extract coherent information from complex auditory environments. In scenarios where multiple sound sources intermingle—like a television playing, the sound of a shower, and distant dog barking—our perception intertwines these elements into a singular, layered auditory scene. Despite their distinct origins, these sounds merge in our experience, demonstrating the entangled nature of auditory perception.

In *Everyday Quantum Reality*, philosopher David Grandy in observing the everyday ways that quantum physics shows up in reality beyond the purely particle level of reality, proposes that music is like quantum physics, and it "folds past and present into the immediacy of the present moment" and that "we do not call up or invoke past and future—they are there already, integral to the [musical] experience."[25] Consider, for instance, a cookout taking place down the street, playing the Black cookout favorite "The Electric Slide" on full blast. The sound of the song remains cohesive, identifiable, comprehensible as "The Electric Slide." Distance doesn't dilute the informational content of the song, that is, the wavelength over which the sound travels to reach you doesn't disrupt the message: *it's electric*. Sound maintains its essence despite alterations in its perceptual qualities.

Grandy's exploration of the "complementary nature of music offers further insight into the temporal complexity of sound."[26] He underscores the pluralistic interplay of individual tones within a musical piece, where each note not only exists in a distinct temporal moment but also contributes to an evolving musical whole. This interplay exemplifies how music, through the entanglement of its notes, integrates successive moments where "each wave gathers up earlier waves," such that "past and future are experientially or subjectively present at every musical moment," of auditory perception.[27] Such a perspective shifts our understanding of sound transmission, moving beyond a linear framework toward a more holistic encounter. It also echoes the principles of quantum entanglement, wherein particles remain interconnected regardless of the distance separating them, influencing one another instantaneously.

A paradigm of sounds as unique and discrete events that entangle in time disrupts conventional notions of unilinear transmission of information through sound stimuli and emphasizes the holistic encounter of auditory sensations. Reconceptualizing sound as a series of distinct yet interconnected events, initiates a move away from the classical metaphysical interpretation of sound. The reevaluation of sound as distinct events catalyzes a departure from the conventional metaphysical understanding of sound, which anchors itself in linearity and causality. This perspective posits sound as a phenomenon that unfolds in a straightforward sequence—where a specific cause, such as a vibrating object, leads to an effect, namely the production of sound waves perceived by the ear. Such a cause-and-effect relationship underpins many of the classical theories of sound, aligning closely with the Newtonian physics framework that views the universe in terms of linear dynamics and predictable outcomes. This reconceptualization challenges the Western predilection for breaking down reality into isolated units and distinct categories (like past, present, and future) and instead aligns with worldviews that acknowledge the interconnectedness of all phenomena binding all aspects of existence. The significance of understanding sound as a carrier of complex information becomes particularly poignant when considering the oral traditions of Black communities, especially in contrast to the predominance of visual culture that is a feature of modern Western European culture, where when words become written and part of the visual world, they lose some of their dynamism, becoming static "symbols without existence in their own right."[28]

In the context of the oral traditions (songs, folk tales, and other spoken word) of Black people, sounds as distinct events creating their own disturbances in space-time gains added significance, where verbal articulation of a thought is inseparable from action, and where "ideas and words are seen as part of the same reality as the events to which they refer." Levine gives the example of the Ashanti culture, where a person who speaks about having a dream of cheating on a partner may be punished to the same extent as a person who actually cheats. In these traditions, "the medium and the message intermesh in crucial ways," in which the "dynamic living quality of the spoken word was conducive to the sense of sacred space and time characteristics of Africans and Afro-Americans in slavery."[29] Singing or narrating the stories of the Bible and relating them orally to dream events and visions, for example, gave them a substance and dynamism that made the stories lifelike, and gave the past a contemporaneity and significance absent from the European worldview, with its "highly segmented and compartmentalized sense of time" and its predominance of the written word on an "abstracted and detached printed page," which diluted the notions of the past that enslaved people.[30] Words are seen as having the ability to manifest or bring forth different times and realities in Afrodiasporic traditions.

The delayed report to enslaved communities in Texas of their legal freedom under the Emancipation Proclamation and of the Civil War's end illustrates the power of the control of information. The awareness that enslavers had of these world-transformative events, systemically kept from those they exploited, through the suppression of literacy and communication, enabled their arbitrary manipulation of waiting time in order to eke out the maximum economic benefit. The time that elapsed between the events following the Emancipation Proclamation and the end of the Civil War, and the enforcement of the outcomes through the order delivered by General Granger was the result of the deliberate obstruction of information. Where information couldn't be manipulated, violence, force, and time itself were used to keep Black people enslaved. Such management strategies by the slave-owning class undermined the capacity of the enslaved population to act collectively and decisively on their own behalf. This uniquely oppressive form of temporal subjugation shackled their claim to their freedom for more than two years. The strategic manipulation of waiting time by enslavers exposed the harsh reality that even awareness did not guarantee liberation.

The Unobjectivity of Facticity and Truth

They waited for justice . . . . And it didn't come. No one talks about that. —**Toni Morrison, on the Rodney King uprisings, *The Charlie Rose Show***

What did it mean to exist between the "no longer enslaved" and the "not yet free"? —**Saidiya Hartman, *Scenes of Subjection***

Facticity means a thing can only take on the feature of being a fact, of being real, of being truth or a part of objective reality, in the Western framework, when it has been pinned to the linear timeline. Anything that cannot be pinpointed to a date on the calendar and time on the clock is not considered real, factual, event(ual), or as having happened. The word *fact* derives from Latin *factum* "an event, occurrence, deed, achievement," and in Medieval Latin as "state, condition, circumstance" (literally "thing done"). From the 1630s, a *fact* is a "thing known to be true" and "something that has actually occurred."[31] A fact is a piece of information that can supposedly be verified and is supported by evidence or logical reasoning.

Truth is then a quality of being in accordance with fact or reality. *Truth* implies a correspondence between beliefs or statements and facts or events. The notion of truth is complex and can take different forms depending on the context and perspective. In metaphysics, truth has been debated and discussed for centuries: some view truth as a correspondence between beliefs and reality while others argue that truth is a matter of coherence within a set of beliefs or system of knowledge. Regardless of its specific definition, truth is often considered a cornerstone of knowledge and understanding, as it provides a means of establishing the accuracy and validity of our beliefs.

Fact and truth, at least in the Western tradition, are meant to be clearly distinguishable from opinion, belief, or subjective interpretation, based instead on evidence and reasoning. Truth in this framework, cannot be determined by a single individual or authority. In scientific inquiry, facts are established through systematic observation, experimentation, and analysis. In domains such as history, journalism, or law, facts are established through research, investigation, examination, and argumentation of evidence.

The scientific method provides a structured process for testing and verifying theories or hypotheses, ensuring that what we consider as fact in our shared understanding of reality is based on objective and reliable evidence. Professor Eve Ruhnau writes that "to test the truth or falsehood of predictions, measurements have to be made. Measurements produce facts. Predictions are about possible future events. Facts are constituted in the present and are retrospectively described as past events with respect to instants which have already passed."[32] This elucidation underlines that facts, within the objective domain of science, are phenomena that can be quantified and measured. However, the status of a claim as fact is subject to ongoing debate and even revision as new information becomes available over time. Ultimately, under this system, the accuracy of a fact is determined by the strength and reliability of the evidence and reasoning that supports it.

By these definitions, in order for the freedom of Black people to become a *fact*, a measurement had to be made: a date and time to mark the moment of Black liberation on the Western timeline, which would be subject to systematic observation, reasoning, and evidence-testing. Here we see "the Gregorian calendar and clock time come together in capitalist social time relations and coalesce into specific hegemonic time forms," and into "the expression of specific forms of historical consciousness."[33] This moment of liberation becomes a point of empirical anchorage in the fluid continuum of time, offering a concrete reference for acknowledging the transition from a state of oppression to one of freedom.

In her study of Black folk narrative, Professor Laura C. Jarmon observes, "The features of time and reality ... may not always operate as criteria stable enough to delineate information status across communities."[34] Instead, Black narratives embody a dynamic and flexible approach to information and prioritize the collective experiences and perspectives of the community, shaping the tenor and essence of news or reports based on participant group interests.[35] This puts Black folkways in direct opposition to the tradition of time reckoning, truth-rendering, and facticity of Western scientism, as "the concept of truth, fact, or realism cannot itself remain stable in the environment of information mythically valorized as fact."[36] This instability challenges the very foundation of Western scientism, suggesting that its claims to objective truth and reality are not only subjective but also exclusionary. The discrepancy between these two worldviews, Black folkways' fluid temporal narratives and Western scientism's rigid linear time, underscores a broader cultural clash. This clash has real-world implications for how histories are written, understood, and valued, and how reality is experienced. The two Freedom Days that the US recognizes (January 1 and June 19th) as historical *fact*, and the idea that on either day enslaved Black people in *fact* became liberated, demonstrates the fallacy of facticity, where the purported "facts" of Emancipation do not align with the material conditions and lived realities of those they were meant to liberate. The narrative of Freedom Days serves as stark evidence of political time as out of sync with the lived experiences of liberation among Black people on the Western timeline, challenging the conventional metric of time that privileges factual observation.[37]

In this context, "out of sync" refers to the dissonance between the chronological recording of freedom and the material conditions that continued to subjugate Black individuals long after these dates passed. It underscores a mechanism of temporal control wherein political declarations and legal enactments fail to immediately alter or improve lived experiences. This temporal gap reveals how Western timelines, predicated on the sequential documentation of events, often mask the complexities and continuities of oppression that persist beyond symbolic moments of "liberation."

The mechanism through which this temporal misalignment occurs is multifaceted, manifesting both in delayed communication of Emancipation (as seen on June 19th) and in the sustained socioeconomic and legal structures that effectively prolonged Black people's disenfranchisement. "Out of sync" thus encompasses, not just a delay in the transmission of legal freedom, but also the enduring legacy of systemic barriers that inhibit Black individuals' full participation in the promise of that freedom.

This temporal discordance exemplifies how Western constructs of linear time, focused on progress, factual milestones, and a forward-moving trajectory, often exclude or marginalize Black experiences and histories. Progress and the accumulation of facts as points on the linear timeline always comes at the expense of Black lives. This leads us to conclude that one goal of Western linear time is to lock Black bodies out of the future, to remove them from the timeline of civilization. In other words, by emphasizing discrete points of historical "progress," this timeline obscures the ongoing processes of resistance, survival, and self-determination that define Black people's relationship to time and liberation. It reflects a deliberate effort within Western temporality to confine Black presence to the past, thereby excluding Black people from the narrative of future-making and civilization. There is still a third liminal space between legal freedom and de facto subjugation for enslaved people, where yet another 800,000 enslaved people still were not able to call themselves free from the tyranny of slavery. This was an insidious kind of temporal violence, where those trapped by it were simultaneously free and unfree, known and unknown, seen and unseen. The slaveholding states that pledged allegiance to the Union, including thirteen parishes in Louisiana and forty-eight counties in Virginia, were allowed to keep their slaves. This meant 800,000 people waited even longer for political time to unfold. These individuals waited for the Thirteenth Amendment abolishing slavery to pass into law on December 6, 1865—nearly six months after Juneteenth. Freedom Day celebrations for those liberated in this third wave are often consolidated under the January 1 anniversary. So, in *fact*, we have three waves of liberation: January 1, 1863 (the issuance of the Emancipation Proclamation); January 31, 1865, to December 6, 1865 (the passage and ratification of the Thirteenth Amendment); and June 19, 1865 (the issuance of General Order No. 3 in Galveston), all overlapping despite their discrete calendar dates.

Freedom from bondage, and the end of white terrorism via slavery, was declared "fact" in a written document, which stated that "all persons held as slaves . . . shall be then, thenceforward, and forever free ..."[38] However, Black people still had to wait "for their actual freedom." They had to wait for the violence of war to end, wait for the master's clock to strike midnight on January 1, wait for Lincoln to sign the

Proclamation, wait for the news to travel, wait for the sun to rise on June 19, wait to escape, wait for General Granger to leave Louisiana and march upon Galveston with his troops, then wait for him to read General Order No. 3. All of this before liberation could become "fact" and before freedom could become "truth."

Enslaved Africans traversed time and space to liberate one another long before the date on the Emancipation Proclamation—during the time of the Civil War and after the time of so-called freedom. They ingeniously employed "waiting time" and communication in codes, symbols, songs, chants, and other means of obscuring the message—a social network relying on Afrodiasporic technologies their white colonialist human traffickers thought they had stripped them of. This network thrived on the principles of the Black folk narrative, its rich temporal layers, communal significance, and oral traditions becoming a powerful conduit for liberation. They carried with them the weight of fact, history, and myth simultaneously. These narratives operated within a unique temporal dimension, one where the past, present, and future were interwoven into a collective memory and aspiration for freedom.

The rituals of Watch Nights and Freedom Days bound together waiting time and political time. Black people have always needed to be vigilant of political and institutional time. Whether in the legislative process or the effective dates of proclamations, there are many other ways in which time does violence, in which the Western linear timeline is openly hostile to Black lives.

Wading Time: Stilling the Movement of Time in the White Linear Timestream

> *wade (v.): Old English wadan "to go forward, proceed, move, stride, advance" (the modern sense perhaps represented in oferwaden "wade across"). Specifically, "walk into or through water" (or any substance which impedes the free motion of limbs) c. 1200. Figurative sense of "to go into" (action, battle, etc.) is recorded from late 14c.* —**The Online Etymology Dictionary**

Oceanos-Chronos, Greek god of the primary substance and the eternal river of time, controls all change. He is creator and destroyer of everything. As water Oceanos encircles the world, forms its boundary and is the origin of all things. —**Barbara Adam, *Time***

The amount of time it takes for a substance to enter the ocean and then leave the ocean is called residence time. Human blood is salty, and sodium, Gardaluski tells me, has a residence time of 260 million years. And what happens to the energy that is produced in the waters? It continues cycling like atoms in residence time. We, Black people, exist in the residence time of the wake, a time in which 'everything is now. It is all now' (Morrison . . .) —**Christina Sharpe, *In the Wake***

Sailing over a vast body of water for many days in a huge canoe with gigantic flapping wings. —**Redoshi's dream the day before she was kidnapped onto the ship *Clotilda* and trafficked into human bondage in Alabama in 1860 at age twelve, quoted in the Africatown History Museum in Africatown, Alabama**

As human beings traveling along the arrow of time, many of us feel that we do not have immediate access to experiences of the past or of the future. With the past behind us and the future always moments, days, months, years ahead, we feel essentially resigned to the sensations of the immediate present. This is embedded in the conception of time's motion as a continuous flow, which has been a feature of European ontological thought for centuries. In 167 ACE, the Roman philosopher Marcus Aurelius called out the inescapable, unstoppable, and uncontrollable advance of life: "Time is like a river made up of the events which happen, and a violent stream; for as soon as a thing has been seen, it is carried away, and another comes in its place, and this will be carried away too."[39] The Sanskrit roots of the word "time" reveals its connection to notions of "tides" and "high water."

The idea of water being used to mark time can also be found in the Negro spiritual "Wade in the Water," which is said to contain coded instructions for escape.[40] Though the lyrics vary, its refrain goes:

Wade in the water,
wade in the water, children,
wade in the water.
God's gonna trouble the water.[41]

Often attributed to Harriet Tubman and her ingenious strategies along the Underground Railroad, "Wade in the Water" embodies a narrative that both veers into the realm of the apocryphal and anchors itself in tangible tactics of evasion and resistance. Despite the absence of explicit confirmation from Tubman's accounts regarding the utilization of this song, the oral tradition and the song's eventual documentation in 1904 by John Wesley Work II, through the vocal harmonies of the Fisk Jubilee Singers, underscores the dynamic and fluid nature of Black narratives. These narratives prioritize the collective experience and wisdom over the rigid facticity often demanded by Western scientism.[42]

The mythologization of such songs within the abolitionist cause speaks to a broader tradition of Black temporalities, where the distinction between myth and fact becomes a site of resistance and reclamation. Black narratives, as seen in the oral tradition of "Wade in the Water," embody a dynamic approach to truth, one that values the collective memory and experience of the community over the individualistic and empirical validations of Western scientism. This approach challenges Western constructs of time reckoning and truth-rendering, proposing instead a nuanced understanding of history and reality that accommodates the complexities of Black experiences. It also permits a backcasting, where the future imprints information in the past that works to entangle the truth. In some quantum parallel reality that was made possible by the intra-action between the relative past, present, and future, Tubman sang the song in at least one version of reality made possible through Black temporalities. There are firsthand accounts of Harriet Tubman using religious songs in her oral storytelling performances and as plot elements in sharing stories about the Underground Railroad.[43]

Jean M. Humez documents that when recounting the story of the Combahee River Raid on June 2, 1863, Tubman ended it with a song that she had improvised in order to assure over 700 enslaved people that they had support from the Union soldiers as they escaped to freedom.[44] In this context, the factual precision of whether Tubman specifically used "Wade in the Water" becomes less significant than the song's symbolic essence and its alignment with known evasion tactics that leveraged the natural landscape. The call to "wade in the water" (and wait in the water) suggests getting off the path to cover your scent and evade the bloodhounds used by slave patrols, which aligns with known tactics that exploited natural landscapes for evasion. The act of wading and waiting/in the water permitted liberation-seekers on the run toward freedom to steal back time and create an interstitial moment of rest and safety amid their dangerous journeys.

Used as a tool of resistance, this wading time averts the gaze, avoids the surveillance of the slave system, of forced labor and according to the clock of capitalist production. Unobserved, they could exist in infinity possibilities, even if only for a moment. But in the wading/waiting, that moment can be stretched out as long as needed until it is time to change again, to move time along its stream. To wade/wait in the water, to rest against the current, to still the tide, and submerge the master's clock, was a revolutionary act within the greater revolutionary act of escape. In the sacred act of "wading in the water," we see a powerful expression of reclaiming time and space, crafting moments of safety and possibility amid the perilous journey toward freedom.

The rivers and streams of the American South provided a natural protective barrier and many enslaved Black people risked drowning, being attacked by animals, and other dangers crossing these waterways in search of freedom. "Wade in the Water" is then as a technology designed to hack the European time stream: wading, or waiting, was an act in the war for liberation that created a temporary time portal, a vortex of protection in the water, where each heartbeat brings a moment of respite from the mechanical grind of the master's clock.

It is also a path cutting through to the other side (spatio-temporally), closer to escape off the plantation and away from the plantation management of time. This interpretation further enriches the mythic narrative of Tubman by framing her actions as a form of temporal rebellion, where moments of waiting or wading through water become acts of defiance against the chronological constraints of slavery. In her work as a revolutionary, Harriet Tubman's scientific abilities, nursing skills, strategic prowess, as well as her trust in her own intuition, helped hundreds of freedom-seekers to access liberation. Calling Harriet Tubman an "Unsung Naturalist," Maryland park ranger Angela Crenshaw shows how Tubman's intimate understanding of the natural world helped ensure the safety of those under her care. One notable example is her mastery of bird calls, including the distinct call of the Barred Owl, which she employed as a means of communication, signaling the presence of danger or a safe path to follow.[45] Information about the natural environment also showed up in her dreams and visions. In an 1863 interview she recalled that, prior to escaping slavery, she had a recurring dream of flying over fields, rivers, mountains, and towns "like a bird" and at points in the dream, beginning to sink down, where she would then encounter a group of women all dressed in white, who would out their arms and pull her across. Tubman claimed that when she came up to the North, the same places she had seen in her dreams appeared in real life, while she met and became friends with several of the women who helped her across in the dream.[46]

Tubman's upbringing in the swampy terrains of Maryland cultivated the skills that allowed her to navigate at night, a strategic choice, tactically exploiting the temporal qualities of her surroundings and the limitations in communication technologies of the time. During Tubman's main years operating the Underground Railroad (1851–62), information traveled primarily through physical means, such as letters, which were slow and could take days to reach their destination. Even with the telegraph becoming more popular during the 1840s, these were still mostly only used by the government. Advertisements for runaway slaves, therefore, were primarily run in newspapers. This delay in the spread of information was particularly pronounced during nighttime, when most activities, including the transportation and delivery of messages, slowed down or ceased entirely, unlike the twenty-four-hour world we live in, where one gets emails and texts at any time of the day or night. This delay in information transmission meant that news of Tubman's movements and the escape of enslaved people would not be immediate. By moving under the cover of night, Tubman significantly reduced the risk of immediate pursuit or interception, as any information about her activities or any of the enslaved people she was helping, would only be known and acted upon the next day.

Tubman operated with a profound understanding of the importance of temporality to the success of her rescue missions. A precise sense of timing was key for all escapes and journeys along the Underground Railroad, and familiar with the night sky, she aligned her journeys with celestial cues such as the North Star as a guiding beacon toward freedom. Tubman's ability to operate in darkness and sustain profound silence played a crucial role. Walking for miles undetected, the absence of sound and visibility allowed her to move swiftly and stealthily, minimizing the risk of detection and effectively erasing her presence in the eyes and ears of pursuers. This strategic inversion of the norms associated with visibility and audibility shattered the conventional boundaries of movement and freedom dictated by the oppressor's clock. Tubman not only circumvented the physical barriers placed before her but also transcended the conventional boundaries of time and space imposed by a slaveholding society. This audacious defiance of the expected rhythms of day and night, and the master's time, opened up a realm of possibilities for liberation, proving that the constraints of time and space, as dictated by the oppressor's regime, were not insurmountable barriers but rather obstacles that could be navigated and overcome with ingenuity and determination.

At twelve or thirteen years old, a violent beating caused Harriet Tubman a lifelong disability in the form of severe headaches, seizures, dizziness, and possible narcolepsy. Hired out to a textile factory, Tubman was hit in the head by a heavy metal weight, thrown by an overseer aiming it at someone else.[47] The injury was life threatening and Tubman was unconscious for days. Despite the lasting impact on her health, which made it difficult for her to work and participate fully in daily life, Tubman would go on to become a leader in the abolitionist movement.

She also had a reputation for having prescient visions and a prophetic ability: many accounts tell of Tubman drifting off for hours, sometimes falling asleep mid-sentence, and waking up with detailed visions. Jean M. Humez's 2003 work, *Harriet Tubman: The Life and the Life Stories*, offers a comprehensive biographical overview based on extensive research and compiled stories Tubman told about her life, including reflections on her spiritual and prophetic experiences. A contemporary in 1865, quotes Tubman describing an experience of riding home in a cart with two other companions when she suddenly heard music fill up the air and began describing a vision "in language that sounded like the old prophets in their grand flow." When questioned, upon coming out of what appeared to be a trance, Tubman claimed not to have been asleep. Humez writes that Tubman spoke of her own "special gifts" of foresight and ability to consult directly with God in interviews, documented accounts by journalists and biographers, and "dozens of conversations with Northerners."[48] Humez further situates this in a context and tradition of "use of religious vision as a spiritual, psychological, and even political resource," particularly by women of the African Methodist Episcopal religion largely situated in the Northern States. Such religious visions, Humez claims, allowed those women who were called to preach to convene directly with the spiritual realm without having to mediate it through a male authority.[49]

Although some reports attribute this precognitive gift to her disability, this subtly undermines Tubman's intentionality in refining and deploying her gifts. In other words, there isn't necessarily a causal relationship between Tubman's injury and her abilities as a prophetess or diviner, especially given her vivid knowledge of the natural world. Harriet Tubman herself asserted that "her father could always predict the weather, and he foretold the Mexican war," and that "some of her intense attributes were founded on the premonitive power, which she said was inherited from her father."[50]

Tubman believed her seizures were a sign that she was about to receive a message from God, messages that helped her make important decisions and avoid danger.[51] She remarked to friends and confidants that "she talked to God every day, and He talked with her everyday of her life." Other stories of Tubman recount how she manifested what she needed through prayer, often seemingly instantaneously or shortly thereafter. Unexpected boons such as "incredible physical obstacles . . . removed from the route to freedom," or "the sudden availability of provisions, monies, and supporters along the way," were not surprising to her because "her faith in God allowed for all these things to occur."[52]

Following these accounts of her skills and abilities, I, too, am compelled to consider Harriet Tubman a powerful diviner, one who used a form of hydromancy—or water divination—to help facilitate her travels back and forth on the Underground Railroad. Her frequent comparison to Moses extends beyond abolition and escape from bondage to the legend of Moses parting sea waters.

Hydromancy, also called water gazing and water divination, an ancient practice appearing in various cultural traditions, interprets the movements and patterns of water for insight into future events. As described by astrologer and author Jewels Rocka, divination is an experiential process that hinges on "merging with the feelings of things rather than mental constructs," which allows the diviner to sense the "emotional undercurrent in a situation or place," or even object, which in turn provides valuable indicators regarding its overall suitability.[53]

Water gazing is one of the main types of divination practices used in Indigenous African cultural and spiritual practices, and seen throughout the diaspora, with many belief systems relying on water spirits for protection and guidance. In the Benin Republic, water gazing practices are used by Mami Wata diviners to communicate with water spirits who will share information about the future. In the Tiv society, living along the Benue River in Nigeria, diviners employ a diverse set of natural materials and everyday items "such as water, mirrors, regalia; cowrie shells, snail shells, tortoise shells, bird feathers" to send and receive communications that help them gain insight into other temporal dimensions (such as the past or the future) and provide guidance on the decisions the community should make.[54] In the Xhosa community, of Southern Africa, traditional healers went down to the river before others in the village, to wash, prepare for daily ritual ceremonies, and convene with the ancestral spirits living beneath the river water.[55]

Nguni-speaking diviner-healers in South Africa believe in "living water" and water divinities as a source of spiritual power. In this tradition, diviner-healers are selected by their ancestors and undergo lengthy periods of training to open communication channels with their ancestors through dreams and altered states of consciousness. This training includes "cleansing rituals using plant-based medicines (often performed at water sites), night-time dancing and singing, animal sacrifice, food taboos and strict adherence to correct moral behavior."[56] Despite cultural transformations brought about by colonialism and

Christianity, the practice of diviner-healers continues into the present, sustaining their connections to "deep pools, the sea, waterfalls and natural lakes."[57]

If Tubman engaged in a practice of water divining or water healing, it would have been seamless alongside her other skills for traveling on the Underground Railroad. By studying the patterns of the rivers and streams around her, she "became familiar with the tides and learned how to find fresh water."[58] Serving as a nurse and a cook in the Union Army, Tubman knew how to treat dysentery, a highly infectious disease often caught from contaminated water, by preparing a medicine from the roots of a plant that grew on riversides. Her knowledge of the healing properties of water and her resourcefulness in deciphering and using the natural resources available to her were all tools in her fight for liberation.

To determine the safest possible route, Tubman employed a variety of techniques—among them, divine guidance. According to the story Harriet Tubman told her biographer Sarah Bradford, on one journey, she was traveling with two men when she received guidance from God to stop and divert from her normal route, which she obediently followed, changing direction, and leading them to a small stream with no bridge or boat to cross. Asking God what she should do, she was instructed to cross the stream, which she did despite the cold March water rising to her armpits. The men with her hesitated until they saw her safely reach the other side. After wading across a second stream, they stumbled upon a cabin where a Black family provided them with shelter and comfort for the night. Later, Tubman and her group discovered that the master of the two men had set a trap for them, with a large reward for their capture, which the change in plans enabled them to avoid. The intercession of a guiding voice and Harriet Tubman's willingness to trust in her intuition through the high water ultimately allowed the men to continue their journey to freedom.

Weighting Time: Pandemic x Uprising Timescapes

weight (v.): *"to load with weight," 1747 (figuratively, of the mind, from 1640s)* weight (n.): *Old English gewiht, "weighing, weight, downward force of a body, heaviness."* —**Online Etymology Dictionary**

A system that is under constant observation cannot decay. In such a situation, it is not possible for the system to undergo any change, it is frozen in time. —**Eve Ruhnau, *Time, Temporality, Now***

The sheer force of the utterance "black" seems to assert a primacy, quiddity, or materiality . . . an acknowledgement of the sheer weight of a history of terror that is palpable in the very utterance "black" and inseparable from the tortured body of the enslaved. —**Saidiya Hartman, *Scenes of Subjection***

I asked that boss-man for to gimme my time; Sez he, "Ole Nigger, you're a day behin" —**Lawrence W. Levine, *Black Culture and Black Consciousness***

Time scholar Kevin Birth points out that the clock and the Gregorian calendar prioritize the idea of uniform durations for measuring time, treating time as a series of empty vessels waiting to be filled. With globalization and the forceful imposition of Western timekeeping standards onto the rest of the world, he argues that sacred holidays became tools to manipulate and quell resistance to political issues.[59] Take, for instance, the commercialization of holidays like Christmas and Eid al-Fitr. In many cultures, these celebrations traditionally center around communal gatherings, spiritual reflection, and familial bonds. However, under the influence of Western time standards, these sacred occasions have increasingly become opportunities for consumerism and profit-driven endeavors. Rather than fostering cultural and spiritual enrichment, they serve as vehicles for economic exploitation and social conformity.

Furthermore, Birth's analysis extends to the manipulation of time to suppress dissent and reinforce political hegemony. Consider how governments strategically schedule elections or public events to distract from controversial issues or to control public discourse. By prioritizing a linear, uniform concept of time, those in power can exert greater influence over societal narratives and limit opportunities for collective resistance.

Waiting, Wading, Weighting Time

The notion of "weighting time" is a critical concept, in its application to the experiences of Black communities. This can be understood as the tangible force and downward pressure exerted by the passage of time, akin to the physical weight or heaviness of a body. It encapsulates the gravity and heaviness of time as experienced through the lens of historical injustices and their enduring impact on the present. Just as a physical weight can influence the shape and movement of a body, the weight of time against Black people signifies how the accumulation of historical disparities and systemic inequalities continue to shape their lived realities. This gravitational pull of time not only bears down with the enormity of past wrongs but also with the persistent challenges faced in the present, creating a continuum where the past, present, and future are inextricably linked by the density of experience and memory. The concept of weighting time, therefore, offers a profound framework for understanding the unique temporal experiences of Black communities, marked by a distinct sense of urgency and resilience in the face of ongoing adversity.

For this reason, holidays such as Juneteenth and Emancipation or Freedom Day represent a powerful counternarrative to state-sanctioned holidays. These celebrations hold profound meaning. Both holidays originated within the African American community, arising organically as expressions of joy, resilience, and collective remembrance. However, the white gaze has played a significant role in shaping dominant narratives of Black culture and the legal recognition of these holidays.

In quantum physics, space-time collapse occurs when a wave or particle, initially in a superposition of all its theoretically possible states, suddenly appears to reduce to a single state after interaction with an observer, that is, when measured, gives a result corresponding to only one of the possible configurations. Uncollapsing, then, would theoretically reverse this process. Restoring the particle to its original quantum state of all possible realities is to allow for a condition of pure potentiality, where every outcome remains viable, and every path is still a possibility.

Similarly, the concept of the white gaze, disguised as the so-called objective observer, is particularly insidious for Black people. Under the watchful eye of white hegemony, a space-time collapse occurs when we are "measured," observed by the white gaze. Then our unique space-times collapse into the Western linear timeline, limiting our possible configurations to what can only be predetermined in line with the hegemonic framework. Uncollapsed, unobserved, unmeasured, and left to act on our infinite possibilities, we contain the degrees of freedom to exist in all states and to manifest all possible futures. Mainstream media has often undermined the importance of Freedom Day and Juneteenth, devaluing their significance and perpetuating stereotypes. Both are reduced to mere opportunities for Black people—the American demographic most heavily burdened by the weight of time—to take a day off work or engage in reckless behavior. Their dismissal, as inconsequential holidays, is part of the systemic erasure of Black history, a legacy that perpetuates the wholesale devaluation of Black lives. Stereotypical depictions of Juneteenth celebrations portray the gathered crowds as rowdy, lazy, and dangerous. An article published in *the Austin American Statesman*, on June 19, 1930, lamenting the "old order" wrote: "It's June 19—and suddenly there's a reason why every cook and yard man in the city can't appear for work that day."[60] An earlier, 1896 report from Wilmington, North Carolina observes an Emancipation Day celebration, writing, "New Year's Day, January 1st is the colored people's time to recognize in some manner their emancipation, and this they did by marching with music and some shouting. But their celebration was generally without any special importance or interest."[61] These distorted, apathetic portrayals seek to invalidate the significance and legitimacy of Black people's experiences of joy and the profoundly felt commemoration of their "waiting time" for freedom.

Despite this marginalization, Black people have continued to honor these holidays over the intervening 160 years as a means of reclaiming our history and preserving our identity. The journey from organic celebrations to state-sanctioned observances has not been without its challenges. In many cases, the struggle for recognition has been met with resistance, skepticism, and systemic barriers erected by those in power. The process of turning organic holidays into state-sanctioned events can lead to a dilution of their potency. As these holidays are integrated into the official calendar, they may be subjected to whitewashing or become opportunities for performative allyship, stripped of their historical context and reduced to mere tokens of inclusivity. It is essential that the true spirit of these celebrations is preserved, respecting their cultural roots and the mass struggles they represent.

During the 1960s civil rights movement, the holiday gained national attention as a celebration of Black history and to promote social justice. In 1980, Texas became the first to declare Juneteenth an official state holiday, and other states have gradually followed suit. It was around that time that Texas-based advocate, Ms. Opal Lee first launched a campaign to make Juneteenth a national holiday. In 2016, Ms. Lee, at age eighty-nine, walked about 1,400 miles from her home in Fort Worth, Texas, to Washington, DC, to raise awareness of the holiday. In 2019, Pennsylvania joined the growing number of states recognizing Juneteenth as a holiday, though businesses were not obligated to treat it as an official holiday.

This would start to change in Philadelphia not long later, when, a few months into the COVID-19 pandemic, on June 16, 2020, the city's mayor, Jim Kenney, declared that municipal workers in the city would have the 19th off with pay.[62] In a press release, Mayor Kenney is quoted using the language of racial reckoning that would come to be repeated across many government, nonprofit, and corporate statements, and media headlines: "The only way to dismantle the institutional racism and inequalities that continue to disenfranchise Black Philadelphians is to look critically at how we got here and make much-needed changes to the governmental systems that allow inequality to persist. This designation of Juneteenth represents my administration's commitment to reckon with our own role in maintaining racial inequities and our understanding of the magnitude of work that lies ahead."[63]

Even before the pandemic's full impact was felt, the problem of structural racism, wages, and housing was an everyday feature in the lives of many. In 2019, half of all renters across the country were paying more than they could afford on housing. Seventy-seven percent of renters and 58 percent of homeowners who are housing cost-burdened are people of color, meaning they spend a disproportionate share of their income on housing, typically defined as 30 percent or more of their monthly income. Black and Latina women are the most severely rent-burdened tenants in the US, experiencing the highest rates of eviction and housing displacement.[64] Despite their higher participation in the workforce in impoverished Black neighborhoods, Black women's earnings consistently lag those of men.[65]

In Philadelphia, the pandemic created circumstances that could no longer be disregarded or attributed to less consequential factors than poverty or race. Notably, neighborhoods with elevated COVID 19 positivity and hospitalization rates were largely occupied by Black renters, while zip codes with the highest eviction rates were three times more likely to experience the virus's impact.[66]

The decision by Mayor Kenney to recognize Juneteenth as a municipal holiday was influenced by George Floyd's murder on May 25, 2020, and the subsequent uprisings that unfolded across the nation. Floyd, a Black man, was killed in Minneapolis, Minnesota, during an arrest when a police officer knelt on his neck for over nine minutes, despite Floyd repeatedly crying out "I can't breathe." This act of violence, captured on video and widely disseminated, became a catalyst for a global movement demanding an end to systemic racism and police brutality. Just days after this tragic event, on May 30, 2020, a significant uprising took root at city hall in Philadelphia, manifesting the community's collective grief, outrage, and demand for justice. The protest rapidly expanded, with participants weaving through the streets of Center City in a powerful demonstration against police brutality racial injustice.

It was the next day, May 31, around 5:48 p.m., when I and everyone in my house got a loud emergency alert on our phones. It was an announcement from the Police Department of a citywide curfew starting just twelve minutes later at 6 p.m. and ending twelve hours later at 6 a.m. Only "essential personnel" were allowed outside. Curfews, the explicit time restrictions placed on people to stay within certain boundaries during designated hours of the day or night, bear a historical and present-day legacy of temporal oppression, one particularly weighted against Black communities. Curfews are inextricably intertwined with slavery, the Jim Crow era, and the ominous threat of sundown towns. Curfews on Black communities have long been a deliberate tactic for controlling their movements and curtailing their access to public spaces.

For enslaved people, curfews were a means of quelling any notion of autonomy. These curfews functioned not only to physically confine the enslaved, but to further strip them of their humanity and remind them of their perpetual subjugation. With every tolling of the bells that regulate time on these forced labor camps, the message was clear: the master owned and controlled the time and space of the slave. While visiting the Bellamy Mansion, a former plantation in Wilmington, North Carolina, I came across a sign explaining how curfews were enforced in the area:

> The Market House bell set the schedule and rhythm of antebellum Wilmington. An enslaved worker rang the bell at 5 a.m. to wake all city slaves, at 9 a.m. to open the business day, and at 1 p.m. for lunchtime. The Bell was rung again at 7 p.m. to indicate the close of business and at 9 p.m. to summon slaves off the streets. A 1765 city ordinance established a 10 p.m. curfew for all enslaved workers lest they had a "Ticket, or a Lanthorn and Candle" indicating permission from their owner. Any enslaved worker found violating curfew was whipped, imprisoned, or both.[67]

In instances of slave rebellions, curfews took on an even more malevolent role. Any anticipation of uprising cast a pall over the plantations, triggering stricter curfews that sought to suppress whispers of insurrection. Another informational marker at the Bellamy Mansion read, "A very few [black workers], as for instance, the mulatto 'Artis' on the Bellamy house construction, were freedmen . . . but even those were restricted by special laws made for freed negroes and were also subject . . . to observation by the day and night patrol."[68] However, both enslaved and freed people found ways to circumvent curfews by creating clandestine spaces of unity and resistance, using the cover of darkness to gather, share stories, and nurture their collective spirit, forge connections, and plan for future liberation.

During the Jim Crow era, curfews persisted as tools to enforce segregation and racial hierarchy. Sundown Towns, notorious for their exclusion of Black people after sunset, used curfews to solidify their racial boundaries. These towns, scattered across the United States, forbade Black residents from remaining within their borders after dark, which upheld an atmosphere of racial terror and dominance through constant threat of violence, harassment, or even death.

In the present, curfews maintain their historical functions in response to social unrest, protests, and demonstrations, such as those that implemented in Philadelphia in 2020, first in May and again later that year, during the protests following the Philadelphia police slaying of Walter Wallace on October 2020, several months after the murder of George Floyd.[69] In Ferguson, Missouri, curfews were imposed in August 2014 amid widespread demonstrations following the fatal shooting of Michael Brown by a police officer. Similarly, in Baltimore, Maryland, curfews were implemented in April 2015 following the death of Freddie Gray while in police custody. Not incidentally, George Zimmerman, the man responsible for Trayvon Martin's tragic murder on February 26, 2012, purportedly acted under the guise of enforcing a community curfew.

While the stated goal of these curfews is to maintain public safety and prevent property damage, the reality is that they are disproportionately target Black and Brown youth, who are more likely to be stopped by law enforcement and who face harsher penalties for violating curfew laws, from imprisonment to death. Curfew violations often criminalize young people who are simply trying to access public spaces or who may not have safe home environments to retreat to. Ultimately, these curfews exacerbate the very same inequalities in their access to opportunities for socialization, recreation, and education. In some cities, based on policy and practice, curfews are selectively enforced in certain neighborhoods or areas.[70] Just as the weight of historical injustices continues to shape the present, the weighting of time through curfews does no less than stifle the temporal agency and mobility of Black people.

Temporal Currents: Shadows Through the Hourglass

In 2021, a cultural milestone was reached when President Joe Biden signed a bill that declared Juneteenth a federal holiday after decades of Black activist campaigning. Yet, the celebration of Emancipation and the recognition of its significance bear the weight of a convoluted reality. Control by the state can have a profound impact, imposing specific narratives, rituals, or expectations that can limit the freedom and creativity of communities in celebrating their heritage and history. It can also hinder the full realization of the radical and transformative potential that organic commemorations like Juneteenth and Emancipation Day hold. While some may find respite and family time during holidays, essential workers—often disproportionately Black people—remain tethered to their duties, carrying the burden of weighted time on their shoulders. Nor are private employers required to give employees the day off on federal holidays.

The recognition of Juneteenth as a federal holiday paradoxically upholds a timeline that belongs to the victors and the colonizers of Black time. This imposition extends to the commodification and regulation of Black labor time, perpetuating a cycle that intersects with present-day dynamics of work and rest. The analogy of the master clock to slave clock mechanisms, drawn from clockworks, is particularly illustrative in this context. Just as a master clock synchronizes the time for all connected slave clocks, ensuring uniformity and control over the temporal order, in this case the ritualized performance of recognizing Juneteenth is representative of the dominant societal forces that dictate the terms of commemoration and rest. In contrast, the slave clocks symbolize the diverse experiences of Black communities, whose time, labor, and very beings have been historically subject to external control and valuation.

In 2022, my partner Camae and I, as Black Quantum Futurism, were the only American artists represented at documenta fifteen, the quadrennial, sprawling international art exhibition that takes place throughout the small city of Kassel, Germany. There, Black Quantum Futurism presented the "Clepsydra Stage," which stood as an homage to Juneteenth's profound significance of Black SpaceTimeMatters. It manifested as a deconstructed water clock floating on the banks of Fulda River, named for its Greek root *klepsydra*, meaning "water thief." The abstracted design comprised three interlocked circular platforms that served as stages, two of which responded to the river's flow, functioning as a temporal indicator set to nature's rhythms. This sculptural timepiece was more than just an object; it was an interactive stage and communal space that echoed the multiplicities of temporalities and identities present. Visitors' movements and the river's flow influenced the sculpture's dynamics. The "Clepsydra Stage" was also utilized by local community members, particularly from marginalized communities in Kassel, as a platform for performances, and other creative expression. The sculpture's symbolic engagement with time underscored the interplay between temporal perception, cultural representation, and community agency, to showcase time as a dynamic force that can be harnessed to reimagine and reclaim spaces for marginalized voices. In doing so, it celebrated the resilience of Black temporal agency illuminated the power of communal expression in reshaping the narrative of time itself.

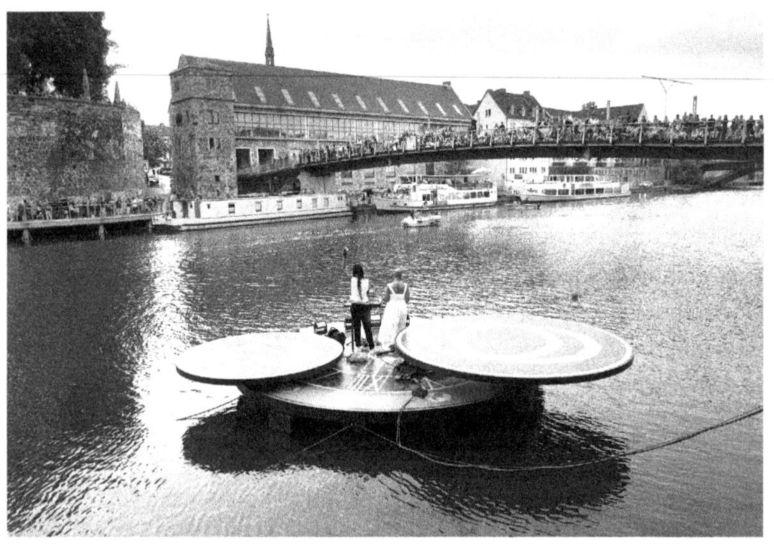

Camae Ayewa and Rasheedah Phillips performing on the "Clepsydra Stage," designed by Black Quantum Futurism, during the event Waiting Time/Watch Night Service with Irreversible Entanglements and Black Quantum Futurism on June 19, 2022, as part of Documenta 15 at the Rondell in Kassel, Germany.

One of the main visions of the "Clepsydra Stage" unfolded on Sunday, June 19, 2022, when Black Quantum Futurism collaborated with the free jazz quintet Irreversible Entanglements to stage a performance called Waiting Time/Watch Night Service in honor and memory of Juneteenth. The performance harnessed the symbolic and literal movement of the river, invoking waiting and wading time. It drew out Black histories and their implications for Black futures, revealing the interpenetration of present and historical times of resistance and oppression, a temporal bridge between past struggles and current challenges, connecting them to futures of boundless possibilities. Despite being observed by a large audience of several hundred, spread along a bridge crossing the river and down the riverbanks, the incantations and sound we generated called up a vortex large enough to suck us in or forge a barrier of protection. The circular motion of the stage, powered by the river, became a time machine on which we transcended the limitations of the present moment, threw off the gaze, held time in superposition, and opened a portal to endless degrees of temporal freedom. Our performance was a demonstration of the possible reimagination of time, offered in reverence of Harriet Tubman's command of water in service of guiding liberation-seekers toward better futures.

Through strategic use of waiting/wading/weighting time, Black people have always crafted modes of adaptation and resistance in the face of varied forms of oppression, temporal and otherwise, to loosen the confines of the Western timeline and to reclaim our own temporal realities. This resistance is both a testament to our resilience and a reminder that the measurement of time does not define our liberation, that it cannot be confined by the constructs of clock or calendar time.

This prompts the question: "What does it mean to be emancipated, pulled through the portal and out of slavery, only to be pulled back in by indentured servitude, or redlining, or forced sterilization, or police murder, while giving birth, or while sleeping, or while playing, or while protesting, or while...?" The journey from slavery into supposed freedom often feels like a perpetual cycle of being pulled back by the gravity of systemic oppression, a stark illustration of the "weighting" of time. This weight is a constant reminder of the battles fought and the ongoing struggle for a liberation that is complete and unequivocal.

The "waiting" time for this complete liberation is marked not by passivity but by active engagement and resistance, a testament to the enduring spirit and agency within Black communities. "Wading" through time speaks to the resilience required to navigate and survive often hostile environments shaped by systemic injustices. These experiences of waiting, wading, and weighting time are not simply about enduring hardship but about the active reclamation and redefinition of time itself. They are about asserting agency over one's narrative and existence in a world that persistently seeks to dictate the terms of Black life and liberation. The collective experience of Black people, caught in the ebb and flow of progress and setback, suggests that perhaps liberation cannot be measured in terms of "when." The notion of "when" presupposes a linear progression toward a definitive endpoint, a concept that seems increasingly inadequate in capturing the complex reality of Black liberation. Instead, this journey toward liberation is an ever-evolving process, a continuous journey defined not by the constraints of time but by the collective spirit of endurance, defiance, and hope which transcends imposed temporal boundaries.

CHAPTER 7

Project: Time Capsule

The Macon Housing Authority says they may have found a time capsule buried in the ground. The CEO of the authority, June Parker, says they discovered a box that looks like a safe underground by a flagpole outside of the Technical Service Building. Parker says the box could be empty, but she says it also could be some kind of time capsule. The Macon Housing Authority will open the box Monday at 4 p.m. to reveal what is inside. —
Chelsea Beimfohr and Mary Grace Shaw, 13WMAZ

In the summer of 2017, a mysterious safe with time capsule–like contents was discovered beneath the grounds of the public housing site Tindall Heights, which was being redeveloped in Macon, Georgia. Several others have also been unearthed: a time capsule, dating back to 1925, was found by contractors at the site of an affordable housing development in Cumberland, Maryland in 2011; another, dating back to 1937, was unearthed during the demolition of the Brand Whitlock public housing complex in Toledo, Ohio in 2013; one from 1941, was discovered as the "blighted" Charter Oak Terrace public housing site came tumbling down in Hartford, Connecticut in 1997; and a capsule from 1909 was found in 2018 at the Garfield Park Lofts in Grand Rapids, Michigan, which is managed today by Michigan State Housing Development Authority and is the former site of the Burton Heights Methodist Church.[1]

While the act of burying a collection of items for preservation can be traced thousands of years back to Egyptian and Chinese burial practices of placing valuable artifacts inside of tombs, contemporary or "modern-day" time capsules, where a date and time are set for opening the capsule, are predominantly associated with Western linear time-marking rituals and traditions.[2] First popularized at the 1939 New York World's Fair, in the United States, the burial of time capsules have become a popular practice for preserving constructed historical timelines, at baby showers, building dedications, weddings, school functions, and other personally significant occasions. In Western contexts, time capsules function along the trajectory of a progressive timeline—items from the present are buried for future generations to gain insights into the past. The anticipated opening dates for these capsules can range from months to years, or even centuries. As described by professor and librarian William E. Jarvis, a time capsule, in the American tradition, must be deliberately sealed with a specific opening date chosen. It must be constructed to endure the passage of time, to notify future discoverers of its existence and location, and to carefully select and safeguard its contents. They are intended to document the past for the benefit of future generations, transmitting a sense of progress from the past to the future.[3]

A comprehensive examination of documented time capsule contents reveals a telling absence. Most American time capsules rarely consider Black future generations, and historical records stored within these capsules rarely acknowledge the presence or experiences of Black people. Black communities are erased from the futures intended by those who bury these capsules. This striking pattern of omission raises the crucial question: Why are Black people and Black histories so often excluded from these imagined futures?

Time capsules at affordable housing sites, by contrast, often contain alternative, obscured, or forgotten histories, offering a corrective counternarrative to dominant historical accounts. Marginalized Black and Brown communities are often disproportionately impacted not just by material and spatial inequalities, but also by temporal inequalities, or what Jeremy Rifkin refers to as "time ghettos."[4] Time capsules buried at housing projects sites tend not to have an evident or specified "opening" date attached to them, which makes them fall, by some accounts, outside of the traditional definition of time capsules.[5] This deviation is not mere happenstance, but a reflection of the nature and intentions of the communities that created them. The absence of a specified opening date in these capsules correlates with the long-term aspirations of the residents: the housing as a permanent settlement, a stable foundation for future generations. The idea of demolition or redevelopment was not part of the community's envisioned future; thus, the concept of a future or specific unearthing date was perhaps irrelevant. It also invokes the sense of the future held in some African conceptions of time, where the future is a space of open possibility, not defined by any specific clock time or calendar date.

Uprooted amid redevelopment, these time capsules work to resurface Black people as active agents in the timeline of Western progress. Simultaneously they bring to light the enduring impacts of "root shock"—the profound dislocation experienced by communities displaced. In this context, the unearthing of these capsules is often a byproduct of upheaval and loss. The demolition or significant alteration of the housing signifies more than just physical restructuring; it represents a disruption of the community's continuity and the shattering of a collective vision of permanence. This phenomenon speaks to the irreversible transformation of these communities, underscoring the reality that even a hypothetical return would not restore their original state or erase the scars of displacement.

For example, the time capsule found at the Brand Whitlock Homes in Toledo, Ohio, held documents dating back to 1937. The homes opened in 1938, as one of the nation's first public housing complexes for workers, constructed under the Public Works Administration. The documents within give a then-present snapshot of the racially restrictive covenants that prevented property owners from selling homes to Black people and other people of color, effectively locking them out of affordable, habitable homes on the rental market, and forcing them into segregated areas of racially concentrated poverty.

> The capsule's contents tell the background of how the Brand Whitlock Homes came to be built: a 1934 study of housing in Toledo noting many central-city homes' poor condition and the

> high number of tuberculosis cases in the area, one of the few parts of the city where blacks were permitted to live at the time; newspaper clippings about the New Deal–era program to build the housing; the Public Works Administration's blueprints for the complex; a program from the Aug. 2, 1936, groundbreaking ceremony; and well preserved copies of *The Toledo Blade* and *Toledo News-Bee* from Aug. 25, 1937, and the *Toledo Morning Times* from Aug. 26, 1937.[6]

As Black people were driven further into segregation in neglected and crowded housing, rentals became associated with poverty, blight, transiency, and lower property values. According to one document in the capsule, the Brand Whitlock Homes were built in one of the "four sections of the City of Toledo where Negroes are permitted to rent or purchase homes," and where "many of those homes lacked running water or electricity. The conditions of the area fostered poor health conditions, including many instances of tuberculosis, as well as high rates of vice and crime."[7] Another document in the capsule was a transcript of a 1937 speech by Black civil rights activist and pharmacist Mrs. Ella P. Stewart, which included a survey of the types of occupations Black people had.[8]

The Brand Whitlock time capsule contains both the evidence of an inadequate present in 1937, as well as the hopes for a radically changed future for the Black people in that community. Its eventual unearthing amid demolition of the Brand Whitlock Homes due to their severe neglect might be seen as a failure of the promises made at the burial of the time capsule. To put it another way, had the visions in the time capsule manifested, it would have never been found, as the Brand Whitlock Homes would never have reached such a point of disinvestment and neglect. But the uncovering of the Brand Whitlock Homes time capsule is ultimately a revelation of the nonlinearity of progress for Black people when measured against a standard timeline. It demonstrates the need for different understandings of time and the ways that Black people transmit memories and future visions across generations.

Quantum Time Capsules

Memory "belongs" to the future as well as the past, offering new techniques for a politics of future making. —**Rosalind Shaw, "Provocation"**

Out there at the county farm, they bust you open. They bust you up till you can't work. There's a lot of people down at the state farm at Cummins . . . that's raw and bloody. They wouldn't let you come down there and write no history. —**Henry Blake, Federal Writers' Project**

To counter the erasure of Black lives from conventional time capsules, it becomes imperative to reconceptualize these capsules as tools that can transcend the limitations of linear time, reaching back into the past to impart messages and cautionary tales, or unveil histories that will materialize in future moments long past. Quantum physics offers a framework for such a radical reimagining.

Quantum physics introduces a paradigm where particles, such as electrons and photons, exist in states of probability rather than certainty. In this quantum domain, particles don't possess precise, fixed properties until they are observed or measured. They are instead described by a wave function, a mathematical formulation embodying all potential states a particle might inhabit, including its position, momentum, or spin. The intriguing nature of the wave function lies in its probabilistic nature; it doesn't pinpoint the exact state of a particle but provides probabilities for each possible state. Upon measurement, this wave function collapses, narrowing down to one definitive state. Observing a particle forces it into a singular, linear timeline, erasing all other possible histories. However, until such a measurement occurs, particles reside in a superposition, embodying all potential states simultaneously.

This quantum superposition is vividly demonstrated in two experiments: the classic double-slit experiment and its intriguing variation, the quantum eraser. The double-slit experiment illustrates how particles traverse multiple paths simultaneously until observed. It is through observation that a particle is compelled to collapse into a singular, linear timeline, thereby erasing all other potential histories. It is fundamental in illustrating the quantum principle that reality is not fixed until it is observed. Building upon this foundation, the quantum eraser experiment opens up another enigma of quantum mechanics. It explores the notion that the act of measuring or observing a quantum system can be "undone" to restore the system's superposition state. In this experiment, information about which path a particle has taken is initially recorded and then subsequently erased. Remarkably, the erasure of this information allows the particle to revert to a state of superposition, as if it were never observed. This outcome challenges conventional understanding of time and causality, suggesting that future actions can influence past events in the quantum realm.

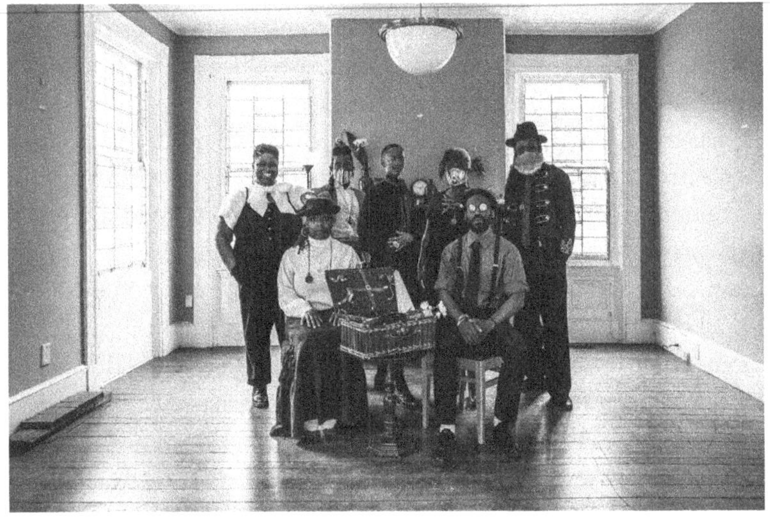

Write No History (dir. Black Quantum Futurism with Bob Sweeney, 2021) is a short, three-panel film featuring found and archival footage of the Temporal Disruptors at one of their meeting lodges, the Hatfield House in Philadelphia. Pictured are Dominque Matti, Iresha Picot, Marcelline Mandeng, Vernon Jordan III, Angel Edwards, Vitche-Boul Ra, Sheena Clay, Camae Ayewa, Alex Farr, Rodnie King, and Riot Dent.

The exploration of quantum time capsules in the 2021 triptych film *Write No History*, created by Black Quantum Futurism with the filmmaker Bob Sweeney, for a site-specific art installation at the historic

Hatfield House in North Philadelphia. The film features speculative found footage of members of an ancient secret society of Black scientists, healers, and writers known as the Temporal Disruptors. The Disruptors harness quantum time capsules to send artifacts and technologies across time, with members planted in every decade, setting up a finely woven communication network which operates on principles of quantum physics and Afrodiasporic features of space and time. Quantum time capsules allow us to subvert this dominance of a singular, observed history. They mirror the quantum eraser's suggestion that past, present, and future are interconnected and mutable. The Temporal Disruptors, existing in every decade, metaphorically and practically embody the quantum eraser's implications, blurring the lines between observation, information, and the malleability of temporal reality.

In the film, the Temporal Disruptors navigate through several crucial junctures in the past, present, and future, which act as gateways or locations for convergence. Here they perform rituals involving the burial and retrieval of quantum time capsules. This strategic distribution of knowledge and resources across time, akin to reversing a wave-function collapse, is an act of hacking colonized timelines. By manipulating their quantum state, the Temporal Disruptors work restores and celebrate histories and futures that have been erased or altered by colonial and oppressive forces. This quantum-inspired approach underscores a larger theme of the film: the power of reclaiming and rewriting one's history and future by understanding and manipulating the fundamental principles of reality, much like how quantum physics reveals the malleability and interconnectedness of the universe at a subatomic level.

Most of the scenes were filmed at The Hatfield House because of its unique features, having been dismantled, transported from its original location, and rebuilt. The quantum time capsules contain information and items that will help the secret society archive and share information to help warn and protect Black communities against harm and keep the communication/warning/healing loop going. Timeless degrees of freedom emerge, creating conditions by which Temporal Disruptors can collapse all eras, instances, and possibilities for Blackness across time and into the present, borrowing freely from any temporal dimension. Through a study of the Unknown, and the development of Black and Afrodiasporic ritual temporalities and codes, Temporal Disruptors activate portals, shadows, and black holes as sites of rememory, future memory, and temporal liberation.

In scientific discourse, the theoretical concept of a quantum time capsule is discussed in a 2007 paper by B. T. Kirby and J. D. Franson examining the unique and nonclassical properties of a quantum system's phase. The paper posits a fascinating aspect of quantum mechanics: the generation of entanglement outside the forward light cone. This phenomenon, which defies the constraints of local realistic theories, implies the potential for creating entangled states in a timeframe shorter than what light would require to travel the same distance. Such capability points to the feasibility of novel quantum information protocols, such as a quantum time capsule. The idea of a quantum time capsule in this context means that information or states could be "stored" in a quantum state and "retrieved" or realized in another location, faster than what would be possible through conventional means. However, the author does not elaborate on the specifics of this concept, as it is not the focus of the paper.[9]

In 2012, before co-founding Black Quantum Futurism (BQF), I was absorbed in cultivating a vibrant Afrofuturist community through my organization The AfroFuturist Affair. This grassroots initiative was dedicated to celebrating, amplifying, and fostering Afrofuturism and science fiction in diverse creative forms, particularly through writing and hosting dynamic events. We first developed the concept of the quantum time capsule during a workshop titled "DIY Time Travel," which I crafted for an event organized by Camae, known as the Rockers BBQ Weekend. The quantum time capsule, initially introduced in this workshop, eventually evolved to become a cornerstone of our artistic and theoretical work within BQF. Blending science, technology, and cultural heritage into our unique brand of temporal exploration and community empowerment, Camae and I planted the seeds of what would eventually blossom into a central element of our BQF practice.

The essence of quantum time capsules, as we conceived them, was their ability to transcend temporal boundaries. This technology would not only facilitate a profound connection with ancestors but also establish a direct line of communication with future generations, thus bridging temporal divides and enriching the cultural and temporal fabric of Black communities. At a time when the term Afrofuturism had not yet reached the mainstream, this concept symbolized a powerful teaching tool for connecting the continuum of past, present, and future, embodying a transformative approach to understanding and interacting with time in the context of Black cultural and historical experiences. Our conception of quantum time capsules was interwoven with our ongoing exploration of time and quantum physics. During that period, I was also immersed in writing stories for *Recurrence Plot: And Other Time Travel Tales*, which fueled our fascination with these themes.

In our workshops, we had participants make a "communal quantum time capsule" out of a shoe box and mirrored paper, while discussing a set of prompts, such as: How would a time capsule differ in your culture? Would you bury it, and if so, where? Who do you intend to unearth it, when, and why? What items would you put in a quantum time capsule to be opened by people in the past versus one to be opened in the future? How could objects in a time capsule maintain their utility and avoid the deterioration of linear time?

We also requested ahead of time that participants bring artifacts that they could share with their community and add to the quantum time capsule, which would be sealed but not buried. Before adding it into the workshop, participants would share why they chose their artifacts, or the stories they invoked, and how these objects represented their personal histories. This collective quantum time capsule could serve as a source of knowledge, both personal and communal. Sometimes we would conduct the workshop in multiple parts, such as ones we did for an organization called Girls Rock Philly. We then conduct an "unsealing" ceremony at the end, opening the capsule after a few weeks or months and sharing what was inside with the entire group, while also discussing any new understandings or connections that emerged as a result of the exercise and our new understandings of time.

Whether born out of quantum physics or Black Quantum Futurism, quantum time capsules serve as radical tools for transgressing linear conceptions of time. These capsules act as conduits, amplifying experiences and narratives typically relegated to the fringes of history and projecting them across a multiplicity of temporal planes. In so doing, they invite us to challenge conventional ideologies, unearthing forgotten histories, and restoring deliberately obscured and erased memories.

In this context, the concept of "erased memories" takes on a significant meaning. It refers to the historical and cultural narratives, particularly of Black communities, which have been systematically excluded, diminished, and distorted within the dominant historical record. These are stories, experiences, and knowledge that have been either intentionally suppressed due to various sociopolitical reasons or inadvertently lost in the passage of time.

Just as the quantum eraser experiment reveals the malleability of quantum states and their histories, the quantum time capsule becomes a symbolic and literal device for reclaiming these memories, giving voice to the voiceless, and restoring to collective consciousness what was erased.

We can therefore navigate the temporal dimensions of Black histories and futures, locating alternative pathways to interpret and interact with the layers of our present moments, much like how the quantum eraser allows for different interpretations of a particle's journey. In the following sections, we will explore the quantum time capsules' transformative potential to carry Black narratives through the corridors of time.

Colored People's Time Capsules

> *I was talking about time. It's so hard for me to believe in it. Some things go. Pass on. Some things just stay. I used to think it was my rememory. You know. Some things you forget. Other things you never do. But it's not. Places, places are still there. If a house burns down, it's gone, but the place—the picture of it—stays, and not just in my rememory, but out there in the world.* —**Toni Morrison, *Beloved***

> *...shards of pottery and broken bottles and old brick and other objects insignificant to sight but actually of a profound meaning and fatal to touch, which no white man could have read.* —**William Faulkner, *Go Down, Moses***

Project: Time Capsule

They regulate space on top of communities
playgrounds on top of graves,
homes on top of landfills,
prisons on top of schools
distorting memory,
collapsing truth,
rendering uncertainty
—Camae Ayewa[10]

Potter's fields, historically known as segregated burial sites for poor, unknown, or unclaimed people, hold significant cultural and temporal implications, particularly in the context of Black history. These sites, often devoid of signage, proper markings, headstones, or memorials, served as the final resting place for many free and enslaved Black individuals in the United States through the twentieth century. Lack of attention and recognition at these burial grounds stands in stark contrast to more privileged or recognized cemeteries, reflecting broader societal attitudes toward marginalized communities. Designed for rudimentary and economical burials, many of these sites have become difficult to locate over time. These sites often lack proper markings, headstones, or memorials, reflecting broader societal attitudes toward marginalized communities and contributing to their relative obscurity today.

For instance, one of the country's largest cemeteries, Hart Island in New York City, has served as a potter's field, with a million burials, including indigent veterans unhoused people, and people claimed by epidemics and pandemics through time, including AIDS and COVID-19.[11] Similarly, the Kings County Potter's Field in New York, active from 1853 to 1917, had over 100,000 people buried there. It has faced threats of being built over, illustrating the disregard for these burial grounds.

Despite being relegated to these unmarked and often forgotten spaces, these fields have become important cultural and historical sites that embody the complicated relationship between Black communities and dominant societal structures. The importance of these sites gives us a window into the burial rituals that offered Black communities "an opportunity to develop African American cultural practices in the New World based at least partially on African practices."[12] Time capsules have roots in ancient practices of preserving memory and sacred artifacts, akin to Egyptian tombs and other ancient repositories, reflecting diverse cultural understandings of time. In this context, potter's fields extend beyond burial sites, transforming into living archives of Black temporalities, capturing the intertwinement of past, present, and future in a manner resonant with the nonlinear, interconnected essence of quantum physics.

The Pennsylvania Historical and Museum Commission shares history on "one of the more infamous potter's fields" in Philadelphia, the "Stranger's Burial Ground" and "Negroes Ground," which lies in a neighborhood now known as Washington Square. There are, however, other notable potter's fields in Philadelphia. In the northwest Philadelphia neighborhood, Germantown, lies a potter's field established in 1755 "for all strangers, negroes, and mulattoes as die in any part of Germantown forever." In 1921, however, a playground was built over it, and as one longtime resident recalled: "Stones that we used for [baseball] bases were old grave stones."[13] Then, in 1955, the Philadelphia Housing Authority erected the Queen Lane Apartments over the site of the Germantown potter's field. In an area that had been redlined and where "white flight" was already underway, Queen Lane was built to be a public housing project, a sixteen-story tower that originally housed 119 low-income "non-white" tenants. Like many other housing projects around the country, federal disinvestment and neglect led to significant maintenance and quality of life concerns, and its eventual demolition.

As the Philadelphia Housing Agency (PHA) readied the Germantown site for demolition and redevelopment, in 2011, community and preservation groups demanded that the cemetery be preserved and memorialized. PHA ensured that construction would only occur outside the boundaries of the potter's field and funded archaeological investigation and preservation. That investigation recovered approximately 6,000 artifacts described as "mostly domestic in nature, and included ceramics, glass, animal bones, architectural items and personal items such as smoking pipes and fragments of musical instruments."[14] These are consistent with historical North American slave practices that included "the surface decoration of graves with ceramics and other objects [a]s the most commonly recognized African-American material culture indicator of cemetery sites."[15]

Fifty-five new housing units were ultimately built on the former Queen Lane site in 2015. The 1921 playground, which was destroyed along with the tower, has yet to be rebuilt, contributing to the pre-existing lack of neighborhood play spaces for youth. As the community, city, and PHA work to find a new location for the playground and decide if and how the potter's field should be used, the site is fenced off with an engraved historical marker signaling its protected status. Neighborhood youth regularly climb the fence and play baseball in the field—a powerful reclamation of the past, its relative present, and future.[16]

In an area to the south of the city, known today as "Queen Village" (unrelated to Queen Lane), another potter's field has laid buried for over a century beneath the Weccacoe Playground and community center. Weccacoe, a re-spelling of the original Lenape name for the area, meaning "Pleasant Place." The neighborhood would later become a haven and community for free Black people living in Philadelphia during the eighteenth and nineteenth centuries; by 1820, nearly two-thirds of all Black families in Philadelphia were settled there. Queen Village had affordable housing, Black churches, and a powerful sense of community. The potter's field located there was built in 1810 by Richard Allen, founder of the nearby Mother Bethel African Methodist Episcopal Church and is arguably one of the most significant African American burial grounds in the country. After a period of thriving, urban redevelopment in the 1950s and 1960s resulted in the decline of Southwark and the eventual demolition of its homes and historic sites. The neighborhood was redeveloped in the 1970s and 1980s. By the early 1990s, it was re-branded by real estate developers as Queen Village, after Queen Christina, ruler of Sweden from 1632 to 1654. The area's original settlers were Swedes, marking the beginnings of "New Sweden," a territory that subsequently became a focal point of contention between England and the Netherlands. After prolonged disputes, control was relinquished to Britain, which in turn handed governance to William Penn in 1681. Penn renamed the area "Southwark." Over time, "Queen Village" emerged not as an official designation but as a popular moniker that gradually gained widespread acceptance.[17] Today the area boasts some of the highest income residents and property values in the city.

The rediscovery of the Queen Village potter's field by local historian Terry Buckalew in 2008, while researching the historical Black figure Octavius Catto, signifies a profound moment in the acknowledgment and preservation of Black historical memory in Philadelphia. Buckalew began a blog called The Bethel Burial Ground Project, documenting as much information as possible about the remains of 5,000 Black people buried beneath what is today a playground, a row of public restrooms, a tennis court, and community center and underscoring the deep, often-overlooked roots of Black heritage in the city.[18] His blog and conversations with local residents helped stir up conversation within the neighborhood and in the local media about the neglect of Black historical memory in Philadelphia.[19] After Buckalew notified the city in 2012, the location was designated a historical landmark in 2013 and renamed the Bethel Burying Ground. A committee of neighborhood residents have since formed to plan for the future of the site to preserve its historical significance and find a new home for the community center and playground. The Bethel Burying Ground Project website by Buckalew has a name directory and shares the stories of some of the people buried there, and public art projects dedicated to memorializing the site.[20]

Set to begin construction in 2024, one memorial project, after extensive community engagement, will bring artist Karyn Oliver's vision, *Her Luxuriant Soil*, to life at the Bethel Burying Grounds Historic Site. This memorial will honor those interred within Weccacoe Playground.[21] The design features a nineteenth-century style cemetery gate, white granite and concrete pavers engraved with the biographies of those buried, based on Terry Buckalew's research. Some pavers will reveal inscriptions only when wet, symbolizing the stories yet uncovered, while others will remain intentionally blank for the unidentified. A brick pathway will outline the cemetery's perimeter, doubling as a wall and bench near the tennis court, with granite "headstones" and inscriptions, including a quote from Richard Allen and words from the site's sole existing headstone. Decorative planters, mimicking nineteenth-century cradle graves, will invite community involvement to maintain them and foster a connection to historical burial traditions. The memorial engages with the concept of memory as something that is dynamic and ever present, rather than static and forgotten. Connecting the Queen Lane and Queen Village potter's fields, and Oliver's memorial, to quantum time capsules, the layering of public spaces and housing developments over potter's fields can be viewed through the lens of quantum superposition, meaning particles exist in multiple states until observed. The layers of history beneath these sites signify the coexistence of various temporalities—from the trauma and struggles of the past to the vibrancy and communal life of the present. This juxtaposition underscores the resilience of Black communities that have continually navigated spaces of marginalization and oppression.

In a society that often seeks to segment and linearize history, the Queen Lane and Queen Village potter's fields are tied by fate, one that places a tension between their respective communities' (re-)memory and preservation of the past, their present needs for community planning and play space, and the future uses of the land. In the context of potter's fields, Toni Morrison's idea of "rememory," which features critically in her novel *Beloved*—the process of revisiting and reliving past experiences, often traumatic, which refuse to be forgotten and continue to impact the present and future—can be particularly powerful in highlighting the ongoing presence and influence of those who were marginalized in both life and death. The existence of these potter's fields, their resilience in the face of being built upon, can be seen as a form of quantum tunneling, where particles pass through barriers that would be insurmountable in classical physics. The histories and memories embedded in these fields have, in a sense, tunneled through temporal and physical barriers, emerging into public consciousness and reshaping the narrative and utilization of these spaces.

According to linear time, these tensions might be rendered flat by what is chosen to be placed in a traditional time capsule, sealed off from the past and simultaneously crystallized into history upon its opening by the future. In a quantum time capsule, however, temporal tensions are expected and can be dynamic, open to influence and possibility, embodying the multifaceted narratives of joy, trauma, and resilience that characterize Black experiences. As cultural artifacts and reclaimed space-times emerge from the dirt, liberated from tombstones of buildings and concrete, potter's fields are open air memorials that, once unburied and reclaimed, serve as quantum time capsules for Black cultural memory, space, and time. Simultaneously, those sacred grounds have been strong enough to hold housing, community spaces, and playgrounds and all the frequencies of joy and trauma that can be found within those communal space-times. These fields demand recognition, preservation, and study, not only for their historical significance but as dynamic continuums of cultural memory, history, and identity.

Subfloor Pits. Cabins, Assemblages, and Time Capsules of the Enslaved

> *Perhaps the most curious personal items from the sites were clock components: a clock winder and pewter key were found at Carter's Grove (CG715B). A toy pewter pocket watch was also found in one of the pits at the late eighteenth-century Utopia quarter. It has been suggested that watches and clocks conferred power on those individuals who owned and understood them, although this power was generally that of the watch-owning planter over the enslaved.* —**Patricia M. Samford, "Power Runs in Many Channels"**

Black cultural artifacts and sites of memory often remain invisible to the dominant gaze unless they intersect with motives of capital appropriation, exploitation, and accumulation. This invisibility persists unless these artifacts and sites present obstacles to or opportunities for the ongoing appropriation of Black bodies and histories by white capital. Such dynamics underscore the community's resistance to the commodification and erasure of Black experiences and memories. In excavating the cabins of enslaved African and Black burial grounds, researchers have come across artifacts that appear to them to be "miscellaneous piles of junk."[22]

Liberating these artifacts from the confines of a commodified lens involves reimagining them as integral components of a broader narrative that reclaims context, subjectivity, and historical significance. These objects, once perceived through a reductive lens, reveal their profound narratives when appreciated as part of quantum time capsules. Within these capsules, the artifacts transcend their assumed material insignificance to narrate stories of survival, defiance, and the unbreakable continuity of Black identity and heritage. Detached from their commodified valuation, these remnants of the past emerge not as "junk" but as powerful testimonies to the complex tapestry of Black history, offering insights that challenge and enrich our understanding of the past, present, and future.

By reframing these objects as valuable testaments to the lives of individuals once reduced to commodity value, we acknowledge their inherent worth and the depth of human experiences they represent. This theoretical linkage to quantum time capsules—where time, memory, and artifacts operate beyond conventional constraints—allows these objects to defy and transform traditional concepts of temporality and significance. In this light, artifacts become not mere relics but vibrant conveyors of memory and identity, challenging a timeline that may not identify their experiences as worthy of historical fact or particular significance, and inviting a multidimensional exploration of Black legacies. The personal possessions in the remains of slave cabins provide a glimpse into the diverse cultural and spiritual practices of enslaved people. As one journalist put it, "while the white family upstairs went about their transplanted English lives, practicing conventional Christianity, African-Americans downstairs cooked, did the laundry and, though baptized, still practiced rituals of their former West African religions."[23] In her study of the Hume Plantation in South Carolina, Sharon K. Moses details the evidence showing how enslaved Africans retained their religious and conjure practices in homes and living quarters, outlining the various symbolic meanings associated with placement in addition to their cloaking mechanism:

> [They] utilized individual agency in spiritual matters, such as placing protective deposits that called upon ancestors or water spirits in the dirt floors, under slat floors, below corner posts, beneath window areas and door jambs—all liminal areas or crossing places that symbolically represent movement from one realm into another. Some deposits were placed near hearths or the proximity to the symbolism of fire; back yards and gardens not only allowed them to supplement their subsistence needs

with vegetables and herbs but provided an outlet for cultivating medicinal plants for healing or magic.[24]

Subfloor pits, for example, are dug-out hollows in the soil beneath the floorboards, which beyond their function as a storage place for root vegetables or "safety deposit box" for personal items, evidence from the seventeenth to nineteenth centuries shows also served as West African spiritual shrines. Some living quarters featured multiple pits.[25] These "sub-floor pits achieve[d] their security function by making access to their contents time consuming, more likely to be publicly observed, and hence socially accountable."[26] They offered effective hiding places for keeping ritual and spiritual activities secret and protected objects from destruction by slave masters and themselves from danger.

Artifacts excavated at these sites include cowrie shells, seashells, colorful glass and clay beads, pieces of iron and copper, ceramic vessels, tobacco pipes, mirror glass, marbles, coins, bone combs, small animal bones, violin parts, jaw harps, talismans, and other spiritual objects. Some feature markings, for example, pottery shards with etchings similar to a Kôngo cosmogram. This cosmogram, also known as *dikenga*, is a central element in Kôngo spiritual beliefs, symbolizing the continuous cycle of life and death. It consists of a cross inside a circle, where the intersection of the cross represents the powerful point of contact between the living and the ancestors. The cosmogram divides life into four stages represented by the sun's daily cycle: dawn (birth), noon (full adulthood), sunset (waning adulthood), and midnight (rebirth). Small circles at each axis end signify these life stages, with counterclockwise arrows indicating the process of reincarnation. The Bakôngo people view life as a perpetual motion through these stages, guided by ancestral spirits (*simbi*) invoked through sacred songs and chants.

Scholars note that these shrines and religious artifacts would have been used for protection from vengeful masters and overseers, for healing, given infrequent access to a doctor or a preference for African healing methods, and for divination to help plans of escape and to foresee other life or community events.[27] In one home in Maryland, excavations found "brass pins, buttons and beads, rock crystals, a piece of a crab claw, disks pierced with holes, a brass ring and bell, pieces of glass and bone, and the arms and legs of a small doll" under the brick hearths and specifically in the northeast corners of the house.[28]

On the Hume Plantation, deposits of buttons, arrowheads, mirror shards, an assortment of shells, and beads of assorted colors were uncovered in the northwest corners of the home or that had north–south orientations. Notably, fragments of colonoware were also found, with one piece displaying a faint "X" possibly symbolizing the Kôngo cosmogram. Colonoware refers to a type of earthenware pottery that was traditionally crafted by enslaved African Americans and Native Americans in the colonial period of the southeastern United States. These hand-built, unglazed ceramics often bear unique markings and are considered significant artifacts of African diasporic culture, reflecting both African influences and the experience of enslavement in America.

The artifacts, including the colonoware, are believed to have ritualistic significance, linked to West African religious practices. As placement of ritual objects is significant in West African religions, the various assemblages were likely associated with a particular spirit or Orisha, with the colors of the beads—blue, red, and white—holding specific symbolic meaning or association with spirits, nature, protection, and the like. Dr. Moses observes that ritual deposits of projectile points found within the foundational beam of an overseer's house and burned cat's teeth with two nails found near its fireplace/hearth suggest "a tone of justice or vengeance."[29]

Gemstones are recurrent objects in excavated assemblages. A quartz crystal, a prehistoric quartz point, and a piece of galena (silver-colored lead ore) were discovered in a tight grouping near the chimney's foundation of the 1870s-era home of an Black family named Nash, located on the Brownsville Plantation in Manassas, Virginia.[30] Afrodiasporic spiritual and religious traditions of the era preserved connection to African cultures relying heavily on the power of crystals and gemstones, imbuing them with good luck, protection against harm, healing, and opening up the spirit world. An excavation of the early 1800s home and slave quarters of slave trader Nathaniel Russell in South Carolina revealed "a glass prism, most likely taken from a chandelier, buried in the floorboards," which were "like quartz crystals discovered in other slave quarters, found by a window in the northeast part of the house and likely placed there to summon the protection of ancestral spirits."[31] The placement of ritual deposits in specific directions (northwest or northeast) within hearths and liminal spaces may be tied to the movement of celestial bodies, or the layout of the spiritual world. The choice of these directions for ritual deposits may reflect inherited cultural knowledge about the significance of these orientations in relation to spiritual practices, protection, and the invocation of ancestral or spiritual forces. However, the precise meaning can vary widely across different African cultures and their diasporic traditions.

Similarly, at the Charles Carroll House in Annapolis, Maryland, several large arrays of quartz crystals were found, dating from 1790 to 1820. The largest of these was a group of twelve crystals and a smooth black stone, covered by a pearlware bowl marked with a large asterisk or sunburst design resembling the Kôngo cosmogram, and located, again, in the northeast corner of the room between the floor and wall.[32] Several other crystals as well as coins, beads, crab claws, ivory rings, and shells native to Florida and the West Indies were found hidden in groupings around the same room, providing evidence "that one, or possibly more, of Charles Carroll's slaves may have been a conjurer or diviner."[33] For enslaved people, these gemstones and architectural talismans would have been understood "as a living, vital symbol that acts as a protector of the individual wearing it . . . especially a gemstone, [which] might be considered a guarantor of fortune, welfare, and prosperity," and which brings sacred benefits to the living.[34] Using these talismans and gemstones were acts of agency, of individuals acting to shape their world—for protection or harm, resistance or communion—operating with subtlety and craft to avoid exposure to the white gaze of the overseer.

Bringing a variety of African cultural practices with them to the Americas, each with its own beliefs and customs regarding the use of objects for spiritual or ritual use, the presence of these items in slave quarters affirms that enslaved people continued to practice their traditions. Long stereotyped as ignorant, uncivilized, passive, and stripped of their cultural heritage, these artifacts showcase the ingenuity, creativity, and resilience of enslaved people to maintain their culture despite oppression. Their practices were alive and well, preserved across generations, nourishing a fragile balance between returning to their own traditions, and resisting the forces that sought to erase and violently suppress their traditions and identities.

The assemblages of artifacts found in subfloor pits, hearths, door jams, and other liminal and secret spaces are representations of rooted memories. Like time capsules, they were ways of burying and storing crystallized moments in the face of psychological, physical, and spiritual warfare, such that they wouldn't be lost in the progress of time, churned through the cogs of the master's clock. They lay in wait, not just in the physical sense, but in a temporal suspension, ready to be reclaimed and reintegrated into the everyday life and spiritual practices of their owners once the opportunity arose.

Temporally transposed, these caches gave space and time for objects of spiritual, emotional, and cultural significance to hold meaning outside the gaze and timestream of white captors.

Freedom's Underground: Caves as Pathways to Temporal Liberation

our death like our birth means something.
a way to it, preparing a body all ours
ancestors returning again
this time only to themselves
—Camae Ayewa

It was of course a closely guarded secret at the time, but today there is increasing documentation of the underground cave systems that formed the routes of the Underground Railroad, in addition to the tunnels, cellars, and basements more commonly used to hide escaped slaves as they traveled northward. In *Free Black Communities and the Underground Railroad: The Geography of Resistance*, Cheryl Janifer LaRoche recounts how "at times, caves replaced hollowed trees, forests or mountains," and were "used by escapees and white conductors alike" for "safety and shelter."[35] She names "the caves and iron furnaces along Underground Railroad routes" in Miller Grove, Illinois or Poke Patch in Ohio as examples "distinguished in a geography of resistance approach to the landscape."[36]

According to legend, a group of enslaved Black people in Kentucky were led through Mammoth Cave by an enslaved man named Stephen Bishop, who used his knowledge of the cave's extensive network of tunnels and chambers to travel undetected and guide the group to freedom. LaRoche also shares the story of Winey Petty and her daughter, who endured a damp, cold cave as a hiding place for five months starting in October of 1855, while they waited for their chance to escape Norfolk, Virginia.[37] Then there is the mystery of a cave near Butler County, Ohio, that has not yet been found, which is rumored to have been used as a hideout for liberation-seekers. Oral history and a mysterious 1892 article, penned in the *Middletown Signal Newspaper* by someone named only "John," the proclaimed son of an abolitionist sympathizer, tells the harrowing story of twenty-one enslaved Africans who died in the cave where they were hiding due to toxic natural gases.[38] The article alleges the cave was sealed after their remains were found, along with the bodies of four other geologists who had ventured into the cave.[39]

The state of Missouri is home to a vast network of underground caves where, over millions of years, water has eroded the limestone underneath to create a network of caves and underground rivers. The city of St. Louis itself boasts twenty-nine caves, many of which were used for commercial purposes during the city's early years. The Lemp Mansion (3322 DeMenil Pl) is a historic and infamous building in St. Louis, known for being the former home of the Lemp family, who immigrated to Missouri by way of Germany in 1838, and made their fortune after founding William J. Lemp's Western Brewery. Part of the property includes an underground cave system, then called Lemp's Cave, which was used for beer storage and cooling and hosted a beer garden, theater, and heated pool for guests and visitors.[40] The brewery was closed in 1919 during Prohibition and permanently shuttered its operations in 1922. This cave system also extends beneath the Chatillon-DeMenil Mansion (3352 DeMenil Place), though its official history denies there is an entrance from the mansion into the caves.[41] Originally built by prominent trapper and businessman Henri Chatillon, the house was later sold to physician and chain drugstore owner Nicolas DeMenil.

A few years after its sale to Lee Hess in 1945, the Chatillon-DeMenil property was opened as a tourist attraction and the underlying cave renamed Cherokee Cave. While developing the tourist attracting, construction work on the old brewery tunnels unearthed a large number of ice age fossils embedded throughout the various layers of sediment, and the owner of Cherokee Cave turned it into a natural history museum.[42] This was short lived, however, and the property was purchased in 1961 by the State of Missouri Highway Commission and the cave partially destroyed to make way for the construction of Interstate 55—the construction of which also destroyed parts of the Lemp Mansion, though the Chatillon-DeMenil Mansion was spared from total destruction when the Landmarks Association purchased the land and home. While there were once multiple entrances to the cave scattered throughout the neighborhood, all the others have since been sealed off.

According to local oral history, Cherokee Cave served an additional purpose: as one of the stops along the Underground Railroad. Its proximity to the Mississippi River and its underground landscape offered ideal spatial and temporal shelter for freedom-seekers looking to cross the river into the free state of Illinois. Cherokee Cave is connected via natural tunnels to a more extensive network of caves called the English Caves, which run beneath Benton Park. This network of tunnels spans over three miles and extends all the way to the old Federal Reserve Bank in downtown St. Louis. Several potential entrances and exits for Cherokee Cave have also been mapped, including one close to the Mississippi River that enslaved peoples could have used to potentially escape to freedom in Illinois. Local historians and longtime residents believe these tunnels served as part of the Underground Railroad, connecting the cave system to a building located at 3314–3318 Lemp Avenue—squarely on the DeMenil property.[43]

In 2000, local high school teacher and archaeologist Chip P. Clatto led an excavation of the Lemp Avenue site with his students, where crystals, cowrie shells, small carved bones, and other African spiritual and ritual objects were discovered. The excavation also uncovered a hole large enough to be the entrance to a tunnel with a shallow room beyond it.[44] On his website documenting the excavation, Clatto suggests that the site may have operated as slave quarters for the DeMenil property. He notes, however, that although the DeMenils were listed as slaveowners in the 1850 census, they were not listed as slaveowners in the subsequent 1860 census, making it unclear whether enslaved people actually lived on the property.[45] Despite ample indication of the connections between the Underground Railroad and the caves running below St. Louis, the city government has deemed these links circumstantial and have refused to further preserve the excavation site on Lemp Avenue, where today, several remodeled houses sit. These shrouded histories show that more than just a means of escape caves were literal portals to another time and place, an exit point from slavery to freedom, where potentials for liberation could be collapsed into reality.

Like giant icicles emerging from the cave roof and floor, stalactites and stalagmites at Cherokee Cave closely resemble Ghanaian divination objects, crafted with groupings of cowrie shells cocooned around a stick or base. Stalactites collect water and time, incrementally forming into crystals.

Quantum physics has confirmed the enigmatic nature of crystalline structures and their play with light and time. One recent discovery shows "an infinitesimally small world composed of a strange and surprising array of links, knots and winding," while another experiment on an ancient Namibian crystal called cuprite (and purchased off eBay) produced the largest hybrid particles of light and matter ever created.[46] This hybrid is a unique combination of an electron and a phonon, exhibiting a bond strength ten times greater than any previously known electron-phonon hybrid. This potent interaction hints at the possibility of manipulating both electronic and magnetic properties simultaneously through external stimuli such as voltage or light. Gemstones, such as diamond and sapphire, which can create special types of particles and quasiparticle that can manipulate the properties and interactions of light and matter, have led scientists to such seemingly mystical terrain as experiments on quantum entanglement and quantum teleportation.

The journey of these stones, mined from the depths of the earth in Africa, tells a story of paradox and exploitation. In scientific research, these gems are highly sought after, their unique energies harnessed for groundbreaking experiments. Yet there exists a glaring contradiction in how these same stones are perceived when used by Black people for spiritual healing and metaphysical practices rooted in Afrodiasporic belief systems. Within scientific communities, such practices are ridiculed and cast off as primitive or superstitious. Here, the same gems that are celebrated in laboratories are dismissed or ridiculed as mere superstition when they form the cornerstone of spiritual healing rituals intrinsic to Black cultures.

The spiritual erasure of Black metaphysical traditions whitewashes cultural practices for new age consumption, effacing the history and contributions of African and enslaved communities. The theft of age-old spiritual practices and their presentation to new audiences as novel discoveries compounds this injustice, perpetuating the resource exploitation, both mineral and cultural, that defines colonialism. This is a form of "spiritual erasure." This phenomenon not only strips these practices of their rich history and significance, but also sanitizes them for palatable consumption, erasing their African origins. It's a modern iteration of colonialism—a cultural and spiritual plunder parallel to the physical extraction of minerals.

This double standard highlights a broader issue of cultural and scientific disenfranchisement. The very minerals that are stripped from African soil are employed to propel scientific endeavors across the globe, often without acknowledgment or inclusion of the people from whose land these resources come. Black people all over the globe find ourselves systematically marginalized from the scientific narrative, our contributions overlooked, and our traditions often deemed irrelevant in the chronicles of scientific advancement.

Is it any more valid for scientists to use these ancient materials extracted from caves and mines in Africa to appropriate their properties for their quantum experimentations with light and time? If crystals can be used to experiment with—and break—time, perhaps we can regard the cave as a quantum time capsule of sorts or a giant quantum computer. Imagine liberation-seekers encoding messages in cave crystals with firelight, to be preserved for all time, or recognizing the substance of the stalactites and stalagmites as the stuff of their sacred tools, as they moved through underground cave networks toward freedom.

In 2023, Black Quantum Futurism drew on the physics of crystals, the structures of caves, and the histories and artifacts of the Black liberation-seekers who navigated the perilous paths beneath the surface of St. Louis to create the *SLOWER-THAN-LIGHT SHRINE: IN REMEMBRANCE OF THE UNDERGROUND RAILROAD* sculpture as part of Counterpublic, the St. Louis public art triennial. The work derives its name from the way I imagined liberation-seekers moving slower than light, inside the shadows, to avoid visibility and the "watch"-ful eye of slavecatchers. Suspended structures inside the shrine echoed the stalactites and stalagmites found in images of Cherokee Cave. The shrine's foundation is a mosaic of potent symbols, blending the Kôngo cosmogram and the Mmere Dane Adinkra symbol, which signifies the fluidity and transformation inherent in time (*time changes, times change*). Adinkra symbols also adorned the gates, weaving a tapestry of cultural heritage and historical memory. The design of the shrine's main structure, with its windows and arches, referenced the architecture of the lost homes of Mill Creek Valley and Pruitt-Igoe, in resonance with those displaced communities.

The Pruitt-Igoe housing project, a once-promising beacon of modern public housing in the 1950s, deteriorated into a symbol of systemic failure, collapsing under the weight of neglect and poor management. Its demolition in 1972 left behind a void, both physically, in the form of an overgrown vacant lot, and metaphorically, as a stark reminder of the intersection of racism, poverty, and urban policy. The site, while devoid of structures, remains as a silent witness to this tumultuous chapter in St. Louis's history, inviting introspection and dialogue about the legacy of public housing.

The nearby Mill Creek Valley was once a bustling African American hub, home to thousands of residents and hundreds of businesses. In the 1950s, this vibrant community fell victim to the city's urban renewal initiatives, resulting in widespread displacement and the erasure of a cultural landmark. The repercussions of this forced exodus reverberate to this day, with many families uprooted and unable to regain their footing in the face of systemic housing inequalities, forced to live in overcrowded, substandard conditions in other parts of the city.

We offered the *SLOWER-THAN-LIGHT SHRINE* as a space for contemplation on the interplay between history, culture, physics, and the urgent pursuit of liberation. The work is now permanently housed at the Vashon Museum, a museum which is itself an exploded time capsule with a collection of over 10,000 unique artifacts, spanning 250 years of African American history in St. Louis, Missouri.

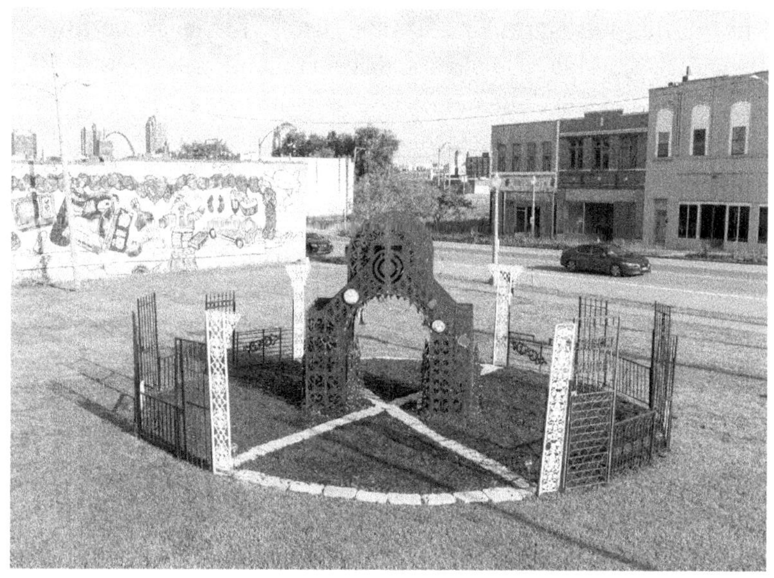

"SLOWER-THAN-LIGHT SHRINE: IN REMEMBRANCE OF THE UNDERGROUND RAILROAD" installation by Black Quantum Futurism (2023), as part of Counterpublic (St. Louis).

Freed People's Time Capsules

When a construction crew's backhoe in 1991 uncovered a time capsule planted by former slaves, some of this mill city's notions and symbols of the Old South began to crumble. The capsule, a three-inch-deep tin box, was nestled in a granite block in what had been a downtown department store. It contained an array of coins, biblical tracts, newspapers, and personal artifacts, including an 1868 lapel pin that reads "U.S. Grant for President." —**Bonnie Winston, "Time Capsule's Treasures at Home in Museum Buried by Former Slaves"**

Under the church
Time is a hymn
An offering of freedom
—**Camae Ayewa**

The Danville Museum of Fine Arts and History, nestled in the heart of Danville, VA, resides in a historic mansion notoriously known as the Last Capitol of the Confederacy due to its history as the temporary home of Confederate president Jefferson Davis. Roughly a century later, in the 1960s, it became a whites-only library, before becoming the fine arts museum in 1974. This landmark has stood as a poignant emblem of segregation and the lingering shadows of the Old South with Danville's Black community. Within its walls the museum houses a time capsule. Found in 1991, by a construction crew inside of a granite block that belonged to a former downtown department store, this relic was originally concealed in 1870 by an assembly of emancipated Black people and members of the Society of True Friends of Charity.

This capsule, far more than a mere repository of historical artifacts, represents a quantum time capsule, functioning within the realms of Black temporalities to excavate and bring to light the buried narratives of Black experiences that might have remained obscured. The unveiling and exhibition of the time capsule in 1993 transcended a simple act of historical revelation; it was a deliberate invocation of Black temporal dynamics, an effort to stitch together the fragmented histories of Danville's Black community and bridge the chasms between Black and white residents.[47]

By aligning the act of uncovering this capsule with the principles of Black temporalities—where time is not linear but layered, multifaceted, and deeply entwined with the community's collective memory and identity—the museum's exhibition served as a quantum leap into the past. It offered a unique lens through which the complex tapestry of Black history in Danville could be viewed, appreciated, and integrated into the broader narrative of the town's past. In doing so, the Danville Museum of Fine Arts and History transformed the time capsule into a powerful tool for social unity and historical reclamation. Through this quantum time capsule, the museum facilitated a communal journey back through time, fostering a deeper understanding and acknowledgment of the diverse narratives that together weave the complex story of Danville, thereby attempting to mend the historical rifts and unite the community in a shared appreciation of its multifaceted heritage.

From the unnamed, captive laborers, whose hands dug deep into the soil to build the United States' infrastructure, we may uproot all kinds of hidden time capsules. For their survival, enslaved Black people and post-liberation Black laborers came to understand the complexities of linear time better than others, learning to navigate white Western timelines just as our ancestors did the stars. They deftly traversed time and space to liberate one another long before the "effective date" of the Emancipation Proclamation, throughout the Civil War, and well after the time of so-called freedom came. Their time capsules were visions planted into the soil or cast into concrete cornerstones, seeds safeguarded to grow into futures they themselves were never meant to reach. In whatever future they emerge, time capsules erupt from outside the timeline, subverting it—reworking the past, loosening their own present, and changing all possible futures.

> When Reverend Christopher Rush laid the cornerstone of the First African Methodist Episcopal Zion Church in 1853, he placed in it a time capsule, a box that contained a bible, a hymn book, and copies of two New York papers, *The Tribune* and *The Sun*. These were mementos for future New Yorkers. Rush, who escaped slavery and became the second ordained bishop of the AME Zion Church, also delivered the church's first sermon.[48]

Unbeknownst to the reverend, just two weeks prior to laying a time capsule in the cornerstone of the new church, the land on which it sat had been condemned by eminent domain to make way for Central Park. In 1825, a Black man named William Andrews bought three plots of land in the area now known as 82nd and 88th Streets, while on the same day, trustees from the first African Methodist Episcopal (AME) Zion Church bought six lots in the same area for use by the church as a cemetery for Black people.[49] Within seven years, twenty-five more lots had been purchased by Black people, and by the end of the decade over one hundred Black people were living there.

Where whites refused to sell land to Black people due to restrictive covenants, the land that became Seneca Village enabled free Black people to buy land, build homes, and eventually build a thriving community. In other parts of New York City, they faced substandard and unaffordable housing—property in the uptown area of the city, where Seneca Village was located, was cheaper than downtown land.[50] Owning property meant that its residents enjoyed voting rights, quality education, religious freedom, refuge from racial violence and surveillance, and the freedom to celebrate their cultural heritage. Such freedoms made the community a prime target for destruction by white politicians concerned with, among other things, liberated Black people gaining too much political power.[51] Although Seneca Village was thriving with three churches and a school by 1856, a media campaign begun politicians was used to justify seizing the land, where the community was described as a "shantytown" and its residents painted as "squatters and bloodsuckers." The summer of that same year, the residents were given eviction notices, and the neighborhood was demolished by the next year.[52]

Nearly twenty years after it was destroyed, Seneca Village had been mostly forgotten until two coffins containing the remains of Black people surfaced in 1871, as contractors were building a new entrance to Central Park. The new entrance was in fact on the site of the AME Zion Church graveyard, as well as a former potter's field.[53] No further efforts were made to preserve or excavate the area until the early 2000s.

The lost time capsule of Seneca Village's AME Zion Church demonstrates how Western linear timelines are openly hostile to Black lives, Black bodies, and their graves. It openly denies us access to our own futures and pasts. And yet again, Black burial grounds serve as literal infrastructure for white progress, triggering a wave of gentrification that stretches forward and backward in time, that invades Black people's living space-times and our death space-times. Even in death we are not allowed time or space to rest.

Monumental Time Capsules

> *Someday you be walking down the road, and you hear something or see something going on. So clear. And you think it's you thinking it up. A thought picture. But no. It's when you bump into a rememory that belongs to somebody else . . . if you go there—you who never was there—if you go there and stand in the place where it was, it will happen again; it will be there for you, waiting for you.* —**Toni Morrison, *Beloved***

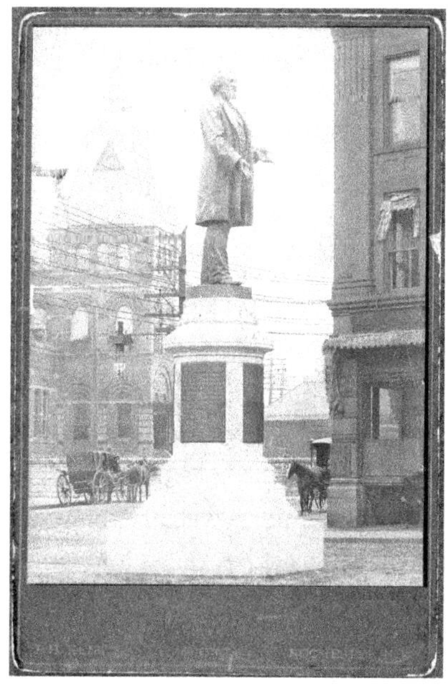

The Frederick Douglass monument in Rochester, NY, photographed circa 1900, shortly after its construction.

In 2019, as workers prepared to relocate a Frederick Douglass statue in Rochester, New York's Highland Park to make way for a memorial plaza in his honor, a time capsule was discovered in a small cutout area inside the statue's granite base. The statue—thought to be the first memorial dedicated to a Black person in the United States—was first unveiled in 1899 in front of Grand Central Terminal in New York City, after being commissioned by Black activist John W. Thomas, and moved to Highland Park in 1941. Among the contents of the beat-up tin box were: two suffragette leaflets by Susan B. Anthony, alive at the time of the monument's original dedication; a copy of the "Declaration of Sentiments," penned in 1848 by Elizabeth Cady Stanton, demanding equality for women; a road map of Monroe County, New York; the 1856 book *Slavery Unmasked*; a letter from the government of Haiti, acknowledging a donation of $1,000 (approximately $31,000 today) toward the cost of the statue; and an 1898 calendar. It also contained newspapers from 1941, added when the statue was moved.[54]

While the contents were ultimately unsalvageable due to water damage they'd sustained, perhaps the true time capsule is the statue itself. It is an unburied quantum time capsule of monumental size, open to revision, able to contain and generate new and old memories across manifold time scales. The bronze representation of Douglass is engraved with an 1863 speech he gave in Rochester, shortly after the Emancipation Proclamation was signed. The memorial's inception traces back to before Frederick Douglass's passing in 1895, ignited by John W. Thompson, a key figure within Rochester's African American community, who initiated a fund for a tribute to African American Civil War soldiers. It is thought that Douglass himself may have originally proposed the idea for the memorial, drawing from his experience speaking at the Lincoln Civil War statue's unveiling in Rochester's Washington Park, where he noted the absence of African American soldiers' representation.[55]

Ensnared in the statue-cum-capsule's temporal web are the years of 1863, 1898, 1899, 1941, and 2019, as well as other dates and times too numerous to be known. The watch chain on Douglass's body is a symbol of authority and power. He is surrounded by pillar sculptures of constellations, including the *North Star*, the name of the newspaper Douglass published in Rochester, in honor of the enduring spatial-temporal marker that enslaved Black people followed on the path to liberation.

In 2018, commemorating the two hundredth birthday of Douglass, thirteen replicas of the original statue were made and installed at key locations around the city as part of a history trail. Two of the replicas were vandalized in separate incidents, but both were eventually replaced. In 2020 a replica was removed from its base and tossed into a gorge, either by anarchists—as was claimed by then-president Donald Trump—or, according to the NAACP, in an act of retaliation by white supremacists for the wave of removals of Confederate statues, seen by many as symbols of racial oppression, that came about following several fatal acts of police brutality around the country. This latter interpretation draws a parallel with the broader movement to dismantle Confederate monuments. This tumultuous period underscores the complex interplay between historical commemoration and contemporary social tensions, revealing how acts of remembrance and the spaces they inhabit can become battlegrounds for competing narratives and ideologies.

Preceding the Frederick Douglass time capsule discovery by four years was the recovery of a time capsule hidden in a cornerstone of the controversial Confederate Vance Monument in Asheville, North Carolina, during its restoration and repair. Constructed just two years before the Douglass monument in 1897, the sixty-five-foot granite obelisk was a tribute to the Civil War governor, senator, slave owner, and possible KKK Grand Dragon Zebulon Baird Vance. Engraved in the base of the Vance Monument are the words "SO THAT THE FUTURE MAY LEARN FROM THE PAST," a testament to the ways in which traditional time capsules send their information forward from the past to the future only.

It is curious, then, that among the contents of the time capsule was a powerful piece of counterhistory: the only known copy of *The Colored Enterprise*, a Black newspaper which ran for two years in the 1890s.

> In March, a time capsule in the base of the Vance Monument yielded a voice from Asheville's 1890s African-American community. *The Colored Enterprise*, a newspaper representing about a third of Asheville's population in its day, lay concealed in a box at the base of the Vance Monument for more than a century. It was put there secretly by Masons in 1897, when the monument was dedicated, and recently discovered during restoration efforts. The time capsule contained the only known copy of *The Colored Enterprise*. Although scholars such as Dr. Darin Waters, a professor of history at UNC Asheville, have found references to it during their research, they've never actually seen a copy.[56]

The local Freemasons who assembled the capsule did not specify an opening date in the future-to-come, unlike traditional time capsules. When a current member of the same local lodge was interviewed about the finding, he reflected that "the time capsule was probably intended to represent the entire community," and while "historically, people have thought of Masons as a white, male organization . . . the only thing Masons ask of a man is belief in a deity."[57] This was the same lodge to which Vance himself belonged.

While the monument was being restored in 2016, a petition signed by over 2,000 local community members called for a marker honoring Black history to be erected nearby. The simmering controversy over the monument's presence spilled over after the murder of George Floyd in 2020 and the nationwide racial uprisings that followed. This reinvigorated calls for its removal, and activists projected messages on the monument and created protest art in the streets surrounding it. In early 2021, Asheville City Council overwhelmingly voted to remove the monument, though debates continue regarding what to do with the monument or its granite remains once dismantled.

The Vance and Douglass monuments are both relics that needed to be troubled—physically and symbolically—to disrupt their status as frozen testaments to one time and instead reveal the time capsules within. Much like the sci-fi Temporal Disruptors, these time capsules hack linear time, fundamentally altering the conditions of the future and allowing Black people to leave their mark, to plant ourselves where we have otherwise been erased. In retrieving these time capsules, we also engage with the principles of quantum physics, where the past and the future can exist in a kind of superposition, influencing each other in unpredictable ways.

While delving into newspaper archives in search of Black time capsules, I came across an October 1, 1949 edition of the *Carolina Times*, a prominent Black newspaper, that documented what it called a first-of-its-kind time capsule, buried in a statue of Dr. James E. Shepard, founder of North Carolina College. The article records the time capsule's purpose being to "embalm records of Negro life—films, newspapers, maps, clippings, news article and similar documents—at the base of the proposed monument of the educator" as a statement to "Americans who live in the twenty-first century that Negroes made valuable contributions to American life."[58]

Situating these monuments with their embedded time capsules as *quantum* time capsules allows us to ask: What information can the past glean from the future? What can the future transmit back to the past?

North Philadelphia Mean Time

In May 2019, BQF showcased an exhibition called *All Time Is Local* at the Center for Emerging Visual Arts in Philadelphia. The art pieces that made up the show, including a short experimental film, collaged clocks, and a mini sculpture of a house, explored the intimate relationship between time and space in their impact on historic Black futurist projects in North Philly. The goal was to shine a light on the efforts of initiatives like Progress Aerospace Enterprises, now nearly forgotten, as well as on more enduring projects like Progress Plaza and Zion Gardens. We argued that the temporal legacies of these projects, which intersected with local spatial politics, created a local space-time.

Co-founded in 1899 by Dr. Caroline Anderson and Reverend Matthew Anderson, the Berean Presbyterian Church, Berean Institute, and the Berean Enterprise Movement served as a nexus for medical, educational, and social activism. Dr. Anderson was one of the first Black women to earn a medical degree in the United States as well as a teacher and social activist alongside such contemporaries as Lucretia Mott, W. E. B. Du Bois, and Sarah Mapps Douglass. While maintaining her own private medical practice, she co-founded the Berean Institute in North Philadelphia with Rev. Anderson, in opposition to the racially discriminatory policy at Girard College, across the street. Girard was a boy's school that restricted enrollment to "poor, white, male, orphans" in accordance with founder Stephen Girard's will. At the Berean Institute, Dr. Anderson was the assistant principle, and taught elocution, hygiene, and physiology, while also being an organizer and administrator for Rev. Anderson's Berean Enterprise movement. This movement, underpinned by a commitment to educational excellence and community upliftment, sought to empower African American communities through a comprehensive approach that included education, economic development, and social welfare. The Berean Institute building still stands on Girard Avenue, but has since changed ownership, though its use as a training institute persists. Unfortunately, the historical marker that commemorates the history of the Berean Institute near the building fails to bear Dr. Anderson's name, but there is an extensive collection of her letters archived at Temple University and biographical information about her is displayed prominently at the Berean Presbyterian Church.

Other Black spatial-temporal landscapes of Philadelphia are presently undergoing a form of "temporal gentrification." Monuments, historic homes and markers, murals, and public art dedicated to Black history are being erased and replaced by luxury housing. A mural depicting local North Philadelphia civil rights activist Florie Dotson, painted to protest the lack of affordable housing in the neighborhood was, tellingly, covered up by a luxury townhouse. Local Black women historians Faye Anderson and Jackie Wiggins have also recently uncovered the destruction by developers of a historical marker at the former North Philadelphia home Jessie Redmon Fauset, a prominent figure in the Harlem Renaissance, a prolific fiction writer, poet, educator, and literary editor of *The Crisis Magazine* whose work on race, identity, and the African American experience was published by the NAACP from 1919–26. Fausset had a home at 17th and Berks in North Philadelphia, where she died three days after her seventy-ninth birthday on April 30, 1961.

Another prominent subject of this piecemeal erasure is Dox Thrash, a pre–civil rights era artist and activist who lived in the Sharswood neighborhood of North Philadelphia at 23rd Street and Columbia/C. B. Moore Street through the 1940s and 50s. Activist and community leader Shaykh Muhammad would purchase the Dox Thrash home in 1959 and open Muhammad's African Asian Cultural Center in it. On two separate occasions in recent years, murals dedicated to the legacy of Dox Thrash have been destroyed: one, located on the side of his deteriorating house, was painted over by the Department of Housing and Urban Development; and the other, placed at 16th Street and Girard Avenue meant to replace the one destroyed by HUD, has since been three-quarters obscured by luxury condos. The Dox Thrash home sold at a bank foreclosure auction, but through the efforts and legal battles of local activists, architects, students, and preservationists, as well as the daughter and granddaughter of Shaykh Muhammad, the building is now in the process of being preserved as a future community arts space.

In another neighborhood of North Philadelphia BQF created *Reclamation: Space-Times*, a multi-part sound installation for the 2021 Monument Lab exhibition *Staying Power* at the Village of Art and Humanities. This venerated community space evolved from the Ile Ife Black Humanitarian Center. Ile Ife a name which translates to "House of Love" in Yoruba, was founded by Arthur Hall in 1968. Hall, a trailblazing dancer, choreographer, and community organizer inaugurated the center as a cultural, artistic, and social nexus for the North Philadelphia community and beyond, fostering collaborations that nurtured a culturally rich and socially engaging environment. With an array of programs ranging from dance and visual arts to educational workshops and mentorship schemes, the center orchestrated collaborations with local artists, scholars, and community organizations to cultivate a culturally salient and socially resonant environment, until its closing in 1989 when Hall moved to Memphis Tennessee.

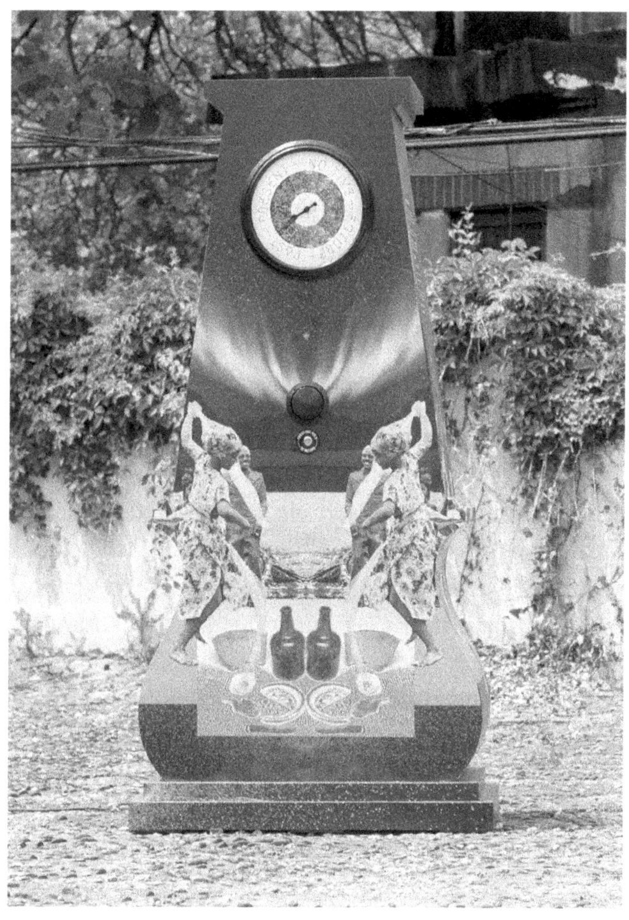

"Black Grandmother Clock, Reclamation: Space-Times" installation by Black Quantum Futurism (2021), as part of the group exhibition *Staying Power* at the Village of Arts and Humanities and Monument Lab (Philadelphia).

In 1986, the transformation of a vacant lot which bordered Ile Ife by Lily Yeh, then hired by Arthur Hall, marked the beginning of the Village of Arts and Humanities.[59] Yeh, inspired by Hall's vision, developed this space into a thriving art park and community center, enriching the neighborhood with gardens, murals, mosaics, and sculptures.[60] This collaboration was crucial in establishing a creative and revitalizing force within the community, leading to the expansion of the Village to encompass a wider array of cultural, economic, artistic, and educational programs, continues the mission of Arthur Hall and Ile Ife.

BQF was one of five artists in the *Staying Power* show, for which we created a multi-part installation called *Reclamation: Space-Times*. This included a public sculpture, a monumental version of our original *Oral Futures Booth*, which had occupied a small room in the Community Futures Lab where we recorded "oral futures" interviews with neighborhood residents. Called the *Black Grandmother Clock* and sitting in the center of Meditation Park within the Village, the giant wooden clock housed a button in the middle that, when pushed, started a recording from the oral futures interviews at CFL. Participants were prompted to share their memories and visions for the future of housing, land, and public space, visitors also contributed memories on the clock, weaving a tapestry of sound that chronicled the community's past, present, and aspirational futures.

The *Black Grandmother Clock* functioned as a quantum time capsule, where memories of the past and visions of the future could be recorded, stored, and played back. It extended both backward and forward along the long AfroFuturist timelines that undergird North Philadelphia.

Complementing the giant clock was a sound installation radiating from a set of directional speakers hidden inside of two small wooden sculptures situated above the *Tree of Life Mosaic* within Meditation Park. The soundscape emanating from the *Sonic Shades*, was an evolving temporally layered soundscape created by Camae, and that would grow and transform over the course of the exhibition. This evolving sound collage interwove archival recordings from the Ile Ife Center of performances with interviews with the founders, blended with contemporary sounds recorded in collaboration with Village arts volunteers prior to the exhibition opening, in which we asked residents and community members surrounding the Village of Arts and Humanities about their memories of the neighborhood, with the addition of recordings from the *Black Grandmother Clock*. In doing so, the installation blurred the boundaries of time, weaving a rich tapestry that encapsulates the unique temporalities of North Philadelphia. Here, time is as local as politics and the weather.

Both the *Black Grandmother Clock* and each sound sculpture was wrapped with collages incorporating and interpreting archival images from the Arthur Hall Afro-American Dance Ensemble, collaged with images of the original Ile Ife Center, cosmic images, and other cultural references to Yoruba masks and cultural objects frequently referenced in the dance company's performance, overlaid with images of the archival photos from the neighborhood.

Despite relentless erasures and historical obfuscations, Black monuments and time capsules, whether physical or otherwise, defy the limitations of linear time, like so many quantum entanglements, their impacts reaching backward and forward through time. They preserve a multifaceted, fluid representation of the community's temporal fabric and allow community members, both individually and collectively, to engage in a form of temporal activism. Whether time capsules or "oral futures" projects, these initiatives act as quantum temporal hacks that provide glimpses into the expansive AfroFuturist timescape that sustains these communities. Time in North Philadelphia is not just a linear trajectory along which the life of the neighborhood plays out, but a layered, participatory construct shaped by the political, social, and environmental currents that define the community.

Quantum Time Capsules as Archives That Resist Definition

This don't belong to you
This secret, from before
this hidden for the future
a quantum event, charting the memory,
the journey,
the way out

Dismantling the Master's Clock

Quantum mapping the truth
—**Camae Ayewa**

The concept of a time capsule traditionally serves as a method to preserve and access the past through historical records. However, within Black communities, this notion intersects with the pervasive challenges of institutional exclusion and the systematic erasure of Black narratives and histories. Black people are often relegated to a status beyond history or timelines, marginalized by a dominant narrative shaped primarily by the white imagination. This systematic erasure denies us access to our own truths—historical, futuristic and otherwise—necessitating the creation of Black quantum time capsules that allow us "to assemble countermemories that contest the colonial archive."[61] These capsules confront and subvert the monolithic, white supremacist historical timeline while expanding the possibilities for what can be preserved, and who can be recognized as custodians of this history.

Operating as both a corrective force and a tool for envisioning and shaping future narratives, Black quantum time capsules emerge as time-hacking devices. They seamlessly interweave Black experiences and perspectives into both historical consciousness and future imaginaries. In doing so, they challenge the linear, Eurocentric concept of time and memory inherent in traditional time capsules, proposing a paradigm rooted in the transformative nature of Black temporalities and spatialities. This shift enables time capsules to transcend their role as more than passive repositories of the past locked underground. They are active and dynamic agents in memory, shifting who has access to particular space-times and disrupting dominant temporal structures.

Black quantum time capsules make evident the immense potential of harnessing Black temporalities as vehicles for liberation. By curating our own temporal spaces outside of conventional narratives, we can dismantle oppressive structures that have sought to confine Black identities within rigid historical constraints. Black quantum time capsules ultimately serve not just as historical correctives but as declarations of liberation, affirming the boundless potentialities of Black temporal-spatial autonomy.

After Echoes

A Cosmogram

This book is nonlinear, and therefore, a traditional afterword or conclusion would not suffice. Instead, I invite you to continue to engage with the ideas in a way that transcends conventional narrative structure, approaching these concepts through a cosmogram: a two-dimensional representation of a dynamic and multidimensional framework. Through it, the aim is to foster connections between concepts, realities, and perceptions that may otherwise seem disjointed or incompatible within the dominant framework of reality. This cosmogram is a conceptual map for the book and a practice in making these connections so they may manifest in our ways of thinking, perceiving, and being in the world.

Navigating the Cosmogram

Horizontal Read:

Reading horizontally will introduce and juxtapose dualities. For example, consider the interplay between "TIME" and "SPACE" or "PAST" and "FUTURE." This method highlights contrasts and complements, revealing the tensions and harmonies in these dualities.

Vertical Read:

Vertical reading encourages thematic connections. For instance, following a path from "TIME" down to "MIRRORS" invites a contemplation on how time can reflect or distort perception. This method unearths underlying themes and layers of meaning.

Diagonal Read:

Diagonal reading weaves themes into a narrative web. For example, linking "TIME" to "PARADOX" to "LIGHT" prompts a different understanding of how these concepts interact. Similarly, connecting "ZAMANI" and "SASA" to "PARADOX" highlights their paradoxical relationship within mainstream concepts of time.

Central Node:

"PARADOX" serves as the central node, the fulcrum around which other concepts revolve. It underscores the inherent contradictions or challenges in each theme and in its relation to others, inviting you to explore the layered nature of these ideas.

Outer Loop:

"ZAMANI" and "SASA" are situated on the periphery but remain integral to the central theme of paradox. They introduce an additional layer, prompting reflections on how various cultures perceive and interact with time. These concepts invite you to consider non-Western temporal frameworks and their implications.

Cycles and Recurrence:

The reader is encouraged to loop back to the beginning after reaching any endpoint, thus emphasizing the themes of cycles, echoes, and temporal fluidity. This recursive reading strategy reflects the non-linear, cyclical nature of time and experience.

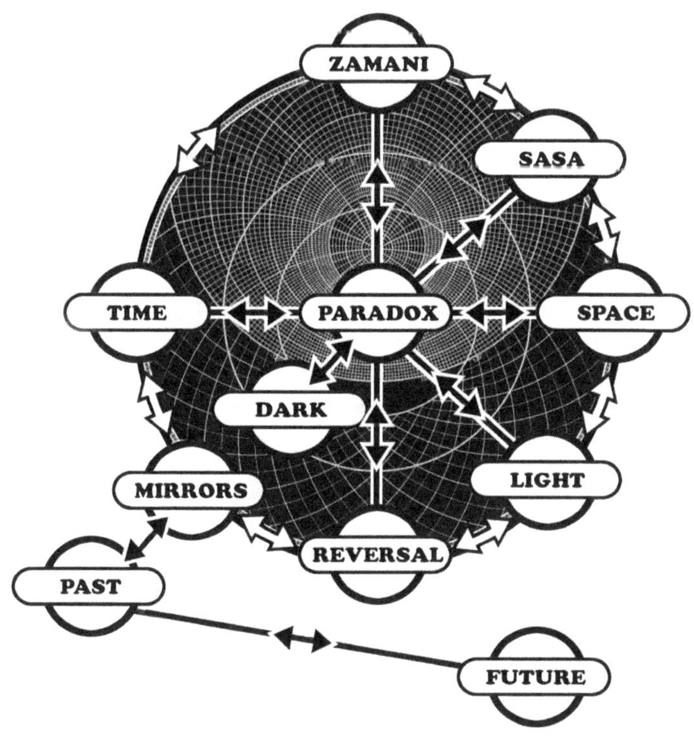

Allow the connections in this book to unfold naturally, letting your intuition and curiosity lead you in your understanding. Resist the urge to force a linear narrative and instead, allow the themes and concepts to interact fluidly and dynamically.

Take moments to reflect on the connections you've made. How have they shifted your own perception of time, space, and reality? Consider journaling your thoughts to deepen your engagement with the material. You can also engage with others who are exploring these concepts. Share your insights and listen to theirs, creating a collective understanding and expanding the network of connections.

Image credits

p. 42: Photo by Brica Wilcox, 2021.

p. 77: Photo by Flip Franssen, 2023.

p. 105: Photo by Harris & Ewing, 1914–1918, Library of Congress, Prints and Photographs Division, LC-DIG-hec-08205.

p. 114: Artwork by the author.

p. 120: Schomburg Center for Research in Black Culture, Art and Artifacts Division, New York Public Library Digital Collections, BU. X.412 and BU. X.409.

p. 124: Courtesy of the Special Collections Research Center, Temple University Libraries. Philadelphia, PA. George D. McDowell *Philadelphia Evening Bulletin* Photographs, P096035B.

p. 127: Courtesy of the Special Collections Research Center, Temple University Libraries. Philadelphia, PA. George D. McDowell *Philadelphia Evening Bulletin* Photographs, P254036B.

p. 155: Naval History and Heritage Command.

p. 167: Library of Congress, Prints and Photographs Division, LC-DIG-ppmsca-50987.

p. 168: Photo by Harris & Ewing, 1918, Library of Congress, Prints and Photographs Division, LC-H25-2437.

p. 179: Photo by Argenis Apolinario, 2022, courtesy of the Vera List Center for Art and Politics.

p. 247: Photo by Chet Pancake, 2016, courtesy of *A Blade of Grass* and *Queer Genius* films.

p. 255: Print by Heard & Moseley, c. 1863, Library of Congress, Prints and Photographs Division, LC-DIG-ppmsca-10980 DLC.

p. 256: Photo by George McCuistion, 1913, DeGolyer Library, Southern Methodist University.

p. 284: Photo by Nils Klinger, 2022.

p. 292: Photo by Bob Sweeney, 2021.

p. 313: Photo by Chris Bauer, 2023.

p. 317: Photo by J. H. Kent, ca. 1900, Schomburg Center for Research in Black Culture, Photographs and Prints Division, New York Public Library, b22766151.

p. 323: Photo by Naomieh Jovin, 2021, courtesy of Monument Lab.

p. 329: Illustration by N. R. Bharathae.

Notes

Introduction

1. Karen Barad, *Meeting the Universe Halfway: Quantum Physics and the Entanglement of Matter* (Durham: Duke University Press, 2007).
2. Barad, *Meeting the Universe Halfway*, 182.

Chapter 1: CPT Symmetry and Violations

1. Plato, *Cratylus*, trans. C. D. C. Reeve. (Indianapolis: Hackett, 1998), 402a.
2. Peter Manchester, *The Syntax of Time: The Phenomenology of Time in Greek Physics and Speculative Logic from Iamblichus to Anaximander* (Netherlands: Brill, 2005), 38.
3. William J. Friedman and Frank Laycock, "Children's Analog and Digital Clock Knowledge," *Child Development* 60, no. 2 (1989): 357–71.
4. James Gleick, *Isaac Newton* (New York: Vintage Books, 2004), 46.
5. Aristotle, "Time Is the Measurement of Change: Part Twelve," *Physics*, Book IV, Part 10–13 (350 BCE), trans. R. P. Hardie and R. K. Gaye, https://faculty.uca.edu/rnovy/Aristotle--Time%20is%20the%20Measure.htm.
6. Thomas S. Kuhn, *The Structure of Scientific Revolutions* (Chicago: University of Chicago Press, 2012), 40.
7. Reinhart Koselleck, *The Practice of Conceptual History: Timing History, Spacing Concepts* (Redwood City, CA: Stanford University Press, 2002), 8.
8. Kuhn, *The Structure of Scientific Revolutions*, 138.
9. Michelle Frank, "A Hidden Variable Behind Entanglement," *Scientific American* 328, April 2023: 4; Richard Webb, "Chien-Shiung Wu, May 31, 1912 –16 February 1997," *New Scientist*, https://www.newscientist.com/people/chien-shiung-wu.
10. Nadja Oertelt, "Meet Chien-Shiung Wu, the Nuclear Physicist Who Developed Revolutionary Experiments," *Massive Science*, December 28, 2019, https://massivesci.com/articles/chien-shiung-wu-manhattan-project-nuclear-physics-nobel-prize.
11. Dr. John Ellis in conversation with the author, 2021.

12. Dan C. Marinescu and Gabriela M. Marinescu, "Classical and Quantum Information Theory," in *Classical and Quantum Information* (Elsevier Inc, 2012), 221–344, https://doi.org/10.1016/B978-0-12-383874-2.00003-5.
13. Rudolf Clausius, *Mechanical Theory of Heat* (1879).
14. Arthur Stanley Eddington, *The Nature of the Physical World* (United Kingdom: Macmillan, 1928).
15. Craig Callender, "Thermodynamic Asymmetry in Time," *The Stanford Encyclopedia of Philosophy* (Fall 2023 Edition), Edward N. Zalta and Uri Nodelman, eds., https://plato.stanford.edu/archives/fall2023/entriestime-thermo.
16. Sir William Thompson (Lord Kelvin), "The Age of the Sun's Heat," *Macmillan's Magazine*, vol. 5 (March 5, 1862), 388.
17. James Gleick, *The Information: A History, A Theory, a Flood* (New York: Knopf, 2011), 271.

Chapter 2: Bending the Arrow of Time

1. Karen Barad, *Meeting the Universe Halfway* (Durham: Duke University Press, 2007).
2. "We must compare the Western linear dead physical timeline (with 'past,' 'future,' and a regularly moving 'now') with the African 'living time.'" Bert Hamminga, "The Western versus the African Time Concept," MindPhiles.com, 2002, now available at https://web.archive.org/web/20020729021514/http://www.mindphiles.com/floor/teaching/timeafr/timeafri.htm.
3. See John Mbiti, *African Religions and Philosophy* (United Kingdom: Pearson Education, 1990); E. E. Evans-Pritchard's study on the Nuer of Central Africa also made the observation: "I do not think that they ever experience the same feeling of fighting against time or having to coordinate activities with an abstract passage of time, because their points of reference are mainly the activities themselves, which are generally of a leisurely character. Events follow in a logical order, but they are not controlled by an abstract system, there being no autonomous points of reference to which activities have to conform with precision." Although what he mistook as leisurely activity may have just been people enjoying themselves in mundane, moments unfixed in mechanical time. E. E. Evans-Pritchard, *The Nuer* (Oxford: Oxford University Press, 1990), 103–4.
4. Nikitah Okembe-RA Imani, "The Implications of Africa-Centered Conceptions of Time and Space for Quantitative Theorizing: Limitations of Paradigmatically Bound Philosophical Meta-Assumptions," *Journal of Pan African Studies* 5, 4 (2012), 106.
5. Imani, "The Implications of Africa-Centered Conceptions of Time and Space for Quantitative Theorizing," 106.
6. Imani, "The Implications of Africa-Centered Conceptions of Time and Space for Quantitative Theorizing," 107.

7. Reginald Crosley, *The Vodou Quantum Leap* (St. Paul: Llewellyn Publications, 2000), 50.
8. It is worth noting that Schrödinger's Cat was intended to demonstrate the absurdity of applying quantum mechanics to everyday objects, suggesting that such a state of being both alive and dead at the same time is nonsensical. Schrödinger's aim was not to propose a serious possibility that such a situation could occur, but to highlight the problems with the Copenhagen interpretation when applied to macroscopic objects; Guido Bacciagaluppi and Antony Valentini, *Quantum Theory at the Crossroads: Reconsidering the 1927 Solvay Conference* (Cambridge: Cambridge University Press, 2009).
9. Crosley, *The Vodou Quantum Leap*, 58.
10. Crosley, *The Vodou Quantum Leap*, 57–8.
11. See Teresa Washington, "*Mules and Men* and Messiahs: Continuity in Yoruba Divination Verses and African American Folktales," *The Journal of American Folklore*, 125, 497: 263–85.
12. Ojo Oludare Oyebisi, *The Mechanics of Ifa Divination System: Highlighting Some Elements of Technological Knowledge in Ifa and Its Divination System* (Columbia, MD: Ajendu LLC, 2019).
13. Barad, *Meeting the Universe Halfway*.
14. Geneva Smitherman, *Word from the Mother: Language and African Americans* (New York: Routledge, 2006), 5.
15. See Kassim Koné, "Time and Culture among the Bamana/Mandinka and Dogon of Mali," in *Time in the Black Experience*, ed. Joseph Adjaye (Westport: Greenwood Press, 1994).
16. "Bamana," in *Encyclopedia of African Religion*, eds. Molefi Kete Asante and Ama Mazama, *SAGE Publications*, 2008, http://ebookcentral.proquest.com/lib/newschool/detail.action?docID=2041979.
17. Koné, "Time and culture among the Bamana/Mandinka and Dogon of Mali," 94–5.
18. "Akan Religion," in *Encyclopedia of Religion*, https://www.encyclopedia.com/environment/encyclopedias-almanacs-transcripts-and-maps/akan-religion.
19. "Destiny," *Encyclopedia of African Religion*, eds. Molefi Kete Asante and Ama Mazama, *SAGE Publications*, 2008. *ProQuest Ebook Central*, http://ebookcentral.proquest.com/lib/newschool/detail.action?docID=2041979.
20. Pierre Verin and Narivelo Rajaonarimanana, "Divination in Madagascar," in *African Divination Systems: Ways of Knowing* (Bloomington: Indiana University Press, 1991), 56.
21. Thomas Buckley and Alma Gottlieb, *Blood Magic: The Anthropology of Menstruation* (Oakland: University of California Press, 2023), 210–11. Some years ago, I took a DNA test with AfricanAncestry.com, a Black-run ancestry service that doesn't store your information and that provides your lineage based solely on ancestry from the African continent. The DNA results came back that my maternal ancestral line traced back to the Temne people of

Sierra Leone. This was separately confirmed by a former colleague who, before I told him what the results said, looked at my face for half a second before guessing Sierra Leone.

22. Buckley and Gottlieb, *Blood Magic.*
23. Omari H. Kokole, "Time, Language, and the Oral Tradition: An African Perspective," in *Time in the Black Experience*, ed. Joseph Adjaye (Westport: Greenwood Press, 1994), 54.
24. Koné, "Time and Culture among the Bamana/Mandinka and Dogon of Mali," 83.
25. "Dinka," *Encyclopedia of African Religion*, eds. Molefi Kete Asante and Ama Mazama (SAGE Publications, 2008), https://sk.sagepub.com/reference/africanreligion.
26. "*ahene*," *Encyclopedia of African Religion.*
27. "*nkonuafieso*," *Encyclopedia of African Religion.*
28. "*Adae*," *Encyclopedia of African Religion.*
29. Koné, "Time and Culture among the Bamana/Mandinka and Dogon of Mali," 95.
30. "Oral tradition," *Encyclopedia of African Religions.*
31. Thomas Albert Hale, *Griots and Griottes: Masters of Words and Music* (Bloomington: Indiana University Press, 1998).
32. Ivaylo Ingov, "African Griot," *ingoStudio*, September 20, 2022, https://ingostudio.com/storytelling/african-griot.
33. "Court Poet," *Encyclopedia of African Religions*
34. David Grandy, *Everyday Quantum Reality* (Bloomington: Indiana University Press, 2010).
35. Robbie Mitchell, *Singer-Storytellers: The Griot Tradition in West Africa*, last modified March 14, 2023, https://www.ancient-origins.net/history-ancient-traditions/griots-0018057.
36. Alfred Korzybski, *Science and Sanity: An Introduction to Non-Aristotelian Systems and General Semantics* (New York: Institute of General Semantics, 1995).
37. Zora Neale Hurston, *Dust Tracks on a Road: An Autobiography* (New York: Harper Perennial, 1996),
38. Hurston, *Dust Tracks on a Road*, 89.
39. Hurston, *Dust Tracks on a Road*, 1.
40. Hurston, *Dust Tracks on a Road.*
41. Alexis McGill Johnson, Rachel D. Godsil, Jessica MacFarlane, Linda R. Tropp, Phillip Atiba Goff, "The 'Good Hair' Study: Explicit and Implicit Attitudes Toward Black Women's Hair," Perception Institute, February 2017, https://perception.org/wp-content/uploads/2017/01/TheGood-HairStudyFindingsReport.pdf.
42. Johnson et al., "The 'Good Hair' Study."
43. This systemic discrimination has spawned federal legislation called the

Create a Respectful and Open World for Natural Hair (CROWN) Act. Introduced in the US Congress, this legislation aims to protect individuals, especially African Americans, from unjust treatment in various settings, including the workplace and schools, due to their natural, textured hair and protective hairstyles. While the CROWN Act has been successful at the state level, becoming law in twenty-four states, it has faced challenges at the federal level.

44. Wayne B. Chandler, *Ancient Future: The Teachings and Prophetic Wisdom of the Seven Hermetic Laws of Ancient Egypt* (United States: Black Classic Press, 2000), 54.
45. See Katherine Blundell, *Black Holes: A Very Short Introduction* (Oxford: OUP Oxford, 2015); Imogen Whittam, "How We're Probing the Secrets of a Giant Black Hole at Our Galaxy's Centre," *The Wire*, December 26, 2018, https://thewire.in/the-sciences/probing-secrets-giant-black-hole-galaxy-centre.
46. Ian O'Neil, "Black Holes Were Such an Extreme Concept, Even Einstein Had His Doubts," April 15, 2019, https://www.history.com/news/black-holes-albert-einstein-theory-relativity-space-time.
47. Albert Einstein, as quoted in O'Neil, "Black Holes Were Such an Extreme Concept."
48. P. S. Joshi, "The Structure of Non-spacelike Curves from a Spacetime Singularity," Tata Institute of Fundamental Research, April 26, 2006, https://core.ac.uk/download/44161179.pdf.
49. G. K. T. Hau, Duncan A. Forbes, "Radial Kinematics of Isolated Elliptical Galaxies," Monthly Notices of the Royal Astronomical Society, Volume 371, Issue 2, September 2006, Pages 633–642, https://doi.org/10.1111/j.1365-2966.2006.10461.x
50. Jean Chevalier and Alain Gheerbrant, *The Dictionary of Symbols* (London: Penguin Publishing Group), 1996.
51. Gen. 1:3–5 (New Revised Standard Version).
52. Hans Blumenberg, History, *Metaphors, Fables: A Hans Blumenberg Reader* (Ithaka: Cornell University Press, 2020), 148.
53. Chevalier and Gheerbrant, *The Dictionary of Symbols.*
54. Roy A. Sorensen, *Seeing Dark Things: The Philosophy of Shadows* (Oxford: OUP, 2011), 4–5, 41.
55. Sorensen, *Seeing Dark Things.*
56. Sorensen, *Seeing Dark Things*, 6.
57. Karen Barad, "Diffracting Diffraction: Cutting Together-Apart," *parallax* 20, 3 (2014), 171.
58. Barad, "Diffracting Diffraction," 171.
59. Jean Chevalier and Alain Gheerbrant, *The Penguin Dictionary of Symbols* (London: Penguin, 1996), 93.
60. B. Thomas and D. Vince-Prue, *Photoperiodism in Plants* (Amsterdam: Elsevier, 1996).

61. R. G. Foster and L. Kreitzman, *Rhythms of Life: The Biological Clocks that Control the Daily Lives of Every Living Thing* (New Haven: Yale University Press, 2004).
62. C. Vetter, E. E. Devore, L. R. Wegrzyn, J. Massa, F. E. Speizer, I. Kawachi, B. Rosner, M. J. Stampfer, E. S. Schernhammer, "Association Between Rotating Night Shift Work and Risk of Coronary Heart Disease Among Women," *JAMA*, April 26, 2016, 315(16). 1726–34, doi: 10.1001/jama.2016.4454; D. B. Boivin and F. O. James, "Circadian Adaptation to Night-Shift Work by Judicious Light and Darkness Exposure." *J Biol Rhythms*, December 2002, 17 (6): 556–67, doi: 10.1177/0748730402238238.
63. Christina Sharpe, *In the Wake: On Blackness and Being* (Durham: Duke University Press, 2016), 75.
64. "Space and Time," *Encyclopedia of African Religion.*
65. Roy Sorensen, "Seeing Intersecting Eclipses," *Journal of Philosophy*, vol. 96, no. 1 (January 1999): 25–49.
66. Laura C. Jarmon, *Wishbone: Reference and Interpretation in Black Folk Narrative* (Knoxville: University of Tennessee Press, 2003), xxx, xxxiii.
67. John Mbiti, *African Religions and Philosophy* (Portsmouth: Heinemann, [1969] 1990), 108.
68. Jarmon, *Wishbone.*

Chapter 3: CPT Symmetry and Violations of Black SpaceTime

1. Hillary Clinton quoted in Erin Durkin, "Mayor de Blasio, Hillary Clinton Ripped for Racist Joke at Inner Circle Show," *New York Daily News*, April 12, 2016, https://www.nydailynews.com/2016/04/12/mayor-de-blasio-hillary-clinton-ripped-for-racist-joke-at-inner-circle-show.
2. Adam Howard, "Bill de Blasio's 'Colored People's Time' Joke Hits Sour Note," *NBC News*, https://www.nbcnews.com/news/nbcblk/bill-de-blasio-s-colored-people-s-time-joke-comes-n554756.
3. Lawrence W. Levine, *Black Culture and Black Consciousness: Afro-American Folk Thought from Slavery to Freedom* (Oxford: Oxford University Press, 2007), 331.
4. Levine, *Black Culture and Black Consciousness.*
5. Nikki Lynette, "'CP Time:' Does My Black Race Indicate I'll Always Be Late?" Becoming Nikki Lynette, December 2, 2009, http://www.chicagonow.com/becoming-nikki-lynette/2009/12/cp-time-does-my-black-race-indicate-ill-always-be-late.
6. Lynette, "'CP Time.'"
7. J. L. King, *CP Time: Why Some People Are Always Late* (New York: Simon and Schuster, 2007).
8. Robert E. Goodin, James Mahmud Rice, Antti Parpo, and Lina Eriksson, *Discretionary Time: A New Measure of Freedom* (Cambridge: Cambridge University Press, 2008).

9. Karel Martens, *Transport Justice: Designing Fair Transportation Systems* (New York: Routledge, 2016).
10. Goodin et al., "Discretionary Time."
11. St. Augustine as quoted in J. G. Pilkington, *The Confessions of St. Augustine* (1876) (New York: Heritage Press, 1963), 301.
12. Jeremy Rifkin, *Time Wars: The Primary Conflict in Human History* (New York: H. Holt, 1987), 146–7.
13. Ecclesiastes 3:1, *The Holy Bible, English Standard Version* (Wheaton: Crossway Bibles, 2016); Ecclesiastes 5:16, *The Holy Bible, English Standard Version* (Wheaton: Crossway Bibles, 2016), https://www.biblegateway.com/passage/?search=Ecclesiastes%203%3A1-13&version=ESV.
14. In contrast, Teresa N. Washington argues in her essay "Mules and Men and Messiahs" that "rather than claiming it to be perfect after six days of creation, the Earth in the Africana worldview is similar to a text that once written is subject to critique, revision, deletions, and addenda." Teresa Washington, "Mules and Men and Messiahs: Continuity in Yoruba Divination Verses and African American Folktales," *Journal of American Folklore*, 125 (2012): 263–85.
15. Jimena Canales, "Clock / Lived," in *Time: A Vocabulary of the Present*, eds. Joel Burges and Amy Elias (New York: New York University Press, 2016), 113–28.
16. Giordano Nanni, *The Colonisation of Time: Ritual, Routine and Resistance in the British Empire* (Manchester: Manchester University Press, 2020), 126–27.
17. Nanni, *The Colonisation of Time.*
18. Maureen Perkins, *The Reform of Time: Magic and Modernity* (London: Pluto Press, 2001), 84–85.
19. Vanessa Ogle, *The Global Transformation of Time: 1870–1950* (Cambridge: Harvard University Press, 2015), 93.
20. Of course, such stereotypes casually persist. To quote Frederick Lamp: "One often hears Europeans in Africa sighing smugly, 'The Africans have no sense of time.' I found in fieldwork that art and the ritual in which it figures reveal almost an obsession with time seen qualitatively, and that spatial constructs and ritual movement in space may be graphed to show a great structural harmony with nonvisual forms of art, such as oral narrative and music, or with common and esoteric notions about the sun and the moon and other natural phenomena." Frederick Lamp, "Heavenly Bodies: Menses, Moon, and Rituals of License among the Temne of Sierra Leone," *Blood Magic: The Anthropology of Menstruation*, eds. Thomas Buckley and Alma Gottlieb (Oakland: University of California Press, 1988), 212.
21. Gerard Dohrn-van Rossum, *History of the Hour: Clocks and Modern Temporal Orders* (Chicago: University of Chicago Press, 1996), 287.
22. Nikitah Okembe-RA Imani, "The Implications of Africa-Centered Conceptions of Time and Space for Quantitative Theorizing: Limitations of

Paradigmatically Bound Philosophical Meta-Assumptions," *Journal of Pan African Studies* 5, 4 (2012): 104–5.

23. Barbara Adam, *Time and Social Theory* (London: Economic and Social Research Council), 61.
24. Adam, *Time and Social Theory*, 61.
25. Stephen Kern, *The Culture of Time and Space, 1880–1918* (Cambridge: Harvard University Press, 2003), 91.
26. Kern, *The Culture of Time and Space*, 91.
27. See Chapter 4 "Time Zone Protocols," for further elaboration on how Western technological space-time compression milestones, such as the development of the chronometer, were inextricably linked to the colonization of both land and time.
28. Thomas Allen, *A Republic in Time: Temporality and Social Imagination in Nineteenth-Century America* (Chapel Hill: University of North Carolina Press, 2008),18.
29. Allen, *A Republic in Time*,18.
30. Barbara Adam, *The Quest for Time Control* (London: Polity, 2004), 137.
31. Thomas Jefferson, "Notes on the State of Virginia" (1788), *The Writings of Thomas Jefferson* (Princeton: Princeton University Press, 1777–1779), 193–4.
32. Jefferson, "Notes on the State of Virginia," 196.
33. Jefferson, "Notes on the State of Virginia," 201.
34. Kodwo Eshun, "Further Considerations on Afrofuturism," *CR: The New Centennial Review* 3, no. 2 (2003): 287–302, 288, http://www.jstor.org/stable/41949397.
35. "Clocked, Clocking In, and More New Senses of Clock," Merriam-Webster.com, July 19, 2019, https://www.merriam-webster.com/wordplay/clock-new-senses-verb-usage.
36. Eyamidé Lewis-Coker, *Creoles of Sierra Leone: Proverbs, Parables, Wise Sayings* (New York: AuthorHouse, 2018).
37. Benjamin Franklin, "Advice to a Young Tradesman," July 21, 1748, https://founders.archives.gov/documents/Franklin/01-03-02-0130.
38. Isaac Granger Jefferson, *Memoirs of a Monticello Slave: As Dictated to Charles Campbell in the 1840s by Isaac, One of Thomas Jefferson's Slaves* (Papamoa: Papamoa Press, 2017).
39. Thomas Jefferson, "To Benjamin Rush Monticello, January 16, 1811," https://www.let.rug.nl/usa/presidents/thomas-jefferson/letters-of-thomas-jefferson/jefl208.php.
40. "A Day in the Life of Thomas Jefferson: Design and Décor—The Great Clock," Monticello, https://www.monticello.org/thomas-jefferson/a-day-in-the-life-of-jefferson/museum-in-the-entrance-of-the-house/the-great-clock.
41. Benjamin Banneker, "Memoir of Benjamin Banneker" (1790), read before

the Maryland Historical Society, at the Monthly Meeting, 1 May 1845; Leonard Price Stavisky, "Negro Craftsmanship in Early America," *The American Historical Review* 54, 2 (1949): 315–25.

42. Bethany McGlyn, "Annapolis's Landscape of Craft: The Roles Enslaved Men and Women Played," *Decorative Arts Trust*, June 24, 2020, https://decorativeartstrust.org/annapolis-enslaved-men-women-post.
43. McGlyn, "Annapolis's Landscape of Craft."
44. William Faris, *The Diary of William Faris: The Daily Life of an Annapolis Silversmith*. (Baltimore: Maryland Historical Society, 2003), 57.
45. Faris, *The Diary of William Faris*, 17.
46. Kevin Sullivan, and Lori Rozsa, "DeSantis Doubles Down on Claim That Some Blacks Benefited from Slavery." *Washington Post*, July 22, 2023, https://www.washingtonpost.com/politics/2023/07/22/desantis-slavery-curriculum.
47. Faris, *The Diary of William Faris*, 57.
48. Caitlin Galante-DeAngelis Hopkins, "Object Lesson: Pompe Stevens, Enslaved Artisan," *Commonplace* 13, 3 (Spring 2013), https://commonplace.online/article/object-lesson-pompe-stevens.
49. Galante-DeAngelis Hopkins, "Object Lesson."
50. Tim Marshall, *The Quaker Clockmakers of North Oxfordshire* (Mayfield: Mayfield Books, 2013).
51. "Peter Hill Tall Case Clock," National Museum of American History, https://americanhistory.si.edu/collections/search/object/nmah_856728.
52. Richard Newman, "An Eighteenth-Century Plantation Owner's Watch," *National Association of Watch and Clock Collectors Bulletin*, 439 2019, https://pubs.nawcc.org/index.php/museum-collection-214/search-the-collection/102-publications/publications-bulletin-tocs-2010s/1895-nawcc-bulletin-no-439-may-june-2019.
53. Walter Johnson quoted in Thomas Bender, *Rethinking American History in a Global Age* (Oakland: University of California Press, 2002), 153.
54. Johnson in Bender, *Rethinking American History in a Global Age*, 153.
55. Johnson in Bender, *Rethinking American History in a Global Age*, 153.
56. See "Three-Fifths Compromise," United States Constitutional Convention, 1787.
57. Robert Levine, *A Geography of Time: On Tempo, Culture, And the Pace of Life* (New York: Basic Books, 1997).
58. *Born in Slavery: Slave Narratives from the Federal Writers' Project, 1936–1938*, Library of Congress, 1941, https://www.loc.gov/collections/slave-narratives-from-the-federal-writers-project-1936-to-1938/about-this-collection.
59. "Slavery Meeting at Colchester," *Essex County Standard*, January 19, 1838, 3.
60. Johnson in Bender, *Rethinking American History in a Global Age*, 153.
61. Mark M. Smith, *Mastered by the Clock: Time, Slavery, and Freedom in the American South* (Chapel Hill: University of North Carolina Press), 130.

62. In Chapter 6, I discuss additional ways that enslaved Africans found to maintain their indigenous spatiotemporal orientations despite the constraints of Western linear time.
63. Anonymous., "Op-ed," *Daily Standard* (Raleigh, North Carolina), May 7, 1867, 2.
64. *The Cincinnati Enquirer*, November 12, 1878.
65. *Sioux City Journal* (Sioux City, Iowa), December 15, 1893, 4.
66. *Asheville Messenger* (Asheville, North Carolina), November 13, 1840, 3.
67. Patikii Gibbs, *Black Collectibles Sold in America* (Paducah: Collector Books, 1987).
68. Filippo Tommaso Marinetti, "Manifesto of Futurism," *Le Figaro* (Paris), February 20, 1909, http://exhibitions.guggenheim.org/futurism/manifestos.
69. D. W. Johnson, *Chicago Defender* (1914), quoted in Kat Chow, "Running Late? Nah, Just On 'CPT,'" *WNYC*, November 23, 2014, https://www.wnyc.org/story/running-late-nah-just-on-cpt.
70. Carl Van Vechten, "Chapter 5," *Nigger Heaven* (New York: Knopf, 1926), https://en.m.wikisource.org/wiki/Nigger_Heaven/Book_1/Chapter_5.
71. Van Vechten, "Glossary," *Nigger Heaven*, https://en.m.wikisource.org/wiki/Nigger_Heaven/Glossary_of_Negro_Words_and_Phrases.
72. Carl Van Vechten, "Glossary," *Nigger Heaven*.
73. "Miss Ovington in Her First Visit to the South Finds 'Colored People's Time' Is Derived from 'Southern People's Time,'" *The Afro-American* (Baltimore, MD), October 29, 1932.
74. Zora Neale Hurston, "Characteristics of Negro Expression," (1934), *Negro: An Anthology*, ed. Nancy Cunard (London: Wishart and Co, 1936–38), 26.
75. "NO C. P. T. ALLOWED THIS SEMESTER," The Telescope, *Weekly Tribune* (Moulton, IA), January 17, 1935, vol. 2, 5.
76. Jules Henry, "White People's Time, Colored People's Time," *Jet Magazine* (Mar 6, 1958); *Negro Digest* (December 1965), 32–33; *Trans-action* 2 (1965), 31–34.
77. The documentary *The Pruitt-Igoe Myth* (2011), directed by Chad Freidrichs, unpacks this in significant detail.
78. Laurie Van Dyke, "The Negro: 'Be Responsible' Urging Heard Often," *Milwaukee Sentinel*, October 19, 1963, pt. 1, col. 1, 1.
79. Martin Luther King, Jr., "I Have a Dream," speech, August 28, 1963.
80. Martin Luther King, Jr., "Remaining Awake Through a Great Revolution," commencement address at Oberlin College, June 14, 1965. The phrase "The time is now" was also used frequently by Barack Obama during his 2007 election campaign.
81. Geneva Smitherman, *Word from the Mother: Language and African Americans* (New York: Routledge, 2006), 56.
82. See James Baldwin in "A Conversation with James Baldwin," *WGBH Educational Foundation*, June 24, 1963, https://americanarchive.org/catalog/cpb-aacip_15-0v89g5gf5r.

83. Martin Luther King Jr., "Where Do We Go from Here?" August 16, 1967, Southern Christian Leadership Conference, Atlanta, Georgia, https://kinginstitute.stanford.edu/where-do-we-go-here.
84. "Billion$ for Space Pennies for the Hungry," *Jet Magazine*, July 31, 1969, https://knowyourmeme.com/photos/2155775-billionaire-space-race.
85. Bernice Jones, "We Refuse to Allow Our Children to Live in Unsanitary and Hazardous Conditions," *Black Panther*, August 1, 1970, 9.
86. Eldridge Cleaver, "Cleaver Scores Apollo 11 as Circus," *Jet Magazine*, July 18, 1969.
87. Josh Pherigo, "When NASA and Its Astronauts Arrived in Houston," Greater Houston Partnership, July 18, 2019, https://www.houston.org/news/when-nasa-and-its-astronauts-arrived-houston.
88. Reverend Sullivan, April 1968, quoted in *Congressional Record—Senate*, February 17, 1969 (Washington: United States Government Printing Office, 1969), 3485.
89. Hillary S. Kativa, "What: The Columbia Avenue Riots (1964)," *Civil Rights in a Northern City: Philadelphia*, Temple University Libraries, https://exhibits.temple.edu/s/civil-rights-in-a-northern-cit/page/the-columbia-avenue-riots--196.
90. Helga Nowotny, *Time: The Modern and Postmodern Experience* (London: Polity, 2015), 23.
91. Kodwo Eshun, "Further Considerations on Afrofuturism," *CR: The New Centennial Review* 3, 2 (2003), 297.
92. "Gang Publishes Newspaper," *Philadelphia Inquirer*, July 28, 1968.
93. *Thirteen* Staff, "Detroit's Colored People's Time, or CPT," *Thirteen, PBS*, February 10, 2009, https://www.thirteen.org/blog-post/detroits-colored-peoples-time-or-cpt.
94. "Black TV and its Promises," *Ebony Magazine*, September 1969, 89.
95. Alvin Toffler, *The Future Shock* (New York: Random House, 1970), 15.
96. Ronald Walcott, "Ellison, Gordone and Tolson: Some Notes on the Blues, Style and Space," *Black World*, December 1972, 4–29.
97. Leslie Lee, *Colored People's Time: A History Play* (London: S. French, 1983).
98. Smitherman, *Word from the Mother*, 24.
99. Joyce Cunneen and Monica Starr, "Cultural Diversity: African American Culture," ELDER Project, Fairfield University School of Nursing, supported by DHHS/HRSA/BHPR/Division of Nursing Grant #D62HP06858, July 14, 2014, https://www.slideserve.com/fia/cultural-diversity.
100. Cheryl L. Woods-Giscombé and Marci Lobel, "Race and Gender Matter: A Multidimensional Approach to Conceptualizing and Measuring Stress in African American Women," *Cultural Diversity and Ethnic Minority Psychology* 14, no. 3 (July 2008): 173–82.
101. Jeremy Rifkin, *Time Wars: The Primary Conflict in Human History* (New York: Simon and Schuster, 1989), 192.

102. Rifkin, *Time Wars*, 192.
103. Michelle M. Wright, *Physics of Blackness* (Minneapolis: Minnesota University Press, 2014), 57.
104. Jeremy Rifkin, *Time Wars*, 190.
105. W. E. B. Du Bois, "The Souls of Black Folk," in *The Souls of Black Folk* (Chicago: A. C. McClurg and Co., 1903), 2–3.
106. John Streamas, "Closure And 'Colored People's Time,'" in *Time: Limits and Constraints*, eds. Jo Alyson Parker, Paul André Harris, and Christian Steineck (Leiden: Brill, 2010), 220, https://doi.org/10.1163/ej.9789004185753.i-378.85.

Chapter 4: Time Zone Protocols

1. Countries represented at the IMC included Austria, Hungary, Brazil, Colombia, Costa Rica, France, Germany, Great Britain, Guatemala, Hawaii, Italy, Japan, Mexico, Paraguay, Russia, San Domingo, Salvador, Spain, Sweden, Switzerland, United States, Venezuela, Chili, Denmark, Liberia, the Netherlands, and Turkey. "International Conference Held at Washington for the Purpose of Fixing a Prime Meridian and Uniform Time: Protocols of the Proceedings," Washington, DC, 1884.
2. Vanessa Ogle, *The Global Transformation of Time: 1870–1950* (Cambridge: Harvard University Press, 2015), 20.
3. "The Prime Meridian Conference," *Nature Magazine*, November 6, 1884.
4. "2020–2022 Vera List Center Fellowships," *e-flux* Education, https://www.e-flux.com/announcements/306773/2020-2022-vera-list-center-fellowships.
5. It is important to note that the word *clock* itself derives from the words *clagan* and *clocca* which means bell in Celtic. A clock was an extremely specific thing: if the timepiece did not have a bell, then the mechanism would be called a *timepiece* instead of a clock. *A Beginners Guide to the Mechanics of Wrist and Pocket Watches* (Baltimore: Patterson Press, 2011).
6. Giordano Nanni, *The Colonisation of Time: Ritual, Routine, and Resistance in the British Empire* (Manchester: Manchester University Press, 2012).
7. Jo Ellen Barnett, *Time's Pendulum: From Sundials to Atomic Clocks, the Fascinating History of Timekeeping and How Our Discoveries Changed the World* (London: Harcourt Brace, 1999), 119.
8. David Rooney, *About Time: A History of Civilization in Twelve Clocks* (New York: W. W. Norton and Co., 2021); Joseph Mazur, *The Clock Mirage* (New Haven: Yale University Press, 2020).
9. Rooney, *About Time.*
10. Dava Sobel and William J. Andrewes, *The Illustrated Longitude: The True Story of the Lone Genius Who Solved the Greatest Scientific Problem of His Time* (New York: Walker and Company, 1998), 72.
11. Sobel and Andrewes, *The Illustrated Longitude.*
12. Edward F. Gilman and Dennis G. Watson, "Guaiacum sanctum: Lignum

Vitae," University of Florida, Institute of Food and Agricultural Sciences Extension, last modified April 6, 2022, https://edis.ifas.ufl.edu/publication/ST286.

13. Allen C. Bluedorn, *The Human Organization of Time: Temporal Realities and Experience* (Redwood City: Stanford Business Books, 2002).
14. Derek Howse, *Greenwich Time and the Longitude: Official Millennium Edition* (London: Phillip Wilson Press, 1997).
15. Harold D. Black, George Gebel, and Robert R. Newton, "The Centenary of the Prime Meridian and of International Standard Time," *Johns Hopkins APL Technical Digest,* vol. 5, no 4 (1984), 382.
16. Kevin K. Birth, *Objects of Time: How Things Shape Temporality* (New York: Palgrave Macmillan, 2012), 162.
17. Sandford Fleming, *Terrestrial Time: A Memoir* (Ottawa: National Library of Canada microform, 1879), 1, https://archive.org/details/cihm_06112/page/n17/mode/2up.
18. Fleming, *Terrestrial Time.*
19. Smithsonian Podcast, "When the Standardization of Time Arrived in America," *Smithsonian Magazine,* December 19, 2016, https://www.smithsonianmag.com/smithsonian-institution/how-standardization-time-changed-american-society-180961503.
20. "Time Zones," Synchronized Time, Smithsonian National Museum of American History, https://americanhistory.si.edu/ontime/synchronizing/zones.html.
21. It is worth noting that the railroads, emblematic of industrial might, were complicit in the use of enslaved labor, particularly in the Southern states. Black men and women were relegated to arduous roles digging track beds, laying tracks, and working as brakemen and maintenance workers, often under extreme and perilous conditions. Under these conditions, this enslaved workforce faced even more egregious exploitation and neglect than on plantations, where, despite the inherent brutality of slavery, the direct proximity of masters or overseers might have ensured a bare minimal standard of living out of a vested interest in sustaining their labor. In contrast, the corporations that rented or purchased slaves for railroad construction were at a great distance and showed little concern for their workers' welfare or safety, treating them as disposable assets. See "African Americans and the Railroad," National Parks Service, last modified November 28, 2022, https://www.nps.gov/grsm/learn/historyculture/african-americans-and-the-railroad.htm.
22. Ian R. Bartky, "The Adoption of Standard Time," *Technology and Culture* 30, no. 1 (1989): 25–56, https://doi.org/10.2307/3105430.
23. Jo Ellen Barnett, *Time's Pendulum: From Sundials to Atomic Clocks, the Fascinating History of Timekeeping and How Our Discoveries Changed the World* (London: Harcourt Brace, 1999), 130.

24. E. P. Thompson, "Time, Work-Discipline, and Industrial Capitalism." *Past and Present*, no. 38 (1967): 56–97.
25. Black, Gebel, and Newton, "The Centenary of the Prime Meridian and of International Standard Time," 387.
26. "Session of October 14, 1884," *International Conference Held at Washington for the Purpose of Fixing a Prime Meridian and A Universal Day. October 1884, Protocols of the Proceedings* (Washington: Gibson Bros., 1884), 25, https://www.gutenberg.org/files/17759/17759-h/17759-h.htm.
27. William Ellis, "The Prime Meridian Conference," *Nature* 31, 784, November 6, 1884: 7–10.
28. *International Conference Held at Washington for the Purpose of Fixing a Prime Meridian and A Universal Day. October 1884, Protocols of the Proceedings*, 5.
29. D. Lewis, "Monrovia, Liberia (1822–)," *BlackPast*, last modified October 8, 2014, https://www.blackpast.org/global-african-history/places-global-african-history/monrovia-liberia-1821.
30. "American Colonization Society and the Founding of Liberia," *Encyclopedia of Race and Racism*, last modified January 8, 2024, https://www.encyclopedia.com/social-sciences/encyclopedias-almanacs-transcripts-and-maps/american-colonization-society-and-founding-liberia.
31. "Liberia," *World Factbook*, CIA, last modified March 13, 2024, https://www.cia.gov/the-world-factbook/countries/liberia/
32. "Lincoln's View on Slavery," Abraham Lincoln Historical Society, http://www.abraham-lincoln-history.org/category/lincolns-view-on-slavery.
33. William Coppinger, *The Continent of the Future: Africa and Its Wonderful Development—Exploration, Gold Mining, Trade, Missions, and Elevation* (Hampton, VA: Normal School Steam Press, 1881), PDF, https://www.loc.gov/item/05008635.
34. Barnett, *Time's Pendulum*, 142.
35. Ian R. Bartsky, *One Time Fits All: The Campaigns for Global Uniformity* (Stanford, CA: Stanford University Press, 2007).
36. Kevin Birth, "Standards in the Shadows for Everyone to See: The Supranational Regulation of Time and the Concern over Temporal Pluralism," in *Law and Time*, eds. Sian M. Beynon-Jones and Emily Grabham (New York: Routledge, 2019), 204.
37. K. Benediktsson and S. D. Brunn, "Time Zone Politics and Challenges of Globalisation," *Tijdschrift voor Economische en Sociale Geografie* 106, 3 (July 2015), 278.
38. Thomas Pakenham, *The Scramble for Africa: White Man's Conquest of the Dark Continent from 1876 to 1912* (New York: HarperCollins, 1992); Records of International Conferences, Commissions, and Exposition," The National Archives, web version based on *Guide to Federal Records in the National Archives of the United States,* compiled by Robert B. Matchette

et al. (Washington: National Archives and Records Administration, 1995), https://www.archives.gov/research/guide-fed-records/groups/269.html.

39. Adam Hochschild, *King Leopold's Ghost: A Story of Greed, Terror, and Heroism in Colonial Africa* (New York: HarperCollins, 1999).
40. Walter Rodney, *How Europe Underdeveloped Africa* (Washington, DC: Howard University Press, 1982).
41. Ogle, *The Global Transformation of Time*, 92.
42. Birth goes on to note that "globalization and locally embedded biological cycles are in arrhythmic relationships because globalization privileges the time and cycles of only a few locations." See Kevin Birth, *Object of Time: How Things Shape Temporality* (New York: Springer, 2012), 139.
43. Benediktsson and Brunn, "Time Zone Politics and Challenges of Globalisation."
44. Benediktsson and Brunn, "Time Zone Politics and Challenges of Globalisation."
45. "Commute Time: All workers should have reasonable commutes," National Equity Atlas (2020), https://nationalequityatlas.org/indicators/Commute_time#.
46. Andrew Aurand, Mackenzie Pish, Ikra Rafi, and Diane Yentel, "Out of Reach: The High Cost of Housing," National Low Income Housing Coalition (September 2023), https://nwlc.org/wp-content/uploads/2023/05/Cutting-rental-assistance-is-harmful-for-women-LGBTQ-people-and-families.pdf.
47. C. G. Stratton, "Slaves of the Time Belts," *Journal of Geography* 46 (1947), 264.
48. "Potential Energy-Saving Impacts of Extending Daylight Saving Time: A National Assessment," US Department of Energy: Energy Efficiency and Renewable Energy (October 2006), https://core.ac.uk/download/492634363.pdf.
49. Michael A. Grandner, Nicole Jackson, Jason R. Gerstner, and Kristen L. Knutson, "Sleep Symptoms Associated with Intake of Specific Dietary Nutrients," *Journal of Sleep Research* 23, no. 1 (2014): 22–34; John H. Kingsbury, Orfeu M. Buxton, and Karen M. Emmons, "Sleep and Its Relationship to Racial and Ethnic Disparities in Cardiovascular Diseas," *Current Cardiovascular Risk Reports* 7, no. 5 (2013); Michelle McDermott, Devin L. Brown, and Ronald D. Chervin, "Sleep Disorders and the Risk of Stroke," *Expert Review of Neurotherapeutics* 18, no. 7 (2018): 523–31.
50. Chandra L. Jackson, Susan Redline, Ichiro Kawachi, and Frank B. Hu, "Association Between Sleep Duration and Diabetes in Black and White Adults." Diabetes Care 36, no. 11 (2013): 3557–65; Shazia Jehan, Alyssa K. Myers, Ferdinand Zizi, Seithikurippu R. Pandi-Perumal, Girardin Jean-Louis, Neomi Singh, Jacqueline Ray, and Samy I. McFarlane, "Sleep Health Disparity: The Putative Role of Race, Ethnicity and Socioeconomic Status," *Sleep Medicine Disorders* 2, no. 5 (2018): 127–33.

51. Brian Resnick, "The Racial Inequality of Sleep," *The Atlantic*, October 27, 2015; Lauren Hale and D. Phuong Do, "Racial Differences in Self-Reports of Sleep Duration in a Population-Based Study," *Sleep* 30, no. 9 (2007): 1096–103; Megan E. Petrov and Kenneth L. Lichstein, "Differences in Sleep Between Black and White Adults: An Update and Future Directions," *Sleep Medicine* 18 (2016): 74–81.
52. M. A. Grandner, N. J. Jackson, B. Izci-Balserak, R. A. Gallagher, R. Murray-Bachmann, N. J. Williams NJ, N. P. Patel, G. Jean-Louis, "Social and Behavioral Determinants of Perceived Insufficient Sleep," *Front Neurol*, 5,6 (June 2015), 112; E. J. Mezick, K. A. Matthews, M. Hall, P. J. Strollo, D. J. Buysse, T. W. Kamarck, et al., "Influence of race and socioeconomic status on sleep," Psychosomatic Medicine 70, 4 (2008): 410–16.
53. N. Slopen, T. T. Lewis, D. R. Williams, "Discrimination and Sleep: A Systematic Review," *Sleep Med*, February 18, 2016: 88–95; R. S. Piccolo, M. Yang, D. L. Bliwise, H. K. Yaggi, A. B. Araujo, "Racial and Socioeconomic Disparities in Sleep and Chronic Disease: Results of a Longitudinal Investigation," *Ethn Dis* 23, 4 (2013 Autumn): 499–507.
54. S. N. Willich, D. Levy, M. B. Rocco, G. H. Tofler, P. H. Stone, J. E. Muller, "Circadian variation in the incidence of sudden cardiac death in the Framingham Heart Study population," *American Journal of Cardiology*, 10 ,60 (October 1987): 801–6.
55. C. G Stratton, "Slaves of the Time Belts," *Journal of Geography* 46, no. 7 (1947): 264–70, https://doi.org/10.1080/00221344708986733.
56. Jane Smith, "Is There a Time Difference in Hawaii?" *Hawaii Star*, August 5, 2023, https://www.hawaiistar.com/is-there-a-time-difference-in-hawaii.
57. David Prerau, *Seize the Daylight: The Curious and Contentious Story of Daylight Saving Time* (New York: Thunder's Mouth Press/Avalon, 2005), 211.
58. Laura Silver, Laura Clancy, and Jenn Hatfield, "Most Countries Don't Observe Daylight Saving Time," Pew Research Center, October 26, 2023, https://pewrsr.ch/3tNdBSZ.
59. Rob Kuper, "Joining the Great Plains in Space, Place, and Time: Questioning a Time Zone Boundary," *Great Plains Quarterly* 31, 3 (2011): 223–42.
60. In 2019, as part of a solo art exhibition called *Black Women Temporal Portal*, I held an event called "Daylight Saving Time Epilogue." Considering the unique, intersectional temporal experiences of Black women, femmes, nonbinary folks, and girls and the ways in which we are being actively erased from the objective, linear future, the *Black Womxn Temporal Portal* is a sculptural portal/booth that serves as a temporary temporal sanctuary for self-identified Black women, femmes, nonbinary folks, and girls. The portal activates the plural, subjective, and quantum nature of the future(s) where Black women, femmes, girls, and nonbinary folks exist and are safe, loved, and valued. The portal contains an open access, interactive nonlinear timescape/tapestry/temporal map/toolkit of Black womanist temporal

rituals and tech preparing us for Black quantum womanist future(s). The event was a ritual for the end of Daylight Saving Time, featuring readings and interventions by Philadelphia based artists and activists. The portal also exists as a web-based platform at www.blackwomxntemporal.net.

61. Matthew J. Kotchen and Laura E. Grant, “Does Daylight Saving Time Save Energy? Evidence from a Natural Experiment in Indiana,” *The Review of Economics and Statistics*, November 2011, 93(4): 1172–85.
62. Austin C. Smith, “Spring Forward at Your Own Risk: Daylight Saving Time and Fatal Vehicle Crashes,” *American Economic Journal: Applied Economics* 8, 2 (April 2016): 65–91.
63. Anne G. Wheaton, Daniel P. Chapman, Janet B. Croft, “School Start Times, Sleep, Behavioral, Health, and Academic Outcomes: A Review of the Literature,” *J Sch Health* 86, 5 (May 2016): 363–81.
64. Cassidy Johnson and Sophie Blackburn, “Advocacy for urban resilience: UNISDR’s Making Cities Resilient Campaign,” *Environment and Urbanization* 26, 1 (2014): 26–52.
65. Drew Dawson and Phyllis Zee, “Work Hours and Reducing Fatigue-Related Risk: Food Research for Food Policy,” *JAMA* 294, 9 (September 2005): 1104–06.
66. T. Roenneberg et al., “Why Should We Abolish Daylight Saving Time?” *J Biol Rhythms* 34, 3 (June 2019): 227–30.
67. Presenters included Mendi and Keith Obadike, Asia Dorsey, Katherine McKittrick, Dr. Walter Greason, Joy Tabernacle-KMT, Kendra Krueger, Ingrid Lafleur, V. Mitch McEwen, Moor Mother (Camae Ayewa), Dr. Danielle M. Purifoy, Ingrid Raphaël, Dr. Thomas Stanley, Ujijji Davis Williams and Dr. Celeste Winston.
68. The *TZP* Surveyors included: Iresha Picot, Kamila Shakur, Muse Dodd, Austen Smith, D’Arcee Charington Neal, Sam Rise, Brennan Robinson, Imani Harmon, Alexis McKenney, Jihan Thomas, Baobab van de Teranga, todd whitney, solıana, Raquel Baker, Nikesha Breeze, Omololu Refilwe Babatunde, Patience Williams, Tarnynon Onumonu, Xenobia Bailey, and assistant facilitators Janelle Dunlap and Sakinah Bramble-Hakim.
69. Documented on www.TimeZoneProtocols.space.
70. Comprehensive recordings and materials from all workshops and the collective set of protocols are available at www.timezoneprotocols.space.
71. Celeste Winston, “Black Fugitive Infrastructures and Cross-Time Space Routines,” Prime Meridian Unconference, April 17, 2022.
72. Joseph L. Paul, “Don’t Gentrify Georgia Avenue,” *Washington Post*, July 25, 2004, https://www.washingtonpost.com/archive/opinions/2004/07/25/dont-gentrify-georgia-avenue/5b85f9ff-8ad6-48f9-81af-86e1367fe00d.
73. Joy Tabernacle-KMT, “Grief Reparations and Temporal Hush Harbors,” Prime Meridian Unconference, April 17, 2022.
74. Joy Tabernacle-KMT, “Grief Reparations and Temporal Hush Harbors.”

75. Tabernacle-KMT, "Grief Reparations."
76. Nicole Van Groningen, "Racial Injustice Causes Black Americans to Age Faster than Whites," August 6, 2020, https://massivesci.com/articles/weathering-hypothesis-black-aging-health.
77. Jamie Wiggan, "New National Study Predicts Lower Life Expectancy for Black Pittsburghers," *Pittsburgh City Paper*, October 6, 2022, https://www.pghcitypaper.com/news/new-national-study-predicts-lower-life-expectancy-for-black-pittsburghers-22556413.
78. Ujijji Davis Williams, "Occupying Vacancy: Looking at Detroit's Grassroot Activation of Vacant Land and Structures," Prime Meridian Unconference, April 16, 2022.
79. Ujijji Davis Williams, "Occupying Vacancy: Looking at Detroit's Grassroot Activation of Vacant Land and Structures."
80. Asia Dorsey, "Bending SpaceTime with Botanicals," Prime Meridian Unconference, April 16, 2022.
81. Asia Dorsey, "Bending SpaceTime with Botanicals."
82. V. Mitch McEwen, "Cloud Time," Prime Meridian Unconference, April 16, 2022.
83. Recording from Amazon Labor Union's formation, played at Nadir Jeevanjee and V. Mitch McEwen, "Cloud Time," Prime Meridian Unconference, April 16, 2022.

Chapter 5: Race Against Time

1. Carol J. Greenhouse, *A Moment's Notice: Time Politics Across Cultures* (Ithaca: Cornell University Press, 1996), 223, 230.
2. Carol J. Greenhouse, "Just in Time: Temporality and the Cultural Legitimation of Law," *Yale Law Journal* 98 (1989): 1631; see also Jeremy Rifkin, *Time Wars: The Primary Conflict in Human History* (New York: Henry Holt, 1987), 146–47, "Western culture has institutionalized its images of the future by way of religion and politics," making sure that "the future can be made predictable and controlled.".
3. Rebecca R. French, "Time in the Law," *University of Colorado Law Review* 72 (2001): 663–64.
4. Renisa Mawani, "Law as Temporality: Colonial Politics and Indian Settlers," *UC Irvine Law Review* 4 (2014): 65–71.
5. See work by Michelle Bastian, Emily Grabham, Renisa Mawani, and Sarah Keenan.
6. "Policy Brief: Evictions in Philadelphia," Reinvestment Fund, January 2017, https://www.reinvestment.com/research-publications/evictions-in-philadelphia.
7. Rasheedah Phillips et al., "Breaking the Record: Dismantling the Barriers Eviction Records Place on Housing Opportunities," Community Legal

Services of Philadelphia, November 2020, https://clsphila.org/wp-content/uploads/2020/12/Breaking-the-Record-Report_Nov2020.pdf.

8. "Reducing Default Judgments in Philadelphia's Landlord-Tenant Court," Sheller Center for Social Justice, Temple University Beasley School of Law, June 2020. The most common reasons cited in cases where tenants tried to open up a default judgment were "lack of notice, medical issues, childcare problems, lateness, and difficulty finding the courthouse and courtroom."
9. Illegal or informal evictions also occur outside of the law, but this analysis is limited to legal evictions that take place through the court system.
10. Editorial Board, "Evicted Without Warning," *Philadelphia Inquirer*, July 28, 2020; Ryan Briggs, "A Philly lawyer evicts people for city courts. She's married to a judge who presides over evictions," *WHYY*, July 24, 2020.
11. Pennsylvania Statutes Title 68 P. S. Real and Personal Property § 250.501, the full text if which can be read at https://codes.findlaw.com/pa/title-68-ps-real-and-personal-property/pa-st-sect-68-250-501-a.
12. Michael Hanchard, "Afro-Modernity, Temporality, Politics, and the African Diaspora," *Public Culture* 11, no. 1 (January 1999): 245, 253, https://doi.org/10.1215/08992363-11-1-245.
13. Cheryl I. Harris, "Whiteness as Property," *Harvard Law Review*, vol. 106, no. 8 (1993): 1707: "the hyper-exploitation of Black labor was accomplished by treating Black people themselves as objects of property. Race and property were thus conflated by establishing a form of property contingent on race—only Blacks were subjugated as slaves and treated as property."
14. Giordano Nanni, *The Colonisation of Time: Ritual, Routine and Resistance in the British Empire* (Manchester: Manchester University Press, 2013), 25, 41.
15. "Slavery Meeting at Colchester," *Essex County Standard*, January 19, 1838. An 1833 article in the Morning Standard discusses the issue of the most economical ways to divide up a "negro's time," should they be emancipated: "three-fourths of the negro's time were to be given to former owner." See also Rasheedah Phillips, "Counter Clockwise: Unmapping Black Temporalities from Greenwich Mean Timelines," *Funambulist* 36, June 21, 2021, https://thefunambulist.net/magazine/they-have-clocks-we-have-time/counter-clockwise-unmapping-black-temporalities-from-greenwich-mean-timelines.
16. Greenhouse, "Just in Time," 1631.
17. Charles W. Mills, "White Time: The Chronic Injustice of Ideal Theory," *Du Bois Review* 11, no. 1 (January 2014): 27, 31, https://doi.org/10.1017/S1742058X14000022; see also Octavia E. Butler, *Kindred* (New York: Doubleday, 1979). Octavia Butler's speculative novel *Kindred* explores the implications of the inaccessibility of the future to enslaved Africans, and the utility and futility of fore- and hindsight when traveling along a progressive worldline. Butler's time-traveling protagonist Dana lands two hundred years into her relative past, pulled back by a soon-to-become slave-owning,

slave-raping ancestor whom she must choose to continue to save to ensure her own time/bloodline. The date of Dana's last trip is the bicentennial of the Fourth of July. Philadelphia, once the ultimate futurist city of the white male utopian vision, is a city built upon the graves, ghosts, hands, and backs of Blackness.

18. Harris, "Whiteness as Property," 1718.
19. Charles W. Mills, "White Time," 28.
20. See generally: Keeanga-Yamahtta Taylor, *Race for Profit: How Banks and the Real Estate Industry Undermined Black Homeownership*. (Chapel Hill: University of North Carolina Press, 2019).
21. James W. Loewen, *Sundown Towns: A Hidden Dimension of American Racism* (New York: The New Press, 2005).
22. Loewen, *Sundown Towns*.
23. "Housing Discrimination Against Racial and Ethnic Minorities 2012," US Department of Housing and Urban Development (June 2013), https://www.huduser.gov/portal/Publications/pdf/HUD-514_HDS2012_execsumm.pdf; Jeannine Bell, "The Fair Housing Act and Extralegal Terror," *Indiana Law Review* 41, no. 3 (2008).
24. Bruce Mitchell, "Philadelphia and the Rapid Gentrification of Downtown," National Community Reinvestment Coalition (October 2018), https://ncrc.org/philadelphia-and-the-rapid-gentrification-of-downtown; finding that between 2000 and 2013, 57 neighborhoods in Philadelphia showed signs of residential gentrification. This includes the influx of large numbers of college-educated residents, booming property values, and rising incomes; see also Jackelyn Hwang and Lei Ding, "Unequal Displacement: Gentrification, Racial Stratification, and Residential Destinations in Philadelphia," *American Journal of Sociology* 126, no. 2 (September 2020).
25. City of Philadelphia and the Philadelphia Housing Authority, "Assessment of Fair Housing," December 23, 2016, https://www.phila.gov/media/20190502115754/afh-2016-for-web.pdf.
26. City of Philadelphia and the Philadelphia Housing Authority, "Assessment of Fair Housing," December 12, 2017, 46; Philadelphia Housing Authority, "Sharswood Blumberg Neighborhood Transformation Plan," 2016, 3.
27. Community Futures Lab interview with Mr. Warren McMichael, 2018.
28. Ukee Washington, "Philadelphia 76ers Award $100,000 Housing Grant to Help Sharswood Neighborhood," *CBS Philly*, October 18, 2021, https://philadelphia.cbslocal.com/2021/10/18/philadelphia-76ers-award-100000-housing-grant-to-help-sharswood-neighborhood.
29. Community Futures Lab Interview with Warren McMichael, 2018.
30. Jonathan Zimmerman, "Fifty Years Later, the Legacy of 1964 Riots Lingers," *WHYY*, August 11, 2014, https://whyy.org/articles/50-years-later-the-legacy-of-1964-riots-lingers.
31. "Philadelphia 2017: The State of the City," Pew Charitable Trusts, April 6,

2017, https://www.pewtrusts.org/zh/research-and-analysis/reports/2017/04/philadelphia-2017.

32. Kelvin A. Jeremiah, "Breathing Life into Blighted Community," *Philadelphia Inquirer*, July 15, 2015, https://www.inquirer.com/philly/opinion/currents/20150715_Breathing_life_into_blighted_community.html.
33. Monique Curry-Mims, "How 100+ Years of Disinvestment Has Led to Today's Philadelphia," *Generocity*, February 9, 2023, https://generocity.org/philly/2023/02/09/how-100-years-of-disinvestment-has-led-to-todays-philadelphia.
34. Bruce Mitchel, "Philadelphia and Business Disinvestment," National Community Reinvestment Coalition, October 1, 2018, https://ncrc.org/philadelphia-and-business-disinvestment.
35. Elizabeth Carlson, "Mapping Inequality and Gentrification in Philadelphia: Visualizing the Spatial Distribution of Inequity," March 18, 2022, https://storymaps.arcgis.com/stories/c7a2cd9db54e4fa5885153246f56bcdc.
36. Ashley Hahn, "Remaking Sharswood: Miller Memorial Baptist Anchors a Changing Neighborhood," *WHYY*, March 18, 2016, https://whyy.org/articles/remaking-sharswood-miller-memorial-baptist-anchors-a-changing-neighborhood.
37. Aaron Moselle, "PHA Demolishes Norman Blumberg High-Rise Towers in Sharswood," *WHYY*, March 19, 2016, https://whyy.org/articles/pha-demolishes-norman-blumberg-high-rise-towers-in-sharswood-video.
38. Philadelphia Housing Authority, "Sharswood-Blumberg Neighborhood Transformation Plan," 2016, http://www.pha.phila.gov/media/163410/2015-blumberg_transformation_-_web23.pdf.
39. Community Futures Lab interview with Ms. K, 2016.
40. Helga Nowotny, *Time: The Modern and Postmodern Experience* (Cambridge: Polity Press, 1994), 23.
41. Bahar Sakizlioğlu, "Inserting Temporality into the Analysis of Displacement: Living Under the Threat of Displacement," *Tijdschrift voor economische en sociale geografie* 105, no. 2 (2014): 206, 208.
42. "Congressman Fattah to Join in Blumberg High-Rise Implosion Saturday," Office of Congressman Chaka Fattah, *PR Newswire*, March 17, 2016, https://www.prnewswire.com/news-releases/congressman-fattah-to-join-in-blumberg-high-rise-implosion-saturday-300237861.html.
43. Kodwo Eshun, "Further Considerations on Afrofuturism," *The New Centennial Review* 3, no. 2 (2003): 297, 301.
44. City of Philadelphia and Philadelphia Housing Authority, "Assessment of Fair Housing," December 12, 2017, http://fairhousingrights.org/wp-content/uploads/2017/12/afh-2016-for-web.pdf, 102.
45. Sakizlioğlu, "Inserting Temporality," 1, 3.
46. Lawrence T. Brown, "Historical Trauma, Colonizing Capitalism and Systemic Racism: Addressing the Damage Caused by Serial Forced Displacement,"

Mariselabgomez.com, July 26, 2014, https://www.mariselabgomez.com/historical-trauma-colonizing-capitalism-and-systemic-racism-addressing-the-damage-caused-by-serial-forced-displacement.

47. Community Futures Lab interview with Ms. K, 2016.
48. Community Futures Lab interview with Mr. M, 2017.
49. "The Philadelphia Race Riot of August 1964," *Philadelphia Inquirer*, August 28, 2013, https://www.inquirer.com/philly/blogs/TODAY-IN-PHILADELPHIA-HISTORY/The-Philadelphia-race-riot-of-August-1964.html.
50. Mindy Fullilove, *Root Shock* (New York: New Village Press, 2016), 14, 70.
51. US Department of Housing and Urban Development, "RAD Key Takeaways," https://www.hud.gov/program_offices/public_indian_housing/repositioning/rad_key_takeaways.
52. Fullilove, *Root Shock*, 70.
53. PHA community meeting.
54. Daryl C. Murphy, "Sharswood Residents Return Home after $28M Tower Upgrade," *Philadelphia Tribune*, March 22, 2019, https://www.phillytrib.com/news/local_news.
55. Jennifer Bennetch and Sterling Johnson, "Biden's Plan Could Be Disastrous for Low-Income Homeowners in Philly," *Philadelphia Inquirer*, April 13, 2021, https://www.inquirer.com/opinion/commentary/low-income-housing-philadelphia-biden-american-jobs-plan-20210413.html.
56. Fullilove, *Root Shock*, 70.
57. "Woe," Online Etymology Dictionary, https://www.etymonline.com/word/woe.
58. Kevin K. Birth, *Time Blind: Problems in Perceiving Other Temporalities* (London: Palgrave MacMillan, 2016), 94.
59. Margaret E. Farrar, "Amnesia, Nostalgia, and the Politics of Place Memory," *Political Research Quarterly* 64, no. 4 (2011): 725–39.
60. Community Futures Lab Oral Futures interview with Ms. K, 2016.
61. Aubrey Whelan, "Blumberg Towers Come Tumbling Down, Raising Memories of Horror and Home," *Philadelphia Inquirer*, March 19, 2016, https://www.inquirer.com/philly/news/20160320_Blumberg_towers_come_tumbling_down_raising_memories_of_horror_and_home.html.
62. Community Futures Lab Oral Futures interview with Ms. T, 2016.
63. Fernand Braudel, *On History*, trans. Sarah Matthews (Chicago: University of Chicago Press, 1980).
64. Adam Barrows, *Time, Literature, and Cartography After the Spatial Turn* (London: Palgrave Macmillian, 2016).
65. Carol J. Greenhouse, *A Moment's Notice: Time Politics Across Cultures* (Ithaca: Cornell University Press, 1996), 230.
66. Michelle Bastian, "Retelling Time in Grassroots Sustainable Economy Movements," *GeoHumanities* 5, no. 1 (2019): 36–53.
67. Hillary S. Kativa, "What: The Columbia Avenue Riots (1964)," *Civil Rights in*

a Northern City: Philadelphia, Temple University Libraries, https://exhibits.temple.edu/s/civil-rights-in-a-northern-cit/page/the-columbia-avenue-riots--196.

68. Jacob Whiton et al., "What's Behind the Racial Homeownership Gap in Philadelphia?" Federal Reserve Bank of Philadelphia, December 2021.
69. Keeanga-Yamahtta Taylor, "How Real Estate Segregated America," *Dissent* magazine, Fall 2018, https://www.dissentmagazine.org/article/how-real-estate-segregated-america-fair-housing-act-race.
70. Maureen Perkins, *The Reform of Time: Magic and Modernity* (London: Pluto Press, 2001).
71. Community Futures Lab Oral Futures interview with Ms. E, 2017.
72. Yvette Taylor, *Fitting Into Place?: Class and Gender Geographies and Temporalities* (Abingdon: Routledge, 2012).
73. Taylor, *Fitting Into Place?*, 2.
74. Community Futures Lab Oral Futures interview with Ms. C, 2017.
75. Kevin K. Birth, *Time Blind: Problems in Perceiving Other Temporalities* (London: Palgrave MacMillan, 2016), 94.
76. Giordano Nanni, *The Colonisation of Time: Ritual, Routine and Resistance in the British Empire* (Manchester: Manchester University Press, 2012), 19.
77. Community Futures Lab Interview with Ms. T, July 15, 2016
78. Fernand Braudel, *On History*, trans. Sarah Matthews (Chicago: University of Chicago Press, 1980), 12.
79. Adam Barrows, *Time, Literature, and Cartography After the Spatial Turn* (London: Palgrave Macmillian, 2016), 33.
80. *Stenger v. Lehigh Valley Hospital Center*, 382 Pa. Super. 75 (1989); acknowledging both a constitutional and common law right of access to judicial proceedings.
81. *Miller v. Cty. of Ctr.*, 173 A.3d 1162, 1167 (Pa. 2017); "[The] principle of openness with respect to public judicial records is . . . also grounded in the Pennsylvania Constitution."
82. Resolution #200531 (October 2020), resolution cowritten by members of the Black and Brown Workers Coalition, including Dominique London and Sterling Johnson.
83. Rasheedah Phillips, Dominique London, and Jenna Collins, "Breaking the Record: Dismantling the Barriers Eviction Records Place on Housing Opportunities," Community Legal Services of Philadelphia and Black and Brown Workers Cooperative, November 30, 2020, https://clsphila.org/housing/report-eviction-record-policy.
84. "Renters' Access Act: Tenant-Screening Guidelines," Pa. Code § 9.1108, 3 and 4 (2021).
85. Karen Barad, "Quantum Entanglements and Hauntological Relations of Inheritance: Dis/continuities, SpaceTime Enfoldings, and Justice-to-Come," *Derrida Today* 3, no. 2 (2010): 240–68.

86. Lars Fuglsang and Jan Mattsson, "Making Sense of Innovation: A Future Perfect Approach," *Journal of Management and Organization* 17, no. 4 (2011): 448–58, doi:10.5172/jmo.2011.17.4.448.
87. Charles W. Mills, "'The Chronopolitics of Racial Time," *Time and Society* 29, no. 3 (2020): 297, 299–300, 303.
88. Community Futures Lab Interview with Ms. C, April 16, 2017.

Chapter 6: Waiting, Wading, Weighting Time

1. "Juneteenth: 'The Emancipation Proclamation—Freedom Realized and Delayed,'" Prairie View A&M University, https://www.pvamu.edu/tiphc/research-projects/juneteenth-the-emancipation-proclamation-freedom-realized-and-delayed.
2. Christopher Klein quotes an August 1862 letter by Abraham Lincoln, in which Lincoln states, "My paramount object in this struggle is to save the Union and is not either to save or destroy slavery. If I could save the Union without freeing any slave, I would do it; and if I could save it by freeing all the slaves, I would do it; and if I could save it by freeing some and leaving others alone, I would also do that." See Christopher Klein, "Congress Passes Thirteenth Amendment, 150 Years Ago," History.com, last modified September 1, 2018, https://www.history.com/news/congress-passes-13th-amendment-150-years-ago.
3. "The House Joint Resolution Proposing the Thirteenth Amendment to the Constitution," January 31, 1865, National Archives, https://www.archives.gov/historical-docs/13th-amendment#:~:text=Passed%20by%20Congress%20on%20January,within%20the%20United%20States%2C%20or.
4. Allison Keyes, "'Watch Nights,' A New Year's Celebration of Emancipation," NPR Weekend Edition, December 23, 2012, https://www.npr.org/2012/12/29/167905308/watch-nights-honor-emancipation-proclamations-anniversary.
5. Christopher Wilson, "Christmas and New Year's Party Like It's 1854 (or 1865)," *Time*, December 25, 2014, https://time.com/3642693/new-year-emancipation-proclamation.
6. Geneva Smitherman, *Word from the Mother: Language and African Americans* (New York: Routledge, 2006), 55.
7. Gerald David Jaynes, "Watch Night," *Encyclopedia of African American Society* (New Haven: Yale University Press, 2005), 870.
8. J. H. Franklin and A. A. Moss, *From Slavery to Freedom: A History of African Americans* (New York: Knopf, 2000).
9. Wanda Ravernell, "African American Watch Night Rings in New Year," *Chronicle*, December 29, 2008, https://www.sfgate.com/entertainment/article/African-American-Watch-Night-rings-in-new-year-3256437.php.

10. "A Letter from a Democrat," *Chicago Tribune*, December 28, 1862.
11. Olivia B. Waxman, "'The Slaves Dread New Year's Day the Worst': The Grim History of January 1," *Time*, December 27, 2019, https://time.com/5750833/new-years-day-slavery-history.
12. Waxman, "'The Slaves Dread New Year's Day the Worst.'"
13. Waxman, "'The Slaves Dread New Year's Day the Worst.'"
14. Lewis Clark, "Leaves from a Slave's Journal of Life," *The Anti-Slavery Standard*, October 20 and 27, 1842, 78–79, and 83.
15. Benjamin Hale, "Emancipation Proclamation: Effects, Impacts, and Outcomes," *History Cooperative*, https://historycooperative.org/effects-emancipation-proclamation.
16. Benjamin Hale, "Emancipation Proclamation."
17. It's important to note that although the Juneteenth holiday is documented as originating in Galveston, Texas, there are many other places where Black people had their freedom delayed for equal lengths of time. Christopher Wilson profiles Ed Mcree, an enslaved person held captive on a forced labor camp in Oconee County, Georgia who didn't learn about the Emancipation Proclamation until 1865. See Wilson, "On Christmas and New Year's, Party Like It's 1864 (or 1865)."
18. R. Green, "Medical Topography of Wharton, Texas–Rowan Green," *Atlanta Med Surg Journal* 6, 8 (April 1861): 445–48.
19. "The Emancipation Proclamation," National Archives Museum, October 6, 2015, archived from the original on February 6, 2017; Gates, Henry Louis Jr., "What Is Juneteenth?," PBS, January 16, 2013, archived from the original on June 11, 2020.
20. "Testimony of Elizabeth Rose Hite," WPA Ex-Slave Narratives, 13, LSU, https://louisianadigitallibrary.org/islandora/object/state-lwp%3A8595.
21. Mary A. Livermore, *The Story of My Life* (A. D. Worthington and Co: Hartford, CT, 1897), 306–7.
22. "Negro Work Songs and Calls," quoted in Lawrence W. Levine, *Black Culture and Black Consciousness: Afro-American Folk Thought from Slavery to Freedom* (Oxford: Oxford University Press, USA, 2007), 219.
23. "Negro Work Songs and Calls," in Levine, *Black Culture and Black Consciousness.*
24. Casey O'Callaghan, *Sounds: A Philosophical Theory* (Oxford: Oxford University Press, 2007).
25. David Grandy, *Everyday Quantum Reality* (Bloomington: Indiana University Press, 2010), 88.
26. Grandy, *Everyday Quantum Reality*, 85.
27. Grandy, *Everyday Quantum Reality*, 87–88.
28. Levine, *Black Culture and Black Consciousness*, 157.
29. Levine, *Black Culture and Black Consciousness*, 158.
30. Levine, *Black Culture and Black Consciousness*, 158.

31. "Fact," Online Etymology Dictionary, https://www.etymonline.com/word/fact.
32. Eve Ruhnau, "The Deconstruction of Time and the Emergence of Temporality," *Time, Temporality, Now* (Berlin: Springer, 1997), 55.
33. Jonathan Martineau, *Time, Capitalism and Alienation: A Socio-Historical Inquiry into the Making of Modern Time* (Leiden: Brill, 2015).
34. Laura C. Jarmon, *Wishbone: Reference and Interpretation in Black Folk Narrative* (Knoxville: University of Tennessee Press, 2003), xxxiii.
35. Jarmon, *Wishbone*, xxxiii.
36. Jarmon, *Wishbone*, xxxiii.
37. Eve Ruhnau, "The Deconstruction of Time and the Emergence of Temporality," 56.
38. Abraham Lincoln, "Emancipation Proclamation" (1863), in Terry Fitzpatrick, "719 Words That Changed History: The Emancipation Proclamation," *Free the Slaves*, December 18, 2012, https://freetheslaves.net/719-words-that-changed-history-the-emancipation-proclamation.
39. Marcus Aurelius, "Book Four," *Meditations* (167 ACE), trans. George Long, The Internet Classics Archive, https://classics.mit.edu/Antoninus/meditations.html.
40. "Wade in the Water," http://41114544.weebly.com/wade-in-the-water.html.
41. John Wesley Work, *New Jubilee Songs, as Sung by the Fisk Jubilee Singers of Fisk Univ*, second ed. (Nashville: Fisk University, 1904), http://dlg.galileo.usg.edu/aaed/do:aarl90.001-001-001.
42. "Secrets: Signs and Symbols—Pathways to Freedom," Maryland Public Television (2002), in collaboration with the Maryland Historical Society and Maryland State Archives, retrieved February 23, 2021.
43. Jean M. Humez, *Harriet Tubman: The Life and the Life Stories* (Madison: University of Wisconsin Press, 2006), 136.
44. Humez, *Harriet Tubman*, 137.
45. The Big Dipper constellation is the focus of another coded freedom song, "Follow the Drinking Gourd;" however, research dates the song back to 1927, according to Fergus M. Bordewich, "History's Tangled Threads," *New York Times*, February 2, 2007, https://www.nytimes.com/2007/02/02/opinion/02bordewich.html; Allison Keyes, "Harriet Tubman, an Unsung Naturalist, Used Owl Calls as a Signal on the Underground Railroad," *Audubon Magazine*, February 25, 2020, https://www.audubon.org/news/harriet-tubman-unsung-naturalist-used-owl-calls-signal-underground-railroad.
46. Humez, *Harriet Tubman*, 212.
47. "Harriet Tubman: Visions of Freedom: Visions Episode 1," *PBS*, October 4, 2022, https://lite.pbs.org/video/visions-slaug4; Gerald David Jaynes, "Tubman, Harriet (1820?–1913)," 825.
48. Humez, *Harriet Tubman*, 180.
49. Humez, *Harriet Tubman*, 6.

50. Joyce Elaine Noll, *Company of Prophets: African American Psychics, Healers and Visionaries* (St. Paul: Llewellyn Publications, 1991).
51. Gerald David Jaynes, "Tubman, Harriet (1820?–1913)," *Encyclopedia of African American Society* (New Haven: Yale University Press, 2005), 825.
52. Noll, *Company of Prophets*.
53. Jewels Rocka, *Divination: Elements of Wisdom* (London: Wooden Books, 2021), 38.
54. Edward Shizha and Gloria Emeagwali, *African Indigenous Knowledge and the Sciences: Journeys into the Past and Present* (Rotterdam: SensePublishers, 2016), 109.
55. P. G. Alcock, *The Stellar Knowledge of Indigenous South Africans* (Rotterdam: SensePublishers, 2016), 126.
56. Penelope S. Bernard, "'Living Water' in Nguni Healing Traditions, South Africa," *Worldviews* 17, 2 (2013): 138–49, https://www.jstor.org/stable/43809484.
57. Bernard, "'Living Water' in Nguni Healing Traditions, South Africa."
58. Dorothy Wickenden, "Liberty or Death: On the Prophetic Visions and Unflinching Will of Harriet Tubman," *LitHub*, March 31, 2021, https://lithub.com/liberty-or-death-on-the-prophetic-visions-and-unflinching-will-of-harriet-tubman.
59. Kevin K. Birth, *Objects of Time: How Things Shape Temporality* (London: Palgrave Macmillan, 2012).
60. "Times Change, But Austin Negroes Find Same Old Fun in Celebrating Juneteenth," *Austin American Statesman*, June 19, 1930, https://www.newspapers.com/article/austin-american-statesman/53340595.
61. *The Southport Leader*, Thursday January 9, 1896, https://www.newspapers.com/paper/the-southport-leader/2863.
62. Sarah Reyes, "Juneteenth Is an Official City Holiday," City of Philadelphia, June 12, 2020, https://www.phila.gov/2020-06-16-juneteenth-is-an-official-city-holiday.
63. Mayor Kenney quoted in Reyes, "Juneteenth is an Official City Holiday."
64. "Housing Burden: All Residents Should Have Access to Quality, Affordable Homes," National Equity Atlas, https://nationalequityatlas.org/indicators/Housing_burden.
65. "Chart of the Week: #BlackWomensEqualPay," National Equity Atlas, https://nationalequityatlas.org/data-in-action/BlackWomensEqualPay-Chart.
66. "Covid-19's Impact on Race and Housing Security Across Philadelphia," *Philadelphia Renters Report*, 2021, https://clsphila.org/wp-content/uploads/2021/02/20210222-Philadelphia-Renters-Report.pdf.
67. Informational sign seen by the author during self-guided tour of Bellamy Mansion in Wilmington, North Carolina on August 8, 2023.
68. This quote at Bellamy Mansion was attributed to Rufus Bunnell, February. 1860.

69. Brakkton Booker, "Curfew in Philadelphia Lifts as City Is Roiled by Protests in Walter Wallace Shooting," *NPR*, October 28, 2020, https://www.npr.org/2020/10/28/928728141/philadelphia-issues-a-curfew-as-protests-follow-police-shooting-of-walter-wallac.
70. Linda Poon, "The Racist History of Curfews in America," *Bloomberg*, June 18, 2020, https://www.bloomberg.com/news/articles/2020-06-18/the-racist-history-of-curfews-in-america.

Chapter 7: Project: Time Capsule

1. "1909 Time Capsule Unearthed at GR Housing Project Site," *Wood TV*, November 20, 2018, https://www.woodtv.com/news/grand-rapids/1909-time-capsule-unearthed-at-gr-housing-project-site.
2. Patricia Seibert, *We Were Here: A Short History of Time Capsules* (Brookfield: Millbrook Press, 2002).
3. William E. Jarvis, *Time Capsules: A Cultural History* (Jefferson, NC: McFarland and Company, 2003), 25.
4. Jeremy Rifkin, *Time Wars: The Primary Conflict in Human History* (New York: Henry Holt, 1987).
5. Nick Yablon, *Remembrance of Things Present: The Invention of the Time Capsule* (Chicago: University of Chicago Press, 2019).
6. Kate Giammarise, "Library Gets 1930s Relics from Project's Time Capsule," *The Blade*, February 21, 2013, https://www.toledoblade.com/local/2013/02/21/Library-gets-1930s-relics-from-project-s-time-capsule-items-will-be-preserved-displayed.html.
7. Ella P. Stewart, "A Snapshot of the Negro in Toledo pre-1930s," Journey:—Toledo's African American Genealogy Group, August 24, 2016, https://journeytoledo.wordpress.com/2016/08/24/a-snapshot-of-the-negro-in-toledo-pre-1930s-by-ella-p-stewart.
8. Stewart, "A Snapshot of the Negro in Toledo pre-1930s."
9. B. T. Kirby and J. D. Franson, "Nonlocal Interferometry: Beyond Bell's Inequality," *arXiv* preprint arXiv:0707.0475 (2007).
10. All poems by Camae Ayewa in this chapter were originally written to accompany this essay.
11. Corey Kilgannon, "A Million Bodies Are Buried Here. Now It's Becoming a Park," *New York Times*, March 24, 2023, https://www.nytimes.com/2023/03/24/nyregion/hart-island-cemetery-park.html; Rachel Sherman, "'Hart Island' Gives Voice to Stories That Might Otherwise Be Lost," *New York Times*, March 16, 2022, https://www.nytimes.com/2022/03/16/theater/hart-island-play-gym-at-judson.html.
12. R. W. Jamieson, "Material Culture and Social Death: African-American Burial Practices," *Historical Archeology* 29, 4 (1995): 39.
13. Cherri Gregg, "Queen Lane Apartments Gone, But History Remains,"

September 13, 2014, https://philadelphia.cbslocal.com/2014/09/13/queen-lane-apartments-gone-but-history-remains.

14. "Queen Lane Archeology," Philadelphia Archeological Forum, https://www.phillyarchaeology.net/research/project-report-index/queen-lane-archaeology.
15. R. W. Jamieson, "Material Culture and Social Death: African-American Burial Practices," 39.
16. Jason Laughlin, "In Germantown, a housing development, a Colonial Graveyard, and a Playground that Wasn't," *Philadelphia Inquirer*, August 27, 2020, https://www.inquirer.com/news/playground-germantown-philadelphia-potters-field-preservation-history-open-space-20200827.html.
17. Stephen Sitarski, "From Weccacoe to South Philadelphia: The Changing Face of a Neighborhood," Pennsylvania Historical Society, https://www.wikiwand.com/en/Queen_Village,_Philadelphia; Samuel Hazard, *Annals of Pennsylvania, From the Discovery of the Delaware, 1609–1682* (Philadelphia: Hazard and Mitchell, 1850), 438.
18. Terry Buckalew, The Bethel Burial Ground Project, https://bethelburyinggroundproject.com.
19. Larry Miller, "Hallowed Ground: Black Colonial-Era Grave Sites," *Philadelphia Tribune*, November 29, 2014, https://www.phillytrib.com/news/hallowed-ground-black-colonial-era-grave-sites/article_604322fa-d743-52cf-8605-78afd4363886.html; Michaela Winberg, "Philly's Black Burial Grounds and the Battle for Preservation," *Billy Penn*, March 24, 2019, https://billypenn.com/2019/03/24/phillys-black-burial-grounds-and-the-battle-for-preservation.
20. Buckalew, The Bethel Burial Ground Project.
21. "Announcing the Winning Bethel Burying Ground Historic Site Memorial Design by Karyn Olivier," The City of Philadelphia's Office of Arts, Culture and the Creative Economy, not dated, https://www.creativephl.org/her-luxuriant-soil-olivier.
22. R. W. Jamieson, "Material Culture and Social Death: African-American Burial Practices," 54.
23. John Noble Wilford, "Slave Artifacts Under the Hearth," *New York Times*, August 27, 1997, https://www.nytimes.com/1996/08/27/science/slave-artifacts-under-the-hearth.html.
24. S. K. Moses, "Enslaved African conjure and ritual deposits on the Hume Plantation, South Carolina," *North American Archaeologist* 39, 2 (2018): 131–64.
25. Patricia Merle Samford, "Power Runs in Many Channels: Subfloor Pits and West African–based Spiritual Traditions in Colonial Virginia" (PhD Dissertation, Chapel Hill, 2000), https://archaeology.sites.unc.edu/wp-content/uploads/sites/187/2020/08/Samford-2000-PhD-UMI.pdf.
26. "A Housing Revolution," Monticello, https://www.monticello.org/research-education/for-scholars/archaeology-daacs/current-research/mulberry-row-reassessment/a-housing-revolution.

27. John Noble Wilford, "Slave Artifacts Under the Hearth," *New York Times*, August 27, 1996, https://www.nytimes.com/1996/08/27/science/slave-artifacts-under-the-hearth.html.
28. Wilford, "Slave Artifacts Under the Hearth."
29. See S. K. Moses, "Enslaved African Conjure and Ritual Deposits on the Hume Plantation, South Carolina," in contrast to the 1997 *New York Times* article "Slave Artifacts Under the Hearth," in which John Noble Wilford doesn't make the connection: "The evidence, archeologists and other scholars say, lay beneath the bricks of the hearths and hidden in the northeast corners of the rooms. (Why the northeast, no one knows.)"
30. "Lost, Tossed, and Found," Manassas National Battlefield Park, National Park Service, https://www.nps.gov/articles/the-nash-site.htm. Some of the excavated artifacts at the Nash site are also believed to have been used for Mancala, a game originating in Africa.
31. John Kessler, "Lauren Northup: The Preservationist," *Garden and Gun*, April/May 2020, https://gardenandgun.com/articles/lauren-northup-the-preservationist.
32. Lynn Jones, "Crystals and Conjuring at the Charles Carroll House, Annapolis, Maryland," *African Diaspora Archaeology Newsletter* 7, 1 (2000), article 2, https://scholarworks.umass.edu/adan/vol7/iss1/2.
33. Jones, "Crystals and Conjuring at the Charles Carroll House, Annapolis, Maryland."
34. "Amulet," *Encyclopedia of African Religion*, eds. Molefi Kete Asante and Ama Mazama (New York: SAGE Publications, 2009), http://ebookcentral.proquest.com/lib/newschool/detail.action?docID=2041979.
35. Cheryl Janifer LaRoche, *Free Black Communities and the Underground Railroad: The Geography of Resistance* (Champaign: University of Illinois Press, 2014), 91–93.
36. LaRoche, *Free Black Communities and the Underground Railroad*, 156.
37. LaRoche, *Free Black Communities and the Underground Railroad*, 92.
38. As recounted in Kevin Williams, "The Legend of a Cave and the Traces of the Underground Railroad in Ohio," *Atlas Obscura*, February 14, 2020, ttps://www.atlasobscura.com/articles/legend-cave-underground-railroad-ohio.
39. Williams, "The Legend of a Cave and the Traces of the Underground Railroad in Ohio"; see also "1849: The Cave: An Underground Railroad Story," *Ohio Mysteries Podcast*, https://ohiomysteries.com/ohio%20mysteries/1849-an-underground-railroad-story-the-poisonous-cave.
40. H. Dwight Weaver, *Missouri Caves in History and Legend* (Columbia: University of Missouri, 2008); Hubert and Charlotte Rother, *Lost Caves of St. Louis: A History of the City's Forgotten Caves* (Columbia: University of Missouri, 1996).
41. See "The Cherokee Cave and Museum of Natural History," Chatillon-DeMenil Mansion, https://www.demenil.org/cherokee-cave#:~:text=When%20the%20cave%20was%20first,of%20Broadway%20and%20Cherokee%20Street.

42. "The Cherokee Cave and Museum of Natural History," Chatillon-DeMenil Mansion.
43. Aimee Levitt, "Secret Passage: Local Cavers Scout the Entrance of Long-lost English Cave in Benton Park," *River Front Times: St. Louis Metro News*, September 12, 2007, https://www.riverfronttimes.com/news/secret-passage-2478123.
44. Craig Savoye, "A Race to Save Pieces of the Route that Saved Slaves," *Christian Science Monitor*, August 10, 2000, https://www.csmonitor.com/2000/0810/p2s2.html.
45. "History of the Lemp Avenue Site," Lemp Avenue Archeological Site, https://users.stlcc.edu/mfuller/lempdig/history.html.
46. "Physicists Discover Strange Array of Links and Knots in Quantum Matter," *SciTechDaily*, May 27, 2022, https://scitechdaily.com/physicists-discover-strange-array-of-links-and-knots-in-quantum-matter; Johanna L. Miller, "An Inexpensive Crystal Makes a Fine Quantum Time Machine," *Physics Today* 72, 11 (2019): 14–17; "Ancient Namibian Stone Could Hold Key to Future Quantum Computers," *PhysOrg*, April 15, 2022, https://phys.org/news/2022-04-ancient-namibian-stone-key-future.html.
47. Bonnie Winston, "Time Capsule's Treasures at Home in Museum Buried by Former Slaves," *Greensboro News and Record*, April 22, 1993, https://greensboro.com/time-capsule-s-treasures-at-home-in-museum-buried-by/article_6cffb139-641a-523d-80d7-df2c4ff89b71.html.
48. Heather Gilligan, "An Entire Manhattan Village Owned by Black People Was Destroyed to Build Central Park." *Timeline*, February 23, 2017, https://timeline.com/black-village-destroyed-central-park-6356723113fa; See also Williams, Jasmin K, "The Village in the Park," *New York Post*, August 13, 2007, https://nypost.com/2007/08/13/the-village-in-the-park.
49. "Seneca Village," *Encyclopedia of African American Society* (New York: SAGE Publications, 2005), 740.
50. "Seneca Village," *Encyclopedia of African American Society*.
51. Leslie M. Alexander, *African or American?: Black Identity and Political Activism in New York City, 1784–1861* (Champaign: University of Illinois Press, 2011).
52. "Seneca Village," *Encyclopedia of African American Society*.
53. Gilligan, "An Entire Manhattan Village Owned by Black People Was Destroyed to Build Central Park."
54. Marcia Greenwood, "Can Frederick Douglass Time-Capsule Contents Be Saved?" *Democrat and Chronicle*, October 24, 2019, https://www.democratandchronicle.com/story/news/2019/10/24/frederick-douglass-time-capsule-contents-rochester-ny/4083662002.
55. Victoria Sandwick Schmitt, "Rochester's Frederick Douglass Part Two," in *Underground Railroad*, ed. Alexander C. Flick, vol. 7 (New York: Columbia University Press, 1935).

56. Emily Patrick, "Black History Emerges from 1897 Time Capsule," *Citizen-Times*, June 3, 2015, https://www.citizen-times.com/story/news/local/2015/06/03/black-history-emerges-time-capsule/28416453.
57. Emily Patrick, "Black History Emerges from 1897 Time Capsule."
58. "Time Capsule To be Placed in Statue of Dr. James Shepard," *Carolina Times*, October 1, 1949, ed. 1, https://newspapers.digitalnc.org/lccn/sn83045120/1949-10-01/ed-1/seq-1/ocr.
59. "Our Mission," The Village Arts and Humanities, https://villagearts.org/about/#more.
60. "Ile Ife Park," Association for Public Arts and Humanities, https://www.associationforpublicart.org/artwork/ile-ife-park.
61. Kodwo Eshun, "Further Considerations on Afrofuturism," *CR: The New Centennial Review* 3, no. 2 (2003): 288.

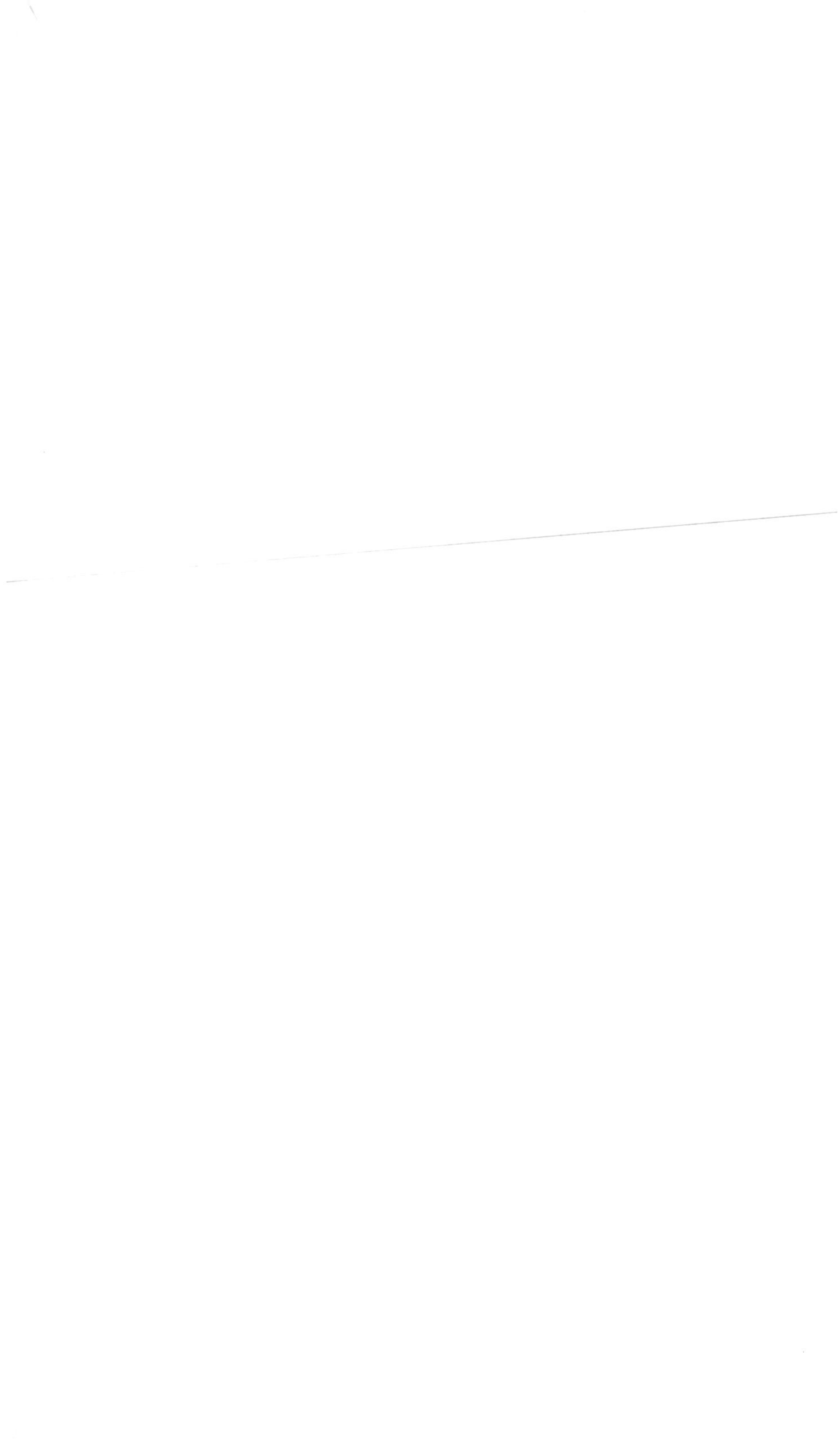

Printed in the USA
CPSIA information can be obtained
at www.ICGtesting.com
LVHW022353140824
788186LV00005B/17

2 370001 914865